US Policy towards Israel

For
John William Haynes

US Policy towards Israel

The Role of Political Culture in Defining the 'Special Relationship'

ELIZABETH STEPHENS

SUSSEX
ACADEMIC
PRESS
Brighton • Chicago • Toronto

2 4 6 8 10 9 7 5 3

First published 2006, reprinted in paperback 2013, in Great Britain by
SUSSEX ACADEMIC PRESS
PO Box 139
Eastbourne BN24 5BP

and in the United States of America by
SUSSEX ACADEMIC PRESS
Independent Publishers Group
814 N. Franklin Street, Chicago, IL 60610

and in Canada by
SUSSEX ACADEMIC PRESS (CANADA)
8000 Bathurst Street, Unit 1, PO Box 30010, Vaughan, Ontario L4J 0C6

British Library Cataloguing in Publication Data
A CIP catalogue record for this book is available from the British Library.

Library of Congress Cataloging-in-Publication Data
Stephens, Elizabeth.
US policy toward Israel : the role of political culture in defining the "special relationship" / Elizabeth Stephens.
p. cm.
Includes bibliographical references and index.
ISBN 978-1-84519-097-2 (h/c : alk. paper)
ISBN 978-1-84519-232-7 (pbk : alk. paper)
1. United States—Foreign relations—Israel. 2. Israel—Foreign relations—United States. 3. Political culture—United States.
I. Title: United States policy toward Israel. II. Title.
E183.8.I7S74 2005
327.7305694—dc22

2005009781

FSC www.fsc.org MIX Paper from responsible sources FSC® C013056

Typeset & Designed by Sussex Academic Press, Brighton & Eastbourne.
Printed by TJ International, Padstow, Cornwall.

CONTENTS

PREFACE

The rationale for Washington's enduring and often forbearing commitment to Israel has long been a puzzle. During the Cold War it was argued that Israel, a "bastion of democracy" amidst a world of semi-authoritarian and often pro-Soviet states, was a natural ally. But the Cold War is over, and the Arab world awash with oil, a resource that is always in short supply in the US. Yet the American commitment to Israel, a small state that is largely oil free, and of little tangible economic benefit, remains. An alternative view is that the US commitment is underwritten by the Jewish lobby which exercises a disproportionate influence on American policy. Yet the Jews comprise little more than six million out of a total of nearly 300 million people. Even when combined with the influence of Protestant fundamentalists who for largely religious reasons, increasingly support Israel, it is still questionable whether interest group politics could determine American foreign policy to such an extent. Yet irrespective of transitions between Republican and Democratic presidents, bureaucratic support for Israel remains relatively constant indicating that support for Israel is not a product of partisan politics but a given firmly ingrained in the political agenda and discourse.

This book proposes to explain the American commitment to Israel in terms of a somewhat imprecise and yet still serviceable concept – that of political culture. This concept best solves the puzzle of an American commitment that is often costly in economic and diplomatic terms. Political culture is not the sole explanatory factor in the development of US policy towards Israel, but it played a key role in serving to shape and define the American approach to foreign affairs, thus contributing to decisions and operations that cannot easily be explained solely in geopolitical, economic or military terms. In perceiving their society to be a beacon of what they like to call 'freedom' and 'democracy', in a world in which these values are largely absent, Americans have been encouraged to believe that they share a political kinship with societies similarly imbued and that they have an obligation to assist where such values are under threat. It is this belief that sets Israel apart from other nations and forms the bedrock of the US–Israeli 'special relationship'.

The relevance of the concept of political culture in accounting for US policy towards Israel is examined in a series of case studies. These focus on crisis decision-making during the presidencies of Johnson, Nixon, Reagan and Bush Sr., when domestic and organisational constraints were somewhat relaxed and decision-makers tended to act on pre-existing values and beliefs. In comparing and contrasting US decision-making both during and following the Cold War, the book attempts to provide an explanation for the relative continuity in US policy towards Israel in times of significant international and domestic change.

ACKNOWLEDGMENTS

The writing of this book would not have been possible without the support and encouragement of my Ph.D. supervisor Geoffrey Stern, Senior Lecturer at the London School of Economics & Political Science. Thanks are also due to Professor Fred Halliday and the late Philip Windsor for their insightful comments and guidance and to all those involved in policy making who kindly gave up their time to allow me to 'interview' them.

I also gratefully acknowledge the support of the London School of Economics & Political Science research fund.

On a personal note, thanks to my parents and grandparents for their support in this endeavour. Thanks also goes to my friends for their endless patience during the research and writing of this book: Helen Humphrey, Mohammed Hafez, Simon Harrison, James Berrill, Claire Saunders and my sister Claire. Particular recognition is owed to Andrew Saunders who discussed ideas and was willing to check the manuscript and to Alison Sands for time spent proof-reading.

The jacket photographs are courtesy of the Israeli National Photograph Collection. President Johnson with Prime Minister Levy Eshkol at Randolf air base in Texas, photographer: David Eldan. Prime Minister Golda Meir and President Nixon at the White House in Washington, photographer: Milner Moshe. Prime Minister Menahem Begin and President Ronald Reagan at attention during the welcoming ceremony on the south lawn of the White House, Washington, D.C., photographer: Saar Yaacov. Prime Minister Ariel Sharon and President George W. Bush at a joint press conference, at the White House, Washington D.C., photographer: Ohayon Avi.

1

THE SPECIAL RELATIONSHIP

> We have deepened our relationship to the point where it is probably the closest that we have with any of our friends and allies anywhere in the world ... We support Israel because it is our major democratic ally with strategic and ideological and cultural ties that grow stronger each year . . . As we work to achieve the goal of peace in the Middle East, we are guided by the fundamental principle which forms the basis for the peace process: our absolute commitment to Israel's security and to close U.S.–Israeli relations . . . The security of Israel is important to us, and we make no bones about it. . . . The U.S. stands by Israel in an unshakeable partnership for peace.
>
> VICE PRESIDENT AL GORE
> "U.S. MIDDLE EAST POLICY: A NEW ERA OF COOPERATION,"
> 35TH ANNUAL AIPAC POLICY CONFERENCE,
> WASHINGTON, D.C., 13 MARCH 1994[1]

THE IDEA THAT STATES, like people, can have a special relationship with one another, is now over half a century old, but the concept of a 'special relationship' remains under-theorised and under-conceptualised. We are left with little more than the assertions of politicians that the relevant relationship "is special. It just is. And that's that."[2]

The notion of a 'special relationship' between two countries was coined by Winston Churchill to describe and if possible consolidate and make enduring the wartime alliance between Britain and the United States. His rhetoric created the belief that the relationship was indeed 'special' and this rhetoric both preceded and outlasted the formal wartime ties between the two countries. More than any other individual it was Churchill who advertised what he saw as the benefits of the relationship and used the notion of a 'special relationship' to dramatise its possibilities in his own lifetime. Before his death but after the end of the Second World War, the relationship may be said to have returned to a more conventional form, with Washington consulting London less frequently on foreign affairs than had been the case during the exigency of hostilities. The closeness of the relationship dissipated in the absence of careful nurturing, but was to be rekindled under the leadership of, first, Harold Macmillan and John F. Kennedy, perhaps most notably under Margaret Thatcher and Ronald Reagan,[3] later under Tony Blair and Bill Clinton, and most recently under Blair and George W. Bush.

What makes an inter-state relationship 'special'? What was important for former US Secretary of State Dean Acheson was not the emotional but the functional:

> I shall not bother you by doing what is done so often on occasions like this, of talking about all that we have in common: language, history, and all of that. We know all that. What I wish to stress is one thing we have in common, one desperately important thing, and that is we have a common fate.[4]

A common fate implies common enemies, and a common interest in defeating or containing them. For example, the Anglo-American relationship was an alliance for a purpose – first a *pax anti-Germanica* and then a *pax anti-Sovietica* – a partnership based on utility not sentimental attachment. Its creation and continuation was not a forgone conclusion, despite the fact that the US had its origins in Britain. It did not evolve organically from an existential sense of community but was constructed and renewed during particular historical periods. The relationship had to be nurtured and above all negotiated. The Anglo-American special relationship was a construct and largely a British or to be more precise a Churchillian one at that.

Despite its relative decline since the Second World War, the Anglo-American relationship is often still alluded to or tacitly acknowledged in rhetoric, if nothing else, as 'special'.[5] Many commentators, politicians and academics have considered the bond between America and Britain to be unique and thought it to embody properties different from those found in relations between other states. The close alliance between the US and Britain in the wars of 2001–2 in Afghanistan and 2003 in Iraq is a testament to the endurance of this 'special relationship'. However, the language that was once the exclusive preserve of those describing Anglo-American relations, has been recently applied in diplomatic or even academic discourse to descriptions of America's relations with other states. This raises the question of whether a state can have more than one 'special relationship' simultaneously and if all those inter-state relationships their leaders claim as 'special' can actually adhere to established and agreed criteria of 'specialness'? Undoubtedly these relationships are unique because the entities that comprise the component parts contain properties that are not identically replicated by any other entity. But are they 'special' in the sense that 'special' implies bonds that go beyond utility to a deeper sense of affinity that transcends, and may on occasions even appear to be detrimental to, the national interest of one of the parties?

Defining Specialness

The *Oxford English Dictionary* offers the following definition: "of such a kind as to exceed or excel in some way that which is usual or common; exceptional in character, quality or degree . . . admitted to particular intimacy; held in particular esteem . . . marked off from others of the kind by having some distinguishing qualities or features; having a distinct or individual character."[6] This criterion is highly subjective and qualitative. There is no definitive article of *the* special relationship and therefore no overarching standard or fixed requirement.[7]

However, it is possible to offer criteria of distinguishing qualities a special relationship can embody, and here Alex Danchev's volume on 'specialness' is particularly instructive. The first attribute is 'transparency', which implies openness in the interaction between decision-making processes of the two governments. For example, it would be assumed that one state would not take significant international action in the absence of consultation, if not agreement, with the other. 'Informality', creates a feeling of at-ease in relations between the representatives of the states. Informality is also a product of personal interaction and fluctuates in accordance with the relationship between the individuals involved. However, the overriding essence of the relationship will be one of familiarity between the official representatives of the two governments. This leads on to the third and perhaps the most fundamental and unique characteristic of a special relationship, that of 'access', where the official representatives of each country enjoy unprecedented mutual access. Through official governmental ties, personal associations between government members and transnational associations, each secures direct access to the leaders and chief decision-makers of the other, bypassing the official bureaucratic process. The fourth attribute, 'generality', explains the wide ranging nature of a special relationship. It is not purely economic, or social, or political, it is all these things. For example, the US may have accorded China special status as a trading nation but this attribute of 'specialness' is strictly limited to the economic sphere. In contrast, Britain receives 'special' treatment in economic, diplomatic and military terms. The fifth criterion is 'reciprocity', whereby both states derive mutual benefits, either perceived or tangible, from the relationship. The sixth is 'exclusivity': the exact terms of the relationship are confined to the interaction between the two states, and not broadened to include third parties. 'Reliability' explains both states' ability to depend on the support of the other in times of need or crisis. Britain was able to rely on US support during the Falklands War (1982) and Taiwan has relied on American military purchases in its quest for independence from China. 'Durability' is the eighth attribute. For a relationship to be truly special it must endure across generations. Short-term 'special' relationships, it can be argued, are not really special at all, but only serve as marriages of convenience (for example, the Anglo-Prussian alliance during Napoleon I's reign). The final attribute is 'mythicisability'.[8] By this is meant the ability to create a legend concerning the origins and history of the relationship in order to justify the relationship and explain why it is special. This 'myth' must be unique to the two states in question and cannot be replicated in relations with another state.

In 1993 the American government inadvertently released a paper ranking states by 'importance to US interests', according to a State Department study completed the previous year. The top ten states in order of importance were Germany, France, Britain, China, Japan, Russia, Mexico, Israel, Canada and Iraq.[9] From this, it is evident that a country can be considered important, without being considered special.

If all the competing claimants to special status had their claims validated, then one must conclude that having a special relationship cannot be culturally specific. It may be a game of governance, to coin Richard Neustadt's term, but it is a game that anyone can play, as long as they have the right cards or attributes.[10] Through diplomatic manoeuvring and the balance of power machinations, many lesser powers have sought to establish special relationships with the Great Powers by attempting to make their services indispensable. The Soviet relationship with Vietnam and the US relationship with Pakistan during the Cold War provide two such examples. As in the case of many Cold War relationships they were, for the most part, the product of a particular historical imperative. They were relationships of mutual convenience or benefit and were not founded on a particular cultural or emotional affinity.

* * *

So far the analysis has examined the notion of the 'special relationship' in general terms. But what of the relationship specifically between Israel and the United States? The Israeli analyst Abraham Ben-Zvi has attempted to explore this relationship be juxtaposing what he terms a 'special relationship paradigm' with a 'national interest paradigm', to try to isolate the elusive element of 'specialness'.[11] He claims that the key criteria for defining a special relationship are durability, pervasiveness and legitimacy. This means that the relationship must be able to withstand conflicts of interest and disagreements, encapsulate all aspects of interaction, be it diplomatic, economic or military, and be widely accepted as justified and valid. However, since Ben-Zvi implies that the parameters of the relationship are determined unilaterally and arbitrarily by the United States, thereby suggesting a hegemonic rather than a 'special' relationship, his analysis fails to explore fully the nature of the perceived advantages to both parties.

International relationships can be both special and unequal. Parity is not a pre-requisite for specialness, especially if one believes in a place for sentiment or cultural influence in international affairs. Even an ardent realist like Henry Kissinger acknowledged that the special relationship between Britain and the US involved "a pattern of consultation so matter-of-factly intimate that it became psychologically impossible to ignore British views."[12] Under these circumstances, power and influence can be wielded in different forms and to different ends. As long as the United States is included in any equation of a 'special relationship', parity, in terms of pure economic and military power, will be non-existent. The closest approximation of parity the United States has experienced in its more recent history was that which it shared with Britain between 1941–42. In March 1941, although war was nine months away, the Lend-Lease Act was a public announcement of the creation of the most productive and co-operative coalition of modern times – the Anglo-American alliance against Nazi Germany.[13] America's potential was much greater than that of Britain, but even US decision-makers acknowledged that this potential would take time to realise. America, as a great power, had gone to war in a state of comprehensive unreadiness, in contrast to the well-organised and experienced, but under-resourced, British. The British and Americans needed each other to ease their respective burdens.[14] Their respective contributions, if not equal, were complementary and necessary. London and Washington were interdependent and both parties knew it. Here was reciprocity in action. Danchev argued that the "perfect alliance would show equality of interest and commitment between the two parties, with a reciprocity of advantage."[15] This is certainly true of the Anglo-American relationship.

In the case of the US and Israel, the relationship does not appear to embody the same reciprocity of advantage. For all Jerusalem's much advertised intransigence, it is a highly dependent relationship and one in which elements of a patron–client relationship exist. America has endowed Israel with many things, including diplomatic support and international legitimacy. However, Israel is in the envious position of being considered both special and important by leading Washington officials, and this has proved sufficient to prevent the relationship being determined unilaterally by the United States. That said, Israel is aware of the asymmetry in the relationship, and as a consequence, one constant theme has proliferated: the importance Jerusalem assigns to equating whenever possible what it sees as the best interests of Israel with those of the US. For example, following the terrorist attacks on the World Trade Center and the Pentagon in September 2001, Ariel Sharon, Israel's prime minister, tried to generate a feeling of shared threat with the US by referring to Arafat as Israel's Osama bin Laden[16] and highlighting Islamic terrorism as their mutual enemy. Despite great disparities in states power, the character of a special relationship cannot be imposed or determined unilaterally.

Within international relations, expectations are crucial. "There are great possibilities for strain and disappointment in a special relationship," but as John Sloan Dickey writes in his work on US–Canadian relations; "nothing is resented quite so much as the unfulfilled expectations of being consulted."[17] Successive Israeli governments have stirred such resentment amongst many American presidents. President Reagan's anger at the Israeli bombing of Osiraq, the Iraqi nuclear reactor, the annexation of the Golan Heights and the siege of West Beirut, stemmed in part from resentment that Israel's Prime Minister Menachem Begin had not consulted him before acting.[18] A willingness to accept criticism and ultimately to be open to influence, a situation that implies a form of transparency, is the exacting requirement of any special relationship. It is a requirement Israel is reluctant to yield. Despite the opportunities for tension in the relationship, there are limits beyond which neither side will push the other, particularly when the vital interests of one of the parties are at stake. For example, immediately after 9/11, when the vital interests of the United States were understood to be challenged by Islamic terrorism, Israel, under immense pressure from Washington, agreed to a cease-fire with the Palestinians.[19] This occurred not because Israel had reached a new understanding with the Palestinian Authority (PA), but because Ariel Sharon, the Israeli Prime Minister, acknowledged that Israel could not "afford to cross the United States in its hour of need and peril."[20] Yet despite concessions of this nature, the US–Israeli relationship is not one of "unremitting and absolute American domination,"[21] as was demonstrated by Israel's subsequent incursions into PA territory in and after November 2001.[22]

The apparent disparity of power between the two states leads to the question of influence in the relationship, its nature and its exercise. Professor Alvin Rubinstein has suggested the following definition of influence: "Influence is manifested when country A affects, through non-military means, directly or indirectly, the behaviour of country B so that it rebounds to the advantage of A."[23] States engage in multifaceted efforts to affect the policies of others, both friends and adversaries, with varying degrees of success at different times. Influence is rarely forceful and open in nature but more often is exercised through subtle means. It is not proportionate to power, in terms of the ability to use military force, but is an element in the relations between two states. Therefore a relationship, though profoundly asymmetrical, can still embody mutuality.[24]

The term 'special relationship' describes the nature of the relationship as developed between the US and Israel since the establishment of the State of

Israel in 1948. This is reflected in the disproportionate and positive attention American candidates for public office give Israel in their campaign rhetoric and the platforms adopted by the leading US parties acknowledging a special status for the Jewish state. For example, the Republican Party platform of 1992 referred to "Israel's demonstrated strategic importance to the United States, as our most reliable and capable ally in" the Middle East. The Democratic Party manifesto of the same year acknowledged that: "The end of the Cold War does not alter America's deep interest in our longstanding special relationship with Israel, based on shared values, a mutual commitment to democracy, and a strategic alliance that benefits both nations."[25] In 1978, Vice-President Walter Mondale went so far as to claim that:

> So long as America believes in its own professed ideals, there will always be a special relationship . . . There is no country anywhere in the world which more accurately reflects our basic values. [It is] the values that we hold in common which accounts for the special relationship.[26]

In turn, Israeli prime ministers have also been quick to acknowledge their country's special relationship with the US. In his 1992 inauguration speech, Prime Minister Yitzhak Rabin commented that:

> Sharing with us in the making of peace will also be the United States, whose friendship and special closeness we prize. We shall spare no effort to strengthen and improve the special relationship we have with the one power in the world.[27]

Similarly, when Ehud Barak became Israel's prime minister in 1998, he also spoke of his commitment to strengthening "[t]he special relationship between Israel and the United States."[28] In contrast to the rhetoric of many American statesmen, it is significant that the dominant Israeli view of the relationship is the 'functionalist' one, that is, Israel's value to the US in concrete not sentimental terms.

Behind the rhetoric of eminent statesmen, the reality of US–Israeli relations, and the type of 'special' relationship they enjoy, is much more complex and multifacted. **'Transparency'**, for example, is apparent in Washington's dealings with Jerusalem, and although this level of openness has on occasions not been reciprocated, Washington consulted closely with Jerusalem about its strategy for confronting the Iraqi invasion of Kuwait[29] and during its operations in Afghanistan. This element of transparency is most notable in the covert operations the two governments have engaged in, both in Central America and the Middle East, of which the Iran-Contra affair is the most highly publicised. This involved the covert transfer of American military equipment to Iran, a country against which Washington had imposed sanctions, in exchange for the release of US hostages held in Lebanon.[30] Israel acted as the intermediary in dealings between Washington and Tehran.

'Informality' is apparent at all levels of interaction between US and Israeli officials. Many American presidents have formed close personal relationships with Israeli prime ministers including Lyndon Johnson and Levi Eshkol, and Bill Clinton and Yitzhak Rabin. Israel also enjoys unprecedented privileged 'access' to the highest echelons of the American decision-making elite, bypassing the official bureaucratic process. In 1971 President Nixon established a special channel of communication between his National Security Council Advisor Henry Kissinger and Yitzhak Rabin, at that time Israeli ambassador to Washington.[31] In 1991, during the Gulf War, President George Bush established a hotline between himself and Prime Minister Yitzhak Shamir that bypassed the bureaucracy.

'Generality' is another attribute of the US–Israeli relationship. Aid to Israel is not limited to the military sphere; Jerusalem has been the recipient of unprecedented amounts of financial assistance, including $10 billion in loan guarantees to settle Soviet Jews in 1992. Israel also receives considerable economic benefit through its status as a favoured trading nation. The two governments have also collaborated in the area of research and development and on 15 March 1993, President Clinton and Prime Minister Rabin announced the establishment of a US–Israeli Science and Technology Commission, designed to increase cooperation in science, technology and conversion programmes.[32]

The fifth criterion, that of **'reciprocity'**, is perhaps the hardest to discern. The US government clearly believes that it receives benefits from its relationship with Israel, but these are intangible. A monetary price tag cannot be assigned to having a democratic ally in the region, in contrast to the tangible economic and military rewards Israel derives from its association with America.

'Exclusivity' unquestionably exists between the two countries; no other state enjoys the same level of commitment or intimacy as Washington and Jerusalem receive from each other.

'Reliability' has been demonstrated by both US and Israeli governments in their dealings with each other. Washington has assisted Israel in military, economic and diplomatic terms both during and after each of its wars with the Arab states. In return, Washington was able to call on Jerusalem not to retaliate against Iraqi Scud missile attacks on its territory in 1991 and to withdraw from Palestinian land, albeit temporarily, in 2001. In the diplomatic sphere, each government can rely on the other to vote with them in international institutions like the United Nations.

'Durability' certainly exists, with government and transnational ties transcending the generations and different political alignments. The final attribute, that of 'mythicisability', includes the creation of a shared religious and moral history, and the belief in a common destiny.

US–Israeli relations are in many respects special. They have come about in part through the existence of significant religious, historical, political and sociological factors, which in many ways account for such a relationship.

The Religious Foundations of the American–Jewish Relationship

In the eighteenth century a number of notable American figures, including Joseph Smith Jr., began to speculate on the possibility of the re-establishment of a Jewish state in former Palestine. Such posturing stemmed not so much from political considerations as from the religious beliefs of the Pilgrim Fathers. Jewish influence expressed itself predominantly through the Hebrew scriptures because the "Englishmen who established themselves in the New World were the most Orthodox Puritans, whose intellectual language consisted of a system ardently Hebraic."[33] When Harvard was founded in 1639, Hebrew was a compulsory subject, with a scholar's ability to translate the Hebrew original of the Bible into Latin a pre-requisite for admission.

This intense respect for the Old Testament led to a high regard for the Holy Land itself. The United States was founded as "New Canaan" and many towns given Hebrew names or named after Biblical places. The early pilgrims thought of America as the "Biblical prophecy come to life."[34] The American–Hebrew–Old Testament–modern Israel connection is not the only determinant factor in the US–Israeli relationship, but neither should it be dismissed. It would be foolish to argue that the United States supported the restoration of Jewish sovereignty merely because many of its more educated Christian citizens studied Hebrew several centuries ago. However, it would be equally misguided not to recognise that the Hebrew–Old Testament element in America's intellectual history provided the foundations upon which US support for the modern Jewish state originated, particularly among American Christians.[35] Many American clergymen, during the founding and consolidation of the state, relied heavily on Old Testament metaphors and images during their sermons.[36] The colonial connection *vis-à-vis* Great Britain was compared with that of the slaves in ancient Egypt, and the struggle against King George III was likened with that of Moses against the Pharaoh.[37] When the Founding Fathers were discussing the seal of the United States, Thomas Jefferson, Benjamin Franklin and John Adams went so far as to submit a design depicting the Israelites crossing the Red Sea.[38] Preaching on 4 July 1777, William Gordon argued that as the Hebrew tribes were driven to rebellion by the tyranny of Solomon's son King Rehoboam, so the thirteen colonies were driven to the same action by the tyranny of the British sovereign King George III.[39]

In a sermon of 1779 entitled *Traits of Resemblance in the People of the United States of America to Ancient Israel*, Reverend Abiel Abbot argued that no country in the late eighteenth century was so much like ancient Israel as was the US. According to Abbot, the two resembled each other in their happiness, in their distinctiveness from other nations, and in their having been favoured with divine presence, divine providence and divine protection from their enemies. Abbot counselled his countrymen to think of the new American nation as a New Zion and to conduct their lives in accordance with the principles of the Gospels.[40] The theory that the Native Americans represented the Lost Tribes of Israel stirred up the imagination of the early settlers.[41] The last verse of Isaiah 18 reads:

> At that time tribute shall be brought to the Lord of Hosts from a people tall and smooth-skinned, dreaded near and far, a nation strong and proud, whose land is scoured by rivers. They shall bring it to Mount Zion, the place where men invoke the name of the Lord of Hosts.

Joseph Smith, a minister of the time, believed that America was the land to which Isaiah was referring and that the people were the Native Americans. Smith spun a tale that enmeshed the Lost Tribes, Native Americans, the US, the dispersion of the Jews and their predestined return to Zion and the Prophet Isaiah. These works related the Judeo-Christian history and theology to the American condition. The equation of America with Israel and the idea of the 'American Israel' was not uncommon.[42] Smith's work differed from other ministers of the time in that he added a political dimension by advocating the bodily return of the Jewish people, presumably in full sovereignty, to the actual geographical area of the Middle East.

However, America's Old Testament-embracing, Zionist Protestant clergy, was not unique to that country. The distinctive aspect of the American experience is that the US was portrayed as a biblical Israel fulfilled by God, in other words, the concept of American Exceptionalism. The Chosen People of the New World knowingly imitated the Biblical saga.[43] Jewish Biblical teachings shaped the development of self-governing institutions introducing religious freedom, and the evolution of the legal codes of the thirteen colonies. As Woodrow Wilson acknowledged:

> Not a little of the history of liberty lies in the circumstances that the moving sentences of this Book [the Bible] were made familiar to the ears and the understanding of those people who had led mankind in exhibiting the forms of government and impulses of reforms which have made freedom and self-government among mankind.[44]

It is a matter of historic record that in the struggle for ratification of the constitution by the legislatures of the various states, the Bible played a decisive role, with the proponents of the constitution repeatedly invoking the scriptures when pleading their cause.

Presidential interest in the cause of Jewish National Restoration dates back to John Adams, the second president of the United States. Although not in office at the time, in 1819 John Adams responded to a letter from a Jewish citizen thus:

> If I could let my imagination loose . . . I could find it in my heart to wish that you had been at the head of a hundred thousand Israelites . . . marching with them into Judea and making a conquest of that country and restoring your nation to the dominion of it. For I really wish the Jews again in Judea an independent nation."[45]

It was the idealised Jew of Scripture, not the contemporary reality that inspired the early Americans. Gentiles like Adams were grinding a Christological axe on a Judaic stone. The Jews' return to Palestine was seen as a theological precondition for the latter's conversion to Christianity and the Second Coming of Christ.[46] From this arose the enduring theme of American social history, concerning the redemption of all mankind. A vision of the special role of America in Jewish destiny emerged with constant connections between modern Palestine and modern Jewry consolidating the psychological foundations for the later Christian acceptance of the modern state of Israel.[47] To this day, American Evangelists perceive their own salvation as inextricably interwoven with Jewish claims to the promised land.

The Historical Foundations of the American–Jewish Relationship

The defeat of the Ottoman Empire in the First World War and the creation of independent nations from its territory fuelled the debate about the establishment of a Jewish National homeland. The British government was aware that Washington looked favourably on the establishment of a homeland and sought President Wilson's advice on the terminology of The Balfour Declaration that set out Britain's position on this issue. The Declaration stated that

> His Majesty's Government view with favour the establishment in Palestine of a national home for the Jewish people, and will use their best endeavours to facilitate the achievement of this object, it being clearly understood that nothing shall be done which may prejudice the civil and religious rights of existing non-Jewish communities in Palestine, or the rights and political status enjoyed by Jews in any other country.[48]

The Balfour Declaration was not, in fact or in intent, a unilateral statement of policy. Balfour himself saw it as a declaration of sympathy for Jewish Zionist aspirations but not as a British commitment to the establishment of a Jewish state. Washington participated in the preparation of the declaration and every American president since Woodrow Wilson has endorsed it. The Declaration received the approval of all the Allied Governments at the Versailles Peace Conference and Wilson registered his formal endorsement in a letter addressed to the American Zionist leader Rabbi Stephen S. Wise on 29 October 1918.[49]

The US was prevented from participating in the Allied Conference at San Remo in April 1920, convened to deal with the disposition of territory conquered from Turkey following the First World War, because Congress refused Wilson's petition to join the League of Nations. Furthermore, the US had not declared war on Turkey, only severing diplomatic relations. In April 1920, Great Britain was awarded the Mandate over Palestine, based on the terms of the Balfour Declaration. However, the US claimed that its participation in the war entitled it to some privileges in the disposition of enemy territory, including that for Palestine. Britain eventually accepted American claims, and in a 1924 treaty effectively gave Washington the formal right to intervene in matters relating to the Mandate territory. Washington's attitude towards Palestine and Zionist and Arab objectives was indicated in the section on Palestine in a Report and Recommendations[50] officially submitted to President Wilson and to the American Delegation at the Versailles Peace Conference in 1919. The report recommended that

> there be established a separate State of Palestine. The separation of the Palestinian area from Syria finds justification in the religious experience of mankind, the Jewish and Christian churches were born in Palestine and Jerusalem was for long years at different periods the capital of each. . . . It is recommended that the Jews be invited to return to Palestine and to settle there. It [Palestine] was the cradle and home of their vital race, which has made large spiritual contributions to mankind, and is the only land in which they can hope to find a home of their own; they being in this respect unique among significant people.[51]

Taking advantage of the growing interest in Zionism, on 11 June 1918, the Zionist Organization of America, addressed a letter to all members and representatives of the United States Senate and the House of Representatives, requesting their opinion on the Zionist question. Most senators and representatives indicated that their support of the Balfour Declaration was based on the belief that the Jews were entitled to the same national rights enjoyed by other peoples, including the Arabs. The statement of Representative William E. Cox of Indiana reflects the attitude of many of his peers:

> For more than thirty centuries unique and alone Judea has stood among the countries of the globe. A nation's greatness is not measured by its gold, its numbers, . . . but it is determined by its ideals, by which it has stood, and the benefits it has conferred on mankind such as Judea has stood for. Rome taught mankind a government of law, . . . but it remained for Judea and her people to give mankind the true Christian religion. These ideals and teachings given to searching mankind makes Judea and her

people the greatest on earth. . . . But just as Moses has led the Israelites out of bondage, so the Allies are now redeeming Judea.[52]

In early 1922 the British House of Lords rejected claims that Jewish rights to Palestine should be recognised according to the terms of the Balfour Declaration, and in so doing challenged Zionist perceptions of the British commitment to a Jewish homeland. Politically, this was a major blow for the Zionists, who had long counted on British support. The Zionists now turned their attention to Washington. They reasoned that the official recognition of the Palestine Mandate by the American Congress would stabilise the situation, so they began to refocus their campaign on the US Congress and Senate. This change of strategy was rewarded on 12 April 1922, when Senator Henry Cabot Lodge of Massachusetts, as Chairman of the Committee for Foreign Relations of the Senate, introduced a Joint Resolution that was reported back to the Committee on 3 May 1922, stating that it is

> resolved by the Senate and House of representatives of the United States of America in Congress assembled, that the United States of America favours the establishment in Palestine of a national home for Jewish people, it being clearly understood that nothing shall be done which may prejudice the civil and religious rights of Christians and all other non-Jewish communities in Palestine, and that the holy places and religious buildings and sites in Palestine shall; be adequately protected.[53]

This 'enhanced Balfour Declaration' was more favourable to Israel than the original document[54] and was adopted unanimously by the Senate, and subsequently passed by both Houses of Congress. Thus as early as 1922 the United States formally endorsed the principle of the creation of a Jewish state in Palestine. United States support of Israel had begun.[55] Yet, as former Ambassador Richard Murphy points out, this was a minor event in American constitutional history.[56] Soon after the passing of the Resolution, the State Department issued a statement claiming that the Resolution "did not constitute a commitment to any foreign obligation or entanglement."[57]

In June 1924, Harding's successor, Calvin Coolidge, added his name to the list of American presidents supportive of Zionist aspirations for a Jewish state. Herbert Hoover followed likewise in 1929.[58] After completing his term in office, Hoover put forward the most radical proposal of any American president regarding the future of Palestine, publicly stating that he was in favour of resettling Palestine's Arabs in Iraq to make way for a Jewish homeland.[59] This plan was significant for two reasons. First, because it reveals the true depth of feeling this issue provoked and secondly because it was proposed by a non-Jewish former American president who was no longer subject to the imperatives of electioneering and had never been personally involved in the Zionist movement.

The Holocaust and the Transformation of American Jewry

With the adoption of the Congressional Resolution advancing the Jewish cause in Palestine, American prestige and national interest became interwoven with British decisions as the mandated power. The issuance of the last British White Paper on 17 March 1939, limiting Jewish immigration to Palestine to 100,000, created tensions between the two governments. British and American Jews and members of Congress, thought that the Paper posed an immediate threat to the development of a Jewish National Home by withdrawing basic pledges and altering the conditions on which Jews had proceeded to rebuild the land and recreate their lives in Palestine. Congress protested the White Paper claiming that, "the contemplated action, if carried out, will be regarded as a violation of the British-American convention and will be viewed with disfavour by the American people."[60]

The White Paper, the Honourable Lyle H. Boren, Representative for Oklahoma claimed, was "an appeasement to the pro-Axis Moslems"[61] and at the time it appeared that the imperatives of fighting a world war took priority over previous sentimental and humanitarian commitments to a Jewish homeland. A senior British official explained the situation to a Zionist leader in March 1941, "[t]hey [the Arabs] are not reliable but they are a power. It is true this is appeasement. Terrible as it is for you, you must take it in good part."[62] Ironically, when America entered the war in December 1941, political questions were subordinated to military considerations. The War Department adopted the cardinal tenet of the British government that the goodwill of the Arabs was vital to the war effort.

The response of the Roosevelt administration to the Jews' desperate need for sanctuary outside Europe was one of virtual inaction. Despite the emergence of concrete evidence and eyewitness accounts of the Nazis wholesale murder of European Jewry, US officials either refused to believe what they were told or to act upon these accounts. Roosevelt did nothing to assist the passage of persecuted Jews out of Europe by either pressurising Britain to rescind the White Paper limiting Jewish immigration to Palestine or by pushing Congress to liberalise, if only temporarily, America's then racist and anti-Semitic immigration laws. In the 1930s, emigration quotas were determined according to ethnic and religious origin and only a certain number of people of each nationality and religion were permitted to enter the country. In April 1943, British and American representatives met in Bermuda to discuss the refugee question, but as one British participant noted, the talks were "a conflict of self-justification [and] a façade for inaction."[63] Rarely did the issue intrude on the correspondence between Churchill and Roosevelt and although it was occasionally discussed, no decision was ever reached.[64] The American president did not do everything he could have done (at least before 1944) to release funds and transport to save those Jewish lives that still could be saved.[65] In his defence it should be noted that even organised Zionism did not seriously contemplate the rescue of European Jewry[66] as a viable strategy. This lack of concrete action was not matched by a lack of internal debate about the Jewish question and by 1945 the Roosevelt administration had come up with 666 possible sites around the globe for the resettlement of displaced Jews after the war.[67]

Like presidents from John Adams onwards, Roosevelt considered the fate of the Holy Land out of all proportion to its geographic significance or its objective relation to the American national interest.[68] He also suffered from the chronic propensity of politicians to say things that would be well received and in so doing courted the favour of both Arabs and Jews in the debate over Palestine. During the early 1940s Roosevelt assured King ibn Saud of Saudi Arabia that he would "take no action, in my capacity as Chief Executive of the Executive Branch of this government, which might prove hostile to the Arab people"[69] and "do nothing to assist the Jews against the Arabs."[70] Yet in March 1944, he stood on the White House steps with his personal friend Rabbi Stephen Wise together with Rabbi Abba Hillel Silver, leader of the American Emergency Zionist Committee, and authorised them to issue a statement that "[T]he American government has never given its approval to the White Paper of 1939 . . . When future decisions are reached, full justice will be done to those who seek a Jewish national home."[71] Perhaps Roosevelt accepted the Zionist position that the creation of a Jewish national home was not a 'hostile move' against the Arabs, but ibn Saud interpreted Roosevelt's assurances differently. For the Saudi king, the immigration of one single Jew and the purchase of one dunam of Arab land by a Jew was a hostile act. Rabbi Wise was dismayed that Roosevelt could act in such a way, while simultaneously claiming that his position on Zionism had not changed. Only after Roosevelt's death was the full extent of the duality of his Palestine policy revealed.

By macabre default, Hitler's holocaust resulted in American Jewry becoming the largest Jewish community in the world, with its subsequent transformation into a political force occurring as a product of political necessity. While Zionist leaders across Europe were being slaughtered and those in Palestine were both co-operating with the British because of Hitler and in conflict with them because of the White Paper, the locus of Zionist public relations and diplomatic activity shifted to the US. This shift was symbolised by the convening of an Extraordinary Zionist conference at New York's Biltmore Hotel in May 1942, organised by America's four largest Zionist groups.[72] The convention was the result of the efforts of Rabbi Wise and David Ben Gurion, then Chairman of the Jewish Agency, leader of the ruling Mapai party and dominant Jewish personality internationally,[73] who later became the first prime minister of Israel. They had made numerous trips to the US in the early war years to begin the process of transforming the American Jewish community into a pro-Zionist pressure group.[74]

Despite their best efforts, it was not the minimalist tradition of pushing for relief measures for oppressed Jewry, whilst avoiding the awkward political question of statehood that proved successful. In establishing the American–Jewish Conference, Wise and Ben-Gurion paved the way for the ascendancy of Rabbi Hillel Silver to the leadership of the American Zionist Emergency Council in the summer of 1943. It was Silver, a Lithuanian born, fifth generation rabbi, raised in Cleveland,[75] with the toughness of a man who did not care whether or not he was liked, that brought the Jews of America to a position of power. It was Silver who galvanised the deeply divided Zionist movement,[76] founded the lobby and made it work. He based his actions on his belief that instead of relying on the good will of American leaders, a mass power base of public opinion pressure should be created to persuade Roosevelt to respond favourably to Zionist demands." On 1 September 1943, at the Biltmore conference, a declaration was unanimously adopted demanding that Palestine be established as a Jewish Commonwealth and integrated into the framework of what was envisaged as the new postwar democratic world.[77]

In mobilising American Jewry, Silver had tapped into a very important political asset. His goal became the conversion of "a club of well intentioned but politically passive Zionist personalities into the nerve centre of a revolutionary programme with a mass following."[78] As Bernard Baruch, a leading American Jewish businessman, acknowledged:

> The only thing which will matter in Washington . . . is if the people in the Bronx and Brownsville and Borough Park begin to mutter in their beards, they'll be damned if they continue to cast their votes to a party that breaks its pledges to them . . . You let me have the Jewish vote of New York and I will bring you the head of ibn Saud on a platter! The Administration will sell all seven Arab states if it is a question of retaining the support . . . of the Jews of New York alone; never mind the rest of the country.[79]

The efforts of American Zionists bore fruit in 1944, when they succeeded in forcing the issue of a Jewish state on to the agenda of both political parties.[80] In June and July, of that year, Silver and Neumann used the parties' national conventions as a forum to test their strategy of encouraging Republican and Democratic competition for the Jewish vote. If the two national parties could be induced to vie for the Jewish vote through their stand on the Palestine question, then another force, Zionist political power – a new form of bargaining power – could be created. Their strategy was successful. The Republicans called for a "free and democratic Commonwealth" in Palestine, while the Democrats went even further by specifying that they favoured a "free and democratic *Jewish*

Commonwealth."[81] As will be shown, from this moment on the political parties position on Israel became a key electoral issue, with the Democrats coming to be seen as the party of the American Jewish people. It was to be the Democratic President, Harry S. Truman, who pledged full recognition of the State of Israel in July 1948.[82]

Truman and the Recognition of Israel

When on 12 April 1945, Roosevelt died in office, he left a question mark about his true feelings, intentions and actions towards the Jews, the Arabs and Palestine. It was left to Harry S. Truman his successor, to determine how far the US should go in helping to transform the Jewish national home into the Jewish commonwealth or the Jewish state.

Truman's first social and business associations with American Jews occurred in his hometown of Kansas City, where his business partner Eddie Jacobson was Jewish. His earliest political action involving the Palestine question dates back to 1939 when, as a Senator, Truman spoke briefly on the floor of the Senate against the White Paper. Later at the Potsdam conference, even though the question of Palestine was not on the official agenda, Truman took the opportunity to urge Churchill to lift the White Paper restrictions on Jewish immigration. In the summer of 1945, Truman announced his support of the immigration of 100,000 displaced persons (DP) from Europe to Palestine.[83]

What moved Truman to take this position in contradiction to that of the State Department and press Britain on the issue of immigration is unclear. His stance is generally attributed to a combination of factors: the Holocaust, congressional pressure and the influence of his advisor Sam Rosenman pressing him in the same direction. Truman's position, like that of so many presidents, was one of attempting to reconcile incompatible objectives and conflicting views. On the one hand, he was in favour of letting "as many of the Jews into Palestine as it is possible to let into that country"[84] but on the other, he was not prepared to use military force to back up his diplomatic position. As president, he had "no desire to send 500,000 American soldiers . . . to make peace in Palestine."[85]

In the spring of 1947 the British terminated their responsibility for Palestine and the matter was referred to the UN, where the partition plan was proposed.[86] Two states, one Arab and one Jewish, were to be established and linked in economic union.[87] Truman instructed the State Department to support the partition plan and the US played an active role in seeking the support of other governments.[88] In his memoirs, Truman described American policy in the following terms:

> My purpose was then and later to help bring about the redemption of the pledge

> of the Balfour Declaration and the rescue of at least some of the victims of Nazism. I was not committed to any particular formula of statehood in Palestine or to any particular time schedule for its accomplishment. The American policy was designed to bring about, by peaceful means, the establishment of the promised Jewish homeland and easy access to it for the displaced Jews of Europe.[89]

This raised the usual problem of interpretation. Many Jews believed that Washington's Palestine policy was the same as the Zionist policy and when it failed to conform, leading British and American Jews claimed that the US had turned pro-Arab.

Partition was met with such violent confrontations on the ground that many governments reevaluated their position on the issue and sought alternative solutions. The American retreat from partition occurred in response to the findings of the National Security Council (NSC) on the question of "the implication of current UN discussion of the problem of Palestine on the security interests of the US."[90] The review concluded that "partition . . . cannot be carried out at this time by peaceful means. We could not undertake to impose this solution on the people of Palestine by the use of American troops."[91] The thought of sending American troops to the Middle East to fight the Arabs, a move that would have legitimised the deployment of Soviet troops to the region as part of an international contingent, was anathema to the State Department and Pentagon. Kermit Roosevelt, the brother of FDR, went so far as to claim that "the creation of a Jewish state in the Middle East [was] not compatible with America's national interest."[92]

Such a statement raised the question of who determines the national interest in the United States. Was it legitimate for ethnic or religious groups whose perception of the national interest differed from that of the Executive to attempt to influence foreign policy decision-making? American Zionists believed the establishment of a Jewish state was compatible with the US national interest and viewed domestic politics as moving hand in hand with foreign policy. Pressure exerted on the White House and the United Nations by the Zionist lobby was a source of annoyance to Truman, and he eventually refused to meet with Zionist leaders. It was the influence exercised by his old business partner Eddie Jacobson that convinced Truman to receive Dr. Chaim Weizmann, head of the World Zionist Commission, and to hear his petition for a Jewish homeland. It is likely that Weizmann's worth in the eyes of Truman was enhanced by the fact that his trusted friend Jacobson had arranged the meeting.

With the failure of partition, the initiative moved out of the hands of the Great Powers and to the local parties themselves. It was in the context of reported violence and chaos on the ground in Palestine that on 14 May 1948, Ben Gurion declared the existence of the State of Israel. Twelve minutes later at 6:12 P.M., Truman, in his capacity as President of the United States became the first foreign leader to accord the state recognition. The extending of *de facto* (though not *de jure*)[93] recognition to the State of Israel was taken against the advice of his advisers and the Departments of State and War, including that of General Marshall, the American war hero who Truman greatly respected.[94] Clark Clifford, the White House Special Counsel was reportedly the only cabinet minister in favour of recognition.[95] Professional bureaucrats considered that overt support for a Jewish state would be detrimental to America's strategic and political interests in the oil rich Arab world and that Washington could be called upon to back up its support of Israel with force.

Uncertainty surrounds the reasons for Truman's decision to recognise Israel. David Bar-Ilan, the Israeli Minister of Communications for the Netanyahu government, argues that the decision was "not done just as a matter of course but as an expression of friendship."[96] Clark Clifford, and Dean Acheson both claimed that Truman's long-held humanitarian concern for Jewish refugees in Europe[97] and horror at the scale of the Holocaust played a role.[98] He was genuinely distressed by the plight of the millions the war had left homeless and particularly the Jews who had no homeland to which they could return. Truman believed that the Balfour Declaration committed Britain, and by implication America, to the creation of a Jewish state in Palestine. He was also a "student and believer in the Bible,"[99] and religion undoubtedly played a role in his decision. From his reading of the Old Testament he believed the Jews derived a legitimate historical right to Palestine.[100]

Emotional considerations aside, evidence suggests that Truman's political concern had to be aroused before he would take decisive action.[101] The catalyst for Truman's decision appears to have been the views of David K. Niles, adviser on national minorities. Niles appreciated the domestic political dimension of the Jewish question and sought to exploit Truman's position as President to the advantage of the Democrat party. As party leader, the President was expected to help congressmen, senators and governors of his party secure re-election. Niles informed Truman that his opponent Governor Dewey intended to issue "a strong statement in favour of Jewish immigration" and urged him to "beat Dewey to the punch because the Jewish vote in New York was going to be crucial."[102] Clifford later claimed that public opinion in support of the Jewish state was decisive because it "permitted Truman, who emotionally supported the Jewish cause in Palestine"[103] to recognise Israel. Forces of public opinion allowed him little choice and he was "happy it had not."[104] Domestic necessity, a genuine humanitarian concern for the plight of Europe's Jewish refugees, a commitment to upholding the Balfour Declarations and Truman's own Christian upbringing were of a high order of magnitude in influencing his decision.

The special relationship between the United States and Israel, that Truman was instrumental in establishing, provides the backdrop against which US foreign policy towards Israel is made. It is not in itself, however, an explanation of foreign policy decision-making which is a product of the interaction of a multiplicity of factors. It is to an analysis of the factors that influence this process that we now turn.

2

FRAMING AMERICAN FOREIGN POLICY

The Components of Policy

IT IS A TRUISM TO SAY that both international and domestic events affect American policy, while individuals and groups with partisan views, both inside and outside the government, compete to influence decisions.[1] But the degree to which such factors mould or reshape government policy, if at all, has to be a product of timing and circumstance. Sometimes they may be largely irrelevant because the President's central political position can enable him to set the parameters of his administration's approach to international affairs.[2] However, within any administration post-1945, Washington's self-image as a global superpower has tended to be paramount in the White House: policy towards Israel and the Arab–Israeli dispute will not knowingly compromise what the administration sees as its global interests.[3] As such, perceptions of the national interest and of how to protect or enhance the country's strategic and economic objectives are crucial in determining the direction of foreign policy decision-making. Perceptions of what such interests require and what takes precedence in the event of conflicting priorities may change over time and are, to a certain extent, a product of domestic pressure and bureaucratic rivalry. Hence the direction of US policy towards Israel may vary over time, in accordance with changing circumstances. This chapter will analyse such factors and the extent to which they may be germane in any framework for explaining US foreign policy decision-making.

The National Interest Perspective

To attempt to explain US policy towards Israel solely by reference to a special relationship is to oversimplify the dynamics of interaction between the two states; consideration of national security and the need to respond to domestic circumstance are also of great, and on occasions, greater significance because they have an immediate impact on decision-makers' perceptions of their nations' vital interests. "National interest," Joseph Frankel writes, "is the most comprehensive description of the whole value complex of foreign policy,"[4] but it is a very loosely defined concept. As a term it derives from the belief that states are the highest political authority and that, lacking any political superior, they must determine national policy for themselves. The question then arises of what it means to say that something is in the national interest. Does 'national' refer to the people or the state, what are 'interests' and who defines them – the head of government, the cabinet, politicians, leading interest groups, the army, the media or the people? In reality, all of the above exert an influence on the national interest, but what counts at any given moment is what those who speak in the name of the state claim as constituting the national interest. As a consequence, it is possible for interpretations to change as one government succeeds another. That said, the term does provide a kind of 'intellectual core' around which policy is framed and suggests the existence of certain aims and objectives that can be identified by both decision-makers and rational observers.[5]

The 'national interest' constitutes an aspect of foreign policy to which statesmen profess to attach great importance. The advancement of what is defined as the national interest forms the basic objective of foreign policy and is "the general and continuing ends for which a nation acts."[6] On the other hand, while the term the 'national interest' is clouded by definitional ambiguity, in this book, the national interest approach will take as its starting point the assumption that a state will use the resources at its disposal to try to guarantee what it regards as its security and well being. This approach draws on the classical realist assumption of scholars such as Kautilya, Machiavelli and Hobbes, which argues that states seek to avoid being overpowered in economic and military terms, and that power in the sense of "the capacity to produce intended effects" provides the common denominator in any assessment of the international system.[7] For other writers, such as Waltz and Bull, power cannot serve as a sufficient basis for the definition of the national interest[8] partly because the term itself is of such conceptual fluidity and partly because the objectives decision-makers pursue are mixed, diverse and sometimes contradictory.[9] Considerations of economic gain, prestige and domestic advantage are often perceived to be fundamental aspects of the national interest, but then in practice they may produce policies that are inconsistent. In this sense, it is more appropriate to speak of interests rather than a single national interest based on a number of often conflicting objectives, in contrast to a single and predominant overriding operational goal.[10]

For any power, great or small, foreign policy is formulated in a context that provides constraints as well as opportunities. The interplay between the enduring features of the international system, which includes balance of power calculations, international trade relations and the geopolitical circumstance of a country, gives foreign policy an element of continuity and imposes limitations on what even the most radical and ambitious leaders are able to achieve. For example, the people of a particular country with relatively unchanging neighbours, will often inherit a framework of perceptions, aspirations and expectations, that give the process of defining the national interest a historical dimension.[11] In Britain, recent disagreements over interpretations of the national interest have to be seen against the background of centuries of conflict with the European powers as well as the colonial experience. In attempting to find an equilibrium between the country's relations with the US, the Commonwealth and with Europe, successive British governments since the Second World War have often seemed less wholehearted about their commitment to the latter than their European partners would have wished, thereby earning Britain the reputation of the "reluctant European."[12]

The interests of a state which comprise the overarching national interest can be subdivided between 'vital' interests which governments consider worthy of sacrifice and are prepared to back up with the use of force and 'secondary' interests from which they can retreat. One of the most fundamental policy objectives of any government is the preservation of the state's territorial integrity and political independence, which includes the perpetuation of a particular social, political and economic order.[13] Since territory is the essence of statehood, decision-makers will generally defend it at any cost, either human or material.[14] There are of course, certain exceptions to this rule as when a state that comprises separate ethnic entities is torn apart by internal tension and the preference of the component nations is to separate into sovereign states. This was the fate of both the Soviet Union and Yugoslavia in the 1990s. Other exceptions in extreme circumstances have also occurred. By signing the 1918 Treaty of Brest-Livtosk, Lenin surrendered large amounts of Russian territory to the Germans in exchange for peace, describing this as a policy of "sacrificing space in order to buy time,"[15] while Czechoslovakian President Emil Hacha allowed the Sudetenland, the German speaking part of his state, to be annexed to Germany in an attempt to save Czechoslovakia as a country.[16] As Hitler's stated objective was to re-unite all German-speaking peoples, Hacha incorrectly believed that in relinquishing the Sudetenland, the Nazis would respect the territorial integrity of the Czech-speaking part of the state. Extreme circumstances aside, the preservation of the state as a unified entity is generally regarded as the most fundamental foreign policy objective.

In recent times, the interpretation of what defines 'security' has been broadened. It is no longer confined to that of military strength because there is increasing acknowledgement that security can be jeopardised both from within and without the states' national boundaries. For example, the awesome military strength of the Soviet Union could not prevent the country's disintegration, while countries with little military defensive capabilities such as Switzerland and Luxembourg flourish, partly because of the diplomatic and economic policies of their governments.[17] We only need to look at the great lengths to which the US and the Western European states went to oust Iraq from Kuwait to understand that resources, in this case oil, are as much a security as an economic priority.

Prestige and national esteem have always been important in international relations. Historically prestige was equated with military power and governments have gone to great lengths to preserve and enhance their military reputations. President Kennedy's willingness to go to the brink of nuclear war with the Soviet Union during the 1962 Cuban missile crisis is said to have been largely attributable to his mishandling of the abortive landing in Cuba's Bay of Pigs in 1961.[18] Kennedy sought to restore both his own personal prestige and that of the US by taking a tough stance in his subsequent dealings with Moscow. Today, in an era of mass communication, international esteem has evolved from emphasis on a purely military reputation to one in which credibility is of increasing significance. For example, many developing countries derive considerable esteem from participation in the UN General Assembly, where their vote technically carries as much weight as that of the Great Powers, even though Great Powers can often exert influence, in economic and political terms, to affect voting patterns.

Paradoxically, the broader a state's foreign commitments and the higher its standing in the international arena, the more limited tends to be its freedom of action in foreign affairs.[19] This is a product of its alliances and treaty obligations, foreign investments and trading interests and commitment to the well being of its citizens resident abroad. For global powers the credibility of commitments is crucial to their continued international standing. If they make threats that they do not follow up or commitments on which they renege, their integrity is thrown into disrepute and their credibility suffers accordingly. In 1939, after reneging on its treaty commitment to Czechoslovakia, Britain's international reputation would have been completely undermined had it also abrogated its obligations to Warsaw by not declaring war on Germany, on 1 September 1939, when Nazi troops entered Poland. The US decision to bomb Afghanistan despite uncertainty that the raids would achieve the stated objectives of destroying Osama bin Laden's power base and reducing the threat of Islamic terror, was in part a product of the need to be seen by the international community to be taking decisive action in response to the September 11, 2001 terrorist attacks on its citizens.

A clear definition of the national interest requires agreement on the nature and priority of values and objectives foreign policy should promote and has to assume that decision-makers behave rationally.[20] This raises the whole question of rationality in foreign policy. Decision-makers are often under pressure of time, inadequate information and simultaneity of issues that all serve to limit their policy alternatives and necessitate decisions in situations of uncertainty.[21] Even if the institutional process has attained a high degree of instrumental rationality in its collection and assimilation of information and in its capacity to handle a number of problems simultaneously, areas of uncertainty still confront decision-makers. Foreign policy issues must be set within a context of other issues and against a framework of the government's prime concerns. Ideally, decisions are a product of a cost–benefit analysis accruing from alternative courses of action[22] based on considerations of the 'value' or 'utility' of alternative sets of consequences[23] and are not capricious or unconsidered.[24] However, there is generally sufficient ambiguity inherent in any international situation, to make more than one interpretation of events plausible. The difficulty lies in determining whether a particular movement of troops, tariff or threat of deprivation constitutes a serious danger to security and if so to decide what level of threat it presents. Decision-makers must then determine which of the state's interests are most affected and which goals are most crucial in determining their response.[25] This criterion of rationality does not mean that governments never act from passion or prejudice. On occasions of course they do, and such emotional forces are themselves often attributable to the perceptions of the state's past experience of international affairs.[26]

The assumption of rationality is even more problematic in assessing the probable motives and behaviour of other states. Increasing cultural diversity means that value systems differ greatly between, and sometimes within, countries. Different governments assign different values or weight to the defence of particular objectives such as the preservation of life, democracy, the institution of private property and the importance of prestige. The weight assigned to each value will affect the direction of foreign policy. As a consequence, one government may have a different conception of rationality from another, with the cultural relativity of values matched by "the cultural relativity of the processes of mind."[27] What is rational for one government in a given situation may not seem rational to another, and what a Western administration reports as rational a non-Western state may not, and vice versa.

The 'national interest', ambiguous though the concept is, is the term given to what those representing states seek to defend. However, despite the great importance assigned to it, an objective national interest common to all cannot be discerned. It is in any case, subject to reinterpretation in the light of changes in inter-state or transnational power relations[28] or the changing values and beliefs of decision-makers. Since the concept of the national interest is composed of different elements, it is to these constituent elements including strategic, economic and domestic interests that we now turn.

The Strategic Interest Perspective

The strategic interest approach to foreign policy decision-making offers a state-centric perspective of foreign policy and looks at the way states mobilise their military and other such capabilities in support of their political goals. It draws on the Clausewitzian tradition that understands military power as an ultimate resource that must be converted into a usable instrument to both advance and defend the strategic interest where necessary. As such states will form alliances or alignments with other states whose perception of the strategic interest happen to coincide.

Perhaps no region of the world has figured as prominently in the strategic calculations of the Great Powers in recent years as the Middle East.[29] The United States is no exception and since the Second World War American decision-makers have come to regard the Middle East as vital to their common perception of the strategic interest, for three main reasons. The first is the role of oil as it pertains to international stability and the prosperity of the Western world. The second is the geopolitical importance of the region as it relates to Great Power rivalry and thirdly is the US commitment to the security and survival of Israel, the only parliamentary democracy in the region. In attempting to advance its interests in these three areas, Washington considers resolution of the Arab–Israeli conflict as essential to the American strategic interest. This is because the conflict is viewed as encroaching upon and threatening all other concerns and in the absence of peace, the US has constantly to juggle its competing interests with Israel and the Arab world.

Since its creation in 1948 until 1990–91, US–Israeli relations were conditioned by an overarching US strategic interest, namely Washington's desire to circumvent Soviet advances in the Middle East. Internal debates within the Truman administration concerning the recognition of Israel focused on the anticipated Soviet response to such a move. In the mid-1940s, Moscow had been eager to recognise the creation of Israel, believing that it would force the British out of the Middle East, thus ending British control over many Arab states and particularly the Arab League. Moscow anticipated that Israel would be a great liberating force,[30] undermining Arab feudalism with the kind of socialist economics advocated by many refugees from Poland and Russia. In the event, the capitalist nature of the Jewish state proved to be a disappointment and

Moscow became further estranged from Israel by the latter's gradual alignment with the United States.[31]

However, a close strategic connection did not immediately follow Truman's recognition of Israel and the US provided virtually no aid during Israel's War of Independence or in the following years. Washington was primarily concerned with preventing Moscow from establishing a position of influence in the Middle East which it viewed as a threat to US access to the region's oil resources and strategic lines of communication, including the Suez Canal. US policy relied on the Arabs to confront the Soviet Union, and Israel was generally not included.[32] It was not until 1962 that the Kennedy administration inaugurated the first significant weapons sale of HAWK anti-aircraft missiles,[33] as a means of demonstrating support for Israel and maintaining the military balance. In return for US support, Israel was expected to practice self-restraint towards its Arab neighbours and US policy elsewhere in the region.[34] The Six Day War of 1967 was an important landmark in the relationship because though there were problems in its relations with Tel Aviv,[35] Washington directly aligned with Israel against its Arab enemies and the Soviet Union. Conflict between the Arabs and Israel was seen as part of the broader confrontation between the two superpowers and the US supported Israel as a means of safeguarding its position in the region. Although the US did not play a direct role in the conflict, it did provide tangential support and moved the Sixth Fleet to counter potential Soviet intervention. Washington also played a crucial role in supporting Israel's position in the diplomatic battle that followed the military conflict.

In 1970, the US was confronted with a new strategic reality: a deteriorating regional position linked to the presence of large numbers of Soviet advisors in Egypt, including pilots and other military personnel who were operating Egypt's missile defence system. It was Washington's preoccupation with Soviet involvement in the region that created a confluence of strategic interests between America and Israel. Nixon pledged US support for the maintenance of the regional balance of power and enhanced Israel's deterrent capability to discourage the Arabs from launching another war that could provoke superpower confrontation.[36]

Though the global power balance conditioned US policy towards Israel, it was also influenced by the administration's strategic analysis of conditions in the region. Thus in 1970, Nixon and Kissinger authorised Israel to act as a proxy to protect US interests in Jordan when King Hussein's throne was challenged by *fedayeen* forces in what was termed Black September.[37] In 1973 the same administration supplied Israel with arms during the Yom Kippur War but did not permit a decisive military victory, because they believed stalemate on the ground between Israeli and Egyptian forces would facilitate peace negotiations. Overt strategic cooperation between the US and Israel developed during the Reagan administration, in response to increased instability across the Middle

East, with the overthrow of the Shah of Iran and the establishment of an Islamic Republic, the Soviet invasion of Afghanistan and the Iran–Iraq war. In an article in the *Washington Post* of 15 August 1979, Reagan criticised the Democrats' approach to relations with Israel and highlighted his perception of Israel's strategic importance:

> American policy-makers downgrade Israel's geopolitical importance as a stabilising force, as a deterrent to radical hegemony and as a military offset to the Soviet Union. The fall of Iran has increased Israel's value as perhaps the only remaining strategic asset in the region on which the United States can truly rely; other pro-Western states in the region, especially Saudi Arabia and the smaller Gulf kingdoms, are weak and vulnerable.[38]

The Reagan administration was the first to formalise and institutionalise the military, economic and political aspects of the US–Israeli strategic relationship.[39] On 30 November 1981, Washington and Jerusalem signed a Memorandum of Understanding (MOU) on strategic cooperation "designed against the Soviet-controlled forces from outside the region introduced into the region."[40] These ties were consolidated in 1984 when Israel was granted permission to compete directly for contracts in the US military market and again in April 1985 when Israel accepted America's invitation to participate in the Strategic Defence Initiative (SDI). The objective of the SDI was to research, develop and test a new generation of high-technology weapons to be deployed in space and on earth, that would create a 'shield' over the US to defend it from Soviet nuclear missiles. The strategic relationship reached its zenith on 14 December 1987, when Israel achieved the coveted status of a 'major non-NATO ally', a position enjoyed by only two other countries, Sweden and Australia.

By the end of Reagan's second term in office, numerous areas of military cooperation had come to fruition that exceeded the bounds of the memorandums of understanding. The US Navy and Airforce were using Israel's live-fire ranges for training exercises, US and Israeli forces were engaging in joint air and sea exercises and the US Navy was making extensive use of Israel's ports.[41] Cooperation was also occurring in a variety of weapons development and production projects including aircraft, electronics, naval vessels, tank guns and terminal guidance bombs.[42]

From the US perspective, strategic cooperation had always been about more than the purely military dimension and included the development of an overall security framework designed to create the conditions for peace.[43] Part of the strategic rationale for supplying Israel with arms was the belief that a strong and confident Israel might be willing to take risks for peace. In reality the reverse often proved to be the case, as when the military balance of power favoured Israel, its leaders were generally reluctant to embark on peace negotiations. It is this linkage between strategic cooperation and peace that constituted one of the most important differences between the respective conceptions of strategic cooperation held by Washington and Jerusalem.[44]

As the majority of the world's known oil reserves are found in the Persian Gulf, petrodollars have made the oil producing states a valuable economic prize and of immense importance to the Western economies. Historically concerns have been raised that support for Israel antagonises the oil producing states, thereby jeopardising Western access to Middle East oil. However, with the exception of the oil crisis of 1973, there is little evidence to support this contention and Washington concluded successful working relationships with the monarchies of the Gulf. While some attempts to create overt and formal alliances, such as the Baghdad Pact of 1955 failed, because the Middle Eastern states refused to join,[45] informal networks based on shared interests but not underwritten by public treaty obligations, like that with Saudi Arabia, have been more successful. Franklin D. Roosevelt's decision to support Saudi Arabia and Richard Nixon's decision to back Iran were based on a pragmatic assessment of America's security requirements. Roosevelt was the first president to publicly acknowledge that "the defence of Saudi Arabia is vital to the defence of the United States" because it is "probably the richest economic prize in the world in the field of foreign investment."[46] Successive administrations acknowledged that if support for Israel was critical for honour and votes, then support for Saudi Arabia was critical for oil.[47] Nixon acknowledged Israel's inability to protect US interests single-handedly and made Iran an important American ally, supplying the Shah with arms accordingly.[48]

In the atmosphere of the Cold War, the protection of the Middle East oil fields were, in their own way, as important to the strategic interest of the United States as the independence of Western Europe.[49] Early in the Second World War, in his correspondence with Roosevelt, Churchill had acknowledged the importance of US interests in Saudi Arabia.[50] The State Department reconciled support for Israel with American oil interests by seeking where possible to delegate to the oil companies themselves Washington's relations with the Arab governments of the Middle East.[51] Confronted with Communist, Islamic and Hashemite threats to his throne, King ibn Saud depended on Washington to guarantee the security of his kingdom[52] and accepted Washington's compromise position of separating economic considerations from the political question of US support for Israel. With oil as the sole source of the monarchy's rapidly expanding wealth and basis for economic development, it was in the monarchy's interest to draw a clear distinction between the operations of Aramco, a purely commercial enterprise owned by four private companies, and the policies of the US government elsewhere in the region. Washington's dual policy with the richest oil state was very successful until the oil crisis of 1973, when under pressure from President Anwar-al Sadat of Egypt, King Faisal imposed an oil embargo on the United States in a show of Arab solidarity. The embargo was a protest against Washington's support for Israel in its war against the Arab states.[53] Yet because the alignment between the House of Saud and the White House was seen as mutually beneficial, the disruption to oil supplies was short lived. Oil derives its value from its sales potential and if stockpiling oil for political ends may damage the Western economies, the financial impact on the oil producing states can be even greater. By 1975, US–Saudi relations had returned to their former equilibrium. Saudi Arabia acted as a bulwark of stability in the Gulf, while the stationing of US troops on Saudi soil during the Gulf War of 1991, was understood by both sides to have defended the regime against internal subversion and attack from external forces.

Historically, the American rationale for describing Israel as a strategic asset derived from the latter's perceived ability to deter radical Arab aggression and with it the prospects for Soviet regional expansion. It was also thought that Israel's existence and military strength buttressed the security of friendly Arab states, thus ensuring Western access to Mideast oil. However, while in theory this may have been the case, the strategic asset explanation suffers from a number of deficiencies. Despite Israel's undoubted military strength and the US perception of Israel as a friend that could be relied upon in an extremity, there are few occasions when actual military cooperation was put to the test. Although US–Israeli cooperation during the September 1970 Jordan crisis provides the most obvious example of direct military collaboration, generally Washington has been reluctant to be seen as openly working with Israel in the region,[54] in case this undermined its relations with friendly Arab regimes. In contrast, examples of technological collaboration or joint research and development projects, such as Reagan's SDI abound, as do examples of covert cooperation as with the Iran–Contra affair.[55] Strategic cooperation with Israel did little to enhance America's ability to project its power in the Middle East. In most circumstances, America was reluctant to use Israeli troops in a conflict with an Arab state, as was the case during the 1990–91 Gulf War. Therefore, while the notion of Israel as a strategic asset contributes to an explanation of US policy towards Israel, the underlying rationale for the policy must be found elsewhere.

The Economic Interest Approach

The viability of a given course of foreign policy action is as much a product of economic factors as of strategic calculations. Economic strength is a pre-requisite for any government wishing to pursue an effective foreign policy. The prevalence and quality of natural resources, the sophistication and diversification of industry, the standard of living of the population and the level of economic self-sufficiency, contribute to any calculation of the economic capabilities of the state. In the formulation of foreign policy, economic interests play a key role in decision-making calculations. In terms of US foreign policy, the costs and benefits of global confrontation are analysed not only in terms of the ability of the industrial complex to sustain the military infrastructure necessary for its defence, but also in relation to the impact a particular foreign policy course will exert on international trade relations. The unwillingness of the population to tolerate the sacrifice of domestic economic growth when priority is given to defence spending has also acted as a foreign policy constraint. By an accident of geography and nature, America has been blessed with a vast landmass and an abundance of natural resources that have enabled its leaders to invest sizeable economic resources in advancing their perception of the national interest. Foreign aid and trade relations are used to protect American interests overseas by supporting friendly governments against internal and external challenges.

The Marshall Plan of 1947 was the greatest foreign aid package in history and provided for the transfer of $13 billion from the US to Europe between 1948 and 1952.[56] It was intended to revive the European economies and stimulate international trade, lest the deprivation and shortages engendered by the Second World War fuel the expansion of Communism across Europe.[57] Since then the Pax Americana has been firmly grounded in the belief that trade produces economic and social change. In this it is not dissimilar from the Pax Britannica which was largely based on the belief that free trade brought enlightenment and with enlightenment liberty.[58] Foreign aid and trade relations continue to be used as a device for promoting stability and creating a world hospitable to American society and its ideals.

Since the mid-1970s, Israel has become the leading beneficiary of America's policy of foreign aid. US–Israeli economic relations did not originate as a product of economic imperatives but as a by-product of the special political and cultural ties between the two countries. The record of US financial and military support for Israel has been unique and historically dependent on a continuous dialogue between the two governments, reinforced by congressional and public support.[59] Over time however, economic relations have expanded in both depth and breadth and they sometimes function virtually autonomously of the political environment.

Initially, US government aid to Israel was low, but increased dramatically as a consequence of the 1973 war and the level of official assistance as of 1990 stood at $3 billion per year – $1.8 billion in military assistance and $1.2 billion in economic assistance.[60] In 1981 grants replaced loans for economic assistance and in 1984, when Israel faced the prospect of repaying past military loans, the US also restructured its military assistance to Israel from loans to grants.[61] This effectively absolved Israel of the obligation to repay the debt. In 1991, following the Gulf War, Israel received an additional $5 billion in aid and in 1992 Washington granted Israel $10 billion over five years in commercial loans to assist with the financial cost of absorbing one million Soviet Jews.[62] Moreover, in contrast to every other US aid recipient, Israel's grants are handed over in full by the Treasury at the beginning of the fiscal year for the Israeli government to invest and use as it sees fit.[63]

Foreign aid, a relatively new political strategy for Washington, was largely a product of the Cold War. It stemmed from the perception that US investment in capitalist countries would be an effective device to thwart the spread of Communism.[64] That Israel has been the recipient of the largest share of US annual assistance of any state in the world since 1976 is directly attributable to its democratic and capitalist status,[65] but has occurred for a number of other reasons – the first being American foreign policy priorities and until recently the exigencies of superpower competition in particular. As the Soviet Union increased arms deliveries to Israel's Arab enemies, Washington reciprocated to maintain the military balance in the region. The American initiation of aid to the Middle East generally followed that of Moscow[66] and escalated in accordance with Soviet arms deliveries to Egypt and Syria.

The second reason for increases in aid stemmed from the need to counterbalance American arms sales to the Arab states. Arms sales were one of the most powerful forms of leverage the superpowers could use to influence regional states. In response to Israeli objections following the supply of arms to friendly Arab leaders, the US claimed that the weapons did not really constitute a change in the balance of power but merely facilitated the recycling of petrodollars. To reinforce this claim, the US supplied additional arms to Israel to maintain its position *vis-à-vis* its adversaries. Thirdly, the US escalated its economic assistance as the *quid pro quo* for persuading the Israeli government to adhere to American strategic priorities, including 'land for peace' deals with the Arabs that it found difficult to countenance.[67] Aid to Israel tended to increase with the signing of each peace agreement and territorial withdrawal, beginning with the Camp David Accords of 1979 and most recently with George W. Bush's Road Map.

That US–Israeli economic relations were originally a product of political expediency is evident by the way they have tended to track political relations between the two governments. Economic factors appeared to have little bearing on aid patterns.[68] Israel was the first country to enjoy a free-trade agreement with the US and it provided a means for Israel to receive preferential access to the US market, as well as ensuring US access to the Israeli market. By 1990, US products comprised one-fifth of Israeli imports, valued at $4 billion annually.[69] Gradually economic relations became somewhat more balanced and included greater emphasis on trade relations and policies to promote and sustain Israeli economic growth. For example, by the mid-1990s, the United States was purchasing 40 percent of Israel's machinery and mechanical appliances and over one third of Israel's optical, photographic and medical exports.[70]

Though economically, Israel would appear to be the main beneficiary of the relationship, there are those like Geoffrey Aronson who argue that support for Israel gives "value for money" according to a non-economic calculus that has been established over time.[71] A. F. K. Organski elaborates on this and provides three main reasons for his argument. First, he claims that in the absence of an Arab ally with the political and military power to defend its regional interests, America was left with little alternative but to fund Israel. Secondly, aid to Israel had been 'cost-effective' because Tel Aviv was victorious in every war against the Soviet-backed Arab states. Israel had effectively blocked Soviet expansion through proxies, while its military strength and potential had defended the moderate Arab regimes.[72] Thirdly, the Arab's successive defeats at the hands of Israel proved the futility of alignment with Moscow. As a consequence, the Arab leaders, beginning with Egyptian President Anwar al-Sadat, concluded that an alignment with Washington was necessary to secure the return of Arab lands conquered by Israel.[73]

But can the 'return' America received on its investment in Israel be so readily quantified? After all, even if Israel successfully contained the radical Arab states, would Arab leaders have been so receptive to Soviet involvement in their domestic politics were it not for their hatred of Israel? Although the brokering of a peace agreement between Egypt and Israel was to America's advantage, to perceive it as a direct benefit deriving from previous military and economic assistance to Israel is somewhat misleading. While the Camp David negotiations had their origins in the 1973 war, the accords were painstakingly and personally brokered by American President Jimmy Carter, and underwritten by $5 billion in annual aid ($3 billion to Israel and $2 billion to Egypt). It was this additional financial commitment to Israel that secured Israeli withdrawal from Sinai, and subsequent Arab–Israeli peace treaties have been underwritten by further economic guarantees. In view of this ongoing financial obligation, it is hard to portray economic support for Israel as a 'bargain' after all. The United States pays a high financial price to its ally for every peace agreement it secures to enhance its perception of its own and Israel's strategic interest.

In terms of the original rationale behind the foreign aid programme that was designed to promote parliamentary democracy and capitalism, Israel is one of America's success stories (even if many Arabs would question the degree to which the democratic rights of Israeli Arabs were respected). However, from a purely economic perspective, America does not receive a tangible financial return on its capital investment in Israel. The first report by the US General Accounting office (GAO), which followed the Lebanon war, analysed the economic aspects of the relationship. Even though it was intended for Congress, the branch of government traditionally most sensitive to Israeli concerns, it emphasised the high financial cost and financial liabilities the US incurred in supporting Israel.[74] This highlighted both complications associated with politically motivated lending and the crucial role domestic politics play in American political decision-making. The importance of popular support for foreign aid to Israel cannot be understated. Foreign policy is often the product of domestic political necessity – one of its basic objectives to reduce domestic political disequilibria. It is to the realm of domestic policy-making that we now turn.

The Domestic Politics Perspective

In any democratic country, domestic considerations play a key role in shaping perceptions of the nation's values and national interest. Michael Donelan argues that "US foreign policy [is] an emanation of domestic politics"[75] because America is not monolithic[76] and the course of foreign policy is deeply rooted in the nature of the political system and the imperatives of electioneering. That is not to say that domestic politics determine foreign policy, but it does provide the immediate context in which decisions are made, defines the rules of the game and determines who is responsible for decision-making.[77] That said, as James Rosenau explains, the influence of domestic factors on decision-making is notoriously difficult to define:

> The premise is that domestic sources of foreign policy are no less crucial to its content than are the international situations towards which it is directed. The dilemma is that links between the domestic sources and the resulting behaviour – foreign policy – are not easily observed and are thus especially resistant to coherent analysis.[78]

The US has a very distinctive political system based on the separation of powers and is home to arguably the most powerful and autonomous legislature in the world. The highly competitive nature of the political system makes it susceptible to pressure from organised lobbyists and voting majorities, where office holders can become a function of their constituents. The separation of powers was designed to prevent the abuse of authority through the concentration of power in one body. In reality the Constitution of 1787 did not create a government of 'separated powers' but a government of 'separated institutions' sharing power.[79] As a consequence, while the American president is often considered to be the most powerful man in the world, in reality his power is severely circumscribed by the other governing organs of the state. Of these governing bodies, Congress has become the institution through which pressure groups attempt to achieve their objectives and have their preferences translated into public policy. Samuel Huntington claims that "the most prominent congressional role is that of prodder or goad of the Administration on behalf of specific programmes or activities. With the executive the decision-maker, Congress becomes the lobbyist."[80] Congress as a whole does not lobby the executive but particular groups within Congress do: committees, blocs, or even an entire house. As lobbyists, congressional groups are in a peripheral bargaining position with the administration. Although Congress is unable to impose its preferences on the executive, through public criticism it can force the executive to pay a substantial price for policies with which it disagrees.[81]

As a result, lobbying, electoral battles and competition between the executive and legislative branches of the government have become an integral part of the foreign-policy process. Robert Art claims that "it is presidential anticipation of Congress and public response that causes [the president] to heed those bureaucratic demands he chooses to accede to."[82] Congress "sets the tone of many policies and limits on many others . . . It seems obvious that Executive proposals are shaped by estimates of how Congress and individual Congressmen will react."[83] The preferences of Congress are only one of a number of different opinions to which the president is exposed. Richard Neustadt describes the president as having five sets of constituents: Executive officialdom, Congress, his partisans, public opinion and the international arena.[84] Each of these forces vie for his attention and policy decisions favourable to their interests.

American Jews and the pro-Israel Lobby

The American Jewish community, together with the pro-Israel lobby (the two are by no means synonymous), exerts one of the most powerful domestic influences on American foreign policy. This is partly attributable to the nature of the American political system that is both integrative and susceptible to religious and ethnic pressure and partly to the highly organised and well funded activities of the pro-Israel lobby. As a result of contemporary Jewish history and early integration into American society, the political system facilitated their socio-economic mobility and operates in a way that enhances their values and interests.[85] Washington has never been a place in which foreign and domestic influences have been separated, a fact that the pro-Israel lobby has been keen to exploit. The social political openness and coalitional political system, which responds to and absorbs diversity, has enabled American Jews to secure an advantage in politics and public office, based on their achievement orientation and their extraordinary level of participation.[86]

Although impossible to quantify, it is often claimed that the pro-Israel lobby, in conjunction with the perceived power of the American Jewish vote, have played a major role in shaping US policy towards Israel. Wayne Owens, a former Senator and now President of the Centre for Middle East Peace, claimed that in Washington "politics is the name of the game and no one plays the game better than the American Jews."[87] Within the US, some hold that a candidate cannot run for Congress without the backing of the Jewish community.[88] This is only partly mythical; it is broadly true, for example, that Congressmen "always feel safe voting for Israel."[89]

Since the 1950s, lobbying in support of Israel has been the preserve of two primary institutions, the Conference of Presidents of Major Jewish Organisations and the American Israel Public Affairs Committee (Aipac). The primary objective of the Conference of Presidents is to define by consensus any grievances the Jewish community harbours towards America's Middle East policy and to present these views to the White House or Department of State. The Conference seeks only to reach a consensus amongst its members on questions concerning Israel and is not involved in direct political action. In effect, the conference is the diplomatic wing of the lobby and is responsible for managing relations between the American Jewish community and the governments of the US and Israel.

Aipac is the official lobbying body of Israeli interests on Capitol Hill. It has over 55,000 members and an annual budget exceeding $15 million.[90] By the mid-1990s it was considered to be the second most powerful lobby in the United States.[91] It is a highly centralised organisation, dedicated to securing the unconditional support of both the executive and legislature for what the Israeli government conceives of as the country's interests. In this endeavour, the lobby maintains daily contact with members of the administration, Senators and representatives. These contacts serve a dual purpose. First, they act as a valuable source of information about policies affecting Israel prior to an official announcement by the American government. This provides the opportunity for early intervention to harmonise American and Israeli positions or to counsel Israel on what it can realistically expect to gain from Washington.[92] David Bar-Ilan, the Israeli director of communications under the Netanyahu government, asserted that a crucial reason for the lobby's success is its timing. It is not enough to be pro-Israeli, you have to know when and where and how[93] to make your power truly felt.

Secondly, regular contact with decision-making personnel provides Israel's supporters with the access necessary to apply pressure to steer policy to what the Israeli government asserts to be Israel's advantage and to secure favours from Congress.[94] For example, in 1985, when the Reagan administration considered selling arms to Jordan and Saudi Arabia, Aipac began the attack long before the administration even announced its intention to sell the arms. It used a time-tested formula: "get insider information on the proposals, give them to the press of friendly Congressmen and use the resulting publicity to generate opposition."[95] The power of the lobby was such that the arms sale was vetoed before the administration even submitted it as a bill to be debated by Congress. This phenomenon is partly attributable to the "law of anticipated reaction"[96] whereby the mere existence of the lobby is enough to encourage Congress to adopt a pro-Israeli line based on the untested assumption that the proposed action would ignite major protests.

The perceived power of the pro-Israel lobby is reinforced by the importance placed on the American Jewish vote. Walter Etyan wrote that Israel's security rests on two pillars, the army and the American Jewish community. He quotes an Israeli spokesman who explained to a state department official that "[t]he Almighty placed massive oil deposits under Arab soil. It is our good fortune that God placed five million Jews in America."[97] The fact that America is home to just 5.5 million Jews, constituting only 3 percent of the population,[98] conceals the actual weight of the American Jewish vote. The intense concern and political activity of this relatively small sector of the population compensates for lack of numbers and is a major source of strength for several reasons.

First, the American Jewish population is not equally distributed throughout the country but is highly concentrated in key electoral states. Jewish influence is strongest in states where Jews provide the critical mass of voters.[99] In New York 12 percent of eligible voters are Jewish, in New Jersey 6 percent and in California 3 percent. Even more crucially, the Jewish population is concentrated in the politically most important zones of those states. More than 90 percent of New York's Jewish population reside in New York City, 70 percent of Pennsylvanian Jews live in Philadelphia and in Massachusetts, 68 percent of Jews reside in Boston.[100] As the number of representatives a state is allocated is determined by the size of its population, in electoral terms these states have greater weight than many others because of their large number of state representatives. The state of California, for instance, can nominate 45 representatives. Therefore, California, which hosts some 970,000 Jews, representing 2.9 percent of the state's population, but a full 6 percent of the electorate, according to a 2000 *Los Angeles Times* exit poll.[101] Secondly, American Jews are highly politicised. In the 1960s and 1970s, more than 90 percent went to the polls, in contrast to the rest of the American population, where almost half the eligible voters fail to cast their vote.[102] This had the effect of increasing the general weight of the Jewish vote by at least one percentage point and by a higher percentage in those states in which Jews are highly concentrated, rising to between 2 and 6 percent in New York City.[103] Since political campaigning is a long-term endeavour where candidates seek to ingratiate themselves with politically organised groups, politicians have found it expedient to sensitise themselves to Jewish community feelings.[104]

Thirdly, the significance of the Jewish vote is further increased because it tends to be located at the centre of the electoral configuration. While generally voting for the Democratic Party, in a close run race the Jewish vote can be the margin of victory or defeat, encouraging politicians to be responsive to the concerns of the Jewish community.[105] In the 2000 presidential election, Florida was one of several "swing states" where Republicans and Democrats expended most of their energies, on the theory that these electorates could be swayed to either party. Joseph Lieberman's potential to draw Florida Jews was cited as one of the reasons for his nomination as vice-president.[106] In any case, support for Israel is a strong motivational force for American Jews and increases their disposition to vote as a bloc for candidates considered to be pro-Israeli. During the Reagan presidency, opinion polls indicated that more than 70 percent of all Jews believed that "Jews should not vote for candidates who have a hostile attitude towards Israel." Jimmy Carter, who in 1976 captured 70 percent of the Jewish vote, secured less than 50 percent in his re-election bid of 1980 because he was perceived by a portion of the Jewish electorate to be unsympathetic to Israel.[107] However, irrespective of the factors outlined above, many Jews tend to vote in accordance with their other concerns, such as the education and standard of living of themselves and their family.[108]

Israel has presented a radical test to the capacity of American exceptionalism to tolerate ethnic activism in support of a foreign state – something it has been more unwilling to do for other large ethnic groups such as the Irish and the Greeks.[109] However, it is not only American Jews for whom Israel is an emotional issue; Protestant Christians have also become increasingly vocal in their defence of the Jewish state.

Christian Evangelicals and the State of Israel

Given the numerically small Jewish population in the US, Israel has never relied solely on this community to maintain political and public support. This is because many non-Jewish citizens are also committed to the Israeli cause. While perceptions of Israel amongst the religious community are by no means uniform, a powerful tendency exists within many Protestant sects to see the Jews as 'God's chosen people'.[110] The alliance of Israeli lobbyists and Christian Zionist fundamentalists began in 1978 with the publication of a Likud plan to encourage fundamentalist churches to give their support to Israel. By 1980, there was an "International Christian Embassy" in Jerusalem; and in 1985, a Christian Zionist lobby emerged at a "National Prayer Breakfast for Israel" whose principal speaker was Binyamin Netanyahu, later Prime Minister of Israel.[111]

One of the most notable and numerically powerful organisations is the Christian Evangelicals, a movement with more than 40 million members. The majority of American Christians that align with Israel are members of the National Council of Churches (NCC) of Evangelical Fundamentalists, who adhere to a literal interpretation of the Bible and fervently believe that God himself wants Israel to take possession of all the Arab lands it can capture. For these Christians, support for Israel has little to do with the endorsement of the government's political strategies or the maintenance of the state as a safe haven for world Jewry. The relationship instead is one of mutual convenience, based on circumstances of a political and military nature, in which both parties are nationalistic, militaristic and advance a dogma centred on Israel and a cult of land.[112] This confluence of interests is necessary purely because, in religious terms, the two movements are, from a theological perspective, worlds apart.[113] The religious characteristics of the Jewish state are based on strains of Judaism that regard Christian proselytising – a basic premise of fundamentalism – as a profound threat to the existence of the Jews as a community.[114] Nevertheless, many people in Israel and amongst the American Jewish community believe that the Evangelicals offer an important source of political and economic support even if they take exception to the latter's underlying motivations.

In the 1980s, during Reagan's time in office, Irving Kristol, a Professor of Social Thought at the New York University Graduate School, urged American Jews to generate additional support for Israel by forming an alliance with Jerry Falwell, the leading American Evangelical Fundamentalist.[115] The Reverend Jerry Falwell's Moral Majority, one of the major political organisations of the New Christian Right,[116] and other fundamentalist/evangelical political groups, campaigned hard for Reagan in the run-up to both the 1980 and 1984 presidential elections. They portrayed Reagan as a defender of traditional Judeo-Christian values, in contrast to the Democrats who were depicted as agents of 'secular humanism'[117] – the sinister cabal supposedly ruining America.[118] The power of the Religious Right reached its zenith under the Reagan administration when the President directly linked himself to the NCC and proclaimed 1983 "The Year of the Bible".[119] His appeal to the fundamentalists appeared to have translated into votes with 22 million Christian fundamentalist and evangelicals shifting from a pro-Democratic 56–43% margin in 1976 to an 81–19% Republican sweep in 1984.[120] Reagan is now commonly portrayed as one of the most staunchly pro-Israel presidents to occupy the White House.

Arab Americans and the pro-Arab Lobby

There is a danger in the above analysis in that the reader may draw the conclusion that the support of American society for Israel is beyond doubt. However, not all Americans share these feelings of empathy for the Jewish state, and the Arab Americans are one such group. The Arab American community had not traditionally been involved in political activity partly because of the more recent emigration of many of its million and a half members and partly because of their disparate origins.[121] Intensified feelings of ethnic awareness amongst the Arab American community emerged in response to the 1967 and 1973 Arab–Israeli wars and the subsequent oil crisis this provoked.[122] By the early 1980s, The

Action Committee on American Arab Relations (ACAAR) and the Washington-based National Association of Arab Americans (NAAA), the two main Arab lobbying bodies, were firmly established. The impact of these associations was limited because the Arab community is highly fragmented and lacks the unity and consensus of their Jewish counterparts on basic political and tactical issues.[123] Internal problems hamper the Arab lobby's efforts and their potential power is curtailed by their failure to agree amongst themselves.[124] A former president of the NAAA, James Baroody concluded that:

> We can't represent the Arabs the way the Jewish lobby can represent Israel. The Israeli government has one policy to state, whereas we couldn't represent the "Arabs" if we wanted to. They're as different as the Libyans and Saudis are different or as divided as the Christian and Moslem Lebanese.[125]

The acknowledged weakness within the political community of the Arab lobby *vis-à-vis* the pro-Israel lobby is demonstrated by the following example. In 1988 John Sununu, an American of Arab origin, had to declare that he did not harbour anti-Jewish sentiment when he was chosen as a candidate for the position of White House Chief of Staff under president-elect George Bush.[126] It is inconceivable that an American Jew, in the same position, would be called upon to make a similar pledge in relation to the Arabs. However, this gap began to close and in the mid-1990s, when for the first time in history, a US President, Bill Clinton, addressed the NAAA.[127]

In purely economic terms, the Arab contribution to the US economy is far more important than that of Israel, but the Arabs have singularly failed to appreciate how to exercise their annual contribution of $27 billion as economic leverage to achieve their political objectives.[128] In contrast, American businessmen have long since realised that being pro-Arab is not a precondition for making money in the Arab world and therefore have no particular economic interest in lobbying Congress to adopt a more favourable policy towards the Palestinians and the Arab states.[129] The minimal involvement of many Arab Americans in domestic politics is attributable to the undemocratic nature of the Arab states; their inadequate understanding of how to manipulate the American democratic process to their advantage has also worked against them. The Arabs are also hindered by the cultural divide between themselves and many Americans, by internal disputes and the tendency of Arab governments and the State Department to bypass Congress and conduct business through American embassies in Arab capitals.[130]

Limitations of Domestic Political Influences on Foreign Policy Decision-Making

Domestic politics have the potential to influence policy towards Israel in a myriad of ways, but in reality this potential is limited to constraining the policy alternatives open to the Executive, not determining the president's actual course of action. As a result of domestic and congressional pressure, a president will generally not be overtly anti-Israeli, will ensure the regional balance of power continues to favour Israel and will not force its government to make concessions in the Arab–Israeli peace process that cannot be justified to the population at large. It should not, however, be construed that Israel has free rein to demand anything it wants from Washington and that it is immune from any kind of pressure. As Assistant Secretary of State Joseph Sisco pointed out in 1970, the American "national interest goes beyond any one state in the area"[131] and successive administrations have exerted pressure on Israel to advance Washington's perception of the national interest. In 1956 Eisenhower forced an Israeli withdrawal from the Suez Canal, in 1973 Nixon insisted that Israel allow supplies to reach the encircled Egyptian army and in 1981 Reagan proceeded with the sale of AWACS to Saudi Arabia despite virulent pressure to the contrary. Similarly, in 1991 Bush Sr. pressured Israel to adopt a policy of non-retaliation during the Gulf War and in 2002 Bush Jr. set out his "road map" to peace which the Likud government strongly objected to. However, Israel can be assured that a US president will never knowingly take action that will threaten Israel's fundamental security interests.

Public opinion, as reflected in opinion polls, does influence American foreign policy but often in very indirect ways. Politicians are more likely to be responsive to their perceptions of the overall public mood as opposed to reacting to preferences on specific issues. In the sphere of foreign affairs the public mood is often volatile and can vacillate between interventionism and isolationism.[132] Yet with regard to the Arab–Israeli dispute, public opinion has remained relatively constant, favouring the Israeli cause above the several causes of the Arabs.[133] It is this generally high level of public support for Israel and popular distrust of the Arab states that has set the tone for America's Middle East policy and influenced the government's approach to the region.[134] But what is the origin of this positive perception of Israel and negative image of the Arab world, and how does it relate to America's perceptions of its broader values and interests in the world?

Defining Political Culture

Since political culture is but one dimension of culture, it seems appropriate first to elucidate the latter concept. The term culture generally encompasses the customs and civilisation of a particular time or people and embraces widely shared ideas of what is and is not regarded as socially acceptable, as expressed through social, religious and educational institutions and other forms of social interaction. A society's culture is also expressed through literature and the graphic arts, music, the press and other forms of media. While cultural expression is often to be found in a common understanding of the meanings of terms, these may be altered under pressure of experience, contact with other societies and scientific and geographical discovery. In sum, culture may be defined as "systems of meaning, . . . including not only the beliefs and values of social groups, but also their language, forms of knowledge and common sense, as well as the material products, interactional practices, rituals, and ways of life established by these."[135] In this sense, to quote Raymond Williams, culture is expressed in the "whole way of life"[136] of a society. It is precisely because culture permeates virtually all aspects of life, that it is through an understanding of the culture of a society that we can understand decision-makers' responses to both national and international events. As Clifford Geertz explains: "culture is not a power, something to which social events, behaviours, institutions, or processes can be casually attributed; it is a context, something in which they can be intelligibly described."[137] For the purposes of this thesis, which explores the influence of beliefs and perceptions on foreign policy decision-making, culture will be defined as the ideas, values and images which are transmitted from one generation to another and serve to shape the way of life of the society.

It follows therefore, that political culture is that aspect of social experience that focuses on the political dimension of a society, shaping the political system and framework of political ideas. To understand political culture therefore, it is necessary first to define politics. The word 'politics' is derived from the Greek word for government of the city state and is concerned with government, rule, regulation or authority. A political arena is a social framework in which the structure of authority, and the purposes, procedures or priorities of government of the society are debated and contested. In its narrowest interpretation, politics is the science and art of government. It is an activity or process under formal government as in a cabinet meeting, a parliament or a local council. In its broader connotations politics is non-violent contention within an ordered framework and can occur in any social situation, so that one can speak of the politics of the classroom or office politics.[138]

Political culture refers to the ideologies, beliefs, values, attitudes, opinions, institutions, operational norms and methodologies governing political behaviour and which give structure and coherence to a political system. As such it may serve either to sustain and promote an existing political framework or to undermine one. The concept of political culture is not a new phenomenon in political discourse. It has a long history and was alluded to in differing forms by the prophets in their oracles and the historians and poets of ancient Greece and Rome. Classical theorists including Plato, Aristotle, Montesquieu, Rousseau and de Tocqueville viewed custom, tradition, mores and religious practice as significant factors in the explanation of political action. In *Republic,* Plato describes the political structure and characteristics of the state as deriving from the values and experiences of the citizens. He writes that:

> governments vary as the dispositions of men vary, and that there must be as many of one as there are of the other. For we cannot suppose that States are made of 'oak and rock' and not out of the human natures which are in them.[139]

Classical theorists, therefore, tended to regard political culture as a given, something inherited and acquired from a historical or traditional approach to the 'good society' and its attainment. In *The Social Contract,* Rousseau highlighted the importance of political culture by claiming it has independent authority because it is akin to a law that is "engraved on the hearts of the citizens. This forms the real constitution of the state . . . and insensibly replaces authority by force of habit."[140]

In contrast, modern sociologists influenced by the Marxist tradition have tended to see political culture as part of the 'superstructure', largely constructed, manufactured and manipulated by what C. Wright Mills called 'The Power Elite'[141] to produce a compliant mass population which accepts its subordination to the power holders as 'natural', part of the eternal social order and unchallengeable. To Gramsci, bourgeois rule was at its most successful (as in the US) when the majority of the people internalised philosophies, sciences, legal and sociological theories propagated by the hegemon, that is the dominant forces in society, and came to see them as common sense.[142] "The bourgeois class poses itself as an organism in continuous movement, capable of absorbing the entire society, assimilating it to its own cultural and economic level. The entire function of the state has been transformed: the state has become an 'educator'".[143] Barrington Moore puts the position more starkly.

> Culture or tradition is not something that exists outside of or independently of individual human beings living in society. Cultural values do not descend from heaven to influence the course of history. . . . To maintain and transmit a value system, human beings are punched, bullied, sent to jail, thrown into concentration camps, cajoled, bribed, made into heroes, encouraged to read newspapers, stood up against a wall and shot, and sometimes even taught sociology. To speak of cultural inertia is to overlook the concrete interests and privileges that are served by indoctrination, education, and the entire complicated process of transmitting culture from one generation to the next.[144]

For him, the 'continuity' of identity, affinity and animosity depends on the mechanisms of selection, amnesia, reformulation and invention manipulated by the powerful.

Yet the notion that a political culture can be entirely manufactured from above and imposed on an unwitting population has been discredited by the fall of the Soviet Union and the collapse of Communist regimes throughout Eastern Europe. Religious values, patriotism, habit and tradition play such a significant role in determining political structure and legitimacy that not even the most persistent propaganda machines of the Soviet Union could completely overcome. This is because education or even re-education is not an antidote to culture[145] and "[i]f the law cannot change culture then culture operates as the defining limit of government power."[146]

In the 1960s and 1970s, theorists such as Almond, Verba and MacIntyre began to rethink the concept of political culture[147] arguing that traditions of beliefs and practices are what bind a society together within a framework of a common language, rules of life and techniques of discourse.[148] Though this might appear to be a reversion to the ideas of the classical theorists referred to above it was not, for these theorists saw political culture as the product of reciprocal interaction between history and current politics and between the elites and the masses. For them what was significant in a democracy, was the diverse and complex origins of opinion formation on policy issues and the often competing agenda of governments, political parties, businesses, interest groups, lobbies, churches and the media in manipulating minds.

As against such approaches there are rational choice theorists who would deny altogether the importance of cultural predispositions. For them calculations of interest take precedence. Richard Rogowski claims that there are clearly defined and, more importantly, rational relationships between socio-economic, ethnic and religious interests and political structure, which the political culture literature fails to identify.[149] While this may be true, perceptions of what constitutes a rational act are based on pre-existing ideas and beliefs and as not all societies share the same beliefs, rationality is not always defined in the same way. For example, in October 1973, Sadat launched a war against Israel which the US had not anticipated since in its calculations of military strength, Egypt could not win, and therefore such an act was considered irrational. However, Sadat's interpretation of rationality differed from that of the Nixon administration and as Kissinger later noted in his memoirs, "[O]ur definition of rationality did not take seriously the notion of starting an unwinnable war to restore self-respect."[150] Here, of course, Kissinger was thinking entirely in terms of military ratios and dispositions. Others, however, might claim that since the war produced a stalemate and US intervention to broker a cease-fire between the parties, Egypt had not lost the war because it had won US patronage – a not inconsiderable achievement.

As has been shown, political culture is an amorphous concept beset with definitional ambiguities that does not provide the researcher with a systematic theory of political action that can be subjected to the scrutiny of scientific rigour. Nonetheless, political culture does offer a set of variables that may be used in the construction of theory.

The Construction and Development of Political Culture

As defined here, political culture evolves over time and "is the product of both the collective history of a political system and the life histories of the individuals who currently make up the system."[151] It is therefore, as rooted as much in private experiences as in public events and it is what people collectively make of their history that gives each society a distinct political culture, giving meaning, predictability and form to the political process. But of course, the shaping of political culture is complex. For popular political attitudes and sentiments are variegated, some too ephemeral to play a significant role in the socialisation process. By contrast, some apparently non-political beliefs such as orientations towards time, human trust and camaraderie and a belief in future progress may be critical in shaping political culture, because they exert an influence on the nature of society.

But political culture is shaped not merely by domestic factors but also by interaction in a world society that is increasingly inter-dependent despite the diverse cultural heritage of its constituent members. In an era of global communications and media, it is no longer possible for a society to remain entirely isolated from the outside world, as the opening up of twentieth century China and Albania demonstrate. As cultural dialogue between societies expands, preconceptions and understandings of the world and interpretations of reality cannot remain unaffected. For example, when an Islamic culture is challenged on the issue of human rights, it has to try to locate the concept of human rights within its own structure of meaning. While many Islamists may reject the concept as alien, at the very least, the cross-cultural dialogue obliges it to define itself against this alien concept.

The notion that a political culture can be reshaped by its exposure to the vicissitudes of global politics is thrown into especially sharp relief as countries face threats of secession from aggrieved minorities. It was in 1941 that Winston Churchill told parliament that he had not become prime minister to "preside over the liquidation of the British Empire" – a theme taken up by L. S. Amery, when introduced to thunderous applause to the Conservative party conference of 1947, as the "greatest imperialist in our midst." Yet despite the evident popularity of imperialism, in the same year, 1947, the jewel in the crown of the British Empire was partitioned into India and Pakistan, Burma was to gain independence the following year and the liquidation of the Empire that had seemed unthinkable only a generation before was being welcomed in Britain. What had begun with different interpretations of British political culture – the Conservatives wanting to retain an Empire they conceived of as providing stability, education and enlightenment to backward peoples, Labour interpreting democracy in terms of granting independence to indigenous populations, was ultimately to end in a grudging consensus.

Adaptation and Change at Different Levels of Political Culture

As has been exemplified, political culture is in part derived from the way in which a shared experience is interpreted. Such interpretations constitute an 'irreducible core' of fundamental beliefs that form the intersubjective meanings which constitute a society's identity. They make the social life of a society distinctive by expressing the kinds of common values associated with a sense of national identity which large numbers of citizens share. Such values concern the nature of society, the obligation of the individual to that society and the relationship of a society to other societies. The beliefs they encompass include culturally defined concepts of historical progress and perceptions of the way in which the world works. It is through these beliefs that a society comes to understand itself and the world of which it is a part.

This sense of belonging is the crucial element in an overarching framework Brian Girvin has termed a macro-political culture. The macro-level 'establishes the rules of the game' that the majority of participants consider acceptable. In Girvin's view, macro-level political culture is the least susceptible to change or adaptation particularly in the short to medium-term. For him, the presence of an overarching political culture enables social conflict to be mediated without the disintegration of either the political culture or the shared sense of identity. Thus, serious political upheaval as experienced in the United States during the 1960s did not culminate in the disintegration of the system, in contrast to the former Soviet Union where the absence of a shared identity led to the collapse of the polity.

In contrast, Girvin explains that at the micro-level of the political culture, numerous sub-cultures are evident. A sub-culture is a significant regional, class, ethnic, religious, occupational, gender-based or other cultural variant subsumed within an overarching framework. Such sub-cultures are often shaped and defined by macro-political cultural beliefs and orientations and are held together by a common source of values that inform those beliefs. The existence of sub-cultures does not invalidate the notion of an overarching political culture. It does mean however, that an apparently homogeneous political culture includes diverse sub-cultures not incompatible with the wider cultural framework. Changes at the micro-level can create a climate in which fresh ideas of what is possible, desirable and necessary can emerge.

The macro-political culture and micro-culture begin to interact and interconnect at what Girvin called the meso-level.[152] While the macro-level is relatively stable, the meso-level is susceptible to influence from political developments and social evolution that occur at the micro-level. These changes are gradually incorporated into the meso-level or even the macro-level of the political culture. To apply Clifford Geertz's analogy, "culture moves rather like an octopus . . . not all at once in a smoothly coordinated synergy of parts . . . but by disjointed movements of this part, then that, and now the other which somehow cumulate to directional change."[153] Often the process of the rise and fall of various elements within a political culture can be equated with the rise and fall of the use of common myths and symbols which express and elucidate core beliefs and values.

Myths & Symbols

Cultural representation, that is the visible representation of a culture, is one of the most pervasive ways in which the government of a society can reinforce the nation's political culture in the minds of its citizens. Symbols and myths are among the most common forms of cultural representation.[154] Symbols, such as flags, anthems, historical monuments and ceremonies, provide a form of political cultural expression on which ideas of 'national identity' are constructed. Their importance resides in the fact that they embody meaning and are the "material vehicles of thought."[155] Symbols provide a reference point[156] and play a role in the perception, understanding, judgement and manipulation of the world. In many new nations or authoritarian regimes a charismatic leader may survive politically as much by being regarded as a symbol of collective national identity as by achieving concrete goals. For example, Yassir Arafat symbolises for many the embodiment of Palestine, while Nelson Mandela symbolised the anti-apartheid movement in South Africa. Both leaders have been widely represented as the personification of nations in the process of coming into being. Mythicised figures can also personify the nation – for example, Marianne of France and Germania as well as cartoon stereotypes such as Uncle Sam and John Bull.[157] Symbols are of great significance to any culture, since as Clifford Geertz explains, they "are felt to sum up, for those for whom they are resonant, what is known about the way the world is, the quality of the emotional life it supports, and the way one ought to behave while in it."[158]

However, symbols only have meaning if they have resonance for a population. In this sense it is necessary to contextualise symbolic references in order to locate meaning. For example, a red card shown by a referee on a football pitch has a very definite meaning within the context of the sport. The red card itself does not have intrinsic meaning, but has been assigned a particular meaning within a given context. Symbols and traditions are an important part of nation building because they assert common heritage and cultural kinship.[159] As such they are incorporated into everyday life and are a representation of a community's mental construction of its place in the world.[160] The Statue of Liberty represents America as the land of freedom and liberty, but in so doing, is seen by some to represent the US in opposition to the rest of the world, which is by implication less free. Many symbols are culturally specific, be they religious, philosophical, aesthetic, scientific or ideological. For example, the cross or crucifix is of symbolic importance to Christians while the crescent is of symbolic importance to Muslims. At the same time, symbols are a visual representation of a belief system that provides a template or blueprint for organising social and psychological processes[161] that transform individuals into members of a community.

In *The Invention of Tradition,* the historian Eric Hobsbawm claims that the nation is an artificial creation in so far as it "can be sited, planted and tended to a conscious design."[162] The creation of a nation's apparently seamless history, a mix of fabrication and reality, is designed to create a type of nationalist sentiment and unity. He writes that:

> The history which [becomes] part of a fund of knowledge or the ideology of nation, state or movement is not what has actually been preserved in popular memory, but what has been selected, written, pictured, popularised and institutionalised by those whose function it is to do so.[163]

This is true with regard to the American experience, where the dominant culture is based upon the positive values of liberty, freedom and democracy as symbolised by the American flag and not the past institution of African-American slavery. Such symbols and myths can be created and manipulated by those with access to political power to provide a sense of unity and shared identity within a society to maintain political integration and stability.[164] In the process, elites may fabricate traditions, ceremonials, institutions and structures that are in effect quite novel but which appear to be or are of ancient lineage.[165] For example, the origins of the traditional British Christmas celebrations with Christmas trees and Santa Claus are a product of the nineteenth century and are not steeped in centuries of British history as is often assumed. Prince Albert, who fondly remembered earlier Christmases in Germany, imported into Victorian England this 'British tradition',[166] while Charles Dickens in *A Christmas Carol* provided a further sentimental overlay. Similarly, the world renowned Scottish kilt was invented in the 1730s by an English cloth merchant, while the tartan colour that is supposed to indicate allegiance to a particular clan was designed for an early nineteenth century pageant.[167] One of the most recent 'invented British traditions' is the reconstruction of a Shakespearean theatre in Southwark, by the River Thames. The theatre, while marketed as 'Shakespeare's Globe' is yards from the original site, is built with modern materials and includes safety features never dreamed of in Elizabethan England.[168] Nevertheless, such 'invented traditions' in Hobsbawm's words, play a role in shaping collective identity and culture,[169] their significance lying "precisely in their undefined universality."[170]

Elite and Mass

This book adopts the view that there is a mutually reinforcing role between individuals and the collective in the formation both of political culture and foreign policy, although it does accept the prevalent conclusion of the literature on political culture or belief systems that elites play a particularly central role in the creative synthesis of political culture.[171] As Philip Converse asserts: "The shaping of belief systems of any range into apparently logical wholes that are credible to large numbers of people is an act of creative synthesis characteristic of only a minuscule proportion of any population."[172] In this vein Gellner argued that meaningful national identity emerged out of an elite high culture of which the masses were passive recipients.[173] This elite group is both highly educated and politically active. Ideas, as Max Weber insisted, must be carried by powerful social groups to have powerful social effects.[174] In the United States, the elite refers to the policy-making elite, those actively engaged in political lobbying and those journalists, business executives, intellectuals or religious leaders that contribute to the cultural dialogue out of which relevant values and attitudes are developed. It is this elite that attempts to resolve the dissonant elements within the political culture which are continually arising as a result of new realities. It is they that lead the process of reinterpreting symbols and myths. It is therefore to their discourse that we must turn in order to gain an awareness of this process.

Nevertheless, one cannot wholly detach the elite political culture from the larger cultural environment, as described in the previous section. According to Asher Arian, politicians and citizens tend to emerge from the same political culture. At least at the level of general orientation, national traumas and collective memories are widely shared. Therefore, when viewing international problems both elites and masses will be conditioned by similar dispositions.[175] Thus, no elite can simply manipulate the mass and impose its values; rather its values must, in some sense, resonate with the broader public mood. In a democracy like the US, the elites may attempt to shape minds, but at the same time they have to act within a framework of generally accepted ideas. If the ideas of the elites fail to resonate with the mood of the country, as occurred when Woodrow Wilson tried to take America into the League of Nations, they risk losing their power. As Aldous Huxley notes, "Propaganda . . . may give force and direction to successive movements of popular feeling and desire; but it does not do much to create these movements. The propagandist is a man who canalises an already existing stream. In the land where there is no water, he digs in vain."[176]

While the elites cannot impose an alien value system on a population, one of the most important ways in which political culture will filter into policy is through the consciousness of the decision-making elite. Leaders such as Napoleon, Churchill and Hitler and statesmen like Kissinger played crucial roles in the conduct of their state's foreign policies. The conglomeration of their existential and instrumental values informed a policy strategy that was used to define objectives and provide a framework for implementation. This strategy may have been constrained by outside factors and eventually abandoned, but it nevertheless provided a workable, if temporary, framework for action. Within any elite, different strategies will exist representing different emphases and different values within a political culture. The predominance of one strategy over another will depend not only on the official power wielded by the various members of the elite within the policy-making structure, but also on their ability to make their strategy appear successful in achieving common overarching goals and values.

Political culture will also impact on foreign policy through its role in legitimating the decision-making elite and their policies. Francis Fukuyama explained that in order to act effectively, even an authoritarian ruler needs genuine support from at least some elements of the population.[177] Subordinates that enact the will of the dictator are necessary to enable a regime to implement its policies. In the realm of foreign affairs, political culture enables the elite to legitimise its foreign policy to its citizens or at the very least to its active political supporters and domestic political allies.

Although the elite may be viewed as the most important element in the generation and construction of political culture, their innovations will only be successful in legitimising policy to the public if they resonate with the mass by tapping into pre-existing themes. As Henry Kissinger acknowledged: "No foreign policy – no matter how ingenious – has any chance of success if it is born in the minds of a few and carried out in the hearts of none."[178] Eric Hobsbawm asserted that the most successful leaders exploit traditions that meet a genuinely felt, though not necessarily clearly articulated or understood, need.[179] The masses are therefore attracted by what the elite appears to stand for, even if this does not always represent the true motivation behind its policies. Public opinion has been shown to be susceptible to manipulation by the elite, yet conversely, public opinion can also act as a constraint on policy either of itself or because decision-makers perceive it as such. While public opinion does not determine policy it delineates the option parameters of decision-makers.[180] For example, the decision-making elite's perception of the British public as highly pacifist and generally opposed to a military conflict with Germany in the early 1930s, was a significant inducement for the government to follow a policy of appeasement with Hitler until 1938. It took a number of years, combined with the demonstration of the futility of its diplomacy, to psychologically prepare the British people for war.[181]

To validate the claim that political culture plays a role in influencing decision-making, it has to be demonstrated that a coherent set of ideas about politics and the political system are passed from generation to generation. As Talcott Parsons explained, the influence of political culture resides in the fact that it is transmitted, learned and shared.[182] Firstly, the transmission of political culture means that it constitutes a heritage or a social tradition; secondly, it is learned and is not a genetic inheritance; and thirdly, that it is shared and is broadly speaking, common to the whole society.[183] It is to an analysis of the process of political socialisation i.e. of the way political attitudes are transmitted from one generation to another, that we now turn.

Political Socialisation

The process through which a community transmits, from one generation to another, its social and intellectual character,[184] that is the particular knowledge, attitudes and judgements that affect politics, is referred to as political socialisation.[185] In its broadest sense, socialisation is, as defined by Irvin Child, a

> whole process by which an individual, born with behavioural potentialities of enormously wide range, is led to develop actual behaviour which is confined within a more narrow range – the range of what is customary and acceptable for him according to the standards of his group.[186]

Behavioural patterns are infinitely variable, but regularities can be imposed through the learning process and the induction, or some would say indoctrination, of new members into a society's preferred way of behaviour. Political socialisation is crucial to the longevity of a nation because, as Emile Durkheim explains:

> The stability of any social system and authority of its government is not purely based in structural constraints and balance, but on social norms which were taken into the character of societies members and created a 'collective conscience'.[187]

Political socialisation occurs through both manifest and latent processes. Manifest socialisation is the formal and overt learning of political culture and tends to occur first through the family, formal education and the mass media. Here basic political attitudes tend to be acquired, such as loyalty towards society and nation and recognition of authority.[188] This is generally followed by the acquisition of more specific attitudes towards politics, such as identification with a party and attitudes towards a specific policy. Today this includes observations of the behaviour and conduct of political figures, party political broadcasts and the impact of the image politicians convey via the mass media. One common feature of this method of socialisation is the repetition of simple ideas – American 'freedom' and British 'fair play'. The second process is that of latent socialisation. This involves the more subtle acquisition of values and attitudes that are politically significant through experience in non-political situations. For example, individuals may acquire an attitude towards forms of authority from interaction with parents or teachers, or from the hierarchical structure of a business corporation or firm.[189]

Classical scholars emphasised the role of parents, teachers, priests and other authority figures in the socialisation process. Traditionally the family played the principle role in the socialisation process and the transmission of values and beliefs across the generations, although this could conceivably change with the disintegration of the nuclear family. Children tended to learn through their parent's identification with specific groups. This has been particularly true in terms of religious education where children soon learn that 'we are' people of Catholic, Muslim, Jewish or some other faith.[190] These messages were often instrumental in encouraging children to form a religious orientation that was supposed to last a lifetime. Parents' views have also been influential in the political context, shaping their children's identification and perceptions of the political parties. In the US, a parent's expression of the view that 'Democrats are good in the field of foreign affairs' or that 'Republicans are the party of low taxation' can provide the cognitive basis on which their children receive and process information. Similarly, if the child heard statements such as 'They don't care about people like us', with reference to a political party, this could form the basis of their subsequent affective reactions to politics.[191]

But while children have tended to acquire political identification and attitudes towards authority from their parents, it was generally from the formal education system that they learned the rules and rituals of the political system. Schools would transmit the values and attitudes of society and shape attitudes about unwritten rules of the political game. In Britain, traditional public schools have tried to instil values of public duty, informal political relations and the importance of hierarchical deference, as well as political integrity. The public education system has tended to reinforce affection for the political system and promote symbols of national identity.[192] In the United States, children begin by learning the prevalent interpretations of the American Revolution and Civil War and to accept the symbols of the state through the pledge of allegiance to the American flag.[193] By extension, political socialisation through the education system has been extended to all those who wish to become American citizens. New immigrants to the United States must attend citizenship classes and pass an examination about the history and government of the country before citizenship is granted.

Since the education system has been an important source of political socialisation, during times of regime change, it serves as the focal point of a new leader's efforts to alter the public's belief system. This adheres to the views of Marxist-inspired sociologists who argued that the present cannot be deduced from the past and that popular perceptions of the past have to be 'constructed', through the manipulation of symbols by the power elite and the shaping of mass opinion through history text books. For example, when the Nazis took power in Germany, school history textbooks were rewritten and mention of the Treaty of Versailles removed. Similarly, in the Soviet Union, the 'cult of Stalin' was propagated in the schools. Stalin's work the *Problems of Leninism* was required reading in schools and universities, while a volume on *Stalin, the Liberator of Eastern & South-Eastern European People* was translated into the relevant languages and distributed free.[194]

Through the process of political socialisation, decision-makers, like all citizens, are inducted into their society's preferred way of viewing the world and their beliefs are shaped by the cultural environment of which they are a product. Political culture feeds into the foreign policy decision-making process because it provides the political and psychological environment through which decision-makers view the world. The psychological dimension of human behaviour, including the ideas, meanings and beliefs people hold of the world, play a crucial role in determining action because they shape decision-makers' perceptions of the external environment. Harold and Margaret Sprout analysed the way in which human behaviour depends upon perception. They pointed out that while the consequences of state behaviour can be understood predominantly in terms of the decision-makers' operational environment, i.e. the world 'out there' the capabilities and intentions of the relevant actors, must be understood in terms of their psychological environment – their beliefs about the world and other actors.[195] "What matters in the process of policy-making is not conditions and events as they actually are (operational environment) but what the policy-maker imagine them to be (psychological environment)."[196] Decision-making may have unintended consequences when the operational and psychological environments diverge.[197] Yet, merely by being born into a society and cultural milieu we are conditioned to hold certain images of the world. The purpose of an image is to provide a simplification and ordering of the external environment that makes it comprehensible to the individual.[198] Such images are not static constructs but are adapted and refined when an individual brings opinions, interpretations and experience to bear.

In the United States, as in many societies, this process of socialisation has perpetuated a predominant view of the world and of America's place within it. Within American society a set of prevalent views or a communal way of looking at the world may be said to exist and because certain notions have persisted through time we can talk of them in terms of a political culture. To fully appreciate American policy makers' approach to foreign policy, their perception of their role in the world, coupled with the values and beliefs that underpin their actions, it is necessary to have a greater understanding of both the American decision-making process and the basic elements of American political culture. It is to an analysis of the operation of the American political system and the content of American political culture that we now turn.

3

AMERICAN POLITICAL CULTURE

The Evolution of American Political Culture

WHEREAS THE FIRST SETTLERS were predominantly from the British isles, subsequent immigrants came from Continental Europe, Africa and Asia. Some settlers originated as slaves, while others came to escape war, poverty and religious persecution. Nonetheless, despite the considerable diversity of the peoples comprising it, the United States was able to develop an overarching political culture that has survived the centuries. One contributory factor was the desire of virtually all the immigrants who remained in the colonies of their own volition to become Americans and to embrace what they understood to be the American way of life,[1] apparently transcending the country's vast size and geographical diversity. Yet even as an 'American identity' was under construction, the achievement of which is described below, the immigrants were never obliged to forego all traces of their original heritage. To be regarded as an American citizen may have required considerable conformity in overt behaviour; yet people were permitted within limits to preserve the religious beliefs and sense of national identification of their countries of origin,[2] not least because the notion of being an 'American' has always existed on the basis of consent and was not intended to replace all other forms of identification.[3] This is, of course, how the notion of the 'hyphenated American' originated. At the same time, if American society did not rest upon ethnic homogeneity, it did presume acceptance of 'a set of principles and ideas'[4] about America's place in the world. In effect the US was to become if not a 'melting pot' then a kind of 'salad bowl' of peoples.

As a consequence of the pattern of colonisation, in which immigrants tended to congregate in adjacent settlements, ghettos or shelters and continued to settle together when they or their descendants moved westward, regionalism and sectionalism have always been important forces in American politics, acting as a constraint on the actions of federal government, including its foreign policy. Over time, as one religious or ethnic group succeeded another in establishing their settlements in the same location, some regional cultural patterns were eroded or modified, while others were intensified. There was also some diminution in regional cultural difference because of geographical mobility between the states and changes in interests and attitudes.[5] The tangible factors such as wealth and social status that contributed to the social and geographic separation of ethnic groups tended to diminish during the twentieth century. As third and fourth generation immigrants were assimilated into American society, their wealth and status often far exceeding those of their parents and grandparents, they tended to identify with people of similar economic and social circumstance, rather than those of the same religious or ethnic origins. Such tendencies to homogenisation were also engendered by the increasing demand for national policy to tackle such global issues as the environment, international trade, terrorism and illegal immigration, affecting the nation as a whole and not just individual states.

Meanwhile, the transition from an individual-based to a more group orientated, but distinctively 'American' political culture was assisted by four factors. Firstly, the gradual development in American business of a corporate culture in which the idea of a 'rationalised conformity' in behavioural and spending patterns was prized, and loyalty to the firm was considered a prime virtue.[6] Secondly, the growth in scope and influence of the mass media, national as well as regional, which had the effect of both moulding and reflecting public opinion and shaping the flow of information between the government and the people.[7] The media contributed to the diminishing of significant regional and sectional differences and disparities of view, as people in locations as diverse as Miami, Alabama, Seattle and Boston were able to watch the same programmes and read the same journals.[8] Thirdly, the increasing use by commercial concerns, lobbyists and party politicians of psychoanalytic techniques designed to influence mass opinion, affect consumption patterns and shape or reshape domestic and foreign policy agendas. In drawing on the insights of Pavlov and conditioned reflexes, Freud and his father images and David Riesman and his conception of the modern American voter as a spectator-consumer of politics,[9] Vance Packard spoke of 'the hidden persuaders', who sought to tap into 'the fabric of men's minds', to condition the hidden emotions that motivate behaviour and to create a group consciousness which would make people "easier to guide, control, cope with and herd."[10] Motivation research, the field of study from which such techniques were derived, was originally used by advertisers to encourage the mass consumption of their products. When subsequently employed by those with political agendas, it fed into the popular political culture and helped to mould a more collective concept of what it meant to be an American.[11] Fourthly, the gradual increase in the power of the federal agencies to determine policy, often at the expense of the state governments, contributed to a more uniform political culture. As the civil rights legislation of the 1960s and beyond took effect and the federal courts prohibited the vestiges of segregation and other violations of minority rights hitherto in common practice in many of the southern states,[12] the process of cultural homogenisation proceeded apace, and with it the refashioning of the American national identity to become much more collectively and nationally self aware. But while the above discussion reveals how American political culture came to permeate society it tells us little about the essence of that culture and it is to an analysis of its content that we now turn.

Defining American Political Culture

Culture plays a very significant part in US foreign policy, more so than in countries with a longer and more complex political heritage. The establishment of an 'American political culture' and the concept of what it means to be an 'American' provided the means through which a rootless society of immigrants consolidated and retained its sense of identity.[13] In America, more than any other country, political speeches resonate with allusions to history and to God. The leaders of today exercise power, by making repeated references to the ideals of the Founding Fathers from which they seek to derive legitimacy. This reveals how great a role historical myth, images and metaphors play in American political life, both consciously and unconsciously. The interpretation of this history acts as what Christopher Coker describs as a "strait-jacket, of a political culture which is unyielding in its forcefulness and all-embracing in its scope."[14]

The past continues to inform the present. Yet the past to which successive American politicians make appeal to win public support for their actions is not necessarily an accurate reflection of history. Often it is a past which Americans have not lived but which to an extent has been manufactured. For the United States, as Coker explained, can be attributed with not one past but three. The first depicts America as a unique country that is set apart and therefore has little to offer the world and no obligation towards it. The second portrays America as a country founded by Protestant fundamentalism from which it inherited a historical mission to redeem mankind from tyranny whether imposed by eighteenth century monarchs or twenty-first century commissars. The third views America as a country blessed with an abundance of natural resources and political liberty which has bestowed on it a duty to show the world that freedom can produce an efficient government and economic growth.[15]

Exceptionalism

The legacy of the Pilgrim Fathers and the unique development of the American nation created the image of America as a country apart, a model to be emulated, but destined to stand alone. This sense of exceptionalism was the product of the secularising of Calvinism and the belief in a divine dispensation in a land where nature had bred a purer more sterling individual – the archetypal American.

The process of creating an 'American' identity began with the landing of the Pilgrim Fathers at Massachusetts Bay. The Pilgrims were highly religious, having fled to the colonies to escape religious persecution in England, and the laws and values of the colonies they helped to shape were based on Biblical teachings and the literal interpretation of the Bible. As discussed in Chapter 1, the Puritans believed themselves to be creating a 'New World' in accordance with Biblical prophecy and tended to polarise the world into the 'good' and the 'evil'. Such religiosity permeated many aspects of life in the colonies and continues to resonate to this day, giving rise to claims such as that by Samuel Huntington that "Americans gave to their nation and its creed many of the functions and attributes of a church."[16] Robert Bellah compares the power of Puritan moralism to permeate society to that of a 'civic religion' that provided a "religious dimension for the whole fabric of American life, including the political sphere."[17] In creating a sense of cohesion to unite an otherwise diverse population together as Americans, the 'civil religion' bestowed a sacred character to national ceremonies and civic obligations. The 'civil religion' can be described as the "lowest common denominator,"[18] providing a set of transcendent beliefs that have tended to bind together what might otherwise have been an excessively individualistic and diverse group of peoples. As Michael Novak explained:

> The Trinity becomes a vision of the importance of individualism over and against the constraints of community; the Incarnation becomes a reality principle that warns us against the utopian hopes of socialism; the value of many biblical narratives is that they 'envisage human life as a contest'; the doctrine of Original Sin serves mainly to convince us that no economic system can ever be free of some evil; the doctrine of the Two Kingdoms becomes an argument for laissez-faire; and the principle of love in the Judeo-Christian tradition mainly suggests that we should respect the freedom of the individual.[19]

Applied in this way, a religious aura embraced establishment values, endorsing attempts to integrate diverse beliefs under the rubric of the 'religion of democracy'. As such it contributed to the formation of an American national identity that took hold and was politicised by the revolution and independence from Britain in 1776.

Although the thirteen states that unanimously declared independence from Britain were vast and disparate, they constructed a sense of identity from the relatively unique experience of the process of colonisation and settlement of the United States and of being situated in the New World.[20] The Declaration of Independence played a crucial role in the construction of an American collective memory, and its preamble set the tone for the legitimacy of the government and the existence of the United States. When Jefferson wrote the words: "We hold these truths to be self evident, that all men are created equal, that they are endowed by their Creator with certain unalienable Rights, that among these are Life, Liberty, and the pursuit of Happiness", he was heavily influenced by the recent injection of ideas of political as well as commercial freedom, that followed independence from Britain. The political element provided the crucial distinction between the two worlds, Old and New, despite the fact that much of the reason for revolution had centred on 'taxation without representation' that had restricted commercial opportunities.[21] Jefferson enshrined the 'exceptionalism' of the American people by making the thirteen colonies the first country to find God's truths 'self-evident'.

This is why the Founding Fathers did not refer to their actions as 'revolutionary'. The American Revolution was never conceived of being for export and throughout the eighteenth century the term 'revolution' referred to a change of power within a state, not the creation of a new one. They believed themselves to be charting a new course through history and did not think it was one that other nations could replicate. As the American ambassador to France stated at the close of the eighteenth century: the French "want an American constitution, without realising they have no Americans to uphold it."[22]

This conception of American exceptionalism is derived from the notion that America was created differently, developed differently and thus has to be understood differently from other states – essentially on its own terms and within its own context.[23] American exceptionalism assumes that not only is America set apart and different from other nations, a "shining city on a hill,"[24] but also that it is exceptional in the sense of being exemplary and "a beacon among nations."[25] Within the domestic context, Americans have deemed their identity exceptional, and their tendency to polarise political issues into an overly simple dichotomy between good and evil led them to believe they had created something new and set apart from the Old World. Such a mindset was to have deep implications for the future of US foreign policy. The 'exceptionalist syndrome' assumed that the New World was created by divine providence which bestowed on America a 'providential destiny' and a 'universal mission' to 'civilise' the world.

But how far has this belief in exceptionalism translated into American foreign policy? Isolationism in the inter-war years derived much of its legitimacy in the public eye from the need to keep the country's virtue intact. The frontier had been reached and the majority of Americans were content to protect their exceptional standing by retreating inside the shield created by their great nation that defended them from the evils of the outside world.

But the recourse to isolationism provided only an illusion of security. In 1941 the outside world sucked the US inexorably into the Second World War in a conflict that was sold to the American people in terms with which they could easily identify: a contest between good and evil. By 1945, Americans had been convinced that a second retreat into isolationism would not be a legitimate response to the demands of the modern world. America was now depicted as a member of the international community with a moral responsibility to help its allies, a responsibility that the inter-war interpretation of exceptionalism had obscured. Roosevelt and Truman, in respect to very different enemies, appealed to both the sense of exceptionalism and redemptionism, to rally the people to their respective causes.

The assumption of leadership of the 'free world' was not synonymous with American integration into the international system and institutions. Its statesmen still maintained that its unique characteristics made it morally superior to organisations like the United Nations, whose laws were drawn up by other states. Protracted debates surrounded the decision to join the International Court of Justice and the United Nations Human Rights Committee in 1948. More recently, Washington's procrastination in signing the UN resolution on the Genocide Convention in 1981 and the Kyoto protocol was attributable to its belief in its own exceptionalism and its unwillingness to submit to the will of other nations. Americans believe that they are only subject to their own national laws and often resist close integration with the UN, for example, because it is perceived to be an undemocratic institution that lacks a mechanism for democratic input into its deliberations. As Senator Jesses Helms explained: "we have a unique development of legal history, the result of our traditions, our religions, our moral and ethical values and our experience. [Therefore there was] no justification for submitting this tradition to the judgement of the world."[26] The decision of the administration of George W. Bush to launch an attack on Iraq on 20 March 2003 in the absence of a second UN resolution is the most recent demonstration of this.

Redemptionism

Redemptionism is the second historical cannon of the US and is by far the oldest. It promotes the belief that America should encourage positive change. The image of the US as a "redeemer nation,"[27] that "right will prevail over might"[28] and the Manichian perception of a world divided into the 'children of Light and the children of Darkness', are intrinsic to the deeply religious sensibilities that permeate the nation. The preaching of John Winthrop and Cotton Mather may have been replaced by Billy Graham and successive tele-evangelists, but the message remains unchanged – Americans, according to Graham "were created for a spiritual mission among the nations."[29] The depiction of America as a 'city upon a hill' reinforced the belief that a unique American destiny serves as a kind of vanguard of a universal destiny for the world.[30] The United States presents itself as a nation convinced of its own ability to treat all other nations justly, objectively and equally and of its capacity to handle problems alone.

The extent to which, in its more subtle manifestations, redemptionism has influenced American foreign policy should not be under estimated. In 1952, as the Cold War intensified, Truman announced to the American people that they had stepped "into the leadership which Almighty God intended us to assume a generation ago."[31] President Eisenhower was similarly preoccupied with America's mission. As he told the American Legion in 1955, the most basic expression of Americanism was recognition of God. Without God there could be no American form of government, or an American way of life.[32] His Secretary of State John Foster Dulles held fundamentalist beliefs. He believed that the US had been founded as an experiment in human liberty and that its survival was dependent on it showing men the way to a better life.[33] Zbigniew Brzezinski commented in his last year at the National Security Council that the US "can help history along by positive deeds."[34]

The belief that America has a mission amongst the nations has its origins in the Puritan tradition. Puritanism was Americanised by the challenge the untamed wilderness presented to the first settlers. The terrain of New England was so harsh and unwelcoming that to prosper there the settlers had to be graced by God and in that sense, the taming of the frontier took on a religious manifestation. Christopher Coker notes that their very survival created a vision amongst the American people of themselves as a "providential people destined to expand, to redeem the land to the west, the frontier."[35] Such beliefs gave rise to the religious concept of manifest destiny which did not come to an end when the frontier was reached in 1890. In his work, *The Significance of the Frontier in American History,* presented to the American Historical Association in 1893, Fredrick Jackson Turner argued that the frontier was the defining feature of American political culture. In pushing across the American continent, Turner claimed, the balance between civilisation and savagery, wilderness and garden, lawlessness and law formed the crucible of the frontier and contributed to the formation of American political culture.[36] While the validity of this argument is a subject of debate, the rhetoric of the frontier is evident in modern day American discourse, the frontier experience having made America fundamentally different from Europe. Creating a new society from nothing, including the establishment of new social, political and economic institutions, made demands on the political system quite unlike those experienced by the European states that had evolved over the course of many centuries.

The concept of 'manifest destiny' has continued to inform American political life, with successive generations reinterpreting its meaning and applicability to themselves. The corollary of this is the assumption that the assertion of American power and rights were natural, with the often brutal treatment of other peoples, the American Indians included, justified by references to 'destiny', 'progress', 'civilisation' and 'modernisation'. Its continued influence is evident in the wars the nation has chosen to fight. It has compelled Americans, on occasion, to embark upon an interventionist foreign policy seemingly based on the tenets of the Protestant faith[37] – a tendency Lipset describes as 'utopian moralism' i.e. viewing foreign affairs essentially as morality plays, with the need for goodness and greatness inextricably linked. President Johnson was influenced by the redemptionist past and a strong biblical compulsion that America had the opportunity to extend its frontier to southeast Asia and to rescue the Vietnamese people from Communist tyranny. Manifest destiny instilled in the American people the belief that they had the right to intervene in the internal affairs of other nations, of which George W. Bush's preference, in 2003, for regime change in Iraq is the most recent example.

The redemptionist approach to foreign policy and its attendant moralistic connotations underpins the standards to which America must adhere (at least rhetorically) and the image it must project in its external relations. As Scott Lucas noted, "however calculated the geopolitical strategy, however base the pursuit of profit and economic control, US foreign policy has to be perceived as 'right' at home and abroad."[38] But although much in the official (and sometimes unofficial) rhetoric is derived from Christianity, its basis is not itself Christianity.[39] While successive presidents never fail to mention God in their inaugural address or in rousing speeches to the nation, Christ is rarely spoken of.[40] The God of what can be described as America's 'civic religion' is much more related to law and order than to salvation and love.[41] Robert Bellah described this God as unitarian and one that "is actively interested and involved in history, with a special concern for America."[42]

The belief of American decision-makers that God had carved out a special role for the US has led to their frequent claim to know without doubt what is good and evil in relations between states.[43] In this respect, moralism and moralistic terminology becomes an expedient, if subconscious, way to cloak political activity based on power politics in the garb of universal principle. On the other hand, the tendency to moralise must be distinguished from respect for moral principle, which also has deep cultural roots in the US and embodies popular values and beliefs. Cecil Crabb offers a revealing definition of the differences between moralism and morality:

> Moralism is not the same as morality . . . Morality has to do with the substance of behaviour. It is conduct in accordance with a predetermined code of behaviour, and throughout Christendom this refers to behaviour sanctioned by the Christian faith. Moralism [in the political sense] is concerned with [the] appearances, with the concepts and language employed in foreign relations, with the symbols used, and with the way ends and means are visualised and expressed publicly.[44]

Moralism, as distinct from morality, tends to have a political base, and in consequence Washington's censures have tended to be somewhat selective. towards its allies or in respect of countries perceived to be offering important political or commercial opportunities, Washington's official rhetoric has tended to be far less censorious, even if their regimes endorsed practices anathema to American values. In the past half century for example, whilst maintaining the rhetoric against the 'evils' of the Castro regime in Cuba, US administrations chose largely to disregard the political misdemeanours of the authoritarian regimes in Guatemala, El Salvador and Chile that they courted. Similarly, whilst Washington was constantly pointing to what it perceived as the political misdeeds of the Soviet Union, there was comparatively little criticism of Communist China when the State Department sought to curry favour with the administration of Deng Xiaoping. Scarce wonder, then, that Washington has often stood accused of applying double standards – and not least in its dealings with Israel.

Such interpretations of American redemptionism have provoked condemnation from the Left who criticise what they see as the distortion of the past and the manipulation of moral purpose as a shroud for an aggressive foreign policy, the demonisation of America's foreign enemies, and the tendency to view conflicts as stemming from matters of principle rather than of interest. After all, official rhetoric would often dwell on the 'evils' of America's opponents – on their 'tyranny', 'despotism', 'abuse of power' and the like. Historically, the US had portrayed itself as a nation set apart and 'fighting the good fight': in the revolutionary period against the monarchy and British imperialism, in President Monroe's diplomacy against the machinations of the Old World, in the late nineteenth century against Spanish colonialism, during the Second World War against the 'Godless' Nazis and Fascists and afterwards, against the 'Godless' Communists and their 'dupes' at home and abroad.

Yet such was the rhetorical force of America's professed principles that even when aligned with regimes opposed to the very values for which the US was supposed to stand, Washington would tend to invoke the notion of 'freedom' in support of its policy. As Bellah explained, those nations that at any moment are "on our side become 'the free world'"[45] – an expedient which allowed Portugal under the authoritarian government of Salazar to be admitted to NATO, a repressive military regime in South Vietnam to be defended against

Communist opponents and unelected administrations in the Middle East to be given financial and military assistance against militant Islamic groups.

Despite the rhetoric of 'freedom' and 'democracy', in practice the fundamental concern of US foreign policy at least since the First World War appears to have been world order,[46] defined in terms of an international system conducive to the enhancement of the American way of life and the establishment of foreign governments favourable to that process.[47] Washington tended to limit its support for 'democratic movements' to areas where it was assured that what the electorate sought would be congenial to the American model and that the governments that resulted would be friendly to the US.[48] As a consequence, the application of the notion of 'freedom' has been "highly elastic."[49] Washington had grave doubts about the 'democratic process' when the electorate chose left-leaning regimes as in Guatemala in 1954 or Chile in 1970. At the same time, Washington's interest in buttressing friendly dictatorships[50] such as those in Saudi Arabia and the UAE, stemmed from the perception that their demise could result in their replacement by governments hostile to US and Western interests and in this sense could be understood as serving the cause of 'freedom'.[51] To its critics however, the US was no more principled than any other state and its rhetoric could not disguise the degree of self-interest and ambition underlying its foreign policy.

The redemptionist approach to foreign affairs has also been combined with 'legalistic' rhetoric, thus giving rise to what George F. Kennan described as the "legalistic-moralistic" approach to international problems.[52] This can be defined as the belief that through the acceptance of a system of legal rules and restraints, as practised in the US, it should be possible to suppress the self-interested aspirations of governments in the international arena. In this Washington was attempting to impose on an international scale the Anglo-Saxon concept of domestic law that is said to govern and constrain the behaviour of individuals.[53] This tendency found expression in attempts to outlaw war by international legislation, as in the case of the Kellogg–Briand Pact of 1928, and if this failed to determine principles upon which wars were fought. 'Democratic' international institutions such as the League of Nations and the United Nations were seen by the proponents of this approach as forums in which debating and voting procedures would be used to settle international disputes in much the same way as they were believed to resolve disputes within American society.[54]

Though Washington would bend or even break international law when it was regarded as expedient to do so, American decision-makers nonetheless considered themselves to be very law abiding in their approach to international affairs. John Foster Dulles, Secretary of State from 1953 to 1959, was the personification of the 'legalistic-moralistic' approach to international affairs. He applied legalistic rhetoric to justify the non-recognition of China and the construction of a system of alliances to isolate the Communist states and moralistic rhetoric to condemn neutral states (those not aligned with either East or West) as 'immoral'.[55] More recently, in the 1990s, President Clinton argued that there existed both a legal and moral basis for the continued imposition of sanctions against Iraq, while President George W. Bush tended to shroud the US bombing of Afghanistan in 2001–2 and Iraq in 2003 in, the legalistic-moralistic rhetoric of a "just cause".[56]

Exemplarism

The third version of the American past – perhaps of lesser moment in recent years – is of a secular nature and is based on the belief that by setting an example and providing a model worthy of emulation, the US can redeem mankind without recourse to direct intervention. Such a conception rested on the need to preserve American 'purity' which would be jeopardised were it to exercise its power to assist other nations, however moral the cause. Those associated with the exemplarist tradition feared that association with non-democratic regimes would compromise the democratic experiment that is America. They were also apprehensive of the potential repercussions were the US to attempt to democratise a nation and to fail in its endeavour. As Kissinger explained: "There are certain experiments that cannot be tried, not because the goals are undesirable but because the consequences of failure would be so server."[57]

Yet the hopes of those like William Fulbright[58] that nations across the globe who lived under tyranny and repression would adopt moral principles derived from the American constitution have proved a disappointment. In the case of the fall of Communism in the former Soviet Union and Eastern Europe, it was as much the American example of capitalism and consumerism that provided the impetus for political reform and upheaval as the desire of the people to live under a democratic form of government. And when the initial euphoria of the election of government leaders and the writing of constitutions failed to generate a great increase in economic growth, many of these countries opted for a reversion to the security of the socialist state and elected former Communist party members.

In the modern age, non-intervention or isolationism, has ceased to be considered a viable policy. Washington has often found itself in a position where it needs to act even against its better judgement, as occurred in Somalia and Kosovo in the 1990s. As the only remaining superpower, America is actively engaged in defending its interests overseas and its former distaste for intervention has been largely cast aside.

'Americanism'

The national images that pervade American life are drawn from three very different conceptions of the past. Perhaps this should not be considered surprising because nations constantly, albeit subtly, rewrite themselves. This is because a country is not just one personality but a multitude of personalities which are in constant movement.[59] The shifts in which aspects of America's role have been dominant since it became a nation are a good illustration of Sorokin's principle of 'permanent change'. Change is inherent in any dynamic society and society itself produces it. Change is endogenous not exogenous and can be a response to an internal as well as an external challenge.[60] No conception of America's past comprises the whole truth and neither is it entirely false. But the American past, in its various interpretations, continues to inform the present, its foreign policy and its relations with other states. This heritage has given rise to another culturally derived concept, that of 'Americanism'.

'Americanism' is a belief in doing what is necessary to preserve and promote what is defined as the 'American way of life.' As Leon Samson explained:

> When we examine the meaning of Americanism, we discover that Americanism is to the American not a tradition or a territory, not what France is to a Frenchman or England to an Englishman, but a doctrine – what socialism is to a socialist.[61]

For Gramsci, 'Americanism' was the product of the bourgeoisie's most successful attempt to establish ideological hegemony. An ideology is a theory or belief system regarding existing society, the desirability or otherwise of its replacement and methodologies for change. According to David Apter, the mythical elements of an ideology cement the solidarity of society and buttress the moral authority of the rulers. An ideology also creates a world image that contributes to the individuals sense of identity. These functions interact to legitimise the authority of political elites.[62] Hegemony is the use of seductive, non-coercive inducements and co-optation to secure the masses compliance to a political and social system. In analysing American culture Gramsci contrasted the US experience to that of nineteenth century Germany or Italy, and saw the country as a dynamic material culture based on corporative, bureaucratic and technologically innovative forms of rationality, with no feudal remnants (monarchy, nobility or peasantry) and a form of religion which, unlike Catholic conservatism, was conducive to the notions of the dignity of labour, efficiency, profit and property which sustained capitalist endeavour. It had produced a worker who was effectively a 'trained gorilla' – the product of social conditioning not only through the state and its bureaucracies but through the legal system, the schools, churches, boardrooms, workplaces, cultural and leisure activities and the mass media. Together, the conditioning legitimated the competitive individualism of liberalism, the social atomism and depoliticisation of bureaucracy, the fatalism of religion, the states worship of nationalism and the patriarchy of the traditional family. Gramsci believed that in the US, the masses had been lulled into complete acceptance of the bourgeois system through the 'manipulation of consent' by means of an adroit use of ideology. In this sense 'Americanism' is akin to an ideology,[63] a belief system that encompasses America's self-styled values of democracy, freedom, anti-colonialism, self-determination and so forth.

One does not have to be a Marxist like Gramsci to believe that there is a kind of 'Americanist' ideology, not as rigidly presented, or as systematically developed perhaps as Marxism–Leninism or Maoism, but to some extent providing the parameters for political, economic, military and cultural activity in the US.[64] Furthermore, that it has persuasive power not merely because of its innate appeal throughout a country struggling to find an identity, but because it is buttressed by a state which has grown geographically, industrially, commercially and militarily for over two hundred years,[65] to become the world's only superpower.

If there is a theoretical component to American 'ideology' it is derived from Lockean liberalism. Traditionally Locke held a particular attraction for Americans and in his *Second Treatise on Civil Government* he wrote "In the beginning all the world was America." The affinity of American society for Locke's writings stemmed from two principles: the first is the morality of proprietary accumulation and the second is the collective right to self-defence.[66] The tie between morality and self-defence culminated in Locke developing a doctrine of just war and protective reaction. These concepts have been turned into ideological precepts by Americans as a result of Locke's philosophical tendency to integrate moral, social, economic and political realities. Louis Hartz argued that Lockean liberalism had become so embedded in American life that it has become a political ideology.[67] This ideology fed into the nation's foreign policy which has been criticised alternately for being too economically driven and imperialist, too moralistic and interventionist, too utilitarian and isolationist. All paradoxically are true, "for the concern with wealth, power, status, moral virtue and the freedom of mankind were successfully transformed in to a single set of mutually reinforcing values by the paradigm of Lockean liberalism."[68]

Ironically the commitment to both 'Americanism' and 'Lockean principles' has often led to the apparent neglect in practice of the country's professed ideals and its policies of protective reaction have often culminated in an interventionist foreign policy grounded in more conventional notions of 'national interest'. Yet even here, the tendency has been to use the language of moral rectitude by way of justification,[69] though whether this is also a 'screen' for geopolitical and economic objectives is a matter of contention.[70] The overthrow of the democratically elected President Arbenz of Guatemala in 1954, like the blockade of Cuba in 1962, the intervention of US Marines in the Dominican Republic in 1965, the support of the Pinochet coup in Chile against an elected Left wing government, its assistance to the Contras in Nicaragua and the despatch of US troops to Grenada in 1983 were all justified in terms of fighting Communism, as if the US were combating some kind of contagious disease on behalf of the American people and the whole of humankind. But in this kind of rationale lies a peculiarity of the American system. For in contrast to the European powers, the US has tended to view not a country, its government and its citizens as a threat, but a particular ideology. Washington was never at war with Germany, Japan, the Soviet Union or China, but with German Nazism, Japanese militarism and Russian and Chinese Communism. This may explain the propensity of the US to bomb countries including Panama, Grenada, Afghanistan and Iraq, without first declaring war on the state. In certain respects, the great foreign policy battles the US has fought have involved its own ideology of capitalism and 'freedom' against an external ideology. Communism was perceived as a source of evil because America rhetorically deplored the way in which a state could subjugate its own people and tended to conceive of what it saw as the forces of 'international Communism' as a single regime.

To Washington, the Soviet Union had forced the countries and peoples of Eastern Europe against their will into a 'Communist Empire', in the process putting in jeopardy the kinds of institutions and regimes for collective action and for constraining force on which it believed international order should be based. In addition, 'Communism' represented an affront to America's prestige and sense of honour since it actively opposed the very principles underlying the American way of life. Indeed, the spectacle of what it perceived, often against the evidence, as a monolithic Communist bloc, controlled by Moscow, continually expanding and taking over one country after another by 'indirect aggression' was to remain of fundamental concern to Washington[71] until the mid-1980s when Mikhail Gorbachev took over the reins of Soviet power and showed earnest in dismantling the political and institutional edifice of the Cold War. Ironically, though Gorbachev was to become a partner in building the UN based 'New World Order' that President Bush Sr. had called into being, his own political security was in jeopardy as was that of his state, and their political demise was to usher in the complete collapse of what remained of the Soviet bloc.[72] On the other hand, that Cuba and North Korea remained in the US political vocabulary as 'focuses' or 'axes' of evil' indicates how difficult Washington was to find it to jettison the mindset of nearly a century.

But Communism has not been Washington's only recent demon. Indeed, with the disappearance of so many Communist-ruled governments since the late 1980s, it is no longer regarded as the primary threat. From Washington's perspective it is the ideology of what it calls 'Islamic Fundamentalism', which it associates with terrorism and threats to civilised life, that constitutes the main danger. Once again, the US uses high sounding phraseology to conceal its use of the time-honoured balance of power principal of 'my enemy's enemy is my friend', in the process moulding a tenuous coalition from among a motley collection of states, by no means all champions of 'democracy' and 'free institutions'. As in the case of its opposition to Communism, Washington has tended to define 'Islamic Fundamentalism' with great imprecision, ascribing the term to such broadly secular governments as Saddam Hussein's Iraq and Colonel Qadafi's Libya, of both of which it strongly disapproved. It is in the context of the struggle against this ideology, however, that Israel has gained an especial resonance in American eyes. After all, since the 2001 terrorist assaults on America's World Trade Centre and Pentagon coincided with the suicide attacks on civilians in connection with the second *Intifada*, Israel can be portrayed as a fellow victim and this has given Washington further cause to regard the Jewish state as a 'special relation'.[73]

The Influence of Culture & History in American Foreign Policy towards Israel

Through a process of political socialisation, decision-makers are inducted, as are all citizens, into their society's preferred way of viewing the world and their beliefs are shaped by the cultural environment of which they are a product. Political culture feeds into the foreign policy decision-making process because it provides the political, social and psychological environment through which decision-makers view the world. The psycho-social dimension of human behaviour, including the ideas, meanings and beliefs people hold of the world, play a crucial role in determining action because they shape decision-maker's perceptions of the external environment. Merely by being born into a society and cultural milieu we are conditioned to hold certain images of the world. Such images are not static constructs but are adapted and refined in changing circumstances and when individual opinions, interpretations and experiences are brought to bear on a problem.

Political culture influences foreign policy making as well as domestic affairs through the nature of the relationship a state has with other states. In international relations, the ability of a state to secure allies on the basis of shared values and beliefs and not purely on calculations of realpolitik can be very significant. This is particularly true in the case of the US where the polity defines itself in terms of values and ideals and looks to other states to promote the values it holds dear. If a state can make itself resonate with another state in terms of values, and link that identification with powerful political forces, it will create a lever through which to pursue its objectives. This is the strategy Israel adopted in its relationship with the western world and has proved particularly effective in the case of the US, where, as the case studies which follow will discuss, it has formed enduring alliances with different elements within the political culture.

This thesis does not claim that political culture is the only factor in accounting for US policy towards Israel, but it does argue that the underlying values of American society play a crucial role in shaping policy makers' perceptions of the world.[74] The preceding discussion explored the way in which the values and beliefs on which the United States is founded can influence the approach to foreign policy and perception of America's place in the world. Within a democracy, with the government dependent on popular support, foreign policy must resonate with popular aspirations. Nowhere is it easier for American decision-makers to demonstrate a direct correlation between the country's political cultural values and its foreign policy than in its support for Israel, where there tends to be a convergence of views between the foreign-policy making elites and public opinion. As Abraham Ben-Zvi acknowledged, there is:

> a widespread fund of goodwill towards Israel that is not restricted to the Jewish community, and an equally strong and persistent commitment to Israel's continued national existence, integrity, and security. Comprising a cluster of broadly based attitudes that underscore the affinity and similarity between the two states in terms of their pioneering nature and commitment to democracy, this paradigm emerged as a legitimate and pervasive precept.[75]

For many Americans, the history and culture of the United States is perceived to resonate with that of the Jewish state, which reinforces the feeling of moral responsibility for the preservation of Israel because of the role Washington had played in its creation. This sense of moral obligation is underlined by the media which tends to encourage the discourse of revulsion and horror at the Holocaust and American complicity through disbelief and inaction in its perpetration. After all, in 1943, a Gallup poll revealed that thirty percent of respondents dismissed news of the death of two million Jews in Europe as a rumour, while an informal poll conducted by the *New York Post* in the same year found that a broad range of Americans did not believe the atrocity reports.[76] In more recent times, however, with the plight of the Jews under constant review, it is hardly surprising that the belief is widespread that the Jewish people have a 'right' to their own state as a consequence of Nazi atrocities. At the same time, the constant reminder of the Holocaust is indicative of the power of Jewish and Israeli images to permeate American society. But what is the origin of this connection with an atrocity that was marginalised in the decades following its perpetration and what is the process by which Israel and memories of the Holocaust have come to be such an integral and powerful part of American political culture?

The Marginalisation of the Holocaust

The speed with which the Holocaust was marginalised and concealed in the late 1940s may astound us today, but when considered against the political realities of the time, it is comprehensible. For it was not feelings of shame and guilt that prompted its relegation, but a revolutionary change in the configuration of world alignments. In the aftermath of the Second World War new rivalries emerged and the international battle lines were re-drawn. The conflict was no longer between Nazi Germany and the Allied forces, but Soviet Communism and the capitalist West, and given its geographical proximity to Moscow, West Germany was on the front line. To secure public support for the rapid rehabilitation of West Germany into the Western family of nations, a fundamental ideological retooling of the minds of the American public mind was required. The apotheosis of evil was reassigned from Berlin to Moscow and public opinion had to be mobilised to accept this new reality. Symbols like the Holocaust that reinforced the old view – that of the Germans as the epitome of limitless depravity – were now dysfunctional because they reminded Americans how recently their new allies had been their enemies and their new enemies their friends. Norman Finkelstein argued that reference to the Holocaust was marginalised because it was actively obstructive to this 're-education' process.[77]

The theory of totalitarianism was invoked to explain the apparent change in US policy.[78] The Truman administration argued that from the perspective of western ideological beliefs the Cold War was actually a continuation of the Second World War in the form of a struggle against the transcendent enemy of totalitarianism first in Nazism and then in Soviet Communism. The concentration camps of the Holocaust were not depicted as an atrocity against the Jews as an ethnic group, but as a symbol of the persecution of political opponents, thus creating a connection between the 'totalitarianism' of Nazi Germany and the 'totalitarianism' of Communist Russia.[79]

Washington's demonisation of the Soviet Union was potentially threatening to the survival of the fledgling Jewish state, which in its early years assumed many of the trappings of a socialist society. American Jewish organisations were confronted with the unwanted dilemma of how to limit the association between Jews and Communists in the public mind, particularly when many of Israel's Jewish inhabitants were left wing refugees from Eastern Europe. The identification of Jews with Communists dates back to the Bolshevik Revolution of 1917 when most of the 'alien agitators' deported from America during the Red Scare after the First World War had been Jews.[80] In the inter-war years the Communist Jew was a staple of anti-Semitic propaganda in both Europe and the US. The association was muted during the Second World War when the Soviet Union was part of the Allied forces, but the respite was short lived.

In the late 1940s and early 1950s, American Jewish organisations worked to counteract the popular Jewish/Communist equation that was being reinforced by the relatively high number of Jews appearing in espionage prosecutions. The ultimate public relations disasters for Jewish organisations in the 1950s were the trials of Julius and Ethel Rosenberg, Morton Sobell, Harry Gold and David Greenglass,[81] all of whom invoked the Holocaust as justification for their association with the Soviet Union. Holocaust rhetoric was a staple of Communist Party policy and American Jewish organisations were determined to distance themselves from it.

Throughout the 1950s and 1960s, Jewish organisations worked on a variety of fronts to alter the American frame of cultural reference by limiting the association between Jews and Communists in the public mind. Their principle co-operative venture was the 'Hollywood Project', in which they jointly employed a West Coast representative to lobby film producers to portray sympathetic images of Jews. For example, the producer of *I Married a Communist* agreed that no Communist character would be given a "name that can even remotely be construed as Jewish,"[82] while in *The Red Menace*, the only sympathetic character in the film was a Jew.[83]

Simultaneously with this, Jewish organisations conducted a purge of their members, expelling their leftist chapters and anyone who could remotely be considered to have Communist sympathies.[84] During this period it was the American Jewish Committee that was the most active and its monthly magazine *Commentary* published hard-line anti-Soviet articles that were, according to its editor Norman Podhoretz, "part of a secret programme to demonstrate that not all Jews were Communists."[85] The Committee also secured agreements from *Time* and *Life* magazine and a number of New York newspapers not to publish letters from readers commenting on the Jewishness of accused Communists. The American Jewish Committee also participated in and financially supported the McCarthyite All-American Conference to Combat Communism and, like many other mainstream Jewish organisations, remained aloof from the campaign for clemency for the Rosenbergs.[86]

While the disassociation of Jews and Communists in the public mind was a powerful imperative it was only one of a number of factors that explain the reticence of American Jews to draw attention to the Holocaust during this time. Involvement in the Second World War had united Americans and the post-war years were a time of upbeat optimism. American Jews shared wholeheartedly in this ebullient mood. "An integrationist rather than a particularist consciousness was the norm in the postwar decades"[87] and the 'victory' over Nazism drew many Americans, particularly the sons and daughters of recent immigrants, into a shared experience of the mystique of the American nation.[88] The 1950s and 1960s saw a precipitous decline in anti-semitism in the United States, in part, because Jews were increasingly seen as far less 'foreign' than in the past.

Generally they were no longer the new immigrants, but third generation Americans and by the 1950s three quarters of American Jews were native born.[89] American Jews were energetically engaged in becoming integrated into American society and seizing the opportunities available to them. It was not until this process was complete, Alan Mintz argues, and Jews felt comfortable in America as Americans, and the lustre of America itself had dimmed, that American Jews were ready to acknowledge the full extent of the Holocaust.[90]

In their earlier marginalisation of the Holocaust, Jews were also repudiating their status as victims. While identification with the struggle and pioneering spirit of the new state of Israel was positive and had parallels in the American society of which they were a part, the victim status of Holocaust Jews was shameful and dispiriting. How and when this avoidance of confronting the Holocaust, shared across many sectors of society, was overcome, was a truly fundamental shift and one for which the reasons are many.

The Integration of Israel into American Culture

A crucial factor in this change was a shift in the very conception of America as a paragon society. In the post-war years America was viewed as the richest, freest, most powerful and most just nation on earth and it is obvious why Jews would wish to be fully integrated into such a society. Yet with the advent of the civil rights movement and the embroilment in Vietnam, the idealist image of America was brought into disrepute. The critique of the justness of American society and its controversial use of power opened up the vista of America, not as a shining example to the world, but as a country that had inflicted suffering both at home and abroad. A growing awareness of the consequences of 'man's inhumanity to man' was epitomised by the apparent hopelessness of the plight of the American black underclass and televised images of the burned limbs of the Vietnamese peasants. The vocabulary used to describe the more unpalatable aspects of American life replicated that more commonly associated with contemporary images of the Holocaust. The urban slums in which the poor existed were called ghettos, the attempt of a strong nation to destroy another peoples was called genocide and the potential for a conflict using atomic weapons was called a nuclear Holocaust. As American culture began to absorb this new reality and the survivor figure emerged as the hero of culture, Jews were conferred with the moral prestige of being the ultimate victims of mans evil.[91]

The 1960s was the decade in which the concept of American society as a single nation comprising citizens from different backgrounds was severely challenged.[92] Difference was being articulated and prized more highly than conformity. As African-Americans articulated their unique status, constraints on the public expression of Jewishness and the Jewish historical experience were lifted. American culture was profoundly, if belatedly, influenced by the Second World War and the Holocaust. One explanation for this, was enumerated by Morris Dickstein in an article on black humour novels of the early 1960s: " . . . it's because the unsolved moral enigma of that period and that experience most closely expresses the conundrum of contemporary life fifteen years later."[93] Parallels were drawn between the Jewish underclass of Nazi Germany and the black underclass of 1960s America.

Yet, the real catalyst for increased discourse about the Holocaust came with Israeli Prime Minister David Ben-Gurion's announcement on 23 May 1960 that Israeli agents had captured Adolf Eichmann in Argentina and secretly transported him to Israel where he would stand trial.[94] For many Americans, Jews and non-Jews alike, Eichmann's trial, which was broadcast around the world, was the first time the reality of the attempted annihilation of European Jewry was revealed. As the full horrors of the Holocaust were recounted, the image of Israeli Jews as activists took precedence over the image of Jews as victims. The public and unrelenting nature of the trial which lasted for over a year, conveyed a plethora of information and heralded the entry of the Holocaust as a distinct entity, perpetrated against a specific ethnic group, into American consciousness.[95] The recognition of the Holocaust by the gentile world had an important impact on American Jews, giving them licence to analyse this aspect of their past.

Yet Israel's actions, including the breach of Argentinean sovereignty in the capture of Eichmann, provoked censure in the Western world. It was noteworthy too that the liberal press in Britain and America that had lauded the Nuremberg trials, expressed reservations about Israel's behaviour.[96] To be sure, in the 1960s criticism of Israel did not take the form of anti-Semitic hatred. On the contrary, it was based on friendship and philo-Semitism and the fact that the world had expected something better of the Jews. Yet whatever the course of the intellectual debate, Argentina was the only country to demand Eichmann's extradition and European countries and the US expressed in their various ways their conviction that the trial would be pursued fairly and justly. In the event, the prisoner was allowed to select his own counsel from any nation he chose, the Israeli government paid all the bills and expenses[97] and when the defendant appealed against the verdict his appeal was heard in the Supreme Court. In their adherence to jurisprudence the Israelis firmly positioned themselves as a part of the Western family of nations.

The trial also placed the Holocaust on the moral radar of the Christian community in America and prompted renewed scrutiny over Christian collaboration and responsibility. The silence of the Vatican and the failure of Pope Pius XII to publicly denounce the Holocaust during its perpetration were re-established in the public mind. Yet while raising questions of gentile culpability, the trial itself created the opportunity for a positive theological connection to the Jews as victims of affliction and torment that resonated with the Christian imagination, making the Jews once again an active and relevant presence in the Christian mind of America.[98]

Cultural change in American society coincided with new political realities that gradually led to a diminution of the constraints in publicising the Holocaust. By the 1960s, the Cold War mentality that had previously limited public discussion of the Nazi genocide had become so institutionalised that it could no longer be jeopardised by reminders of Second World War alliances. An environment was emerging where Americans were increasingly receptive to the rehabilitation of memories of the Holocaust that were reinforced in the early 1960s when the East German government revealed the Nazi connections of prominent West German officials. Yet the process through which the Holocaust succeeded in penetrating the layers of American isolationism is complex,[99] and its infiltration into the cultural discourse of society through books, films and television played a crucial role.

Israel and American Popular Culture

Perhaps the first major cultural event that impacted on public perceptions of the Holocaust was the publication of the English translation of Anne Frank's *The Diary of a Young Girl* in 1952 and its subsequent translation to stage and screen. The importance of the diary lay in its ability to do what political events had proved incapable of: creating an empathetic connection between the fate of European Jewry and the average American reader who had little knowledge of the event itself. Yet, the Holocaust does not form the central consciousness of either the book or its various dramatisations and Anne's Jewish identity is depicted in such a way that it seems inessential to her character. The film was also compromised by Hollywood conventions of scoring and casting,[100] with Anne bearing a striking resemblance to the popular 1950s actress Audrey Hepburn.[101] The audience was more likely to associate with Anne's courageous struggle in a time of adversity than to confront the horrors of the Holocaust itself. Americans might empathise with the young girl's plight and blame the Nazis – though none appeared in the play – but they were not asked to implicate their government or themselves for any role in a tragic drama overseas.[102] In the mid-1950s, American audiences were not ready to make that connection.

In early American cinematic responses to the Holocaust, both the Nazi genocide and the Jewish homeland were absent. For example, the 1947 film *Gentleman's Agreement* explored the bloodless anti-Semitic practices of New York and Connecticut, which by implication cast the Jewish experience of the US in a much more favourable light than their experience of Central and Eastern Europe. In the film, gentile journalist Skylar Philip Green posed as a Jew to research an article on anti-Semitism, as it were, 'from the inside'. While posing as a Jew, Green experiences various kinds of hostility including anti-Semite remarks and exclusion from exclusive clubs. Although these might appear to be relatively harmless forms of discrimination, the unspoken backdrop of the Holocaust makes clear that these actions fall along a continuum, the ultimate conclusion of which is genocide.[103] *Gentleman's Agreement* universalised the meaning of the Holocaust to encompass all forms of bigotry, prejudice, hatred and social injustice. By extending its concern with anti-Semitism to prejudice more generally, the film repudiates its perpetration not only because it is morally objectionable but because it is the antithesis of American values.

A central objective of the film was to minimise the difference between Jews and others through an exploration of American Jewish identity. When Green's young son asks him "What is an American Jew?" Green adopts the Enlightenment response to the centuries old European Jewry question: religion as distinct from nationality. He describes Jews by their religious label,[104] as members of one of the many religions that have a place on the American urban landscape and explains that anti-Semitism is just one of a variety of hatreds targeted at members of a particular religion. Jews are described as being as American as anyone else: "You can be an American and a Protestant, or an American and a Catholic, or an American and a Jew."[105] By implication, Nazi Germany's repudiation of its Jewish citizens is also a repudiation of its democratic values, and therefore, an example to be rejected. Green explains that: "One thing is your country . . . but the other thing is religion. . . . That doesn't have anything to do with the flag or the uniform or the airplanes." In defining the Jews nationality through the national symbols of flag, uniform and airplanes, Green also marginalises suspicions of dual loyalties for the American Jew.[106]

The absence of any reference to Israel in *Gentleman's Agreement* is representative of a time when Jews were encouraged to embrace an American identity through the adoption of an American universalist vision. The contrast between this 1947 film and Otto Preminger's 1960 film *Exodus* exemplifies the difference in approach and the evolution of American cultural attitudes.

Leon Uris's 1960 book and film *Exodus* treats the Holocaust as a distinctly Jewish event and pairs the quintessential Jewish tragedy with the Jewish triumph of a homeland in Palestine. Crucially for the development of American Jewish identity, the Holocaust and the creation of the state of Israel are shown in the film as the two pillars by which Jews can define themselves. An unarticulated but important triangulation exists between the traditional Jew as remembered, the new Israeli Jew represented on screen and the American Jew off-screen, external to the films plot. The identification of the American Jew with the new Israeli Jew is encouraged by the American English dialogue and the casting of Paul Newman in the lead role as Ari Ben Canaan. While Ari personifies the powerful, virile and handsome Israeli man he also represents the American Jew, thus enabling a positive connection to be made between them.

The film endeavours to make clear that although the Jews have a distinctive religion and history they are no different from anyone else. This 'anyone else' is shown to be the gentile world. While Ari enters into a relationship with an American Christian nurse, that is designed to erase differences between Americans and Jews, more ominously for a Jewish state situated in an Arab world, *Exodus* presents Jewish-Arab difference as unbreachable – Ari will not permit his sister to marry his Arab friend.[107] Simultaneously with this, the connection between the Arab enemies of the Jewish homeland and the Nazi murders of European Jewry justifies this difference. Palestinian terrorism is masterminded with an escaped Nazi in the background.

Exodus is representative of popular American characterisations of Jewish history that, in depicting the state of Israel as the culmination and redemption of the Shoah, conflate the American and the Israeli Jew. For American Jews internalising this discourse, the imagined Israel is not the actual Israel but an Israel of the mind. The virile representation of the Israeli Jew is someone with whom American Jews can identify in contrast to the vision of Jewish impotence of the Shoah that they wish to cast off.[108] It is this idealised image of Israel that American Jews mobilised to defend.

The Entry of the Holocaust into American Life

The most effective means of securing public engagement with the Holocaust was through the depiction of it in terms that had a resonance with the contemporary concerns of the audience. Two of the first films that attempted this were the 1961 film *Judgement at Nuremberg* and the 1965 film *The Pawnbroker*. Both relied on parallels between Nazi Germany and 1960s America for their popular appeal and both enlisted all star casts to ensure that audiences were drawn to the box office.

When *Judgement at Nuremberg* premiered on 14 December 1961 it was a major cultural event. United Artists staged the screening in Kongresshalle in the shadow of the Berlin Wall. The invited audience were Allied commanders, members of the West German government and American journalists who had been flown in to report on the event. The film had already been brought to the attention of the American people by a feature in *Life* magazine[109] and a profile in the *New York Times* of the film's director Stanley Kramer.[110] The premier was also guaranteed an audience because its opening coincided with the verdict in the Eichmann trial and parallels between the courtroom in Nuremberg and the courtroom in Beit Haam, Jerusalem, could be drawn in the public mind.

The film dealt with principles not individuals and its "metaphorical content on the discourse of justice, so relevant to Americans, created an atmosphere of what Pierre Sorlin call[ed] readiness."[111] Nazi symbols and images avail the credits and the audience read the words Nuremberg, Germany 1948, which introduces them to a courtroom scene. We then meet the American judge Dan Haywood (Spencer Tracy) who has come out of retirement to judge four Nazi war criminals. Most of the film is devoted to the trials which are orchestrated by the raging American prosecutor Colonel Tad Rolfe (Richard Widmark) and the charismatic German defence lawyer Hans Clift (Maximilian Schell). The key witnesses are Rudolf Petersen who was sterilised by the Nazi's for political reasons, Irene Hoffman (Judy Garland) who recounts an incident of racial pollution and the most important defendant, the German scholar and jurist Ernst Janning (Burt Lancaster). Judge Dan Haywood respected Janning for his earlier writings on jurisprudence and he now explains that in a period of indignity and fear, Hitler had restored pride to the German people. "I am aware!" he yells. "Were we deaf? Blind? If we didn't know, it's because we didn't want to know."[112]

Rolfe's comeback is that if Janning is guilty then everyone is guilty: the Vatican, Churchill who indirectly praised Hitler in 1938, American industrialists who assisted Hitler in rebuilding German armaments and the list goes on. The judge finally indicts the men in the dock because these men were directly responsible for their actions, irrespective of whether many more people were guilty. He then warns the court that "If these murders were monsters, this event would have no more moral significance than an earthquake . . . how easily this can happen!"[113]

In essence, *Judgement at Nuremberg* is a film in which four stories are told. The first is the manifest submission of the German people, particularly the educated classes to Nazism and the denial of complicity for their willing compliance. The second is the implicit splendour of American justice which provides the moral yardstick for the determination of right and wrong.[114] The third story addresses the issue of responsibility, both individual and national.[115] The fourth is the subtly concealed narrative of the Holocaust and the public interest in its perpetrators.

The Pawnbroker tried to achieve a connection between Nazi Germany of the 1930s and the US in the 1960s by creating an analogy between street violence in Harlem and the murder of European Jewry. The film tells the story of Holocaust survivor Sol Nazerman (Rod Steiger), who lost his wife and children in the camps and now runs a pawnshop in Harlem. It depicts American society as being responsible for the suffering of the blacks and the Jews, and Nazerman, himself so recently a victim, is guilty of complicity, not unlike the Germans responsible for his own suffering and the death of his family.[116] The film focuses on the psychological damage inflicted on the pawnbroker by his wartime experiences that have made him choose a life bereft of human compassion and detachment. At the time of the film's release, *New York Times* writer Bosley Crowther dscribed it as a "drama of discovery of the need of man to try to do something for his fellow human sufferers in the troubled world of today."[117] The story tells of how the shooting of Nazerman's Puerto Rican assistant finally strips off his defences and brings him back to the living world of suffering. This 'regeneration' does not culminate with the alleviation of pain but with a renewed capacity to feel it and the ability to rejoin the world of "fellow suffers."[118] In so doing, the pawnbroker regains his 'social conscience', a newly developing concept in American society.

The film is one of the first in which the 'survivor' is the central consciousness and it played a role in shaping the image of the survivor in American culture.[119] It heralded the emergence of the survivor as a representative type and the onset of the process by which the survivor became the hero of society and popular culture.

The transition from a general consciousness of the Holocaust to its memorialisation was to a certain extent, driven by the pervasive influence of another cultural artefact: the television. Peter Novick, a professor of history at the University of Chicago, contends that the defining moment in the entry of the Holocaust into general American consciousness was NBC's presentation in 1978 of the television mini-series *Holocaust.* The programme reflected the resurgence of ethnic consciousness in America and the strengthening of ethnic identification that had occurred as a product of the black struggle for civil rights in the 1960s.[120] Close to 100 million Americans tuned into the four part nine and a half-hour programme[121] that featured household names including Meryl Streep and James Wood. The series was designed to maximise identification between the American audience and the victims, an educated German Jewish family. The television images showed the 'evil' of societies based on other ideologies and the righteous morality of the United States and its obligation to prevent a repeat of this genocide.

The success of *Holocaust* represented the intersection of a medium that was very American with a virulent mode of Jewish persecution that was seen as exclusively European. A human cataclysm had taken place in the Old World and had gained admittance to American consciousness through the medium of "entertainment that Americans had devised to protect their historical innocence."[122] The incredible power of television universalised the Holocaust in two senses. Firstly, it became the referent for collective suffering and the ultimate standard of describing victimisation. Secondly, in the political sphere, it dramatically became a point of moral consensus. A politician could maximise his political capital by advocating the memorialisation of the Holocaust and rest assured that his actions would generate public support. It was in this vein that on 1 May 1978, two weeks after *Holocaust* had been aired on national television, President Jimmy Carter announced the establishment of a presidential commission to recommend a national Holocaust memorial. Carter responded to the developing consensus within American society that the Holocaust should be memorialised in America. He claimed his decision was a product of changes in American cultural consciousness, brought about by his reading of Arthur Morse's book *While Six Million Died* and his growing awareness that Israel had been born "out of the ashes" of the Holocaust.

Fifteen years later, Steven Spielberg's blockbuster film *Schindler's List* represented "Israel as the historical culmination of Jewish destiny."[123] The film is a work of popular culture that led to an intensification of engagement with the Holocaust in public cultural discourse in the US. Not unlike the mini-series *Holocaust*, the genre was crafted in a way that enabled the public to admit the film into their consciousness in very American terms. Firstly individualism is an integral aspect of American political culture and the portrayal of the individualism of Schindler enabled him to assume the traditional Hollywood role of the strong leading man. Through an oversimplification of history, Schindler becomes the saviour of the Jewish people and with it the personification of goodness against the evil of Nazism. Schindler's perceived success in saving countless Jews from the gas chamber plays to the American conviction that individuals can move history.

Secondly the concept of rescue that is manifest in the films Hollywood style 'happy ending' appealed to an American audience. Alan Mintz argued that the issue was more profound than a standard plot device and was essential to the success of the film because an American audience would not accept the true story of the fate of the majority of European Jews.[124] By choosing Schindler as the focal point of a film depicting the Holocaust, Spielberg was able to focus on the atypical rescue of a group of European Jews, within the overarching framework of Nazi genocide. The concept of survivor-rescuer, facilitated by the rehabilitation of the survivor in the American mind, has led to a new interest in those gentiles who helped make that survival possible. As Lawrence Langer acknowledged, "it is the nature of the American mind, and perhaps human nature in general, to avoid abiding the unremittingly tragic."[125]

In the American mind, the idea of rescue is interwoven with the concept of redemption, a concept that has deep roots in American culture and is commensurate with the theological dimension of some of the country's leading religious groups. Spielberg's film is a story about a rescuer and a fallen Christian at that, who returns to his faith and saves himself by saving Jews. In seeking to appeal to a modern American audience, the focus on survivor-rescuer and the overarching theme of redemption, was a key device through which the film was accepted into mainstream popular culture.

The power of images of the Holocaust to move the American public was convincingly demonstrated in 1992 when fund-raisers asked for donations from individuals for the construction of the national Holocaust museum. An astonishing $168 million was raised, demonstrating the power and commitment of a sector of American society to support a cause in which they came to deeply believe.[126] Situated in the heart of the nation's capital, next to the National Museum of American History, the museum enshrines, by virtue of its placement, not just the history of the Holocaust but what are seen as American democratic and egalitarian ideals as a counterpoint to the Holocaust. James Young, a professor of English and Judaic studies at the University of Massachusetts, explained that "remembering the crimes of another people in another land . . . encourages Americans to recall their nation's own idealised reason for being."[127] It is also a means by which the symbolic importance of Israel is reinforced in the minds of America.

The "Americanisation of the Holocaust", the title of a number of works on this subject, implies that this event has been refracted through means of representation that resonate with American culture. Events are only comprehensible to cultures, like people, from within the confines of their own experiences, interests and values and the willingness to engage in an external event is generally motivated by an internal exigency.[128] The Holocaust was admitted into American life in American terms and has gradually been assimilated into public discourse and political culture.

Shared Values and Practices

Americans have come to feel a strong empathy for Israel as a society imbued with the liberal values and humanistic culture of the West. Viewed as a democratic and open society, the Jewish state is perceived as sharing the concepts of individual freedom, and in this regard is identified as a 'Western' state. In some respects, Israel is seen as a reflection of the American self not just because many of Israel's more vociferous citizens were radicals raised in the US, but because shared values, cultural affinity, a common ethical and religious heritage, the Judaic tradition and the Judeo-Christian heritage bind the United States and Israel together.[129]

Israel has a parliament elected by free and secret ballot and a government that is perceived as changing in accordance with the will of the governed. Debates between the different political and ideological persuasions of the political parties characterise Israeli political life and these ideas are also central to western political systems. The United States has an interest in the survival of the relatively few democratic states outside of Europe and believes it has a moral obligation to protect such an exposed democracy in a sea of Arab feudalism. Characteristically, in the 1992 presidential election, Clinton drew on Israel as an example of a 'democratic ally' and claimed that "Democracy has always been our nation's perfecting impulse . . . democracy abroad also protects our own concrete economic and security interests here at home."[130]

Washington's professed concern with Israel's fundamental values includes support for what are seen as human rights, minority rights (there are Arab members of the Knesset), pluralism, popular participation in government, and the rejection of extremism, oppression and terrorism, and whatever misgivings some Americans may feel regarding Israel's ability to deliver on these values, the country is generally believed to honour them where possible. Successive US administrations have believed that Washington can have close and enduring relations with countries such as Israel that are believed to share America's fundamental values.

Like America, Israel is a nation of immigrants who left inhospitable lands for a new one where they endeavoured to build a just and free society. The American experience in striving to escape persecution and establish an independent national homeland had a parallel in a Jewish state that appeared to reaffirm those ideals through absorption and immigration. A parallel is also seen between the struggle of the Israelis against the Arabs and the struggle of the Pilgrim Fathers against the American Indians.[131] There is, in addition, a corresponding dedication to the values of pioneering peoples – the United States placed great importance on those who heeded the call to 'go west' and Israel attributed equal salience to the settlers who moved to and developed the frontier lands.[132]

The importance of political culture in influencing foreign policy is evident in the pronouncements of senior American decision-makers such as former Assistant Secretary of State Edward Djerejian: "The U.S.–Israeli relationship [is based on] shared democratic ideals and values . . . and we remain unshakeably committed to Israel's security and to preserving Israel's qualitative edge." The perception of such cultural similarities and shared values clearly contribute to the strength and endurance of the US–Israeli relationship. As former Secretary of State Henry Kissinger explained:

> For Americans, co-operation among the free nations is a moral and not merely a practical necessity. . . . America, to be itself, needs a sense of identity and collaboration with other nations who share its values. . . . The solidarity of the democratic nations in the world is essential both as material support and as a moral symbol.[133]

This is very revealing of decision-makers' attitudes towards international affairs in general and, in the context of this book, of their understanding of relations with the Arab states in general and Israel in particular.

The Selection of the Case Studies

This book focuses on United States policy toward Israel during times of hostilities between Israel and her Arab neighbours, which tended to create tensions in relations between Washington and Jerusalem and also between Washington and Moscow. As most of the events under consideration occurred during the

Cold War, tensions in the Middle East both reflected and impacted on the relationship between the superpowers, when their leaders perceived the national interest of their respective states to be threatened to a far greater extent than under normal circumstances. It is particularly revealing to analyse inter-state relations during periods of intense strain between Israel and the United States, when their respective national interests often appeared to demand different courses of action. Under such conditions, the real flow of influence, willingness to compromise and commitment of both parties to the security and interest of the other is most apparent. As Quandt acknowledges:

> By definition, crisis involves surprise, threat, and enhanced uncertainty. Previous policies may well be exposed as flawed or bankrupt. Reality no longer accords with previous expectations. In such a situation, a new structure of perceptions is likely to emerge, one that will reflect presidential perspectives to the degree that the president becomes involved in handling the crisis.[134]

It is because of the crucial role that US presidents and their key decision-makers tended to play in crisis situations that their perceptions and actions form the main focus of this book. As was discussed in Chapter 1, it is apparent from an assessment of the available evidence of the foreign policy-making elite's pronouncements on Israel that the relationship is perceived to rest on a "moral basis".[135] The United States' commitment to Israel is seen as transcending the bounds of realpolitik, and an emotional affinity and spiritual connection is perceived to exist between the two nations. The rhetoric of successive American leaders indicates that Israel is considered to be one of the United States' greatest allies and that a "commitment to the security and survival of Israel is an essential element of . . . global policy."[136]

An analysis of the public rhetoric and private sentiments of the United States foreign-policy elite reveals recurrent themes, values and resonant notions that are indicative of the cultural premises on which elite perceptions of Israel are based.[137] The analytical challenge is to assess the complex relationship between ideas and action, by comparing public pronouncements with private statements to determine whether the rhetoric of successive administrations acts as a reliable guide to policy or if serious contradictions exist between words and deeds. Comparisons will also be made between the statements and actions of successive presidents to illuminate the priorities of different administrations' and to reveal both continuities and changes in policy.

The selected case studies focus on the Johnson, Nixon, Reagan and Bush Sr. administrations, and therefore analyse the policies of both Democratic and Republican governments. Particular emphasis is placed on crisis situations and their impact in shaping issues for Presidents and their advisers, particularly the Secretary of State, National Security Adviser and Secretary of Defence. Consideration will be given to the extent to which their actions have been a rational response to the defence of the perceived national interest, the product of domestic pressure or the outcome of a cultural frame of reference and of Washington's special relationship with Israel.

During the Suez crisis of 1956, Eisenhower forced Israel to withdraw from Egyptian land it had captured as part of a joint Anglo-French operation to control the Canal zone. By opposing what Washington viewed as the 'imperialist' actions of other Western states in Afro-Asia, Eisenhower hoped to win the support of the regions newly independent states and to discredit the Soviet Union's 'colonialism' in Eastern Europe.[138] Yet by the time Kennedy assumed the presidency in 1960, Eisenhower's decision had been discredited. The Soviet Union was increasing its influence in the region, most notably with the assistance of President Gamal Abdul Nasser of Egypt, who had benefited from American actions a decade earlier. While continuing to court the Egyptian leader, Kennedy began the process of re-establishing friendly relations with Israel and supplied it with small quantities of arms.

The failure of both Eisenhower and Kennedy to lure Nasser into the Western camp and Kennedy's agreement to the sale of US arms to Israel, provides the context for the first case study that begins with President Johnson and the response of his administration to the June War of 1967. This has been taken as the starting point because the conditions of more recent ties between the United States and Israel largely stemmed from this event. The 1967 war culminated in the Johnson administration mounting the first American military resupply operation to Israel following the cease-fire, providing Israel with diplomatic support in the United Nations against the Soviet Union and the radical Arab states and tacitly endorsing Israeli occupation of captured Arab territory until the conclusion of peace negotiations.

The second case study explores the policy of the Republican administration of Richard Nixon towards Israel during the Yom Kippur war of October 1973. This period is of particular interest because the Arab–Israeli conflict culminated in the US armed forces being put on nuclear alert, the launch of America's first resupply operation to Israel during a war and the establishment of the financial component of the more recent special relationship, when Congress authorised Nixon and Kissinger's request for $2.2 billion in financial aid to Israel.

The third case study analyses the Reagan administration's approach to the Israeli invasion of Lebanon in 1982. This was Israel's first 'war of choice' and has parallels with Suez because Israel was widely perceived as the aggressor state. Despite this, Reagan continued to support Israel and even deployed US Marines to keep the peace between the warring Lebanese factions, many hundreds of whom were killed in a terrorist attack in Beirut – more than the number of US servicemen killed in the Gulf War of 1991.

The final case study provides an overview of the administration of George Bush Sr. and its attempts to balance American, Israeli and Arab interests during the kaleidoscopic changes in the international landscape that characterised the post-Cold War world. The objective of this and the other case studies is to explore the dynamics of US policy towards Israel in terms of the politics, sociology, economics and strategy of commitment.

4

THE JOHNSON ADMINISTRATION

THE POLICY LYNDON JOHNSON'S administration pursued towards Israel reflected a combination of the shifts that occurred in American political culture during the 1960s, and the trauma of Vietnam. Johnson assumed office as leader of a troubled nation whose president had just been assassinated and which was beginning to question the conception of itself as a paragon society. The violence associated with the reaction to the civil rights movement and the move to end racial segregation in the southern states challenged the unity of the nation at a time when the Vietnam War undermined the belief in American military superiority and the righteousness of its foreign policy. The questioning at home and abroad of the exemplary nature of American society and its controversial use of power undermined the perception of America as an 'ideal' nation.

As majority leader in the Senate, Johnson had built consensus through ingeniously constructed compromises,[1] using his power to further his objectives for social reform. But the confidence he exuded in domestic politics contrasted sharply with his inexperience in foreign affairs, an area that required his increasing attention with the escalation of the US commitment in Vietnam during 1964–65 and the Middle East crisis of 1967. Perhaps as an acknowledgement of this, Johnson continued the foreign policy strategy of his predecessor, President John F. Kennedy,[2] and in the Middle East, sought to balance American interests with those of Israel and those of the Arab states. It is perhaps because he initially pursued Kennedy's approach that the contrast was so great between his reluctance to act decisively to avert war in May 1967[3] and his later support and alignment with Israel as the war intensified. The extent of his personal belief that the Jews had the right to a homeland and his commitment to the preservation of Israel was apparent in his rhetoric but was not truly revealed in practice until the war commenced. By the end of his presidency, the

Middle Eastern map had been redrawn and the United States had become Israel's major arms supplier, tacitly accepting Israel's occupation of Arab land as legitimate.

From his early days in office, Johnson's outspoken defence of Jewish causes distinguished him as a strong proponent of Israel. His assumption of the presidency was greeted warmly in Tel Aviv. In 1938, prior to the outbreak of the Second World War, he had used his position as a congressman to press immigration officials to lift restrictions on Jewish refugees seeking asylum in the United States.[4] A decade later, when Israel was literally fighting for its survival, he worked behind the scenes to facilitate the clandestine flow of American arms to Israel's fledgling army, the Haganah. Following the Suez crisis of 1956, Johnson opposed the Eisenhower Administration's insistence on Israeli withdrawal from Sinai and spoke out in opposition to United Nations sanctions against Israel. He came to Tel Aviv's assistance again in 1958, supporting its attempts to secure American military aid. Johnson's efforts did not go unnoticed by leading Jewish figures[5] and as early as the mid-1950s, Israeli Ambassador Abba Eban claimed that "there was something about Israel that stirred [Johnson's] pious memories." McPherson, a White House aide, went so far as to suggest that "some place in Lyndon Johnson's blood [there were] a great many Jewish corpuscles."[6]

Johnson's early life shaped the basic premises on which he operated as president. Born into a Christian family that had ties to the small Texas Jewish community in his hometown, he was raised on biblical teachings that taught him to believe that the Jews had a right to a homeland in Palestine. As a politician, the influence of his religious upbringing was evident as revealed in a speech he delivered to a B'nai B'rith meeting in Washington in 1968:

> Most, if not all of you, have very deep ties with the land and with the people of Israel, as I do, for my Christian faith sprang from yours. The Bible stories are woven into my childhood memories as the gallant struggle of modern Jews to be free of persecution is also woven into our souls.[7]

Johnson enjoyed close contacts with the American Jewish community; fighting for domestic liberal and social reforms in the Senate, he had discovered in them a kindred spirit with shared values. Israeli leaders capitalised on this to advance the US–Israeli relationship. It was possible to translate this empathy into foreign affairs because in the mid-1960s Tel Aviv was experiencing problems of economic development and challenges from external forces, with which a domestically orientated president, believing his own country to be threatened by Communism, could identify.[8] In his memoirs Johnson acknowledged that he had "always had a deep feeling of sympathy for Israel and its people, gallantly building and defending a modern nation against great odds and against the tragic background of Jewish experience."[9]

The emotional affinity and sense of common heritage Johnson felt for Israel was explicit in his public pronouncements. In a toast he made to President Zalam Shazar of Israel in August 1966, he asserted:

> [O]ur Republic like yours, was nurtured by the philosophy of the ancient Hebrew teachers who taught mankind the principles of morality, of social justice and of universal peace. This is our heritage and it is yours.[10]

The warm sentiments Johnson expressed for the Jewish state contrasted with his emphasis on the differences between the American and Arab peoples. In toasting King Hussein of Jordan in 1964, he claimed that, "in Jordan, he [King Hussein] and his people have brought that ancient land of the camel, the date and the palm to the threshold of a bright and a hopeful and a modern future."[11] He believed many aspects of Arab culture, such as Islam and the lack of democracy, to be incommensurate with American political culture, and a sense of shared history or common identity was lacking in Johnson's image (and the majority of Americans) of the Arab world. He was unsympathetic towards the radical brand of Arab nationalism promoted by Egypt's President Gamal Abdel Nasser and was conscious that the Soviet Union was exploiting Arab nationalism to weaken US interests in the Middle East.[12] He fluctuated between trying to come to terms with Nasser and the belief that the ambitions of Egypt's president had to be curtailed. In general, however, he perceived Nasser's brand of Arab nationalism to be very different from the Zionist nationalism of the State of Israel, and often applied the analogy of the Texans fighting the Mexicans to depict Israel's struggle against the Arabs. Given the president's mindset, in the event of an Arab–Israeli war it was already evident where the support of the White House would lie.

Johnson's commitment to Israel was as personal as it was political, for he valued the friendship of many American Jews for whom Israel was a personal issue.[13] As president he cultivated the close personal relations he had developed with leading Israeli politicians. In 1954, when Johnson emerged as the Senate majority leader, he befriended Abba Eban, the Israeli Ambassador to Washington – a friendship that was to continue throughout his presidency (Eban was the last Israeli official to meet with Johnson prior to the June 1967 war). It was Eban who pressed for US support in the event of hostilities and then reported to the Knesset that Johnson had indeed given Israel the green light to proceed with a pre-emptive strike against Egypt. Likewise, one of Johnson's first foreign policy acts as president was to receive Levi Eshkol, the Israeli premier to Washington, in June 1964. The visit was marked by a considerable cordiality, and over time he and Eshkol established a degree of intimacy Eban described as "unprecedented in previous relations between Israeli premiers and American presidents."[14] It was Eshkol who requested of his friend, and received for Israel, the most advanced fighter planes US inventories could supply.

Perhaps the most controversial question of Jewish 'access' and its potential to influence policy concerned the close friendship between Johnson and the Israeli Minister Ephraim ("Epi") Evron, second-in-command at the Israeli embassy in Washington. Harry McPherson, a Texas Democrat and impeccably Anglo-Saxon, held the Jewish portfolio from 1966 and was responsible for managing White House relations with the American Jewish community and presenting their concerns to the president. He was the only non-Jew ever to hold this position and found it hard to account for the appointment, save that he had worked on civil rights, worked with Jewish liberals and administered several foreign programmes. There also appeared to be no suitable Jewish candidate on the White House staff who was either interested or available.[15] McPherson was close to both Johnson and leading Jewish figures and commented that Evron "developed one of the most unusual friendships with an American President, I suspect, that any Minister has ever developed."[16] The hitherto unprecedented associations between the Executive and the Israeli government laid the administration open to the charge that the national interest was being subordinated to personal affinity in determining matters of state.

Johnson's close association with Israel was replicated by many of his advisers who for a mixture of cultural, political, ideological or religious reasons shared his sympathy.[17] Former members of the "old Left" Democratic liberal-labour alliance identified with Israel as a state founded on the same humanitarian ideals that had given rise to Democratic Party programmes such as the New Deal and the Great Society. Included in this group were Vice-President Hubert Humphrey, White House speechwriters John Roche and Ben Wattenberg, and Sheldon Cohen the Chief of the Internal Revenue Service. Even in the more impartial national security apparatus, Arthur J. Goldberg, US Ambassador to the UN and Eugene Rostow, Under Secretary of State for Political Affairs, fitted into this pro-Israeli framework.[18]

The question of Jewish access to and influence upon the decision-making process extended beyond members of the administration to the many non-governmental American Jews with a vested interest in Israel's future. Amongst the most influential were Ed Weisl, a leading New York lawyer, Abe Feinberg a Democratic Party member, Arthur Krim of Paramount Pictures (whose Israeli wife purchased a ranch near Johnson's in Texas), and David Ginsberg, a Washington lawyer who listed the Israeli embassy amongst his clients. It was these people with whom Johnson spent the final days prior to the Arab–Israeli war and their views he heard before he returned to Washington to direct US policy during the crisis.[19]

Irrespective of personal preferences, President Johnson, as leader of a party whose many members identified the future of Israel as a prime concern, was under a certain obligation to back Tel Aviv. Party pressure was tempered by the fact that as President of the United States he had sworn an oath to place the

American national interest above all else. In this endeavour Johnson tried to strike a balance between the pro-Israeli sentiments of much of the Democrat Party and the oil interests prominent in Texas politics. Even anti-Israeli pressures from companies with Middle East interests were restricted in this period because of the threat Nasser posed to Saudi Arabia, the largest Gulf oil-producing state.[20] However, he did not carry co-operation with American oil interests to the point of pro-Arabism,[21] and until the June 1967 war, tried to moderate support for Israel to avoid antagonising the Arab oil-producing states. Thus it cannot be construed that Johnson's support for Israel blinded him to America's broader interests in the Middle East. As a Senator, he had played a pivotal role in securing the passage of the Eisenhower Doctrine that committed the US to the defence of both the Arab states and Israel.[22] As befitted his office, Johnson looked critically at what Israel's welfare required[23] and, without diluting his devotion to the Jewish state, sought to balance it against America's other regional interests.

It is unclear how much factual knowledge Johnson had of the Middle East, its history and its politics. As a politician he was aware of the power of the pro-Israel lobby, comprised of Israelis, right-wing Jews and, increasingly, Christian fundamentalists, to shape the political process and was not averse to linking domestic politics to foreign policy decision-making. Likewise, in making personal appointments to high office including the White House staff or the United Nations, he was aware of the effect his choices could exert on the attitudes of ethnic, religious and social constituencies.[24]

Global and Regional Perspectives

The foreign policy of the Johnson Administration was to a considerable extent a product of the redemptionist interpretation of the American past and a continuation of the sentiment that had imbued the rhetoric of the Kennedy years. That the US was fighting a war in Vietnam was largely due to Kennedy's almost messianic redemptionism and his conception of the frontier. He took his country into Vietnam arguing that the US had no other motive than the defence of "freedom" and that a nation raised in "freedom" could not be oblivious to the "freedom" of others.[25] Redemptionism bestowed on America the God-given mission to redeem a sinful world and gave it the moral authority to lead. This belief manifested itself in a foreign policy designed to shape an American world order and to prevent the spread of Communism, yet the belief in its righteousness distorted America's perception of the world. The war in Southeast Asia may have been fought to save South Vietnam from Communism[26] but it was based on an American idea: that the people of South Vietnam were eagerly awaiting the coming of the Americans to save them from Communist tyranny.[27]

Johnson inherited the idea of South Vietnam as a nation that required American protection, and under his leadership the ideological tradition of Lockean liberalism reached its fruition. The verbal strategy of the president and his advisors invoked the ideological norms of liberalism to justify a succession of escalated commitments in Southeast Asia. The administration could legitimise the military activities that inflicted vast material damage and human suffering on the Vietnamese people because it was less concerned with the welfare of those it was trying to help than with the abstractions – 'freedom', liberation from Communism and stability – that it believed justified the war.[28] However, Johnson's attempts to fulfil the redemptionist past were to inflict a far greater sense of failure on the American nation, one that was to overshadow his presidency and the lives of a generation.

Despite the protracted conflict in Vietnam, Johnson nurtured the vision that he stood at the head of a great nation with a responsibility for guaranteeing peace and stability across the globe. His belief in the indivisibility of peace resonated throughout his foreign policy.[29] In a speech in May 1966 he explained that, "Surely it is not a paranoid vision of America's place in the world to recognise that freedom is still indivisible – still has adversaries whose challenge must be answered."[30] Johnson was to be frustrated, though, by what he termed "the comparative impotency of the world's greatest power in the face of the tiniest pinpricks from the puniest of nations."[31]

In the heady days of perceived US strength following Khrushchev's climb down over the Cuban missile crisis, some officials felt they had the requisite power to stop all Communist threats and that this power should be used to the hilt.[32] It was against this backdrop of American gains that, in 1965, Johnson abandoned Kennedy's overtures towards the Arab nationalists. He came to equate, as did Thomas Mann, his Assistant Secretary of State for Latin American Affairs, a left-wing government as threatening to American interests irrespective of whether Communists were involved.[33] Johnson's sense of optimism combined with virulent anti-Communism was reinforced by several of his key advisers including Walt Rostow and Dean Rusk,[34] and became a key component of American foreign policy.

Global perspectives were crucial to the unfolding of the administration's policy towards the Middle East and the penchant for addressing regional situations through the prism of superpower confrontation. When President Nasser of Egypt declared, after a brief flirtation with the Vietcong, that "[W]hoever does not like our conduct can go drink up the sea. If the Mediterranean is not sufficient, there is the Red Sea, too,"[35] Johnson responded by attempting to isolate Egypt and court those he saw as more moderate Arab leaders. Since the level of antagonism in American–Egyptian relations was not replicated in the administration's dealings with Israel, Tel Aviv was to show an understanding of the American cause in Vietnam, voting with Washington in international institutions and in turn making the president even more predisposed to support the Jewish state in any conflict with Egypt.[36]

The Evolution of US–Israeli Relations

While Johnson is often credited with enhancing and consolidating the special relationship between the US and Israel, it was his predecessor, President Kennedy, who had reversed what was perceived to be Eisenhower's anti-Israel policy during the Suez crisis, and initiated the chain of events that culminated in America's alignment with Tel Aviv in June 1967.

That the American perception of Israel and the importance assigned to American Jews changed between the Suez crisis and the presidential election of 1960 was demonstrated by Kennedy's willingness to use the issue of Israel for electoral purposes and his need to secure the support of this sector of the electorate. He was the first president to publicly discount charges of 'dual loyalty' that Jews feared made support for Israel incompatible with their integration into American society, acknowledging that, as he had an emotional attachment to Ireland, why shouldn't the Jews identify with Israel?[37] As President, he initiated a major breakthrough in Middle East policy by simultaneously improving relations with Israel while enhancing ties with Nasser, which led him to announce that "the United States . . . has a special relationship with Israel in the Middle East really comparable only to that which it has with Britain over a wide range of world affairs."[38] High praise indeed for a state that had incurred Washington's wrath less than five years before. But what explains this shift in US policy and the increasing assertiveness of the American Jewish community? Strategic calculations were undoubtedly of paramount importance, but Kennedy may also have been influenced at a more fundamental level by subtle changes in perceptions of American culture, fuelled by an increasing discourse about Israel and the Holocaust.

Kennedy's courting of the American Jewish vote and Israel coincided with the worldwide attention given to the trial of Adolf Eichmann, whose capture in Argentina had been announced by the Israelis on 24 May 1960. Eichmann was the SS officer who had directed the Jewish Section of Nazi Germany's Reich Main Security Office, and in that capacity he had presided over a major phase of the Final Solution.[39] The Eichmann trial filled the news and public discourse during and after the presidential election and entered the homes of millions of Americans through the relatively new cultural medium of the television. Media coverage of the Eichmann trial revealed, for the first time to an American audience, the full-scale atrocities of the attempted annihilation of six million Jews and in so doing, served to reinforce in the public mind the legitimacy of Israel as a homeland for the Jewish people.

The level of interest that news coverage of the trial, generated amongst mainstream American viewers did not go unnoticed by the television networks. During the early 1960s, the producers of prime-time television dramas like *The Defenders* and *Dragnet, The FBI,* began to feature the Holocaust as a 'guest topic'. These programmes depicted individual cases involving Holocaust survivors, former Nazis, or neo-Nazis, and explored the larger challenge of coming to terms with the injustices of the Holocaust in the postwar era. The symbols of the Nazi swastika and jackboots and the numbered tattoo on the forearms of concentration camp survivors consolidated the Holocaust as a recognisable concept in American public culture in the 1960s. The larger issues addressed in these 'guest' appearances by the Holocaust were indicative of its "emergence as a moral paradigm in American discourse" and one that could act as a test case in the limits of social justice or the "study of the nature of evil" in society.[40]

The Holocaust also featured as a subject in science fiction, which, considering the genre's conventions of travelling through time and defying the laws of nature, provided an unparalleled opportunity to address the subject. *The Twilight Zone*, one of America's most popular science fiction series, first dealt with the subject of the Holocaust in November 1961 in an episode entitled "Death's Head Revisited." Like most episodes of *The Twilight Zone,* it used supernatural situations and events to explore social and ethical issues of relevance to American audiences, in this case issues raised by the Eichmann trial, in otherworldly "morality plays."[41] The drama tells the story of fictional SS Captain Lutze who takes a nostalgic visit to Dachau. As he walks round the camp he recalls his past, embodied in an apparition of himself wearing his SS uniform. Suddenly a former prisoner in a striped uniform appears and, addressing Lutze as Captain, announces that he and the other inmates have "been waiting for [him]." The prisoner leads Lutze round the camp, describing the suffering of the Nazi victims at each site and then announces that the inmates of Dachau will try him for "crimes against humanity." The sentence passed down on Lutze is that he will be rendered insane, but he is told that this is not revenge but justice and that his "final judgement will come from God."[42]

"Death's Head Revisited" implicitly retried Eichmann in the otherworldly court of the Twilight Zone. In so doing, it offered viewers a less complex but more satisfying account of the Holocaust and the bringing to justice of those responsible for its perpetration, than the four months of televised proceedings from Jerusalem. The technical capabilities of television's special effects and the endless possibilities of the science fiction genre provided viewers with the rewarding spectacle of witnessing the victims of Nazism rising up and bringing their persecutor to justice. This appealed to the American sense of 'justice' and the triumph of 'good' over 'evil' and contrasted with the protracted debate in the international press of how the Israeli court might appropriately punish

Eichmann. In simplifying the symbols and meaning of the Holocaust, mainstream television encouraged Americans to identify with the Jews and Israel in a way that news coverage and political statements never could.

The gradual entry of Israel into American culture and the sense of empathy that was beginning to develop in the minds of many Americans, increased the confidence of American Jews to more actively campaign for the interests of the Jewish state, and created a domestic environment conducive to the enhancement of US–Israeli ties. These developments contributed to the combination of forces operating on Kennedy, when he created the precedent, albeit modest, of arms sales to Israel. When Johnson succeeded Kennedy, a president with closer links to Jewish figures nationally than his predecessor, Tel Aviv endeavoured to exploit the relationship to secure an increase in arms transfers to offset Soviet weapons supplies to the Arab states.

Arms for Israel: The Special Relationship Begins

From the Israeli perspective, the only way it could compete in the new regional balance of power Moscow was creating in the early 1960s was by accessing the US arms market as a permanent source of supply. Planes could be bought in France, but French tanks could not match the Soviet T-54s and T-55s being supplied to Syria and Egypt and the only comparable alternative, British Centurion tanks, were available in very limited quantities.[43] Prime Minister Levi Eshkol and Shimon Peres, a Labour member of the Knesset, visited Washington in 1964 to request a major change in America's arms shipment policy and to discuss for the first time the purchase of an offensive weapon – the tank.

The administration was divided over the appropriate response to Israel's request. Defence experts confirmed that Soviet arms transfers to the United Arab Republic (UAR)[44] had weakened Israel's defensive capability, but were reluctant for Washington to become its major arms supplier.[45] The Pentagon's preference was for Israel to obtain tanks from Europe, while the CIA was concerned that accommodation with Israel in an election year would be detrimental to American interests. Members of the bureaucracy feared that the Arabs would demand greater oil revenues from US companies and cease co-operation on the isolation of mainland China if American policy was seen to favour Israel.[46] The State Department was opposed to the sale on the grounds that the regional balance of power still favoured Israel and that increased arms transfers would only serve to intensify the military build up.[47]

It is interesting to note that it was the career bureaucrats and unelected officials who opposed the sale. Support for Israel's request came from those quarters with a direct personal or constituency interest. At the White House, Myer Feldman, the new holder of the Jewish portfolio, was in favour of shipping tanks to Israel. McGeorge Bundy, the NSC advisor, was also in agreement but wanted to secure a quid pro quo for the US in return. The final decision on reconciling Eshkol's request with Washington's broader regional interests rested with Johnson. After days of deliberation he settled on a compromise position and agreed to assist Israel in securing tanks from Europe, with the proviso that if this failed, the United States would supply them directly.[48] In exchange, the administration secured Israel's grudging permission for a US inspection of its nuclear research and development facilities.[49] The transfer scheme operated on the basis that Washington would send new tanks to West Germany to modernise its defence forces while used German tanks would be forwarded to Israel. The deal was to remain secret to alleviate Bonn's fears that the Arab states would retaliate against a blatantly pro-Israeli policy by recognising East Germany.

The debate surrounding the weapons transfer scheme was indicative of the conflict of interests in a relationship between a small state and a superpower. Eshkol and Peres objected to the exact terms of the deal because the American tanks would be supplied indirectly to Israel via Germany. They were interested not only in American tanks as a weapon, but in receiving them from an American source with all its overt political implications. Peres believed that the direct supply of tanks would demonstrate Washington's support for Israel, thus enhancing its deterrent power and reducing the prospect of an Arab attack.[50]

By January 1965, after the delivery of about forty US tanks from West German inventories, word of the transfer arrangement had leaked out. Embarrassed in the Arab world, Bonn offered Egypt financial compensation – a strategy that proved ineffective and resulted in the strengthening of ties between Cairo and Moscow.[51] In February, the West Germans terminated tank shipments to Israel, and Washington was obliged to fulfil the agreement itself. The failure of the transfer scheme placed the Johnson Administration in the very situation it had sought to avoid. The blatant supply of offensive weapons to Israel undermined its regional arms embargo and set Washington on course to become a major Middle East arms supplier.

Simultaneously with the Israeli–German tank controversy, the United States undertook another initiative that appeared to undermine its commitment to Israel's security, agreeing to supply arms to Jordan. In late 1964, King Hussein of Jordan had also requested weapons supplies from the United States, the cost of which was met by Kuwait as a show of solidarity with the Palestinian cause in the 'war' against Israel. The White House believed that it had no choice but to adhere to Amman's request because a refusal from Washington would have forced Hussein to look to Moscow for assistance, the corollary of which would have been increased Soviet influence in Jordan. Opening a supply line to Jordan reinforced Washington's objective of standing firm against Moscow's attempts to increase its influence in the region at American expense. Yet this policy raised another dilemma: if the United States armed Jordan, a hostile Arab state situated on Israel's borders, while the Soviets were pouring weapons into the UAR, the military balance in the Middle East could be destabilised and relations with Israel undermined.

The Johnson Administration was the first to be confronted with the dilemma of selling arms to the Arab states and the controversy this engendered on both a domestic and international scale. In early 1965, Averell Harriman the Under Secretary of State for Political Affairs and Robert Komer of the NSC, met with Prime Minister Eshkol and Foreign Minister Golda Meir in Tel Aviv and informed them of Washington's decision to sell arms to Jordan. Predictably, Eshkol and Meir were incensed by the suggestion and could not reconcile themselves to the idea of American arms deliveries to a country that might turn against them in the event of war. Israeli acquiescence was eventually secured, not so much as a result of Washington's bargaining power, but because Eshkol and Meir realised that they had little choice but to accept it. The real issue at stake was not whether Jordan was to receive the arms, but from whom it would obtain them – Washington or Moscow, with all the implications that stemmed from either choice.[52]

The paradoxical elements of US–Israeli relations were revealed by Israel's demand for increased aid in exchange for ratifying a decision it had no alternative but to accept. The administration was not yet as tolerant of Israeli demands as future governments were to become and expected Tel Aviv's acquiescence in a matter directly related to the American national interest. However, the influence of Israel and the pro-Israel lobby was steadily increasing, and as early as February 1966, Komer told Bundy that "[Capitol] Hill and Zionist pressure [will] sooner or later force us to sell planes to Israel."[53]

The level of tension the negotiations evoked in a supposedly close inter-state relationship is evident from the acrimonious debate that dragged on for many months, and was indicative of the difficulties that arise when American and Israeli perceptions of the national interest diverge. The negotiations were also a symptom of the different parameters within which a superpower and a small regional state operate. Nonetheless the fundamentals of the US–Israeli relationship, in this case the mutual interest in countering Soviet influence and guaranteeing Israel's security in conjunction with an acknowledgement that each state needed the other, allowed a compromise position to be reached. Negotiations ended with Johnson's agreement to supply Israel and Jordan with Patton tanks, Israel with Skyhawk planes and Jordan with F-104s.[54]

The irony of the US–Israeli relationship and the strength of Israel's negotiating position was attributable to the highly penetrated nature of the American political system and its susceptibility to influence from transnational actors. It was Tel Aviv, not the administration, that convinced the pro-Israel lobby and Congress not to oppose the sale. By communicating informally with their contacts in Washington, Tel Aviv prevented the mobilisation of Israel's congressional friends against the Jordanian arms deal.[55] Israeli access and ability to influence government officials paradoxically gave Israel almost equal weight with the White House in the negotiations. In an all-out confrontation with Israel, Johnson was not guaranteed of success and may have expended considerable political capital and his personal currency as President in securing the support of the Senate in ratifying the sale. President Reagan's 1981 battle with Congress and Israeli Prime Minister Menachem Begin over the AWACS sale to Saudi Arabia vindicates Johnson's determination to secure Israeli compliance in the deal.

The Jordanian arms deal undermined the distinction between defensive and offensive arms sales and signalled a fundamental reconfiguration of America's role in the Middle East. A spiral of superpower confrontation by proxy was unleashed, whereby arms supplies to the region escalated as the regional states exploited their new found power over their patrons to secure an abundance of increasingly sophisticated weapons systems.[56] Washington's official policy of curbing arms supplies was further undermined by the revelation that Jordan was not an exception to the rule and that a number of friendly Arab states, including Lebanon, Libya and Saudi Arabia, had also received weapons from the US.[57] Members of the State Department were also concerned that "if Israel [were] unable to obtain its valid conventional arms requirements, those in Israel who advocate[d] the acquisition of nuclear weapons [would] find a much more fertile environment for their views."[58] The extent to which this fear was replicated in the White House is unclear,[59] but both Kennedy and Johnson made US inspections of Israeli nuclear facilities[60] to ascertain the extent of Israel's nuclear capability, a prerequisite for agreement on conventional arms transfers.

Through accident as much as by design, three broad contours of Johnson's Middle East policy were firmly established by the eve of the 1967 war. The first objective was to create stability in the Gulf region. This was to be achieved through the sale of nearly half a billion dollars' worth of military equipment to Iran and Saudi Arabia to enable them to strengthen their monarchies against internal subversion and to defend the region against Soviet encroachment. The second objective was to promote Israel's security and deter it from seeking a nuclear capability. The third objective was to control the Arab radicalism that threatened to erode Western influence in the Middle East by decreasing aid to Egypt and isolating Syria's pro-Soviet regime.[61] This policy was designed to strengthen pro-American regimes while avoiding official commitments and diplomatic entanglement.

Prelude to Crisis

Despite Washington's effort to buttress what it saw as the forces of moderation, Middle Eastern tensions were heightened in February 1966 when a new radical government, drawn from the minority Alawi sect, seized power in Syria. In seeking to consolidate its hold on power, the regime fell foul of Soviet blandishments and the temptation to substitute foreign adventures for domestic popularity.[62] In so doing, Damascus was instrumental in accelerating the outbreak of the third Arab–Israeli war.[63]

In an endeavour to establish popular legitimacy and support amongst the Syrian people, the government used Ahmad Shuqairi's fledgling Palestinian Liberation Organisation (PLO) in a "war of national liberation" that took the form of guerrilla raids into Israel across the Syrian, Jordanian and Lebanese borders. For the Syrian leaders, the raids and the predictable Israeli reaction had the double virtue of putting both 'reactionary' Jordan and 'progressive' Egypt on the spot and forced Cairo's hand in concluding a mutual defence treaty with Damascus in November 1966.[64] The treaty blatantly aligned the region's two most radical states with Moscow, and by implication, against Israel and the United States.

The explosive nature of the situation was heightened in November 1966 when Israel retaliated against the raids by attacking the Palestinian West Bank village of Es-Samu and killing 30 civilians. Johnson rebuked Eshkol for the severity of the attack and reassured King Hussein of his government's commitment to the territorial integrity of his Kingdom. The administration was so incensed that another democracy could behave in such a way that in the United Nations, the US ambassador Arthur Goldberg condemned both sides for the use of force[65] and on 25 November refused to veto the UN Security Council resolution censuring Tel Aviv. American strategy appeared to have the desired effect when, in January 1967, Eshkol reacted with marked restraint to a Fatah raid on Israeli territory.[66] The effect was short-lived, however, and the scale of Arab terrorist attacks and Israeli retaliation reached new heights on 7 April 1967 when the Israelis shot down six Syrian MIG-21s over Jordanian and Syrian territory without sustaining any losses themselves.

Despite the obvious and abundant warning signs, a beleaguered President, increasingly despised by his people for the escalation of American involvement in Vietnam, failed to appreciate the significance of the explosive situation brewing in the Middle East. By May 1967, when it became apparent that war was imminent, Johnson's credibility with Congress and the American people had diminished to such an extent that he was powerless to commit his country to decisive intervention to defuse the crisis.

The Crisis of May 1967

As if to demonstrate their legitimacy and leadership credentials to their Arab peers, Arab rulers tended to outbid one another in rhetorical outbursts of hatred against Israel. Yet throughout early 1967 the customary posturing began to spiral out of control, ultimately setting the scene for renewed Arab–Israeli war.

By spring 1967, Nasser was growing increasingly aware that his anti-Israel rhetoric lacked credibility while the United Nations Emergency Force (UNEF) that had patrolled the Egyptian–Israeli border since the Suez crisis of 1957[67] prevented an Egyptian attack on Israel. To enhance his status in the Arab world, in a letter of 16 May to Major-General Indar Jit Rikhye, Nasser ordered General Fawzy of the Egyptian army to request the removal of UN posts from the Sinai.[68] Israel's 1957 withdrawal from the Sinai, Gaza and the entry to the Straits of Tiran, had been secured on the condition that the UNEF be deployed to safeguard the border and that it would remain in place until its task had been completed. Since, however, this was to be jettisoned following Nasser's letter,[69] the Israelis believed that what was in prospect was the "precise situation"[70] that had justified Israel's exercise of its "inherent right of self-defence"[71] ten years before.

United Nations Secretary General U Thant compounded the situation by failing to respond to the exact terms of the Egyptian request and limiting the UNEF withdrawal to the Sinai, but ordering its complete removal from Egypt. U Thant argued that he had no alternative but to accede to a request rooted in Egypt's sovereign rights,[72] a decision that took Johnson by surprise.[73] In so doing, he prevented Nasser from exploiting the diplomatic victory of securing a partial withdrawal of troops as a face-saving device, while retaining UNEF troops in Sharm-el-Sheikh as a buffer between Egypt and Israel.[74] Meanwhile, in response to Nasser's moves, the Israelis began to mobilise.

The US administration's reaction to the impending crisis was reminiscent of Truman's approach to partition in 1947 and 1948. Johnson recalled in his memoirs that "[a]s far as possible, I wanted the main thrust of our diplomacy to be through the United Nations. At the same time I was prepared to use American influence in any way that might be effective and helpful."[75] During this period the President sent letters to Nasser, Eshkol and Kosygin, urging a diplomatic solution; Johnson also supported the UN's recommendation of discussions in Cairo.[76] The Israelis, however, were impatient with the low-key American response to Nasser's moves; the administration had rejected their request for public support and even suggested that the UNEF troops be stationed on the Israeli side of the armistice lines.[77]

On 22 May Nasser announced a blockade of all Israeli shipping and strategic goods bound for Israel through the Straits of Tiran.[78] The declaration was technically an act of war since freedom of shipping in the Gulf of Aqaba had been a key objective of the Sinai Campaign,[79] Israel having maintained since 1957 that it would take military action to maintain free access to the port of Eilat.

Washington responded by seeking an Israeli delay and consultation preceding any use of force. In contrast, General Yitzhak Rabin and General Moshe Dayan, Minister of Defence, demanded an early attack against Egypt because Israel lacked the strategic depth to fight any war on its own territory.[80] The military urged a pre-emptive strike which offered military gains that could not be made up later[81] and argued that stalemate worked to the Egyptian's advantage.[82] However, in an effort to avoid a repeat of the tensions with Washington in the wake of the Suez crisis, Tel Aviv decided on 23 May to acquiesce in the President's appeal.

As the international crisis grew, Johnson reaffirmed America's long-held position that the Gulf of Aqaba was an international waterway and that the blockade of Israeli shipping was therefore illegal. Surprisingly, however, the President still did not declare overt support for Israel or offer a solution to the crisis.[83]

Descent into War

Although a military victory for Israel was almost certain, US support would be crucial if Israel were to win the ensuing diplomatic battle. A pre-emptive strike risked isolating Israel politically; the tacit support of the western powers[84] would be necessary to create the international environment in which Israel could "safely and profitably" launch an attack.[85] Eshkol reasoned that as long as the international community was convinced that Israel had been provoked into fighting for its survival and that every alternative political avenue had been exhausted, American political and economic assistance was assured.[86] The importance placed on US support was evident in Eshkol's explanation to the Ministerial Committee of Defence, convened on 2 June:

> We will still need Johnson's help and support. I hope we won't need it during the fighting, but we shall certainly need it if we are to be victorious, in order to protect our gains. I want to make it clear to the President, beyond a shadow of a doubt, that we have not misled him; that we've given the necessary time for any political action designed to prevent the war.[87]

Israel's request for international support received a cool response from French Prime Minister General Charles De Gaulle, who rejected the notion that Nasser had initiated hostilities. De Gaulle took the view that opening hostilities meant firing the first shot.[88] He told Harold Wilson, the British Prime Minister, that he saw no justifiable reason for France or Great Britain to jeopardise their relations with the Arabs because they felt some "superficial sympathy" with Israel because "she was a small state with an unhappy history."[89] This was in sharp contrast to Johnson's use of the analogy of the Texans fighting the Mexicans to depict Israel's struggle against the Arabs. However, Wilson was more supportive of the Israeli position and reassured the Israeli Foreign Minister that London would co-operate with Washington.[90] Thus it fell to the White House to determine and co-ordinate the international response to Nasser's actions. Johnson was gravely concerned that the conflict would escalate into a superpower confrontation, but his power to effectively determine the outcome was significantly weakened by the public and congressional opposition to the growing commitment in Vietnam. The scale of US casualties and public opposition to the war was soon to cause Congress not merely to regret its decision to allow the escalation of American involvement but to make it reluctant to sanction American military operations elsewhere. As a consequence, McNamara claimed, the President believed that the question of who fired the first shot would be of vital significance in mobilising Congress and the people if America were called upon to assist Israel in a war.[91]

In Congress, sentiment strongly favoured Israel, but there was much opposition to intervention. Key senators on the Foreign Relations Committee such as Fulbright, Mansfield and Stennis, opposed unilateral American action, but others, including three Vietnam 'doves', Edward and Robert Kennedy and Wayne Morse, urged the use of force. Senator Stuart Symington suggested that a choice had to be made between the Middle East and the Far East and he favoured the Middle East as meaning more to the US and its allies, "politically, economically and mutually."[92] In this complex international atmosphere, Congress was too divided to take decisive action, although this was the last occasion that the legislature was not fully mobilised in defence of Israel. Already by 1967, through a process of popular cultural representations in novels, plays, films and television productions, Israel was gradually assuming a special place in the American consciousness, particularly amongst Congressmen who were beginning to acknowledge the concerns of their American Jewish constituents. On the other hand, with 500,000 troops committed to Vietnam, the legislature was not prepared to countenance a second war to protect a vulnerable state. The perception of US interests were not yet fully aligned with those of Israel, and American Jewish organisations lacked both the strength and confidence to go against the tide of public opinion and demand US intervention on Israel's behalf.

Washington's hesitant actions and cautious statements conveyed to Tel Aviv a sense of an administration divided, while its inability to assemble an international maritime force to open the Straits sent signals of weakness to both the Arabs and Israel.[93] On the eve of the war, only the Australians, British and Dutch had agreed to participate, and the numbers fell short of the forty to fifty ships

Israel had been promised.[94] In his memoirs Johnson recalled that American action would have been taken if necessary, but that the administration had not had time to prepare the public for such an event. It was one thing to think of principles, commitments and rights, but it was quite another to think of arms and a second-front war.[95] While the Knesset had confidence in Johnson's personal credentials as a champion of the Israeli cause, the President no longer commanded sufficient respect nor sufficient esteem for him to be able to mobilise Congress and the American people in Israel's defence. In military terms, Johnson saw Vietnam and Israel as similar issues and, mistrusting the conversion of "Congressional Vietnam doves" into "Israeli hawks," he discounted many statements backing Israel as merely "political."[96] Rhetoric cost nothing, while committing troops cost money, lives and potentially elections. As he explained to Eban, while he was "aware of what three Presidents have said [that] will not be worth five cents if the people and the Congress do not support their President now."[97]

Johnson believed that the re-opening of the Straits served the American national interest because hostilities were certain to erupt if the blockade remained. He also felt obligated to honour Eisenhower's promise to Israel to keep the Straits open,[98] but felt powerless to act decisively and was assailed from both within his administration and without. Meanwhile, Moscow was exacerbating regional tensions by informing both the White House and the Kremlin's Arab clients that it had evidence that an Israeli attack was imminent.[99] This provoked Hussein to sign a defence pact with Nasser on 30 May, in effect confirming in Israeli minds that in the event of war, Tel Aviv would be forced to fight the enemy on three borders.[100]

As tensions escalated, Washington continued its diplomatic efforts. The US had been without an ambassador in Cairo for three months prior to the June crisis[101] and in a belated effort to avert war an envoy was dispatched to Nasser. A visit to Washington by the Egyptian Vice-President, Zakariyya Muhieddin, was also scheduled.[102] The proposed visit greatly alarmed the Israelis, who feared that any improvement in US–Egyptian relations would occur at their expense and that Washington might defuse the crisis by capitulating to Nasser's demands.[103]

It was against this backdrop that Meir Amit, the head of Mossad, reported to the Israeli cabinet the findings of his 31 May visit to Washington. Based on his meetings with Robert McNamara at the Pentagon and Richard Helms and James Angleton at the CIA, Amit advised the Israeli cabinet that if they launched a pre-emptive strike Washington would accept it as having been their only viable alternative. This appeared to be confirmed by a journalist's report that, when asked if the US was seeking to restrain Israel, Rusk had replied, "I don't think it is our business to restrain anyone."[104]

On 1 June Eban received an account of a meeting between Evron and Justice

Abe Fortas, a close personal friend of both Avraham Harman (the Israeli ambassador) and Johnson, that altered his position in favour of an Israeli attack. William Quandt, a former NSC adviser, claimed that the Israelis had every reason to believe that in Harman they were dealing with one of Johnson's true confidants and that his views deserved careful attention. According to the report, Fortas claimed that: "Eshkol and Eban did great service to Israel by giving the United States a chance to explore options other than Israeli force. If they had not done so, it would have been difficult to secure the President's sympathy." Eban interpreted this as the closest thing to a green light Johnson was going to give and informed General Rabin and General Yariv that the diplomatic reason for military restraint had been removed.[105]

On 2 June Eshkol reluctantly acknowledged that decisive American action would not be forthcoming but that in acting alone, Israel need not fear diplomatic isolation. He realised that American public perceptions and popular representations of Israel had shifted so markedly since 1957 that if Israel were successful in its attack, Congress would not easily allow Johnson to punish it for its actions, in the unlikely event of the President seeking to do so. After all, Israel was taking protective action and exercising the state's collective right of self-defence,[106] a right deeply enshrined in the American belief system. He was also aware that it would be even more difficult for a Democratic President to take a hard line with Israel than it had been for Eisenhower in 1957,[107] since unlike the Republicans, the Democrats had a sizeable pro-Zionist component for whom Israel's security was a prime concern.

In this crisis Israel's supporters founded themselves relegated to the sidelines. The pro-Israel lobby wanted to see Israeli security preserved but, given the atmosphere of the times, they could not call for unilateral American action or Israeli pre-emption. In this respect, some of the problems that inhibited Johnson also inhibited the pro-Israel lobby. Vietnam had created an atmosphere in which any military action elsewhere, especially if not related to the conflict between East and West, could not easily be contemplated.[108]

As war broke out, a sense of sympathy tinged with regret prevailed in the White House, which would explain the President's handling of the crisis both during the war and in the efforts for peace that followed. Johnson recalled in his memoirs that:

> I have always had a deep feeling of sympathy for Israel and its people, gallantly building and defending a modern nation against great odds and against the tragic background of Jewish experience. . . . I have never concealed my regret that Israel decided to move when it did. I always made it equally clear, however, to the Russians and to every other nation, that I did not accept the oversimplified charge of Israeli aggression. Arab actions in the weeks before the war started – forcing UN troops out, closing the Port of Aqaba, and assembling forces on the Israeli border – made that charge ridiculous.[109]

Washington had been unable to act decisively to prevent the slide into war and would be forced to deal with the long-term consequences of its client's actions and territorial conquests.

The Six Day War

On 5 June 1967, Israeli forces launched a surprise attack on Egypt's air force bases, destroying the entire fleet. The Israelis quickly moved on to capture the Gaza Strip and Sinai Peninsula and a cabinet message was sent to King Hussein requesting that Jordan remain out of the war.[110] Hussein considered his position too vulnerable to heed the warning, a decision that would cost Jordan East Jerusalem and the West Bank but, ironically, may have saved his kingdom. With over half his population of Palestinian descent, had Hussein not participated in a war to liberate the lands of Palestine, he risked being deposed by his own people. On 9 June, in contravention of the UN brokered cease-fire, Israeli troops advanced across the Golan Heights, forcing out terrorist militia and capturing the Syrian town of Quneitra. So impressive were the Israeli advances that by 9 June Damascus itself was only thirty miles beyond the reach of its troops and an estimated thirty-six hours away.[111]

A serious challenge to Israel's existence threatened to put the US administration in an untenable position. The nature of superpower confrontation was such that American acquiescence in Israel's destruction at the hands of Soviet proxies was unthinkable,[112] and Washington would have been forced to intervene militarily on Israel's behalf to prevent this. Congress feared that they would be asked to sign another blank cheque for American intervention at a time when public opinion opposed the further deployment of US troops in regional ideological conflicts. Under these circumstances, the administration was more than willing to extend diplomatic rather than military support to reinforce Israel's accomplishments on the ground, by pressing for a cease-fire.[113]

Confronted with the prospect of having a large number of their own advisers and equipment captured in Syria and given the apparent threat to Damascus, the Soviets threatened to raise the level of superpower confrontation if Washington did not rein in its client. In a hotline message on 10 June, Premier Alexsei Kosygin demanded that Israeli operations cease immediately or the Kremlin would take "necessary actions including military."[114] Conscious of the overtones of the message, Johnson responded to the threat by ordering the redeployment of the Sixth Fleet from its position three hundred miles off the Syrian coast to a distance of fifty miles. The US was positioning its warships to attack the Soviets and defend the Middle East against Soviet advances should Moscow take aggressive action. Simultaneously, the administration moved to deescalate the crisis. Rusk ordered the Israelis to halt their advance[115] and

Johnson reassured the Kremlin that his government supported a Syrian–Israeli cease-fire.[116]

At 0600 hours on Saturday 10 June the shooting officially stopped, signalling the end of the first round of hostilities in a war that transformed the geographical and diplomatic contours of the Middle East. Israel's vulnerability to Arab attack had been dramatically reduced. Cairo was now within range of Israeli tanks, and Damascus was in range of Israeli artillery. All of Mandated Palestine and East Jerusalem now fell under Israeli control. On the diplomatic front, the Soviets severed relations with Israel and, when Nasser falsely charged on the second day of the war that British and American carrier-based planes had aided Israel in attacks against Egypt, they as well as Algeria, Syria, Iraq, the Sudan and Yemen severed diplomatic relations with Washington.[117]

The severing of diplomatic relations reflected the Arabs belief that Washington was not neutral in the conflict and had sided with Israel.[118] It also demonstrated that Johnson's efforts to convince the Arabs that his policy was not so much pro-Israeli as anti-Nasser had failed.[119] The position of the US as an impartial bystander in the conflict had been called into question early in the war, when a State Department announcement that "Our [America's] position is neutral in thought, word and deed"[120] provoked controversy within the administration. Congress was outraged by the announcement and passed a resolution that stated: "The people of this country are not neutral in thought and word. Every expression of opinion . . . shows a deep concern for the preservation of Israel."[121] The President had also politically committed his country to Israel's position on opening the Straits and did not propose to be neutral if diplomacy failed to sway Egypt. Johnson recalled in his memoirs that: "We are certainly not belligerents, but our successive guarantees since 1950 to the independence and territorial integrity of all the states in the area made "neutral" the wrong word."[122]

Iraq and Kuwait responded to Nasser's accusation with the imposition of an ill-prepared and ineffective oil embargo against Britain and America. In 1967, the US was not sufficiently dependent on Middle Eastern oil and the producers not sufficiently well organised for the embargo to produce a significant impact on the Western economies.[123] Yet the very fact that an embargo was actually imposed indicates the extent to which Johnson and Rostow had overestimated the pro-Western sentiments of the Arab conservatives and underestimated the collective Arab hatred of Israel. Saudi King Faisal did not allow gratitude for US support in Yemen to deter him from embargoing oil shipments as an act of solidarity with Nasser, his Arab rival. When aligned against Israel and the West, blood proved thicker than ideology, and was something Washington did not fully comprehend until the oil embargo of October 1973.[124]

US–Israeli Relations under Pressure: The USS *Liberty*

During the Six Day War, an incident occurred that, under other circumstances, should have signalled an almost irrevocable breach in US–Israeli relations. On 8 June the Israelis attacked the USS *Liberty*. The American vessel was in international waters in the East Mediterranean on an intelligence-gathering mission when Israeli planes and torpedo boats besieged it.[125] As life rafts were lowered from the ship, the crew claimed these were also fired upon in an apparent attempt to wipe out all survivors and witnesses.[126]

Though Israel's motive is still debated and the government claimed that the vessel was incorrectly identified, the nature of the *Liberty*'s mission as an intelligence-gathering ship, capable of intercepting radio messages between the Israelis and the Arabs in the war zone, offers a possible explanation. If the attack was intentional, Tel Aviv's motivation may have been in keeping outside knowledge of its operations to a minimum, particularly its plans for attacking Syria after the UN cease-fire had gone into effect. It is possible, therefore, that the *Liberty* was targeted to prevent Washington from receiving advanced warning of General Moshe Dayan's order to attack Syria at 0700 hours on 9 June, four hours after Damascus had accepted the UN cease-fire. Had the *Liberty* conveyed reports to Washington that an attack was imminent, Israeli plans might have been thwarted.[127]

Survivors of the *Liberty* incident claim that the Israeli government intentionally ordered the attack. Their argument is based on the fact that, during the morning of 8 June, Israeli aeroplanes had circled the ship and, as visibility was perfect, would have been able to correctly identify it as a an American vessel.[128] In the afternoon, when the *Liberty* was attacked by three Delta Wing Mirage jets, the crew tried to send an SOS but were unable to do so, apparently because their frequencies were jammed. John Hrankowski, a member of the crew, claimed that the attackers needed to know which frequencies the ship operated on in order to jam them and therefore must have known that it was an American vessel, as all ships in the US fleet used the same frequencies.

Eventually the Sixth Fleet picked up the SOS and, in retaliation for the assault on a US vessels, two A-4 bombers from the USS *America* were launched to attack Egypt, the presumed attackers of the *Liberty*. Richard Parker, the Political Consul at the US embassy in Cairo was informed that a US attack on Egypt was imminent. Yet within minutes of the order being given, Tony Hart, the Naval Communications Supervisor on the *America*, passed on a Pentagon message recalling the aircraft.[129] News had reached Washington that Nasser was not responsible for the strike.

Thirty-four crew members were killed and 171 wounded in the attack.[130] A group of US Navy planes from the carrier *America* set out to assist the crew but were ordered back before reaching the stricken vessel. Eventually the *Liberty* reached a US naval base in Malta where several wounded were transferred to a US hospital in Naples. Significantly, the ship's personnel were ordered not to comment on the attack[131] and the naval inquiry that followed was conducted in such away that many dubbed it "cover-up."[132] The US Navy still refuses to comment on the incident.

Israel accepted responsibility for the attack but insisted that it had occurred in error because military intelligence had incorrectly identified the USS *Liberty* as an Egyptian vessel. Transcripts of voice conversations between two Israeli helicopter pilots and the control tower at Hazor Airfield, collected by a US Navy EC-121 following the attack, indicate that Israel was trying to correctly identify the ship as either Egyptian or American.[133] Compensation totalling $13 million was paid to the families of the dead and wounded but Tel Aviv refused to meet the cost of repairing the vessel because the cabinet did not consider itself responsible for the train of events that culminated in the attack.[134] To do so would have been to acknowledge that Israel had deliberately and wilfully attacked a vessel of the US Navy. No one in Israel was charged or court martialled as a result of the incident.[135]

Within the executive branch of the government, interpretations of the event were mixed. Secretary Rusk considered Tel Aviv's version of events an incredible distortion of reality and in a 10 June communication to Israel's ambassador in Washington stated that:

> At the time of the attack, the U.S.S. *Liberty* was flying the American flag and its identification was clearly indicated in large white letters and numerals on its hull . . . Experience demonstrates that both the flag and the identification number of the vessel were readily visible from the air . . . Accordingly, there is every reason to believe that the USS *Liberty* was identified, or at least her nationality determined, by Israeli aircraft approximately one hour before the attack . . . The subsequent attack by Israeli torpedo boats, substantially after the vessel was or should have been identified by Israeli military forces, manifests the same reckless disregard for human life.[136]

According to Joseph Califano, a member of Johnson's White House staff, Clark Clifford, as representative of the President's Foreign Policy Advisory Board (PFIAB), also urged the President to take a tough stance and approach the attack as though the perpetrator were Arab or Soviet,[137] although he did counsel against a permanent break between the two countries.[138]

The US response to the attack was revealing of the strength of the ties that bound Washington and Tel Aviv and the power of Presidential perception of the national interest in determining government policy. In contradiction to the views of his Secretary of State, Johnson, publicly at least, accepted the Israeli version of events[139] and actually downplayed the seriousness of the incident. In the only official Presidential statement about the incident he went so far as to lower the number of dead and wounded and claimed that:

> We learned that the ship had been attacked in error by Israeli gunboats and planes. Ten men of the *Liberty* crew were killed and a hundred were wounded. This heart-breaking episode grieved the Israelis deeply, as it did us.[140]

Califano writes in his memoirs that privately Johnson subscribed one hundred percent to Clifford's view,[141] while McNamara attributed the President's decision not to pursue the event to his "reluctance to embarrass an ally."[142]

Lucius Battle, Director of the Near East Bureau, later said of the incident "we ignored it for all practical purposes and we shouldn't have. The price of winning the war quickly was the *Liberty* ship."[143] Press Secretary George Christian expressed similar sentiments when he wrote that the matter of what caused the attack was not pursued because it was dwarfed by other events. The major concern of the Johnson administration lay not in chastising Israel but in presenting a united front against the humiliated Soviet Union and its clients[144] and stopping the war before it led to a direct superpower confrontation. Johnson also believed that his only hope of restraining Israel was to remain on friendly terms, with superpower rivalry and congressional pressure rendering the severing of relations or the imposition of sanctions politically inconceivable.[145] The imperative of electioneering may also have played a role in Johnson's calculations, as he could not afford to antagonise pro-Israeli supporters in the run up to the Presidential election.

In the legislature, Congress endorsed Israel's position, with the Congressional Record referring to the incident as "the tragic mistake of today – when Israeli forces attacked a United States ship."[146] The Pentagon took a stronger stance and described the attack on the ship as an "outrage."[147]

The silence and lack of condemnation, irrespective of the underlying motivations, which followed the attack on the *Liberty* is highly unusual, given that the death of US servicemen is generally met with condemnation, public outrage and a pledge of retaliation by the White House. Conventional explanations of international relations fail to adequately explain the apparent collusion of the President and Congress in the "cover-up" that surrounds the episode. The matter was officially closed between the two governments by an exchange of diplomatic notes on 17 December 1987.[148]

The lack of media investigation into the attack is perhaps even more surprising than the response of the administration. The relatively small amount of news coverage of the incident was coordinated and centralised by the Pentagon and the surviving crewmen were not permitted to speak independently to reporters. In the first weeks after the attack the American press was often critical of Israel and there was a great deal of journalistic speculation. On

26 June 1967 *US News* stated that some US officials did not subscribe to the view that the attack was accidental and the following day the *National Review* printed the most emphatic denouncement when it asked, "Is the *Liberty* episode being erased from history?" However, neither publication followed up on their original reports and in 1968 the *US News* and the *National Review* printed only two stories about the incident, both of which accepted the findings of the Naval enquiry that the *Liberty* had been incorrectly identified by the Israelis.

In contrast, the coverage in the *New York Times* started from the premise on 10 June that the attack on the ship was accidental. On 18 June the *NYT* printed contradictory stories of the attack, one adopting the Israeli position that the vessel was wrongly identified and the other taking the view of the crew that it was intentional. However, the newspaper did not appear to investigate to see which story was true and the coverage was devoid of the paper's customary journalistic analysis. Subsequently, since 1967, the *Liberty* incident has rarely been mentioned in either the *NYT* or the mainstream American press.

There are several possible explanations for the relative lack of media interest. First, Johnson and McNamara set the parameters for coverage of the incident, and publicly the administration did not waver in its position that the attack was an accident. The official enquiry concluded that Israel had wrongly identified the vessel and the general reluctance of Americans to question the integrity of their judicial system appeared to prevail. Secondly, the attack on the *Liberty* was drowned out by other events. Israel's comprehensive victory filled the news and by the time the findings of the inquiry were published, public attention had returned to the Vietnam war, which was perceived to threaten the lives of many thousands of US servicemen. Thirdly, Israel had been victorious in a war that had defeated Soviet proxies, and Americans preferred to revel in the success of an ally than to condemn its misdemeanours. Israel may also have benefited from a type of moral blindness, whereby the American people failed to take account of the ethical shortcomings of a country with which they perceived themselves to share a sense of political and cultural kinship.[149] People, whether at the individual, corporate or state level, are always more willing to condemn agreed-upon perpetrators of evil than they are to question an ally.[150]

Cultural Change and Israel's Place in America

In the aftermath of the war, Johnson's sentimental feelings for Israel were increasingly reflected throughout American society, as people gave voice to the dramatic change that had occurred to Israel's place within American culture in the decade preceding Suez. The entrance of Israel and the Holocaust into public consciousness, as reflected in the media, altered the frame of reference through which the American public perceived the Jewish state. By the mid-1960s, the reality of the Holocaust was increasingly interspersed with fictitious but gratifying images of events that gave Americans increasing cause to consider the actions of their own country in relation to Israel. By the time of the Johnson administration, the dramatisation of the anti-Semitism that could lead to a Holocaust, as in Bernard Malamud's 1966 novel *The Fixer*, and the theme of complicity through inaction as portrayed in Arthur Miller's 1964 stage plays *After the Fall* and *Incident at Vichy*, contributed to the increasing feeling that Israel was not a socialist state, despite the large number of East European Jews who had settled there, and that Americans should be concerned with its security. This was facilitated by Israel's astounding victory, which enabled the US to support the state diplomatically, safe in the knowledge that American troops would not be called upon to defend it.

The parallel between Israel and Vietnam as weak states in need of American protection, was gradually replaced by the image of Israel as a strong state that epitomised American values. Israel's victory was equated with the reassertion of the power of American ideals and demonstrated that American values could triumph over the enemies of 'freedom'. Israel's defeat of the Arabs was heralded by some as a kind of victory for the US that extended the American frontier into the Middle East, in a way that Johnson had failed to do in Southeast Asia.[151] After all, it had not been Americans but Israelis that had been fighting and dying to protect what were regarded as American as well as Israeli interests, and in contrast to American GIs in Vietnam, "Israeli fighters were not being humiliated by Third World upstarts."[152]

This cultural evolution, *vis-à-vis* perceptions of Israel, generated an increased feeling of security amongst American Jewish organisations. The fear that overt support of Israel might merit the charge of 'dual loyalty' was replaced by the image that support for Israel denoted super-loyalty.[153] With the defeat of the Arab states, the last vestige of Israel as a vulnerable or socialist state were cast off and replaced by the image of the Jews standing on the front line, defending America against the proxies of the Soviet Union. From this point on, American Jewish organisations could devote much of their efforts to consolidating the US–Israeli alliance.[154] This was demonstrated in increased fund-raising for Israel, and between 27 May and 10 June 1967, American Jews had collected over $100 million in emergency funding, and a total of $317.5 million by the end of the year. The year's total dollar transfers placed such a burden on the balance of payments that Johnson was advised to seek Eshkol's assistance in ensuring that a large proportion of it was reinvested in long-term dollar holdings.[155]

Tel Aviv was less diplomatically isolated than it had been in 1956 and public opinion would not permit Johnson to force the kind of Israeli withdrawal that Eisenhower had demanded in 1957. This, coupled with the President's own beliefs, led to the negotiation of UN Resolution 242.

American Diplomacy and the United Nations

Johnson exerted his greatest influence over the Arab–Israeli dispute in the months immediately following the war, when he determined that a genuine peace agreement might be reached on the basis of a land for peace formula. He did not believe that the US should launch an intensive peace-making effort at a time when it was preoccupied with Vietnam and America's standing in the Arab world was at an all-time low.[156] Instead, he saw the establishment of a diplomatic framework for a peace settlement that allowed time to pass until the Arabs were prepared to negotiate with Israel as an interim solution to the crisis. One of his prime concerns was to prevent the balance of power moving against Israel, but with the armed forces of Egypt, Syria and Jordan in ruins, this was not an imminent possibility. However, his administration's relief at Israel's victory did not necessarily translate into unconditional support for its actions and territorial gains.[157]

Johnson's reasoning was a product of the major shift that occurred in US policy in the days immediately following the war. There is no documentary evidence that this change of emphasis was accompanied by debate within the administration and it may have been attributable to his personal recollection of Suez. After all, he had opposed Eisenhower's decision to force an Israeli withdrawal in the absence of tangible Egyptian concessions and his position had been proved right by the outbreak of the June war. Johnson was determined not to emulate what he saw as Eisenhower's mistake, especially when Israel's right to defend itself against Arab aggression appeared much stronger than in 1957.[158] He would not pressurise Israel to withdraw in the absence of a peace settlement to resolve outstanding issues dating back to 1948.

Johnson's land for peace agreement found support in the Knesset. From a military perspective, the planning and execution of the Six Day War was a testament to the ingenuity of Israel's generals and the skill and determination of the country's defence forces. In contrast, the political planning for the post-war situation was negligible. Its cabinet had not anticipated the rapid expansion of Israel's borders and the occupation of land inhabited by Arab peoples. The government was in agreement, from Begin's Gahal on the right to Mapam and former Brigadier General Yigal Allon's Achdut ha' Avodah party on the left, that territory should be traded for peace. The question the parties confronted was which territories[159] and how peace should be defined. Israel was willing to return to the status quo ante with Syria and Egypt in exchange for a peace treaty and the de-militarisation of land evacuated by Israeli forces. The most sensitive issues were that of Jerusalem and the West Bank because their existential religious value "raised problems that transcended strategic interest."[160]

In determining the framework for a peace agreement between the Arab states and Israel, the President played the decisive role. On 19 June, at a State Department address that had been timed to overshadow Soviet Premier Kosygin's opening remarks at the UN General Assembly, Johnson placed the entire responsibility for the war on Egypt and deemed the closure of the Strait of Tiran an "act of folly."[161] He then unveiled his own approach in which the US would not press for an Israeli withdrawal in the absence of Arab diplomatic concessions. While reflecting Israel's post-war popularity, the speech also presented principles that could appeal to the conservative Arabs. Johnson stated that the Israelis should withdraw but only in return for a peaceful settlement. "Certainly, troops must be withdrawn; but there must be recognised rights of national life, progress in solving the refugee problem, freedom of innocent maritime passage, limitation of the arms race, and respect for political independence and territorial integrity."[162] This view became widely accepted in the American government but was subject to differing interpretations on exactly what Arab concessions were required in exchange for Israeli withdrawals.

Between June and November 1967, American diplomatic efforts focused on achieving a UN Security Council resolution based upon Johnson's five points. The negotiations between the US and Israel and between the Soviets and the Arabs revealed very real differences in the positions of the parties. Israel insisted on direct negotiations with the Arab states and a settlement in which withdrawal was one element of a peace agreement.[163] In contrast, the Arabs insisted upon withdrawal as a pre-condition for negotiations. The Soviets backed the Arab position, whereas Washington, in endorsing a land for peace agreement, was less insistent on direct negotiations, but continued to support the Israeli position. After all, the very idea of accommodation with the enemy lay outside the US imagination and militated against the idea of winning, which it perceived as the sole rationale of waging war.[164]

Ironically, the divergent positions of the superpowers were brought closer together by a conflict between the US and Israel over Jerusalem and the West Bank. Johnson was dismayed by the Knesset's unilateral decision to annex East Jerusalem and incorporate it into the State of Israel because it transgressed the Lockean principle of self-determination that both Eisenhower and Johnson had sent American soldiers to war to defend.[165] The Knesset's unwillingness to coordinate its actions with Washington further compromised America's relations with the Arab states. In a meeting between Rusk and Eban, the Israeli Foreign Minister proposed that the future of the West Bank be decided through a settlement with King Hussein or an association between the West Bank and Israel. Rusk was outraged by the Israeli proposal and its blatant disregard for democratic principles and reminded Eban that "there is a constitutional precedent for letting people themselves decide."[166]

In mid-July, in an attempt to break the deadlock, Goldberg and the Russian Foreign Minister Andrei Gromyko advanced a joint proposal that called for an immediate Israeli withdrawal in exchange for a declaration of non-belligerency and the inadmissibility of territory acquired through force.[167] The Israelis were incensed that Washington had agreed to a major reversal in policy without prior consultation and that the potential for reaching an understanding with the Soviet Union took precedence over support for Israel's current position.[168] They were further outraged that the word "Israel" did not appear in the text as this would enable the Arabs to agree to a general statement and then declare its non-applicability to Israel at a later date.[169] Eban claimed that his country had been confronted with a Soviet–Arab–US alignment and a proposal that, if endorsed by the General Assembly, his country would be forced to flout. However, an outright confrontation between Jerusalem and Washington was averted by the Arab rejection of the superpower's proposal. The refusal of the governments of Algeria and Syria to compromise, insisting on a full Israeli withdrawal without acknowledging the rights of all states in the area, resulted in the Arab rejection of the plan,[170] as the Arab league operated on the basis of unanimity of action and understanding.

With the failure of the initiative, the regional states entrenched their positions. On 1 August 1967 the Knesset passed a resolution calling for the establishment of peace treaties through direct negotiation.[171] For the Israelis, victory presented an unprecedented opportunity for concluding a final, negotiated settlement with the Arabs, and they were determined to capitalise on this.[172] The Arabs opposed direct negotiations, which implied at least the tacit recognition of Israel and by implication, its right to exist. In late August, Arab intransigence intensified at the Khartoum conference, where in return for subsidies from the oil-producing Arab states, Nasser and Hussein were pressurised to accept guidelines for a political settlement based on "no negotiations with Israel; no peace with Israel; no recognition of Israel and no bargaining over any Palestinian territory on any terms."[173]

For domestic and diplomatic reasons the Israelis made the alteration of their position contingent on Arab recognition. For a different set of domestic and diplomatic reasons, the Arabs made immobility their common position. The Soviets, seeking to regain a semblance of credibility in the region, were forced to support their Arab clients, while the US could not advance a resolution that was unacceptable to Jerusalem. By insisting on a solution that was acceptable to both Israel and at least some of the conservative Arab states, Washington created a situation in which Israel could effectively veto its policy.[174]

The deadlock was broken by the British, who only eleven years before had been the enemy of every state in the region, but were now seen as the only impartial and trustworthy arbitrator. Lord Caradon, the British delegate to the UN, composed a resolution, the language of which was of such calculated ambiguity that it satisfied the now modest expectations of each party.[175] It differed from the American text in that it did not recommend limiting the arms race but did advise the appointment of a special UN representative to act as mediator.[176]

The result of Caradon's efforts was UN Resolution 242, passed unanimously by the Security Council on 22 November 1967. The Resolution was in part a product of Goldberg's diplomatic efforts because at his insistence the word "the" was removed from the terms of Israeli withdrawal, leaving it free to withdraw from some or all of the territories it had occupied depending on agreements reached with its neighbours.[177] Goldberg, himself of Jewish origin, had manoeuvred for many months to "protect Israel from losing on New York's East River what it won on the battlefield."[178] The resolution fell short of calling for Israeli withdrawal from all Arab territories and on the Arabs to conclude a full peace agreement with Israel. It called for Israeli withdrawal:

> from territories occupied in the recent conflict [and] respect for and acknowledgement of the sovereignty, territorial integrity and political independence of every State in the area and their right to live in peace within secure and recognised boundaries.

The implementation of the resolution was to be achieved through a process of negotiation not forced implementation.

Caradon's text contained three crucial omissions. No reference was made to specific postwar borders, the status of Jerusalem or the Palestinians as a separate people.[179] The fact that the resolution was passed is directly attributable to these ambiguities. Nasser accepted the resolution but kept his armed forces in place and made any solution contingent upon the acceptance of the Palestinians themselves. The "Palestinians" he referred to were the Popular Front for the Liberation of Palestine (PLO), which rejected the resolution on 23 November 1967. Eban accepted on behalf of Israel at Eshkol's behest, but the acceptance was so indirect and discreet that Johnson requested its reaffirmation in April 1968.

The ambiguity of UN Resolution 242 predictably led to a stalemate because the demands of each party were irreconcilable. During 1968, the UN special representative, Ambassador Gunnar Jarring, took centre-stage in the peace negotiations and the administration itself maintained a relatively low profile. In public, American officials said nothing to modify the language of Resolution 242, but in private, Washington repeatedly told the Israelis that a settlement would have to be based on a virtually complete withdrawal.[180] The administration could countenance Israel depriving the inhabitants of the West Bank and Gaza of their right to self-determination and democratic elections because the occupation was viewed as a temporary situation pending a negotiated settlement. Besides, Vietnam was Johnson's foremost preoccupation and after the Tet Offensive of February 1968, he announced his intention not to seek re-election. This initiated an intense campaign for the presidency, first within his own party and, after Hubert Humphrey's nomination, between the two main parties.[181] Domestic considerations took precedence over foreign policy initiatives, and throughout his last months in office, Johnson left negotiations to the UN.

Popular Opinion and the Media

Following the tension of May and euphoria of June 1967 American public interest in Israel had dramatically increased.[182] Opinion polls indicated that sympathy for Israel stood at 55 percent in the few weeks during and after the war in contrast to support for the Arab side which remained at 4 percent.[183] Israel's victory against the Arabs was quick and decisive and the television coverage of the 'heroic' Jewish nation won the hearts and minds of large sectors of the American public. This stood in marked contrast to the situation in Vietnam where, largely to conserve American lives, the US had dropped 90 percent of its bombs on civilian populations. This had the unintended consequence of further alienating the already jaded American television viewer.[184] Identification with Israel was reinforced by the ease with which Americans could associate with the victory of a state which they perceived to share their own values. Initially this new found support was largely superficial in its effects, though it materialised in increased fund raising and attendance at commemorative events. However, by the end of the 1960s it had been transformed into a powerful pro-Israel presence.

By supporting Johnson's efforts to safeguard the Israeli victory through international diplomacy, the American people were encouraged to believe they were acting in defence of a people they had virtually ignored during the 1930s. In 1965, beside *The Pawnbroker* which juxtaposed images of the Holocaust with Harlem, and *Ship of Fools*, in which the ship's passengers disregard a world on the brink of war, *The Sound of Music*, a popular musical about the Trapp family singers who were forced to flee Nazism, was also an overwhelming success. In the same year, the Czech film *The Shop on Main Street* told the story of the deportation of Jews in Slovakia in 1942 and received an Academy Award for the best foreign film. Their popular appeal was attributable to the many parallels that could be drawn between the 1930s, the setting of many of these films, and the social upheaval of the 1960s.

The increase in the number of films addressing the subject of the Holocaust, social inequality and persecution occurred at a time when American society was in great turmoil. By Americanising the Jew, films also began to Americanise Jewish history, with the Jews coming to symbolise more universal ideas. America appeared to be assimilating, and coming to terms with, the history of Nazism through its application to contemporary life.[185] The media, intentionally or otherwise, propagated images that fuelled the protests by many Americans against racial inequality and an unjust war in Vietnam. With the memory of recent Jewish history in mind, the American black underclass intensified their struggle against racial inequality, while US involvement in Vietnam ignited student protests at universities against the war machine. Support for Israel against the Arabs was one way in which this discontent found expression and provided a means through which Americans could believe they were making recompense for both the injustices of their society and those of others.

Furthermore, Israel consolidated its place in the American consciousness not through a perception of its weakness but through a demonstration of its strength, and its victory was represented symbolically in television drama. Aired on 16 February 1968, the cult television show *Star Trek* addressed the subject of ethnic cleansing and racial persecution amidst a plethora of Nazi symbols. The programme offered an encounter between the inhabitants of the fictitious planet Ekos, which had been transformed into a replica of Nazi Germany in the 1930s and was persecuting its minority Zeon citizens, and the crew of the starship *Enterprise.* Symbols of the Nazi era, including jackboots and swastikas, were used to establish in viewer's minds the concept of a totalitarian culture. The programme also included vintage black-and-white footage of the Nazi era interspersed with original images, also in black and white, of characters who appeared in the episode. By the climax of the episode the crew of the *Enterprise* had helped the Zeons throw off their Ekos persecutors and reconciled the two peoples so they could live in harmony on the planet. For the programme's viewers, the depiction of the Zeons rising up to defeat their enemy may have resonated with the recent victory of Zionism over the Arabs in the Six Day War; in this context, the heroes of the *Enterprise,* who supported the persecuted Zeons, were analogous to Johnson's diplomatic support of the Israelis in the UN.

Through media representations, Americans could share in Israel's glorious victory over hostile forces. For America in the late 1960s, Israel had become the heroic, civilising democratic force that it had longed to be for Southeast Asia. In entering into a war in Vietnam, the government had demanded for a second time that the American people support a war rather than a crusade, but once the draft was introduced the ends had to be unlimited and the objective, unconditional victory, underwritten by a peace agreement not an armistice.[186] A hero must have an heroic task and by 1967, the American people conceived of their involvement in Vietnam as anything but heroic. The Six Day War occurred at a time when America was receptive to an Israeli victory and an alliance with a small, but powerful, regional state.

US–Israeli Diplomatic Relations in the Aftermath of War

Despite Israel's enhanced popularity, the outbreak of hostilities had led the administration to embargo all arms transfers to the Middle East in the hope that Moscow would reciprocate. However, the Kremlin refused to deviate from its position that, prior to a political settlement, there could be no agreement on arms limitations. As a consequence, in January 1968, in response to Soviet arms transfers to the Arabs, the US arms embargo against Israel and Jordan was terminated.[187] This presented Washington with the problem of how to balance Soviet weapon supplies with arms transfers to Israel and the friendly Arab states. During the fighting an absurd situation had arisen in which "outside Old Jerusalem, American tanks manned by Jordanians met American tanks manned by Israelis."[188] From this point on, Israel's defence requirements became a crucial aspect of US–Israeli relations and formed an integral aspect of Washington's diplomatic efforts to mediate the Arab–Israeli dispute.

In negotiating arms agreements with Washington, Israel and its supporters were in a stronger position to wield influence than they were in the diplomatic arena. First, the American commitment to a regional balance of power meant that requests for arms were commensurate with Washington's objectives whereas their respective views on a territorial settlement differed. Secondly, although the Israeli aircraft that had defeated the Arabs in 1967 were of French origin, as a consequence of De Gaulle's pro-Arab policy, France was no longer a reliable source of supply. With the French supply route closed, the growing pro-Israel lobby could legitimately argue that US weapons were the only option. Thirdly, the Constitution grants Congress the responsibility for appropriating funds, which makes it easier for any such lobby to campaign for material assistance in contrast to diplomatic support. In addition, it is foreign governments that initiate the weapons procurement process by making a request which its supporters have time to prepare for and act upon. Fourthly, through unilateral action, Israel had demonstrated its propensity for transforming its own security concerns into a potential superpower crisis, and in so doing, aligned US security interests with its own.

The domestic environment created by Vietnam was also conducive to providing arms for Israel. Conservatives and military officials had become more sympathetic towards Israel for displaying characteristics most Americans admired and respected: self-reliance, democracy, anti-communism and idealism. The Israelis were also making a positive contribution to US security as their capture of Russian equipment provided useful information to the American military in Southeast Asia. Israel clearly opposed Soviet objectives in contrast to the majority of the Arab states that were firmly aligned, if not ideologically, at least militarily, with the Communist regime.[189]

The new balance of domestic forces was tested in 1968 by Israel's request for the President's support in purchasing F-4 Phantom jets. The stage was set for what was to become a familiar battle for the President's support between the bureaucracy, which opposed the sale, and the pro-Israel lobby. Within the bureaucracy, the feeling was that the supply of F-4 fighter planes should be dependent upon movement in the Israeli position, and two currents of opinion emerged. Some felt that Israel should be asked to agree to full withdrawal in the context of peace in exchange for US arms. Others, fearful of Israel's nuclear development, argued that the signing of the non-proliferation treaty (NPT) should be a precondition for delivery of the jets.[190] The NPT issue was discussed at length with Israeli representatives, but they would only commit themselves not to be the first to "introduce" nuclear weapons into the region. In trying to ascertain exactly what this meant Ambassador Rabin informed US officials that Israel would not be the first to "test" nuclear weapons or to *publicly* reveal their existence. In response, Assistant Secretary of Defence Paul Warnke sent a letter to Rabin specifying that Washington's understanding of the non-introduction of nuclear weapons meant: "no production of a nuclear device."[191]

To counteract the pressure on Israel and the efforts of the bureaucracy to prevent the sale, the pro-Israel lobby initiated a campaign of its own. Every American Jewish organisation and an array of non-Jewish groups emphasised the importance of the sale, and the American–Israeli Public Affairs Commission (AIPAC) obtained statements from the two presidential candidates, Hubert Humphrey and Richard Nixon, in support of the sale. In fact, there was no real concerted public opposition to the sale, which indicated that many influential Americans and organised groups were beginning to identify with, and support, the Israeli cause. In July the Senate passed a resolution calling for the sale of F-4s to Jerusalem. Finally, on 9 October, Johnson succumbed to the pressure inflicted on his beleaguered administration and publicly announced that Israel would be permitted to purchase fifty Phantom jets to be delivered in 1969 and 1970.

In a futile attempt to offset the inevitable backlash from the Arab states, Rusk informed the Egyptians on 2 November that Washington continued to favour full Israeli withdrawal from the Sinai as part of a peace settlement. This position was subsequently endorsed in the Rogers Plan of 1969, and had consistently been part of the American official consensus on the terms of an Israeli-Egyptian peace accord.[192] The move did little to win the confidence of the Israelis and a distinct chill between the two governments marked the last months of Johnson's term in office, at the head of an administration that had firmly positioned the US as Israel's undisputed ally and major arms supplier.

Assessing Johnson's Middle East Policy

Both Vietnam and the Six Day War exerted a profound effect on the domestic forces that sought to influence Johnson's foreign policy. Vietnam acted as a constraint that all but destroyed his relationship with the legislature and turned the tide of public opinion against him. In its lightning victory against the Arabs, Israel proved that it was able to achieve what the US could not in Vietnam: the defeat of Communist proxies and the expansion of the frontier of American values of freedom and democracy. The Jewish community and American conservatives responded to Israel's success by becoming more deeply involved with the country, while media coverage diffused this enthusiasm throughout the population. A new awareness of the Holocaust and the symbolic importance of Israel as a homeland had rapidly been absorbed into American culture and support for Israel became the new political trend.

Washington was a major beneficiary of the 1967 war, even though it had not risked military action and Israel's defeat of the Arabs had been secured with French, not American aircraft. A US ally had been victorious in a war that directly undermined Soviet interests and Johnson sought to capitalise diplomatically on Israel's military prowess. In seeking to avoid what he perceived as the mistakes of the Eisenhower administration in advancing grandiose conceptions and forcing a complete Israeli withdrawal, Johnson made the mistake of moving too far in the opposite direction, with avoidance and lack of commitment. His administration failed to advance proposals for a genuine peace settlement or a strategy for normalising relations between the Arab states and Israel. In attempting to appease different factions, Johnson's approach tried to unify two irreconcilable strategies: one favoured by the bureaucracy and pro-Arab supporters, the other by Congress, many of his political associates[193] and increasing numbers of the American public. In trying to reconcile the two, Johnson adopted elements of both strategies, to the confusion of all involved. He eventually settled on a policy similar to that pursued by Truman: that of increasing arms sales to Israel to soften the impact of a divergent diplomatic strategy.[194]

"Sentiment and concern" had proved no substitute for innovation and diplomatic skill. Time eventually ran out for the Democrats and the unfinished business of the Middle East passed on to the Republicans. In contrast to Johnson, President Richard Nixon placed a high priority on foreign policy and considered the conduct of international relations to be one of his greatest strengths. Yet even Nixon's knowledge of the Middle East did not prepare him for the complexity and challenges of managing Arab–Israeli affairs.

5

NIXON, KISSINGER AND US POLICY TOWARDS ISRAEL

THE STRATEGY THE ADMINISTRATION of Richard Nixon adopted in its relations with the Arab states and Israel was not noted for its consistency, and the President's attitude and policy towards Israel often mirrored the erratic and contradictory elements of his own personality. The man behind the presidency was something of an enigma. Re-elected overwhelmingly to office in 1972, his foreign policy hailed as a resounding success, within two years the Watergate scandal forced him to resign in disgrace on 9 August 1974, his domestic support in tatters. During his six years in office Nixon had condemned the Israeli government for its intransigence in negotiations with the Arabs and for a time, withheld arms supplies. Yet he had also played a key role in overseeing the most dramatic consolidation of US–Israeli ties of any President. Under his leadership Israel was considered worthy to act as a proxy state to protect US interests, was elevated to the status of a strategic asset and received, on the personal request of the President, an unprecedented $2.2 billion aid appropriation during the 1973 war.[1] On occasions Nixon allowed the imperatives of détente, superpower competition for influence in the Arab world and divisions within his own administration to force a reluctant Israel to compromise with Egypt. Yet on each occasion, while he maintained the power of his presidency, Nixon always provided Israel with a way out of difficult negotiations and alternative policy options that bypassed those in his administration who would have forced Jerusalem to make peace at any price.[2]

Israel's leaders were adept at manipulating Nixon's admiration for the Jewish state, his distrust of the American bureaucracy[3] and his penchant for viewing regional conflicts through the prism of the Cold War, to their advantage.[4] By the time Nixon was elected to the presidency, his religious upbringing and perception of international affairs had conditioned him to believe that the

United States had an "absolute commitment" to prevent Israel from "being driven into the sea."[5] This belief, in conjunction with his view of foreign affairs, as a series of inter-linked developments set against the backdrop of superpower rivalry,[6] meant that, ultimately, his support of Israel was assured.

Nixon was raised in a tight-knit Quaker community by religious parents who adhered to a literal interpretation of the Bible.[7] Religion played an influential role in his early life and was revealed in a paper he wrote while at college under the heading "What Can I Believe?"

> Years of training in the home and church have had their effect on my thinking . . . My parents, "fundamental Quakers," had ground into me, with the aid of the church, all the fundamental ideas in their strictest interpretation. The infallibility and literal correctness of the Bible, . . . all these were accepted facts.[8]

Within the Nixon household, religion and prayer were essentially personal and private and perhaps because of this, Nixon avoided the common practice of so many political figures of quoting the Bible during public speaking. He recalled that as Vice-President, Eisenhower urged him to give greater legitimacy and power to his public speeches by occasionally referring to God, but that he did not feel comfortable in so doing.[9]

Once absorbed by the intricacies of international affairs, Nixon was to be less influenced by his religious heritage. He came to believe, for example, that the pacifism espoused by Quakers was only an option in international life if one were confronting a civilised, compassionate enemy.[10] History had proved that in the face of dictators such as Hitler and Stalin, pacifism had failed to stop violence, strengthened the enemy and weakened morale at home.[11] In foreign affairs Nixon was to take a tough stance against the enemy and in Israel he found a kindred spirit.

Nixon does not appear to have perceived a connection between his view of Israel, American Jews and his personal acquaintance with individual Jews, and his feelings for one group were not necessarily commensurate with his feelings for another.[12] Henry A. Kissinger, his National Security Adviser, claimed that he embodied many of the prejudices of the uprooted, Californian lower middle class from which he came. He believed that Jews formed a powerful, cohesive group in American society; that they were predominantly liberal; placed the interests of Israel above all else; were generally more sympathetic to the Soviet Union than other sectors of American society and that their control of the mass media made them powerful and dangerous adversaries. In this regard, Nixon retained the post-war view of Israel as a socialist state inhabited by Communist Jews from Eastern Europe, which he juxtaposed with the post-1967 image of Israel as part of the western camp with its guns firmly pointed at Moscow. Yet his contradictory image of American Jews as an entity did not deter him from enjoying cordial personal relations with individual Jews and from elevating them to influential positions within his administration. Kissinger went so far as to claim that Nixon felt particularly at ease with representatives of a group that shared his experience of being an outsider.[13]

Yet this view stands in stark contrast to another image of Nixon. On one occasion, at an Oval office meeting, Nixon reportedly complained that the "Jews are all over the government, . . . generally speaking, you can't trust the bastards. They turn on you."[14] He was not averse to expressing his crude views in front of Kissinger[15] and Kissinger himself once said that, "You can't believe how much anti-Semitism there is at the top of this government, and I mean at the top."[16] It was this aspect of Nixon's personality that caused Kissinger to remark that Israeli Prime Minister Golda Meir's announcement within a year of Nixon's election that he was "an old friend of the Jewish people" was "startling news to those of us more familiar with Nixon's ambivalences."[17]

Despite these outbursts, it would be inaccurate to categorise Nixon as an anti-Semite. Long before he became President a leading Jewish group defended him against such charges[18] and, remarkably for a Republican, once in office he filled many senior posts with people of Jewish origin. He appointed Kissinger, a Jewish immigrant and former Harvard Professor, to the second most powerful post in the United States. Subsequently, in 1974, Kissinger was appointed Secretary of State, becoming the only official to hold the two posts simultaneously. Kissinger was a Rockerfeller protégé and his appointment was therefore beneficial to Nixon's standing amongst the 'respectable' Republican wing of the Republican party, where he needed allies.[19] Nixon also appointed other Jewish figures, including Arthur Burns as chairman of the Federal Reserve, Herb Stein as head of the Council of Economic advisors, Leonard Garment as White House counsel and William Safire as a White House speech writer.[20]

Irrespective of his general distrust of American Jews and his ambivalence towards Israel as a spiritual and emotional homeland, Nixon shared the deeply ingrained belief of his generation that Israel could not be abandoned[21] and stood by it more firmly in every crisis that assailed the Jewish state than any President except Truman. He was vocal in his support for Israel, even though his associates later claimed that this was a ruse to conceal his true feelings and policies. Whatever Nixon's real sentiments, Israel embodied many of the attributes he most admired. He respected Israel's determination and courage and its leader's tenacious defence of their national interest. He also considered its military prowess to be an asset for the Western democracies.[22]

However, Nixon's admiration for Israel's tough stance was tempered by his conviction that Israeli occupation of Arab land only strengthened anti-Western radical forces in the region. He believed that Israel had to be forced into a peace settlement because its current posture jeopardised US relations with the Arab states. Yet Nixon was sufficiently astute to realise that pressurising Israel to relinquish territory in apparent response to the demands of the radical Arab states was more likely to promote Soviet, rather than US, interests. He came to share Kissinger's view that America could not mediate an Israeli withdrawal until circumstances made it clear that Washington's actions had not been extorted by Soviet pressure. Under his leadership, the exclusion of the Soviet Union from the Middle East was seen as a pre-requisite for a concerted White House initiative to secure an Arab–Israeli peace agreement.[23]

Kissinger's viewpoint on Middle Eastern affairs began at the opposite end of the emotional spectrum to that of his patron. Whilst not actively practicing his Jewish religion, Kissinger carried with him the memory that thirteen members of his family had died in Nazi concentration camps. His determination not to leave Israel strategically vulnerable and susceptible to the infliction of a second Holocaust was evident in his refusal to countenance a diplomatic strategy that might escalate the regional situation beyond his control.[24] Despite his personal friendship with a number of Israeli leaders and his assertion that "it was not always easy [and] occasionally proved painful,"[25] he subordinated his emotional preferences to his perception of the strategic interest of the country of which he was a citizen. The journalist Jonathan Goldberg claimed that "[T]o many, he embodied the age-old truth that Jews in high places will serve their masters, not their brethren."[26] Yet there is ample evidence that simple fear as a Jew for Israel's safety was a crucial factor in Kissinger's strategy during the tense early days of the Yom Kippur War. Defence Secretary James Schlesinger would later say that, "[a]s Israel began to fall apart, Henry began to fall apart."[27] It mattered to Kissinger that Israel was the only Jewish state and while he was not averse to arguing with its leaders and forcing concessions, there was a point beyond which he would not go. By the end of the Ford administration he had reportedly stated that he would resign rather than push Israel still further.[28]

An astute political realist, Kissinger believed that in the long-term, Israel's security could not be guaranteed by an appeal to the emotional sentiment of politicians and decision-makers, but only by anchoring it to the strategic interest of the United States. These shared conceptions of the national interest solidified the close personal relationship between Nixon and Kissinger[29] and provided the foundations on which the unlikely partnership between the Communist-baiter from California and a refugee from Nazi Germany was formed. By different routes and emotional perspectives, similar perceptions of the national interest brought Nixon and Kissinger to the same conclusion regarding the strategy the administration should pursue in the Middle East.[30] Their relationship was consolidated still further by Kissinger's preference for secret negotiations that played to Nixon's paranoia.

Israeli leaders expertly capitalised on Nixon and Kissinger's pre-existing conception of international affairs and their positive image of Israel to consolidate their control over territorial gains made in the Six Day War. The President was obsessed with the potential for a Soviet–American confrontation in the

Middle East, believing that the Soviet commitment to the Arab radicals and the American commitment to Israel might draw both superpowers into a confrontation "even against our wills – and almost certainly against our national interest."[31] At the same time, he tended to distort the true origins of the Arab–Israeli conflict by asserting that "the Soviets are the main cause of Middle East tensions," thereby ignoring the reality that Moscow was actually fuelling a pre-existing hostility for its advantage. In response, and to ensure the support of a staunchly anti-Communist President, the Israeli government promoted the view that its conflict with its Arab neighbours was a direct result of Arab intrigue and Soviet machinations. By aligning their views directly with those of Nixon, Israeli leaders could be more certain of American support.[32]

The potential for Soviet intrigue in the Middle East was a recurring theme in conversations between Israeli leaders and the President.[33] However, it remains uncertain whether this commonly expressed view of Moscow's involvement in the region was an accurate reflection of the President's position, or a tactic to pacify and reassure the Israeli government. Five years after publishing his *Memoirs*, Nixon acknowledged that:

> [a]lthough the Soviet Union is the cause of many conflicts in the Third World and profits from most of them, it is not the only cause. If the Soviet Union did not exist there would still be regional conflicts and civil wars. The Palestinian people would still fight for their homeland.[34]

Nixon justified his commitment to maintaining Israel's military superiority on his cultural and strategic conviction that it was the "only state in the Mideast which [was] pro-freedom and an effective opponent to Soviet expansion."[35] The image of Israel as a courageous state was prevalent amongst conservatives, like the President, who advocated a stronger stance against Communism.[36] The need to enhance US–Israeli relations to undercut Soviet advances into the region apparently took precedence over potential interests in the Arab world,[37] as the administration did little to improve its relations with the governments of either Egypt or Syria.

Despite this, Nixon's commitment to Israel was tempered by two other factors. First, Israel's attitude of "total intransigence on negotiating any peace agreement that would involve the return of any of the occupied territories." Israel's victory, Nixon claimed "had been too great"[38] because its resounding achievements in the 1967 war had substantiated the belief that Israel's security could most effectively be secured through military force and territorial control. Second, Nixon's perception of what he identified as "the unyielding and short-sighted pro-Israeli attitude prevalent in large and influential sectors of the American Jewish community, Congress, the media, and in intellectual and cultural circles."[39] Domestic politics were a perennial concern to Nixon but he decried the Jewish lobby's tendency to equate moderation in relations with

Israel with anti-Semitism.[40] Irrespective of his declarations that he did not care about the Jewish vote because American Jews would never vote for him, he was painfully aware that the Jewish constituencies in New York, Pennsylvania and California had voted 95 percent against him in 1968 and he was determined to carry these states with him in the 1972 Presidential election.[41] The conclusion could be drawn that both the national interest and domestic political considerations played a role in his administration's Middle East policy. The exact balance of these considerations remains, however, a subject of debate.

The Changing Place of Israel in American Consciousness

Nixon was the first President to be elected to office following Israel's newly elevated standing in public discourse. In formulating policy towards the Middle East, Nixon had to be cognisant of the changing place of Israel in the mind of America. As a conservative he was proud of America's alliance with the heroic Jewish state, even though he did not share the emotional empathy for Israel that many of his countrymen had begun to demonstrate. Positive media representations of Israel and parallels between the depravity that led to the Holocaust and the more unpalatable aspects of American life were fast becoming a staple of popular culture and shaping the expectations, albeit subtly, of the policy the American people expected their government to pursue towards the Jewish homeland.

Some of the most popular films of the early 1970s were set against the backdrop of Nazi Germany and by implication the consequential establishment of the State of Israel. Amongst the most successful American films in portraying the rise of Nazism was the musical *Cabaret* (1972). Annette Insdorf describes the film as "entertaining, engrossing, and ultimately chilling in its stylised tableaux of spreading swastikas."[42] It is set in the Germany of the early 1930s; Germany is seen through the eyes of an English university student involved in a relationship with an American cabaret singer. The story evolves through a juxtaposition of scenes at the cabaret and daily existence in Berlin. Songs and dances provide a social commentary to the film, which depicts the disintegration of the Weimar Republic and the rise of National Socialism.

At both a cultural and political level, *Cabaret* evokes a tenuous parallel between Germany in the 1930s and the chaos of American society in the early 1970s. German expressionism reached its zenith in the 1920s but was outlawed by Hitler in the 1930s. This provided a sharp contrast to contemporary America where the openly permissive atmosphere deprived art of its ability to shock. There is also a parallel between violence, murder and social and political chaos. In Weimar Germany protests tended to be anti-democratic, in contrast to

America, where protestors advocated greater democracy with an end to racism and the Vietnam war.[43]

It was during this period of newly developing social and political consciousness throughout American society that Holocaust survivor Elie Wiesel became an important figure on the Jewish scene. Wiesel's personal memoir *Night*, which told of his experiences in a concentration camp, published in 1960,[44] and his 1966 testimony of the harassment of Jews in the Soviet Union in *The Jews of Silence* attracted the American Jewish youth, who were themselves searching for their own identity. Judith Doneson goes as far to say that, by the early 1970s, Wiesel and his works had built a "cult of the Holocaust" around him. At a time of "spiritual neediness," Wiesel's renditions of the Holocaust "personified a lost culture with a contemporary relevance that was irresistible."[45] As a consequence, Nixon was confronted with an electorate with a higher degree of emotional commitment to Israel than ever before. A connection that was to intensify throughout his term in office.

The Nixon Team: An Administration Divided

In the first year of Nixon's term in office, high-ranking officials became embroiled in an unprecedented controversy over the Middle East. The conflict challenged the assumption that the United States had become Israel's staunchest ally as a result of the resupply operation in the wake of the Six–Day War and subsequent alignment with Israel's position in the United Nations. It also appeared to contradict the cultural ties that had burgeoned at the public level and the increasing confidence of the American Jewish community in using its influence in defence of Israel.

The debate centred on the difference of opinion between Kissinger and the Secretary of State, William Rogers. Rogers was a lawyer by profession and a close personal friend of the President. He had served in Eisenhower's cabinet as Attorney General, but while an excellent negotiator, he lacked the strong, assertive personality and foreign policy experience necessary to compete with Kissinger.[46] Rogers was doubly disadvantaged because his cabinet post created a greater physical and psychological distance between himself and a President who admitted in his memoirs that he distrusted the Foreign Service,[47] partly because he felt unable to control it.[48]

Nixon's personality and leadership style, combined with his suspicion of the bureaucracy, which he perceived to be a bastion of the Democrats,[49] worked to Kissinger's advantage. To increase his control over foreign policy, the President transferred the locus of power, traditionally centred in the State Department, to the White House and the newly empowered and reinvigorated National Security Council (NSC).[50] Nixon and Kissinger's demand for power over all decisions eventually merged both policy formulation and operational functions inside the NSC.[51] As a result, the National Security Adviser had the means to shape foreign policy[52] and ultimately became the foreign policy Tsar.[53] In his memoirs Kissinger described the evolution of the system thus:

> Eventually, though not for the first one and a half years, I became the principal adviser. Until the end of 1970 I was influential but not dominant. From then on, my role increased as Nixon sought to bypass the delays and sometimes opposition of the departments. The fact remains that the NSC machinery was used more fully before my authority was confirmed, while afterward tactical decisions were increasingly taken outside the system in personal conversations with the President.[54]

If relations between Kissinger and Rogers were acrimonious, then Rogers' deputy, the talented and ambitious Under Secretary of State Elliot Richardson, bridged some of the rift. Richardson developed a close working relationship with Kissinger that kept the channels between the White House and the State Department open. Joseph Sisco, a skilled State Department bureaucratic tactician, was appointed as Secretary of State for Near East and South Asia affairs. In his long career at the State Department, Sisco had never served overseas and derived his considerable knowledge of the Middle East from time spent in Washington. Working with him first as office director for Israel and Arab–Israeli affairs and later as Deputy Assistant Secretary for the Near East, was Alfred "Roy" L. Atherton, Jr. Atherton was the embodiment of professionalism and experience and formed a formidable partnership with Sisco in Middle East policymaking.[55]

Nixon's other notable appointees were not directly involved with Middle Eastern affairs on a day-to-day basis. These included Melvin Laird, the Secretary of Defence, for whom Vietnam and the defence budget were his main preoccupation, and the chairman of the Joint Chiefs of Staff, General Earl Wheeler.[56] Richard Helms, Director of the CIA, reported directly to the NSC and provided the President with an alternative viewpoint on international affairs to that of the State Department. As Nixon's presidency progressed, all but one of his advisors exerted a gradually decreasing influence over the administration's Middle East policy. However, these men continued to play a role in reinforcing the President's ideologically imbued image of the world as one divided between friends and enemies and emphasised the links they perceived to exist between Nixon's domestic support and his foreign policy successes.[57]

The Israeli government's perception of Nixon's commitment to their state's security and interests was challenged by this bureaucratic infighting. In organising the foreign policy apparatus in the early days of his presidency, the Middle East was the one region Nixon subcontracted to the State Department. As the State Department was the home of the "Arabists," in the sense that many bureaucrats had served in the Arab Middle East, Israeli officials were concerned that they would encourage the administration to pressurise Israel to sacrifice territory to facilitate a US rapprochement with the Arabs. However, Israeli fears were misplaced and Nixon's decision seems to have been a product of practicality, not grand strategy. In his memoirs Nixon explained his decision in terms of his concern that "Kissinger's Jewish background would put him at a disadvantage during delicate negotiations for the reopening of relations with the Arab states,"[58] a claim with which Kissinger concurred.[59] Nixon's actions were also motivated by his perception of the Middle East as a "powder keg"[60] where the stakes were elusive, the risk of superpower confrontation high and the price of intervention, especially in domestic terms, even higher. Underlying the President's thinking was a desire to distance the White House from an unsuccessful Arab–Israeli initiative and the potentially negative fall-out such a move might entail.[61]

The War of Attrition

As the Four Power talks between Britain, France, the Soviet Union and the United States to reach a settlement of the Arab–Israeli dispute continued, the situation on the ground deteriorated throughout the spring of 1969 and the war of attrition intensified. Moscow attempted to dissuade Nasser from escalating the "mini-war" but its efforts were not backed up with the necessary threat of force to have been taken seriously.[62] Fighting broke out along the Suez Canal, while *fedayeen* attacks escalated, thus provoking Israeli retaliatory raids. Throughout 1969, the Egyptians, armed with superior artillery, inflicted extensive physical and psychological casualties on Israel. Jerusalem's apparent weakness in countering the Egyptian assault appeared to reflect the deterioration of Washington's position in the Middle East relative to that of Moscow. On 1 September, King Idris of Libya, one of the most pro-Western, conservative Arab monarchs was overthrown in a coup d'état by Nasserist army officers led by Muammar Qaddafi. This, in conjunction with the declared state of emergency in Lebanon and the coup in Sudan the previous spring, convinced State Department officials that the trend towards extremism in the Arab world was a response to the lack of progress towards a peace settlement.

The Israeli government was increasingly uncertain of Nixon's position on the growing crisis, because his public response oscillated between the view of his National Security Adviser and those of his Secretary of State. On the one hand, at a meeting in mid-December 1968, he reassured Israeli Defence Minister Moshe Dayan of his support,[63] but on the other, at his first news conference as President, he emphasised the danger of a US–Soviet confrontation in the Middle East and rejected Israel's demand for direct negotiations.[64] These words ignited fear in Jerusalem of an imposed peace. Rabin claimed that the Israeli government "knew perfectly well that if an agreement were reached between the two powers, each would be obliged to 'induce' its 'clients to accept it.'"[65]

By mid-September, Nixon sought expert advice on the effect State Department negotiations were exerting on domestic opinion. He became increasingly sceptical as State officials moved negotiations closer to Arab demands on the 1967 borders.[66] Thus he rejected both Rogers' requests for increasing pressure on Israel and Israel's demands for a joint American–Israeli position to force the Arabs to negotiate.[67]

In the midst of these internal deliberations, Golda Meir, who had become Prime Minister of Israel after the death of Levi Eshkol, arrived in Washington in September 1969. Meir was to enjoy a good working relationship with the Nixon administration and some political analysts claim that she was more popular in the US than she was in Israel.[68] Her fear of a diminution in US support was assuaged by her meeting with Nixon, as he gave his visitors the impression that he did not share Rogers' commitment to the talks now in progress. He even established a special channel of communication between Kissinger and Rabin that circumvented the State Department.[69] This was symptomatic of Nixon's tendency to exploit internal disagreements within his administration when dealing with the Arab states and Israel. Once each side had its "friends," the President sought to balance the competing parties while appearing sympathetic to all.[70] Immediately after Meir's return to Israel, Nixon granted Rogers permission to present Soviet Ambassador Dobrynin with Washington's fallback position, which "would determine a timetable and procedures for [the] withdrawal of Israeli armed forces from UAR territory occupied during the conflict of 1967."[71]

The first public challenge to Israel's confidence in Nixon's support came at the end of the first year of his presidency. Entrusted with the conduct of Middle East policy, Rogers presented a comprehensive proposal for an Arab–Israeli peace agreement, known as the Rogers Plan. This was a rare but dramatic exception to Presidential control over the bureaucracy and heralded a downturn in US–Israeli relations. The Rogers Plan, publicly announced on 9 December 1969, was based on UN Security Council Resolution 242 and upheld the principle that Israel should return the occupied territories in exchange for Arab commitments to end the state of war and respect Israel's territorial integrity. The objective of US policy Rogers declared was:

> to encourage the Arabs to accept a permanent peace based on a binding agreement and to urge the Israelis to withdraw from occupied territory when their territorial integrity is assured as envisaged by the Security Council resolution. . . . Any changes in pre-existing lines, should not reflect the weight of conquest[72] and should be confined to insubstantial alterations required for mutual security. We do not support expansionism. We believe that troops must be withdrawn as the resolution provides.[73]

Israel's leaders were outraged that the new administration's interpretation of Resolution 242 appeared to differ so greatly from that of Johnson. From Jerusalem's perspective, "the Soviets were acting as dutiful lawyers for the Arabs,"[74] while the American representatives were negotiating their own terms at Israel's expense and informing Jerusalem only after the event.[75] Given the psychological environment of the fear of invasion in which Israel existed, any agreement Washington made on alterations to the 1967 borders was considered to be a concession made at their expense.[76] The central provision of the plan, that the occupied territories be exchanged for peace, guaranteed that it would be greeted by hostility in Israel. Rabin claimed that:

> At no stage in the talks did the Russians adopt any position that had not previously been agreed upon with the Egyptians, whereas basic American positions were not co-ordinated in advance with [Israel]. They essentially reflected American interests and concepts that we were more or less expected to adopt.[77]

Israeli objections were as much procedural as they were substantive and the public way in which the proposal was presented was as much a cause of rejection as its substance. Washington had transgressed a very important element of any special relationship – the right to be consulted. The following day Jerusalem rejected the plan and on 22 December the Israeli cabinet issued the following statement:

> Israel will not be sacrificed by any power or interpower policy and will reject any attempt to impose a forced solution on her . . . The proposal of the U.S.A. cannot but be interpreted by the Arab parties as an attempt to appease them at the expense of Israel.[78]

The next day, the Soviet Union also rejected the proposal.[79]

It was at this juncture that the duality of Nixon's policy towards Israel was starkly revealed. Had Rogers' proposals carried the full weight of Presidential backing, Jerusalem may have felt an obligation to be receptive to the Plan. However, Nixon used the Rogers Plan as a device to show the Arab world "that the United States did not automatically dismiss its claims to the occupied territories or rule out a compromise settlement of the conflicting claims."[80] Yet irrespective of the fact that he had both appointed and trusted Rogers with the conduct of Middle East diplomacy, Nixon endorsed Kissinger's and – by implication – Israel's position. To preserve his own standing with the Israelis, Nixon used Leonard Garment, his White House advisor on Jewish affairs, to privately inform both Prime Minister Meir and leaders of the American Jewish community of his doubts about State Department policy. In so doing he demonstrated the increasingly perceived importance of the pro-Israel lobby and public support of Israel in the United States. He also explained that without the willing acceptance of the parties, the proposals would not be enforced.[81] In so doing, Nixon effectively gave the Israeli government the latitude to veto the plan.

Kissinger remained aloof from Mideast affairs during the early phases of this inter-administration dispute. While he was critical of any State Department initiative that placed the onus on Washington to deliver Israeli concessions, he did not align himself with the delegation opposing Rogers. Kissinger's objective was to deny gains to countries aligned with Moscow and to ensure that the Kremlin did not receive credit for any progress made in negotiations.[82] He was not averse to pressuring Israel for concessions but only after the Arab states had been shown the futility of alignment with Moscow and looked towards Washington for progress. Kissinger was "attempt[ing] to create a foreign policy based on permanent values and interests,"[83] and in his memoirs explained that he "wanted to frustrate the radicals – who were in any event hostile to us – by demonstrating that in the Middle East friendship with the United States was the precondition to diplomatic progress." He was only prepared to pressure Israel if "the Arabs showed their willingness to reciprocate."[84]

Reflection and Reassessment

The failure of the US initiative exerted a profound impact on Israeli perceptions of their relationship with the administration and gave rise to a period of reflection within both governments. The White House concluded that it had been foolhardy to believe that the Soviet Union could be separated from Egypt during settlement negotiations and that a confluence of interests between the superpowers could form the basis of an agreement. Even when common ground was found, Washington and Moscow were unable to deliver their clients to the negotiating table or impose a settlement. In submitting the Rogers Plan, Washington had blatantly placed superpower détente above the interests of Israel, and had shown its willingness to distance itself from some Israeli demands. This degree of flexibility had not been reciprocated in Moscow's dealings with Egypt. Events had demonstrated that America's best interests were served by the realignment of its negotiating position with that of Israel, because the administration concluded that every American initiative that failed played into the hands of the Soviets and strengthened the hand of the radicals.[85]

The perceived balance of power between Washington and Jerusalem was also a factor in this decision. Kissinger believed that Rogers had doomed himself to failure by underestimating the will and ability of Israel to resist American pressure. In the domestic sphere, both he and Nixon recognised the strength of congressional and public support for Israel, engendered by popular cultural representations of Israel and its perceived military prowess. While issues pertaining to Israel and the Holocaust were appearing on every mass market medium, from television shows to newspaper articles, a domestic backlash against policy decisions viewed as antagonistic towards Israel was a very real possibility. Israel was now perceived not as a distant, unknown state, but in terms of real people, from Ben Gurion to Elie Wiesel. It was harder to ask the American public to adopt a policy of indifference towards people that entertained their living rooms, and were portrayed in such warm terms, on the evening news. On a strategic level, the White House also considered it misguided to try to exert pressure on a friend as a means for improving relations with an adversary. Indeed, it is the notion of Israel as a friend, a state which for ideological and cultural reasons America could identify, that is crucial to understanding the nuances of US policy.[86]

The administration drew several conclusions from the diplomatic failures of 1969. First, Kissinger came to believe that pressure should only be exerted on Israel if the Soviet and Egyptian position were moderated to such an extent that a permanent settlement could be secured. This gradually became the dominant tenet of US policy. Secondly, circumstances had shown that, as the separation of the Soviet Union from Egypt was not possible during negotiations, it was preferable to bypass Moscow and deal directly with Cairo. Thirdly, as American concessions and movement from the Israeli position had not been reciprocated, the next advance in peace negotiations would have to come from either Moscow or Cairo. The United States and Israel were now in the comfortable position, or so they thought, of being able to sit and wait for their adversaries to moderate their demands. Fourthly, events had shown that the package settlement approach had been too ambitious and that henceforth initiatives should be conducted privately on a step-by-step formula to ensure that the obtainable was not held up in the process of waiting for the unobtainable.[87]

While Washington's reassessment should have reassured Jerusalem, the ramifications of its alignment with Moscow in formulating the Rogers Plan forced the Israeli cabinet to reach a very different set of unpalatable conclusions. Yitzhak Rabin, the Israeli Ambassador to Washington, took the American decision to pursue a diplomatic initiative, apparently at Israel's expense, as a sign of the administration's loss of faith in its ally. Rabin reasoned that the White House felt it was losing ground in the Middle East because its 'client' was incapable of putting an end to the war of attrition, which forced it to adopt a conciliatory position in negotiations with the Soviet Union.[88] Moshe Dayan, the Israeli Defence Minister, wrote in his memoirs that the White House was "very worried by what they called the Sovietisation of the Egyptian war."[89] In an endeavour to redress the regional balance of forces, Israel escalated the conflict and by spring 1970, Israeli planes were involved in deep penetration raids against targets in the Nile Delta and in Cairo itself.

Israel's intensification of the war of attrition culminated in the escalation of fighting along the Suez Canal as Moscow came to the aid of its client. Soviet arms, including the latest SAM-3 surface-to-air missiles, flooded into Egypt and for the first time, Soviet pilots actively defended Egyptian territory.[90] By the end of 1970, 200 Soviet pilots and 12,000–15,000 Soviet soldiers were stationed in Egypt.[91] Reports from the Israeli government that Soviet pilots were flying operational missions from Egypt,[92] in conjunction with the intensification of Israeli deep penetration raids on Cairo, undermined the newly emerged consensus within the administration on how to approach the Middle East. Increasing domestic pressure to abandon the Rogers Plan and grant Israel's request for 100 A-4 and 25 F-4 jets compounded the situation. As congressional elections drew closer, members of Congress became increasingly vocal in their support for Israel and increased military assistance.

Arms for Israel

The escalation of the war of attrition threatened to send US–Israeli relations to an all time low. Far from reassuring Jerusalem of Washington's support, the conflict undermined the fundamental assumption of all Israeli calculations – that if the Soviet Union intervened in the Middle East, the United States would move vigorously to block it. Now what Dayan had feared and many predicted could not happen, had become a reality.[93] The Soviets were militarily intervening on behalf of Egypt, but the assumption about the Americans was not borne out. Washington was hardly reacting. Israel had never wanted or asked for US troops to fight on its behalf but the Israeli government desperately needed the dispatch of the 25 additional Phantoms and 100 Skyhawks Meir had requested during her September 1969 visit to Washington.[94]

The Nixon administration was now confronted with the dilemma of how to de-escalate the conflict while simultaneously acquiescing to Israeli demands for arms supplies. Should the US undertake another peace initiative, Nasser's favourable response was dependent on its non-partisan nature. This was particularly difficult to facilitate when American-made Phantom jets were bombing Egypt and the Israelis were actively pursuing the destruction of Nasser's regime.[95] Yet superpower politics dictated that the administration could not stand by while ever increasing numbers of Soviet personnel and armaments poured into a hostile Arab state. Kissinger argued that the despatch of the jets would serve the dual purpose of reassuring Israel and demonstrating US resolve to confront any Soviet or Arab challenge.[96]

Washington therefore began the process of reversing the debilitating effect that the Rogers Plan had exerted on US–Israeli relations with the announcement of a change in strategy. In his "State of the World" address Nixon emphasised the Soviet threat and the need for direct Arab–Israeli negotiations, a statement that directly contradicted the basic tenets of the Rogers' Plan.[97] This was followed on 30 January 1970 by Nixon's surprise announcement during a press conference that a decision would be made on Israel's request for arms within thirty days.[98]

The sense of relief the announcement generated in Israel was short-lived because the thirty-day time limit passed without a public decision. Nixon then delivered another shock to Jerusalem by further delaying his decision. This change in policy has been attributed to a number of factors. First, the President was outraged that Mayor Lindsay of New York and members of the Jewish American community boycotted the February 1970 visit of the French Prime Minister Georges Pompidou in protest against the recent sale of one hundred Mirage jet fighters to Libya.[99] In response, Nixon flew to New York and took the Mayor's place at a dinner in honour of the French President and his wife. He then ordered Israel's request for Phantoms and Skyhawks to be put on indefinite hold.[100] Secondly, the four-power talks were scheduled to resume in late February and the Soviets had indicated that they and their client might adopt a more flexible approach to negotiations. Thirdly, King Hussein's position in Jordan was growing increasingly unstable and it was feared that arms transfers to Israel could heighten regional instability and exacerbate tension between the superpowers.[101] In March 1970 Rogers announced the "interim decision" to hold in abeyance a final commitment to sell the jets to Israel.[102]

In private, however, the changing balance of power in the region provoked the President to move in a different direction. He instructed Kissinger to inform Rabin that some of Israel's aircraft losses sustained in the war of attrition would be replaced and the balance of forces maintained in Israel's favour. In his memoirs Rabin claimed that Nixon told him:

> Whenever you request arms – particularly planes – all the media sounds off about it and everyone waits for the administration's decision. That's such a superfluous and harmful dramatisation of the matter. . . . You can be sure that I will continue to supply arms to Israel, but I shall do so in other, different ways. The moment Israel needs arms, approach me, by way of Kissinger, and I'll find a way of overcoming the bureaucracy.[103]

However, on 21 May, any illusion that US arms transfers would not be used as a form of leverage came to an end. The Israeli Foreign Minister, Abba Eban, was received at the White House, where Nixon informed him, as he had Rabin, that "you'll get the stuff as long as you don't insist on too much publicity."[104] The quid pro quo for receiving the weapons was a public statement from the Israeli government indicating a degree of flexibility on the terms of an agreement with Egypt. This was forthcoming on 26 May, when Prime Minister Meir formally announced that Israel continued to accept UN Resolution 242 as the basis for a settlement.[105] In his memoirs, Kissinger attributed the President's change in policy not to the presence of Soviet personnel in Egypt, but as a means to secure Israeli acceptance of the cease-fire.[106]

This incident highlighted a paradox in US–Israeli relations that was to become an enduring feature. If military assistance and diplomacy were linked, Jerusalem effectively exerted equal leverage in its negotiations with Washington. While the United States was keen to make diplomatic progress as a means of excluding the Soviet Union, Israel was in a position to demand aid in return for diplomatic concessions. Israel and the United States soon found themselves in a mutually dependent relationship in which the small state wielded almost as much diplomatic leverage as the superpower.

The Cease-Fire Agreement

With the White House preoccupied with domestic and international controversy following the Cambodian invasion, the State Department continued to dictate the tactics for Middle East negotiations. Rogers and Sisco attempted to build on the credibility that the public decision not to sell the Phantoms to Israel had generated amongst the Arab states by inviting Nasser to undertake another diplomatic initiative designed to restore the cease-fire along the Suez Canal.

With the humiliation of the failed Rogers Plan fresh in its mind, the State Department ignored Moscow's bid for a joint initiative and continued to pursue its own unilateral call for a cease-fire. Despite Kissinger's condemnation of a proposal that failed to confront the problem of Soviet combat troops in Egypt, Nixon authorised Rogers to request the parties' acceptance of a ninety-day Egyptian-Israeli cease-fire along the Canal, accompanied by indirect talks through UN Ambassador Jarring. Rogers publicly revealed this, his second peace proposal, on 25 June 1970.[107]

At this juncture, internal differences within the administration erupted publicly. In an anonymous press briefing – something for which he was famed – Kissinger took a stance in direct opposition to the State Department. He claimed that the United States was "trying to expel the Soviet military presence from Egypt, not so much the advisers, but the combat personnel, the combat pilots, before they become so firmly established."[108] In the aftermath of Cambodia, Kissinger's remarks provoked an immediate public controversy over their meaning and a White House spokesman indicated that America did not propose to expel the Soviets by force.[109] However, in a television interview on 1 July, Nixon threatened action if Moscow upset the regional balance of power and suggested that Israel was entitled to defensible borders.[110] This last point implied that Israel should not be forced to withdraw to pre-1967 lines. By the end of the month, seventy-one Senators had endorsed the President's remarks.

Just when Nixon's comments appeared to have strangled the plan, the Egyptians accepted Rogers' proposal. Nasser's motive remains unclear but Mohamed Heikal, former editor of *Al-Ahram*, claimed that the Egyptian President revealed his true intentions to Soviet President Brezhnev when he explained:

> I am going to accept it [the plan] just because it has an American flag [on it]. We must have a breathing space so we can finish our missile sites: we need a cease-fire, and the only cease-fire the Israelis will accept is one proposed by the Americans.[111]

Believing that the Egyptians would instantly violate a cease-fire agreement,[112] the Israeli cabinet's initial reaction was to reject the plan. Rabin refused to deliver this response, giving time for the gradual modification of Jerusalem's position, a change that was aided by reassurances from Washington and a personal letter from Nixon to Meir reassuring her of continued arms deliveries.[113] Once Nixon publicly promised that the cease-fire would not result in an Arab military build-up, and that Israel's "negotiating position" would not be "compromised or jeopardised,"[114] Meir had little choice but to accept the initiative,[115] which she did on 31 July. On 4 August, the Israeli government went a step further in committing to the peace accord with the Knesset's acceptance of Resolution 242 "in all its parts."[116] In reality, the cease-fire agreement was an American commitment to Israel, not a bilateral Israeli-Egyptian agreement.[117]

Once the cease-fire had been implemented, the State Department's pre-existing conceptions of the region undermined its success. Rogers and Sisco continued to view Israel as the major impediment to progress and their approach was dominated by the need to implement the cease-fire proposal before either party could change its mind. This took precedence over the need to make cease-fire arrangements clear and verifiable to ensure the trust of both parties and to avoid violations (and accusations of violations). Starting from the premise that the first outcome of negotiations would be an Israeli withdrawal from the Canal line, Soviet missile movements that would enable the Egyptians to cross the Canal under missile protection were considered immaterial. This analysis failed to acknowledge that the Israelis would not negotiate if the Egyptians could gain leverage by committing cease-fire violations or if the United States refused to underwrite Israeli positions with military and diplomatic assistance.[118]

On 7 August the cease-fire came into effect and provided for a complete military standstill to a depth of 50 km on both sides of the Canal. In his memoirs Nixon acknowledged that the agreement was "[a] major source of accomplishment for Rogers and Sisco."[119] The euphoria in the State Department was short-lived however, as Israeli reports of Egyptian cease-fire violations were received almost immediately.[120] Not wishing to undermine their achievement, the administration was in no mood to listen and "declined to say whom [they] considered to be the truce violators."[121] Acknowledgement of the violations would have undermined the premise of future negotiations and as Nixon reminded Rabin, the American people were in a "peace mood." [122] The need to reassure friends is a far more onerous task than deterring enemies,[123] but on this occasion reassuring Jerusalem was not a priority. Nixon defended the subordination of Israeli interests to those of his government on the basis that even a violated cease-fire "established the United States as an honest broker to both sides."[124]

Jerusalem's sense of vulnerability intensified when Washington's eventual protests to Cairo about the breaches were ignored, prompting Israel's withdrawal from the UN–sponsored talks led by Ambassador Jarring. Confronted with a growing crisis in Jordan, and in order to deter a pre-emptive strike along the Canal, on 1 September Nixon revoked his earlier order and sent additional military aid and supersonic aircraft to Israel.[125] Just hours later, the power of Jewish support in Congress was demonstrated when the Military Procurement Authorisation Bill was passed in the Senate. The Bill contained an amendment initiated by Senator Henry Jackson which gave the President almost unlimited authority to provide Israel with arms to counter Soviet weapons in Egypt.[126] Events were to demonstrate that the Phantoms were inadequate compensation because it was the Egyptian movement towards the Canal during the cease-fire that made the launching of the Yom Kippur war of October 1973 possible.[127]

Crisis in Jordan

One of the greatest casualties of the 1967 war was the cohesion and stability of the Jordanian monarchy. With Palestinians comprising more than half of Jordan's population, the country was vulnerable to external pressures, particularly those relating to the Arab–Israeli dispute. Seeking to challenge the King's already diminishing hold on power, the Palestinian Liberation Organisation (PLO) established its headquarters in Amman in 1969. Elevating its activities to the status of a state-within-a-state, through cross-border raids into Israeli territory and terrorist acts against the state apparatus, by late 1970 the organisation was successfully challenging the authority of the monarchy.

To Nixon's strategic mindset, unrest such as that taking place in Jordan was symptomatic of Soviet machinations and another facet of a "global Communist challenge."[128] The administration had little understanding of the complexities of nationalism and the quest for self-determination of a displaced people. Palestinian nationalism forced itself on to the administration's agenda as a by-product of increasing discontent in Jordan. The US-sponsored cease-fire sent out warning signals to Arab radicals that President Nasser, the guerrilla's most prestigious backer, was moving towards a political settlement with King Hussein that would undercut the position of the Palestinians.[129] Paradoxically, the Palestinian *fedayeen* appeared to place great faith in the ability of the Americans to negotiate an Israeli-Egyptian peace settlement because progress in the talks coincided with an escalation in terrorist activity. By 1 September, two attempts had been made on Hussein's life[130] and the King had gone so far as to enquire about Israeli intentions in the crisis. This implied that the King might agree to Israeli intervention should *fedayeen* activities endanger his throne.[131]

The new Middle East crisis erupted on to the international stage on 6 September 1970, when the Popular Front for the Liberation of Palestine (PFLP), a radical faction of the PLO led by George Habbash, hijacked four Western aeroplanes and forced them to land at an airstrip near Amman. The hijackers held more than 500 people hostage, many of them American citizens. The stated objective of the hijackings was to force Israel to release 450 *fedayeen* prisoners it held and to provoke a confrontation between Hussein and the *fedayeen* movement. With 10,000 Iraqi troops stationed in Jordan, and Syria just across the border, the PFLP believed the Arab governments would come to the aid of the Palestinians in a direct confrontation with the Jordanian monarchy.[132] The hijackings were to be the catalyst that ignited civil war and forced Hussein's hand in confronting the PLO.

Nixon interpreted the crisis as a clash between East and West, a confrontation between Arab terrorism and US–Israeli moderation. It provided an opportunity to finally defeat the guerrillas in Jordan and to demonstrate American strength to the Soviet Union, Iraq and Syria. From a purely military perspective, Secretary of Defence Melvin Laird and chairman of the Joint Chiefs of Staff Moorer opposed unilateral American action. Military commitments in Southeast Asia were so extensive that an additional and unilateral intervention in the Middle East would prove a logistical nightmare, while the absence of US bases in the Eastern Mediterranean made the deployment of ground forces difficult. Kissinger's preference was for using Israel as a proxy in the event of Syrian and Iraqi intervention.[133] He appreciated the logistical obstacles associated with US action but feared that Washington's position would be undermined and the region thrown into turmoil if King Hussein were overthrown. Ironically, the ultimate decision on action was not the President's to take. When Nixon directly ordered the Secretary of Defence to bomb guerrilla hideouts in Jordan, Laird cited bad weather as the reason for his failure to carry out the President's order. When Laird was subsequently asked to explain his inaction, he stated that "[t]he Secretary of Defence can always find a reason not to do something. There's always bad weather."[134]

In the longer term, the preferences of Nixon and Kissinger were destined to dominate purely because of the way in which the decision-making process was structured, with power concentrated in the White House. The response to the

Jordanian crisis is of particular significance because it signalled a turning point in the administration's approach to the Arab–Israeli conflict. On 9 September, Kissinger convened the Washington Special Actions Group (WSAG) which met daily to coordinate America's response to the crisis.[135] Kissinger was the Group's chairman and members included the Deputy Secretary of Defence, the Under Secretary of State, head of the CIA and the chairman of the Joint Chiefs. The formation of WSAG transferred, for the first time, decision-making power from the State Department to the NSC, where it remained.

Given the prevalence of territorial infringements in the Middle East, the belief in state sovereignty and territorial independence enshrined in the Treaty of Westphalia of 1648 does not appear to have taken hold in this region. In evaluating the alternative courses of action available to ward off the challenge to his leadership, Hussein was concerned that Syrian and Iraqi forces would breach the territorial integrity of his state if he moved against the *fedayeen*. Unbeknown to the King, his determination to secure a guarantee of assistance against external aggression was to give impetus to the consolidation of a strategic alliance between the United States and Israel, to the eternal detriment of the Arabs.

The response by Nixon and Kissinger to the crisis was symptomatic of their penchant for subordinating regional events to the imperatives of superpower confrontation. The encroachment of Syria, as a Soviet-backed proxy, into Jordan, was considered a challenge that had to be met because it would determine whether the Soviet-backed radicals or the American-supported conservative states would dominate the region. Irrespective of the fact that Moscow had not instigated the crisis, Washington exerted considerable pressure on the Kremlin to rein in the radicals.[136] The *New York Times* reported a Presidential declaration which stated that "[T]he United States is prepared to intervene directly in the Jordanian war should Syria and Iraq enter the conflict and tip the military balance against government forces loyal to Hussein."[137] Kissinger used this threat of American intervention as a lever to deter Soviet and Arab radicals from seeking Hussein's overthrow.

Tension mounted as the hostage crisis continued. Three of the hijacked planes were blown up and the European governments brokered a deal by which they freed seven Arab prisoners in exchange for the release of three hundred hostages. Finally, on 17 September, reassured by the US military build-up in the Mediterranean, Hussein ordered his army to move against the *fedayeen*. In response to the King's actions, Syrian tanks rolled into Jordan.

Israel as a Strategic Asset

A US response was clearly required to this dramatic new development, but following the incursion into Cambodia, the domestic climate was not propitious to American involvement in another regional war. Laird continued to deny the need for US intervention, while Nixon was preparing for precisely that contingency. The situation intensified when Hussein requested assistance against the invading Syrian forces. In response to the King's request, Kissinger concluded that "[A] quick review of the pros and cons of American military intervention strengthened our conviction that our forces were best employed in holding the ring against Soviet interference with Israeli operations."[138] The invocation of the Nixon Doctrine, whereby the US would provide military and economic assistance to local states,[139] in this case Israel, to enable them to defend regional security on America's behalf, was coming closer to reality.[140] Israel was the ideal proxy, particularly amongst conservative currents and military officials who admired the nation's military prowess and characteristics of self-reliance, democracy and anti-communism.

On 18 September, the Israeli option was finally put to Rabin and Meir, who were in Washington on an official visit.[141] In confronting the crisis, the perceived interests of the US and Israel converged and, based on its performance in June 1967 and its espousal of American values, Washington believed it could rely on Jerusalem in an extremity. The perception of mutual interest was accentuated by the fact that, for the first time, America actually needed Israel to defend its regional position.

By late on 20 September, the administration was united in supporting Israeli air strikes if necessary, but this unity was soon undermined when Rabin reported that the deployment of Israeli ground forces might also be required.[142] Rogers and Laird opposed this because of the potential repercussions an Israeli violation of the territorial integrity of an Arab state could engender. This was countered by Moorer, who argued that insufficient US forces were available to undertake a viable operation in the Middle East. The inescapable conclusion was finally reached that if ground action were required Israel would have to act.

The administration does not appear to have seriously contemplated the fact that an Israeli incursion into Jordan could have resulted in Israeli control of even greater tracts of Arab land. On the contrary, Kissinger worked determinedly to persuade Nixon of the efficacy of Israeli intervention if the crisis intensified.[143] He differed from his predecessors, Dulles and Kennan, in recognising that that US was no longer powerful enough to always act alone. He worked with Rabin to formulate a strategy for the despatch of 200 Israeli tanks into Jordan, in conjunction with air strikes. Rabin guaranteed that Israeli forces would be withdrawn from Jordan on completion of the military operation, but Kissinger remained unconcerned,[144] convinced that the massing of Israeli troops on the Golan Heights would result in a diplomatic solution precluding the need for direct Israeli intervention.[145]

As it became increasingly obvious that Israeli action was the administration's most viable military option, Nixon gave his approval to the plan and a

Presidential pledge to intervene in Israel's defence if the Soviet Union were to become militarily involved. On 22 September, reassured by the promise of Israeli and American support, Hussein unleashed air attacks against the undefended Syrian tanks,[146] forcing a gradual Syrian withdrawal from Jordanian territory. By 23 September it was apparent that the crisis had abated with a victory for Washington.[147] A decisive show of American force had maintained Hussein in power, weakened the *fedayeen* and pre-empted direct Soviet intervention. Judged through the prism of global concerns the outcome of the crisis was a complete success for the United States and its allies.

US–Israeli co-operation during the crisis created new precedents in the relationship and, set against the psychological backdrop of the Nixon Doctrine, Israel acquired for a time the coveted status of strategic asset. The speed and success of the hastily negotiated agreements between Kissinger and Rabin testified to the deep understanding and personal association between the two men and the strategic relationship between the two governments.[148] Jerusalem had shown itself capable of protecting American interests by deterring a full Syrian assault on Amman. Its argument that only a strong Israel could neutralise Soviet influence in the region thus became part of official White House doctrine.

Kissinger had been instrumental in defining the administration's response to the crisis and his success appeared to make the President more sympathetic to his perspective – and more willing to make him the pre-eminent decision-maker on the Middle East.[149] Meanwhile, the emergence of a special relationship between Kissinger and Rabin undercut the position of the State Department. From September 1970 onwards, Kissinger interceded with Rogers on Rabin's behalf, alleviating pressure on Jerusalem to make unilateral concessions during negotiations for the reopening of the Suez Canal.[150]

Standstill Diplomacy

The death of Nasser on 7 September 1970 and Anwar al-Sadat's assumption of the Egyptian presidency created an opportunity for a new, deeper understanding between Washington and Cairo.[151] Sadat demonstrated his willingness to make peace with Israel by accepting all UN Ambassador Gunnar Jarring's points for a settlement.[152] Sadat's quid pro quo for the agreement was the return of Egyptian land and with it the country's honour. However, Meir was adamant "that it is unreal and utopian to think that . . . [Israeli troop] 'withdrawal' will pave the way to peace."[153] Under these conditions of stalemate, and with the State Department deprived of its ability to influence Jerusalem, the Jarring mission, and with it the United States commitment to a comprehensive settlement, came to an inglorious end.

The spotlight for Mideast diplomacy now fell on Henry Kissinger, the newly-appointed Secretary of State. Kissinger adopted a policy of standstill diplomacy that consisted of little more than open support for Israel and effectively foreclosed Egyptian diplomatic opportunities for redressing the territorial balance. In an election year the administration wanted to avoid any bold policy moves that might prove unpopular; as the Secretary of State explained: "What finally got me involved in the execution of Middle East diplomacy was that Nixon did not believe he could risk recurrent crisis in the Middle East in an election year. He therefore asked me to step in, if only to keep things quiet."[154] Translating his global perspective on to Mideast politics and obliterating regional dynamics, Kissinger's preference was "to produce a stalemate until Moscow urged compromise or, even better, until some moderate Arab regime decided the route to progress was through Washington."[155]

It was perhaps ironic that Sadat's acknowledgement that Washington held the key to progress and his genuine interest in reaching a peaceful agreement was ignored. Elliot Richardson, the US ambassador to Cairo, had conveyed to Nixon and Kissinger Sadat's intention to form an entirely new, friendly and co-operative relationship with Washington. He later recalled that he had left the meeting with the impression that what he had said had not been heard.[156] On 18 July 1972, Sadat reversed seventeen years of Egyptian policy and expelled 21,000 Soviet advisors without seeking reciprocity from the United States.[157] This spectacular gesture was a domestic success, secured Moscow's undivided attention and misled the Americans.[158] Israel reacted with slightly more caution and Meir emphasised that the Soviet strategic hold continued.[159] With attention diverted by the Watergate break-in and the forthcoming Presidential election campaign, Washington acknowledged Sadat's move as little more than a bonus for the US. Although perturbed that the Egyptian President had taken such a bold unilateral decision without attempting to extract a price, American officials led him to believe that Washington would respond after the election.[160] In the interim, the administration virtually ignored Sadat's gestures and continued to do little more than enhance Israel's military superiority.[161]

With his landslide re-election in November 1972 and the nominal peace in Vietnam in January 1973, Nixon turned his attention to the Middle East, [162] setting out his position in a memo to his Secretary of State:

> You know that my position of standing firmly with Israel has been based on broader issues than just Israel's survival. Those issues now strongly argue for movement towards a settlement. We are now Israel's *only* major friend in the world. I have yet to see one iota of give on their part – conceding that Jordan and Egypt have not given enough on their side. This is the time to get moving – and they must be told that firmly . . . *[T]he time has come to quit pandering to Israel's intransigent position. Our actions over the past months have led them to think we will stand by them regardless of how unreasonable they are.*[163]

In an effort to move negotiations forward, a secret meeting was convened between Kissinger and the Egyptian National Security Adviser, Hafez Ismail, in New York in February 1973. Ismail reiterated the familiar Egyptian demands that Israel withdraw from all conquered territory in exchange for an end to belligerency; Kissinger continued to claim that the United States could not 'impose' an agreement on Israel. He did, however, hint that there might be ways of bringing pressure to bear which Israel could not ignore, and which his government might be prepared to consider if a "moral basis" for their use existed and could be shown to exist to the American people.[164]

Though Kissinger found little reason for optimism in his discussions with Ismail, this did not deter him from using the meeting as a device for increasing pressure on Meir during her visit to Washington three days later. However, the administration's leverage over Israel was undermined by a deeper reality of the relationship. As the objective of US strategy was to maintain the regional balance of forces and to militarily strengthen Israel to increase its confidence in peace negotiations, Jerusalem could be relatively confident that its arms request would be met irrespective of the country's intransigence on other matters. Nor did it help relations between Washington and Cairo that just as Ismail reached Egypt, the *Washington Post* prematurely leaked news of a new arms agreement between Washington and Jerusalem. In an endeavour to alleviate embarrassment and confusion concerning Washington's intentions, Kissinger moved swiftly to try to persuade Sadat that the article was based on false assumptions. However, the hollowness of such assurances was demonstrated when, a few weeks later, the White House did indeed announce a new arms package for Israel. As a result, the Egyptians became unresponsive to further initiatives and for a time American diplomacy appeared to be stalled.[165]

Kissinger's inability to deviate from his notion of Israel as a friend and Egypt as a puppet of the Soviets prevented him from taking advantage of the opportunity Sadat offered for peace during the period 1971–3. He also disregarded the potential implications of Sadat informing the Saudi government, who had never participated in diplomacy with Israel, of his secret meeting with Ismail.[166] The President himself admitted that "the interests of the Israelis were uppermost" in Kissinger's calculations.[167] He was ultimately successful in his strategy to frustrate Arab attempts to regain their land either diplomatically and militarily to encourage them to break with their Soviet patron and turn to the US for help, but failed in his role as a peace negotiator by leaving Sadat with little option but to resort to war to break the US imposed deadlock. By 1971 the Egyptian President had realised that the Soviets were impotent and were unable to deliver either American or Israeli flexibility.[168] However, Kissinger's disregard of Sadat's initiatives, his increasingly pro-Israeli policy and, following Rogers' resignation, the removal of the State Department as an alternative channel of communication, created a situation of stalemate that substituted for American policy.[169] The Egyptian President concluded that "the US regrettably could do nothing . . . as long as we were the defeated party and Israel maintained her strategic superiority."[170] On 6 October 1973, Sadat resorted to his ultimate political strategy[171] when Egypt and Syria went to war with Israel.

The October War

Washington was caught off guard when war came to the Middle East on 6 October 1973[172] because Jerusalem's expertise in conditioning the administration's mindset culminated in policy being founded on three conceptual misapprehensions. Firstly, it assumed that the military balance of power in the region was the determining factor in war and peace calculations, and that a rationally planned Arab war was implausible in light of Israel's qualitative military superiority. Given Israel's demonstration of strength in 1967 and 1970, the White House was willing to take Prime Minister Meir's claim that "we [Israel] never had it so good" and her insistence that the stalemate was safe because the Arabs had no military option[173] as its starting point. Israeli intelligence had reported that the Arabs would not attack unless the Israeli airforce had been neutralised. Israel did not perceive such neutralisation as a likely scenario. The arrival in Egypt of Soviet SAMs in the canal zone, however, effectively cancelled Israeli air superiority for a time and provided the necessary cover for the initial Arab attack.[174]

Secondly, the US presumed that war was a viable option for the Arabs only if a diplomatic settlement was unobtainable;[175] with Kissinger still in the midst of talks with Cairo and Jerusalem, a settlement was still within the Arab's grasp. US policy-makers were operating on the assumption that Western logic could be applied to the Arab mindset. But as Kissinger later noted in his memoirs, "[O]ur definition of rationality did not take seriously the notion of starting an unwinnable war to restore self-respect."[176] In early autumn the redeployment of Syrian missiles from the Jordanian border to the Golan Heights and the massing of Egyptian troops along the Suez Canal were dismissed as annual manoeuvres.[177] Even the evacuation of Soviet civilians from Egypt and Syria was interpreted as a rift in Arab-Soviet relations, not as a sign of impending war.[178] Thirdly, Washington posited that progress with détente meant that Moscow would notify the US of impending conflicts in the region, once again failing to comprehend the rapidly changing dynamics in the international situation.

When, at 0600 hours on 6 October 1973, Sisco brought Kissinger news that another Middle Eastern war was imminent, the Secretary of State mistakenly thought the Arabs were mobilising to pre-empt an Israeli attack,[179] and wasted valuable time reassuring Soviet and Arab leaders that Israel was not about to strike and urging Moscow to use its influence to restrain its clients.[180] When the

Arabs finally launched their attack, Egyptian troops crossed the Suez Canal in less than an hour and Syrian troops advanced on the Golan Heights.[181]

The administration focused on Moscow's involvement with the Arab states and the international implications of the crisis. Nixon and Kissinger feared that if the Arabs suffered a crushing defeat, the Soviets would enter the fighting.[182] In an effort to avoid direct superpower confrontation, the Secretary of State sought a joint US–Soviet effort in the UN to establish a cease-fire based on the status quo ante.[183] At the same time, he was anxious to prevent the diplomatic debate from reaching the UN General Assembly, where an automatic pro-Arab majority would be available to endorse the Arab's position.[184] For his part, Nixon was convinced that the US should not use its "influence to bring about a cease-fire that would leave the parties in such imbalance that negotiations for a permanent settlement would never begin." He believed that "only a battlefield stalemate would provide the foundations on which fruitful negotiations might begin."[185]

This war was a moment of truth for US credibility in the Middle East. While Israel need not achieve a decisive victory as in 1967, Nixon was determined to prevent the defeat of Washington's most prominent ally by Soviet arms. The United States had to demonstrate to the world that it would stand firmly by its allies and that Nixon personally would "not let Israel go down the tubes."[186] However, with the atmosphere of détente taking precedent,[187] it was also a time to practice restraint and avoid antagonising the Arabs. Nixon took the view that Israel should be supported so that it considered Washington a reliable partner in post-war diplomacy, but "in such a way that would not force an irreparable break with the Egyptians, Syrians and the other Arab nations."[188] The Arabs had to think that the administration was not assisting Israel, while the pro-Israel lobby had to be convinced of the reverse.

Despite their aggressive rhetoric, the Israelis claimed to be in desperate need of arms supplies. From the first weekend of the war Nixon had authorised a modest re-supply operation and had given the Israelis permission to collect US weapons supplies, either in their own aircraft if the markings were obliterated, or in chartered aircraft.[189] His objective was to preserve the image of US detachment,[190] while ensuring Israel received the equipment it required. Members of the State Department were concerned that a major US re-supply effort would be seen as prejudicial and could compromise effective mediation after the war. Deputy Assistant Secretary of Defence James H. Noyes argued that "they [Israel] don't really need the equipment."[191] No one present disputed his judgement. Defence Secretary James Schlesinger suggested delaying the operation because "shipping any stuff into Israel blows any image that we have of an honest broker."[192] Kissinger was the only advocate of immediate and public action, but his motivations appeared to stem from foreign policy calculations rather than military considerations. In the absence of Soviet co-operation in the UN to bring a rapid end to the war, he favoured providing Israel with large-scale aid. If the Israelis defeated the Arabs using US weaponry they would be obligated to Washington and would have an incentive to heed the administration's views on post-war diplomacy.[193] If Washington could prove that in an extremity Israel would not stand alone, Jerusalem could perhaps be persuaded to moderate its position. In contrast, if the Arabs prevailed, there would be no reward for American restraint. Kissinger reasoned that because the outcome of hostilities would determine the course of post-war diplomacy, not whether the US supplied arms, "[T]he time to show understanding to the Arab position [was] after the war."[194]

The administration based its estimate of the adequacy of Israeli resources on the consumption rate of munitions during the 1967 war. However, circumstances were very different in 1973 and with Israel on the defensive, the consumption rate was much higher.[195] On 7 October Meir requested that the US postpone a UN Security Council cease-fire resolution until 10 or 11 October, by which time Israel anticipated it would be on the offensive on all fronts.[196] By 8 October, as Nixon recalls in his memoirs, "it was clear that the Israelis had been overconfident about their ability to win a quick victory."[197] In the Golan Heights the Syrian air-defence system was taking a high toll of Israeli Skyhawks and Phantoms. In the Sinai, over half of all Israeli tanks had been destroyed[198] and Moshe Dayan, commander of the Israeli armed forces, had offered to resign.[199] The Israeli government was concerned that it had insufficient resources to fight the war, but its request for increased supplies created political difficulties for the US administration.[200] There were even suspicions that Israel had readied its nuclear arsenal, if only as an implicit threat, to reinforce arms requests.[201] As a nuclear power in an unstable environment there was always the potential that Washington could become involved in a nuclear exchange with the Soviets.[202] William Quandt recalled that: "Without being told in so many words, we knew that a desperate Israel might activate its nuclear option. This situation, by itself, created a kind of blackmail potential . . . But no one had to say it, and I don't think anyone did."[203]

By 12 October, the Israelis had launched a major counter-offensive into the Golan Heights and were pushing beyond the initial cease-fire line. At this point, with the Israel Defense Forces (IDF) reversing the Arab's fortunes, US and Israeli objectives began to diverge. From the American perspective, the circumstances had been created for the implementation of a cease-fire agreement before the Soviets further supplied the Arabs and the Israelis recouped their losses. In contrast, the Israelis were determined to redress the military balance but were dependent on American arms supplies to do so. This dependency forced Meir and her top military advisers to accept the American-sponsored cease-fire out of concern for both the costs of the continued fighting and the delay in the US re-supply mission.[204] Kissinger's strategy appeared to be coming to fruition. The war could be concluded without a direct American airlift to Israel, American oil interests in the Persian Gulf would remain secure and the basis for future diplomacy would be established. However, Sadat's veto of the initiative ensured that the cease-fire never came into effect.[205]

Re-arming Israel

The decision to launch a massive resupply operation came in response to political realities: the failure of the UN cease-fire-in-place initiative was evident and the extent of the Soviet airlift to Egypt and Syria threatened the regional balance of power.[206] It was the logistical aspect of implementing the President's decision that was problematic. Since 15 October, El Al planes, their markings concealed, had been collecting supplies from US depots in Virginia, but the quantities were insufficient to replace Israeli losses. On 19 October, when Schlesinger reported that Israel was unable to charter planes because no insurance company was willing to issue policies for chartered planes flying to a war zone,[207] it was decided that US C-5s would be used to transport equipment to Israel. The proviso from the President was that the operation took place under the cover of darkness. It was at this juncture that Nixon's attempts to maintain the image of America as an "honest broker" unravelled. For refuelling purposes the C-5 aircraft were flown to Israel via the Portuguese air force base in the Azores. However, adverse weather conditions delayed the departure of the planes, with many arriving in Israel at dawn and not in the dead of night. Visual proof of the US re-supply operation delighted the Israeli public and the media, but the publicity surrounding the airlift unleashed the wrath of the Gulf Arab states.[208]

The reasons for the delay in the resupply are multifaceted; certainly, the decision-making system in the Pentagon was far more complex than Kissinger was willing to publicly acknowledge.[209] Schlesinger, William Clements and the Pentagon were also aware that if US stocks were depleted, they were unlikely to be replenished until 1981.[210] Walter Isaacson, Kissinger's biographer, suggests that a key culprit in the delay may have been Clements, "a Texas oilman with pro-Arab sympathies."[211] Isaacson also portrays Schlesinger as leaning towards Clements' perspective.[212] Many Jewish community activists remained convinced that Schlesinger's feelings towards Israel were influenced by his ambivalent relationship towards Judaism.[213] Of Jewish birth, he was baptised an Episcopalian as a young man. Historically, the act of conversion has been regarded among Jews as a sign of disloyalty, particularly when the conversion is to Christianity. Whether this is an accurate portrait of the psychological state of James Schlesinger during the second week of October 1973 is unclear and claims that he played an instrumental role in delaying the airlift cannot be fully resolved.[214] However, in a press conference on 26 October he stated: "The

United States delayed, deliberately delayed, the start of its resupply operation, hoping that a cease-fire would be implemented quickly."[215]

In contrast, Air Force Chief of Staff George Brown and his intelligence head, George Keegan, worked, on their own authority, to prepare for a military airlift in case the President should order it. Thomas Moorer, chairman of the Joint Chiefs, embodied these conflicting attitudes: while he favoured a military airlift to re-supply Israel, he admitted to finding the Israelis "difficult" and hoped that they would not receive all the hardware they requested. In contrast John Lehman, the Secretary of the US Navy, claims that Washington responded immediately to Jerusalem's request for arms, much as it did for Britain during the Falklands War of 1982.[216] According to his account, everyone helped to expedite arms shipments and Israel was treated as an ally. Delays were not attributable to the Pentagon dragging its feet but to normal bureaucratic friction because a pipeline had to be created for sending arms to Israel that extended through the embassy, the NSC and the Pentagon.

While the precise reasons for the time taken in expediting the operation remain unclear, Kissinger was sufficiently powerful to shield himself from public criticism. In his memoirs, Kissinger admits to deceiving the Israeli ambassador on this and other issues. "When I had bad news for [Simcha] Dinitz, I was not above ascribing it to bureaucratic stalemates or unfortunate decisions by superiors."[217] Most accounts conclude that the Pentagon did not deliberately delay shipments and that the real failure was to recognise the impracticality of the charter scheme from the start.[218] The eventual timing of the airlift did offer one distinct advantage. It could be construed as a response to the airlift undertaken by Moscow to the Arab states and not as a major US provocation.[219]

The Financial Relationship Begins

While geo-strategic factors undoubtedly played a role in determining the administration's response to the October war, its actions also reflected the fundamental shift that had occurred in public perceptions of Israel. In 1957, when Eisenhower had forced an Israeli withdrawal from Arab territory, his actions had reflected the public mood as sympathy for Israel dramatically declined following an overt display of aggression. All vestiges of this were erased following Israel's victory in the Six Day War and American aid to Israel had reached unprecedented levels rising from tens of millions of dollars to $300 million annually. By October 1973, when the administration provided Israel with military assistance, far exceeding that of the past four years combined, the decision was supported by American public opinion.[220] It was evident that the airlift would be expensive and that a way of financing it had to be found.

Kissinger argued that the Arab reaction to an aid package would be the same, irrespective of its size, and that as funding was also required for Cambodia, the request to Congress should be for an unprecedented amount. In a crisis atmosphere it was anticipated that Congress would be compliant and would not hesitate to pass an aid package of which Israel was the main beneficiary.

Against this backdrop of a quiescent political and public environment, Kissinger took the decision at a WSAG meeting to increase the aid level to unprecedented proportions.[221] "For reasons that had a lot to do with US-Soviet relations, Kissinger . . . [argued] that we should come up with a number that was huge, to demonstrate that America was going to make a massive commitment of resources to ensure Israeli security after the war,"[222] recalls William Quandt. As Washington would need political credit with Israel to ease unpopular disengagement negotiations, financial aid was considered an expedient device for demonstrating its commitment in advance. Quandt further claims that emotional considerations also played their part as "[i]n the end he [Kissinger] sort of picked the number [$2.2 billion] out of the air. I don't think anyone in the room had any doubt that there was a real, emotional concern for Israel."[223]

Nixon submitted the request for a massive boost in aid, to which there was no public opposition, to a receptive Congress on 19 October 1973. Once approved, "it had the effect of casting in stone the special US–Israel relationship."[224] The sentimental or moral commitment towards Israel was elevated to a top priority of US foreign policy through the sheer power of the marketplace. By transforming America into Israel's largest investor, Kissinger guaranteed that Washington would stand by Jerusalem, if only to protect its investment.[225] Prior to October 1973, Washington had continually restated its commitment to Israel's security but the commitment consisted of little more than words. When words needed to be backed up by action, as they did during the Suez Crisis in 1956, in May 1967 and the first week of October 1973, "American policy-makers responded by arguing, agonising, [and] weighing their moral commitment to Israel against" a range of diplomatic and strategic objectives. It can be argued that congressional approval of an annual $2.2 billion commitment to Israel effectively ended this debate. As Arthur Goldberg claims, "America was now signalling to the world that it stood behind Israel's survival and security with the same faith that it put behind the dollar itself."[226]

It is perhaps ironic, given Nixon's tense relationship with American Jews as an entity, that he was responsible for promoting the pro-Israel lobby to the status of a major player in Washington politics and securing congressional approval of the $2.2 billion aid bill. Only in Washington could such an aid package become entitlement and as a result, Israel and its affairs became big business and the pro-Israel lobby became established, important players.

Israel, the Holocaust and the Palestinians

That the President could conceivably request that Congress would approve and the public accept, such an enormous and unprecedented aid appropriation, gives some indication of the dramatic evolution that occurred in American perceptions of Israel between June 1967 and October 1973. By the outbreak of the Yom Kippur War, Israel had become firmly established as a heroic and courageous US ally that had joined Western forces in the battle against Communism.

Meanwhile, Egyptian gains on the battlefield had increased the Arab's negotiating power. After all, the 1947 UN partition plan had given equal weight to Jewish and Palestinian claims to the land and had therefore voted to divide it. After the 1967 war and increasingly after 1973, many outside observers came to understand the conflict in terms of the competing claims of two peoples for a homeland and the Palestinian's quest for a state. But in mobilising grassroots support for Israel, many Jewish organisations marginalised the Palestinian claim and attributed Israel's diplomatic difficulties in retaining control of the land, to the world having forgotten about the Holocaust. On occasions references to the Holocaust were evoked to make criticism of Israel illegitimate and as a device for diverting attention away from the complexities of the issue.

Numerous discourses surrounding the Holocaust and its relationship to Israel emerged, with different authors adopting different approaches to suit varying audiences and needs. The objective was to situate the Middle East imbroglio in a Holocaust framework that submerged the complexities and ambiguities of the situation. The Holocaust bestowed a moral clarity that Peter Novick argued, "came to be for the Israeli cause, what Israel was said to be for the United States – a strategic asset." [227]

Beyond a diffuse relationship between the Holocaust and Israel's objectives, specific themes were developed. One prevalent theme was the establishment in popular culture of a connection between Arabs, and more particularly the Palestinians, with Nazism. In Leon Uris's *Exodus*, Palestinian terrorism is masterminded with an escaped Nazi in the background and in numerous thrillers, most notably Frederick Forsyth's seminal work *The Odessa File*, devious Nazis collaborate with Arabs to bring about the destruction of Israel.[228] Popular cultural equations of Nazism and the Palestinian nationalist movement were also advanced in more serious forums and by 1978 the then head of Aipac, I. L. Kenen, felt able to credibly state that "The Arabs cannot pretend that they played no role in the Holocaust."[229]

Assertions of Palestinians complicity in the Holocaust were to a certain extent a pre-emptive response to the Palestinian complaint that if a Jewish homeland was recompense for the Holocaust, it was unjust that Muslims should pay the price for the actions of European Christians. The historical validation for claims of Palestinian complicity in the wholesale murder of European Jewry is predominantly attributable to the Mufti of Jerusalem, a pre-Second World War Palestinian nationalist leader who fled to Germany during the war to escape incarceration by the British. That he resided in Nazi Germany is beyond doubt but allegations that he played a significant part in the perpetration of the Holocaust have never been validated. Despite this, set against the backdrop of the Middle East conflict, claims of the Mufti's involvement were considered politically expedient to the extent that in the four-volume *Encyclopaedia of the Holocaust* the reference to him is longer than the articles on Goebbels, Goring and Eichmann.

In the tense atmosphere of 1973, it was not only the Arabs who were condemned for complicity through inaction in the Holocaust. Coming amidst condemnation that the US administration had not responded swiftly enough to Israel's requests for help, charges of wartime silence and abandonment assumed a contemporary relevance. Arthur Morse's *While Six Million Died* (1968), a searing indictment of America's wartime policy, gained in relevance with the October 1973 war as it was perceived by some American Jews to embody their contemporary fears that the US would abandon Israel.[230]

Oil Politics

To maximise the impact of the Egyptian attack on Israel, and to keep American support for Israel at a bearable level, Sadat needed to exert some form of pressure on Washington through a third nation. He had focused the military training of his forces on crossing the Canal quickly and efficiently in the first phase of the attack, but knew that the Israeli army and air force, resupplied by the US, would defeat Egyptian forces once on Israeli soil. In an effort to moderate Washington's response to the war, Sadat convinced King Faisal of Saudi Arabia to implement an oil embargo designed to threaten and damage Western oil-consuming nations and cause them to press the US and Israel for a compromise outcome.[231]

Between the 1967 and 1973 wars, demand for oil had increased and pressure was brought to bear on prices. As a consequence, bargaining power shifted from the American oil companies in favour of the producing nations, thus giving Sadat's strategy a realistic chance of success. The tightening of the market, in conjunction with a strong feeling amongst the Arab oil producers that their relationship with the Western oil companies was ripe for change, set the scene for a confrontation that he was able to exploit. By 1973, OPEC felt sufficiently strengthened to consider using the termination of oil supplies as a form of leverage against the West. On 13 October, six days before King Faisal announced an oil embargo against the US, Nixon received a letter from the chairman of Aramco's four constituent companies, Mobil, Exxon, Chevron and Texaco, warning of the King's restlessness with the situation between Israel and the Arabs.[232] The letter stated that:

> We are convinced of the seriousness of the Saudis and Kuwaitis and that other actions of the US government at this time in terms of increased military aid to Israel will have a critical and adverse effect on our relations with the moderate Arab producing countries . . . Much more than our commercial interest in the area is now at hazard. The whole position of the United States in the Middle East is on the way to being seriously impaired, with Japanese, European and perhaps Russian interests largely supplanting United States presence in the area, to the detriment of both our economy and our security.[233]

Based on prior experience that Arab rhetoric would not be accompanied by action,[234] Nixon did not heed the warnings of the oil executives.[235]

On 16 October the *New York Times* reported that the White House had received a letter from King Faisal requesting that the US terminate arms shipments to Israel and call upon it to withdraw to pre-1967 borders, otherwise US–Saudi relations would become "lukewarm."[236] On 17 October, when a positive response was not forthcoming, OPEC announced that it would cut "oil production by ten percent and then 5 percent a month thereafter,"[237] until Israel withdrew from the captured territory. The following day, when Kissinger met with Arab representatives, the impending aid appropriation was not mentioned, which may have lulled the administration into a false sense of security regarding the Arab response. On 19 October, following Nixon's official request for an appropriation of $2.2 billion to cover the cost of the airlift, the Arabs gave their response. King Faisal announced an embargo on oil shipments to the US, a policy that was soon replicated by the other producers.[238] But despite the economic implications, Nixon maintained his commitment to Israel claiming that, "[E]ven so, I felt that we could do no less for Israel at such a critical time."[239]

In reality, the administration had little option but to deal with the implications of the embargo. By abandoning the Rogers Plan and any semblance of "even handedness," and failing to develop an alternative policy, the administration had no choice but to place support for Israel above domestic oil interests.[240] The deepening energy crisis and the concerns of the oil companies did not have as profound an impact on policy as Sadat would have wished, because attention was focused not on potential price increases or production cuts, but on relations with Moscow and the survival of Israel. However, oil politics was a consideration in Washington's calculations and in a press conference on 26 October 1973, Nixon acknowledged that without a settlement, Europe and Japan would have frozen to death that winter and emphasised the "need to avoid another Mideast crisis so the flow of oil continues."[241]

Nuclear Alert and the Cease-Fire Agreement

Fortified with American weapons, the Israelis launched a successful counter-offensive against the Egyptians across the Suez Canal. When Cairo and Moscow became aware of the extent of the destruction of Egyptian forces on 18 October, Brezhnev sent a message to Nixon to convene urgent consultations.[242] Kissinger departed for Moscow and en route received a message from Nixon advising him that Brezhnev had been notified that he was authorised to negotiate a cease-fire without further consultations with Washington. Nixon instructed Kissinger that the US and Soviet Union "must step in, determine [the] proper course of action to a just settlement, and then bring the necessary pressure to bear on our respective friends."[243] Kissinger was outraged that Nixon had deprived him of the ability to stall, to buy the Israelis more time and to find a way of excluding the Soviets from the negotiations. Yet a telephone conversation with Sisco restored Kissinger's confidence in his own authority. Nixon was so preoccupied with Watergate and the task of self-preservation that he did not have time to intervene in the Middle East, thus enabling Kissinger to ignore his instructions.[244]

With their client's position in jeopardy, the Soviets were eager to reach a swift resolution. The final cease-fire, based on Resolution 242, was passed by the Security Council as Resolution 338 and provided the legal basis for ending the October war. Once the agreement was concluded, Nixon sent Meir a letter of regret that there had been insufficient time for consultation and described the provisions of the proposed agreement: it called for a cease-fire in place within twelve hours, implementation of Resolution 242 "in all its parts" and negotiations between the parties. This was of particular note because it was the first occasion the Soviets had agreed to direct negotiations between the Arabs and Israel without conditions or qualifications.[245] The lack of consultation and the presentation of a *fait accompli* offended Meir, but she had little option but to comply. In her memoirs she wrote: "In the final analysis, to put it bluntly, the fate of small countries always rests with the superpowers, and they always have their own interests to guard."[246]

Despite his apparent diplomatic success, Kissinger demonstrated uncharacteristic naïvety towards the realities on the ground. Given the entanglement of the Egyptian and Israeli armies, the temptation was too great for the Israelis to resist; within hours of his return to Washington, the encirclement of the Egyptian Third Army was complete. Kissinger was incensed because he had assured the Soviets that Israel would respect the cease-fire – now he was concerned that violations would lead to a lack of US credibility in the Arab world. Brezhnev, for the first time during the Nixon presidency, used the hotline to request Presidential intervention. Both Soviet and US credibility was at stake.

As Kissinger told the Israeli ambassador, "[T]here were limits beyond which we could not go, with all our friendship for Israel, and one of them was to make the leader of another superpower look like an idiot."[247]

The Security Council called for another cease-fire otherwise known as Resolution 339. When this was again breached by Israel,[248] the US was taken to the brink of direct confrontation with the Soviet Union. Brezhnev threatened unilateral action if the US found it "impossible to act jointly." As Congress, under the terms of the War Powers Act, had restricted the President's authority to use military force, Kissinger convened a meeting of senior aides to formulate the administration's response.[249] On 25 October, the decision was taken to move US forces to alert status on DefCon 3, the highest state of peacetime readiness. On a psychological level, the impact was immense. Washington had signalled its preparedness to go to war with the Soviet Union to preserve both Israel and its own position in the Middle East.

While observers claimed that the military alert was nothing more than a show of strength from an embattled President,[250] it was successfully employed to force Israeli co-operation. Moshe Dayan stated in his memoirs that Kissinger made clear to Dinitz that the administration would take the destruction of the Third Army as a personal blow to their prestige and threatened the Israelis with an American resupply operation to the Egyptian forces if all else failed.[251] As Jerusalem discovered, "the trouble with friends is not what they can do for you, but what they prevent you for doing for yourself."[252] By abandoning the Soviets, Sadat had given the US a "stake in him"[253] and therefore American commitments were expanded to include both Israel and Egypt. In requesting a $2.2 billion aid appropriation, Nixon's aim was to create a military stand-off that would lead to diplomatic compromise.[254] The resupply of the Third Army was part of that compromise. Jerusalem was presented with little alternative but to comply.

On 25 October the UN Security Council passed Resolution 340, calling for an immediate cease-fire, a return to the 22 October lines and the implementation of Resolution 338. On this occasion the cease-fire held and the Arab–Israeli war was finally brought to a close. Kissinger had become the leading force in America's Middle East diplomacy. At a news conference the morning after the alert, Kissinger presented his position: "The conditions that produced this war were clearly intolerable to the Arab nations, and . . . in a process of negotiations it will be necessary to make substantial concessions."[255] The following day he convinced the Israelis to permit the re-supply of the Third Army. Kissinger had succeeded in preventing a decisive Israeli victory and achieved the military stalemate for which he had worked throughout the war.

Step-by-Step Diplomacy

A parallel can be drawn between Kissinger's cease-fire talks with Moscow during the Yom Kippur War and Goldberg's during the Six Day War. Both parties put forward formulations to advance their client's interests, but the framework for negotiations was largely determined by the military configuration on the ground. This similarity ended in Moscow on 21 October when Kissinger accepted a cease-fire that theoretically prevented Israel from encircling the Third Army and apparently placed Egyptian interests above those of Israel. A diplomatic opportunity was created by leaving the warring factions in a battlefield stalemate that a total Israeli victory would have precluded. The White House had been in continuous contact with Sadat throughout the war and sought to facilitate his break with Moscow and move him towards the West. Sadat had gone to war to regain Egypt's dignity; achievement of that goal would enable him to disassociate his country from Nasser's radicalism. The infliction of another humiliation and Washington's continued disregard of his overtures of peace, however, would have forced him to return belatedly to Moscow's protection.

Kissinger once said that "if the world is in flux we have the capacity and hence the obligation to help shape it."[256] This was true of the Middle East in October 1973 and Kissinger seized the initiative. The word 'obligation' holds the key to understanding Kissinger's statecraft. His success in engineering the battleground stalemate between Israel and Egypt created a situation whereby he could deliver Cairo from the clutches of the Communists, which he believed he had a moral and strategic obligation to do. By aligning Egypt with the United States and turning away from the Soviet Union, Sadat had adhered to the criteria Nixon and Kissinger had set for working with an Arab state to reach a peace agreement with Israel. The spotlight now fell on Washington: the administration had to demonstrate that it would be as good as its word by delivering Israel to the negotiations. This meant that Kissinger had to pressure each side equally or at least be seen to do so,[257] although from Jerusalem's perspective, it appeared that their only friend had abandoned them. In March 1975, Kissinger took his strategy to the ultimate extreme by arranging for the Ford administration to announce "its reassessment" of US–Israeli relations as a device for increasing pressure on Jerusalem.

In the final analysis, Kissinger can be seen as Israel's greatest friend because he secured for them the peace they had so desperately sought. That the price was tangible Israeli concessions for intangible Egyptian commitments on paper was taken as a sign by many that Kissinger had betrayed his Jewish roots. Kissinger offered the contrary view in his memoirs when he wrote that "[T]he Geneva conference of 1973 opened the door to peace through which Egypt and

Israel walked."[258] Throughout the remainder of his tenure as Secretary of State he used a step-by-step diplomacy technique to broker a series of disengagements between the parties and to build the framework for a peace settlement. Although Brezhnev charged that Kissinger had disregarded the UN negotiating framework in favour of one of his own,[259] ultimately, this process culminated in Sadat's historic visit to Jerusalem in 1977 and the signing of the Camp David Accords in 1979. Kissinger's strategy in the Middle East succeeded "in relating our [US] commitments to our interests and our obligations to our purposes."[260] While motives and strategy have remained the subject of debate, Washington secured a peace agreement between Israel and Egypt that neutralised the only Arab country capable of threatening Israel's existence at that time.

Public Opinion, Israel and the War

The October war completed the transformation of the Arab–Israeli dispute from a regional diversion into a conflict central to American diplomatic and strategic concerns. Regional and superpower politics collided in the Middle East and negotiations were treated as central to global foreign policy.[261] The course of the war had a dramatic effect on the activities, arguments and positions of all the parties involved. The pro-Israeli camp was thrown onto the defensive because its cherished assumptions of Israeli strength had been compromised and Arab forces appeared to have gained the upper hand.

Nixon was in the enviable position of not having to seek re-election, but once Watergate challenged his political survival, domestic pressures exerted a greater influence on foreign policy. He could no longer afford to alienate the American Jewish community by being seen to pressure Israel, but conversely, the war had proved that an Arab oil embargo could undermine the American economy and to avert a repeat of this, Washington had to be cognisant of Arab feelings. This fear counterbalanced the pro-Israeli sentiment that had become prevalent in the preceding decade and even public opinion polls reflected a decline, albeit temporarily, in support for Israel.[262]

Even in the Pentagon, support for Israel declined in response to losses in the first days of the war. The credibility of officials who had warned that effective diplomacy provided the only means to avert another war was greatly enhanced. At a lecture in October 1974 at Duke University, George Brown, the chairman of the Joint Chiefs of Staff, said:

> Jewish influence in this country . . . is so strong you wouldn't believe [it]. We have the Israelis coming to us for equipment. We say we can't possibly get the Congress to support a programme like that. They say, "Don't worry about Congress. We'll take care of the Congress." Now this is somebody from another country, but they

can do it. They own, you know, the banks in this country, the newspapers . . . you just look at where the Jewish money is in this country.[263]

That the chairman of the Joints Chiefs could make such a statement indicates that the pro-Israel lobby had been weakened by the perception of increased Arab strength and their own loss of credibility. The fallibility of the central tenet of their argument had been revealed; Israeli strength had not deterred the Arab attack.[264]

Yet the notion of a diminution in Israeli influence was balanced by displays of Israeli strength. After all, it was the Arab states that had unleashed the devastating oil embargo on the US economy, while Israel had sustained casualties fighting Communist-backed forces that were the mutual enemy of Washington and Jerusalem. Israel continued to garner some support at the Pentagon amongst those officials who could foresee an advantage in aligning themselves with the demands of some Jewish leaders for increased defence expenditure to offset losses incurred during the war. In addition, Israel's experience in fighting against the latest Soviet armoury was an invaluable source of information for US military planners.[265]

Popular cultural representations of Israel remained positive. The triangulation of Israel, America the Holocaust was made explicit in the 1974 television film, *QB VII,* based on the novel by Leon Uris. The film followed the libel suit brought by the Polish-born physician Adam Kelno against Abraham Cady, a Jewish American writer, who made allegations that Kelno was involved in medical experiments at a fictional concentration camp. Cady's need to gather proof to acquit himself of libel charges allowed the film to present the Holocaust through the testimony of survivors and footage of Yad Va-Shem. *QB VII* ends with a trial scene in which the Holocaust is narrated at length and demonstrated the new-found strength of the Jewish people as justice is served.[266] Throughout the film Cady's attachment to Israel is designed to reflect the growing public attachment of American Jews to the country following the Six Day War. The pride he takes in Israel's military prowess is symbolised by an Israeli air force formation flying overhead, protecting the state from its hostile neighbours. One significant element of the film for post-1973 America was the way in which it counteracts images of Israeli weakness that emerged as a result of its initial losses in the war. The death of Cady's son, a paratrooper in the Israeli air force, in the Yom Kippur War was depicted as a heroic act that contributes to the strengthening of the vitality of the Jewish state. Despite the loss of his son, Cady continued to work in support of Israel, and in so doing, was able to bring new meaning to his life as an American Jew. The implicit message conveyed is that viewers should work harder in defence of the Jewish state in its hour of need.

The Holocaust and American Life

The Holocaust truly entered American life following the October 1973 war. Though Israel was ultimately victorious, this came after substantial Israeli casualties and considerable Egyptian gains. The victory was in large part attributable to the US airlift of new supplies during the war, thus undermining the illusions of Israeli invincibility and self-sufficiency. A related casualty was the distinction traditionally drawn by Zionists between the vulnerability of Jews in the Diaspora and the security Jews could find in their homeland. For some, the events of the Yom Kippur War appeared to demonstrate that there was nowhere less secure for Jews than Israel.[267]

The war also provoked considerable concern over Israel's increasing international isolation. Washington was Jerusalem's only real supporter and many American Jews feared that rising oil prices and the sought after détente with Moscow could threaten this support. There was also doubt amongst the American Jewish community that the American people, just emerging from the Vietnam nightmare, would respond positively to calls to defend another small state half way around the world. Leonard Fein, the editor of the Jewish magazine *Moment*, summed up the situation thus: "We cast about uncertainly for a way of making the case for Israel, . . . a way sufficiently compelling to persuade a post-Vietnam America to assume the burdens and risks of Israel's defence."[268] The memory of the Holocaust provided the solution.

Many Jewish organisations intensified their activities to counteract negative publicity resulting from the war. Arab gains in Washington did not adversely diminish Israel's long-term popularity with the American people or its strong support among American Jews. Coverage of Israel and the importance of the Jewish state as a safe haven intensified as the 'Holocaust memory' moved to centre stage. Norman Finkelstein argued that this transition occurred in response to Egypt's impressive military performance, which convinced the administration that a diplomatic settlement with Sadat, including the return of Egyptian lands seized in 1967, could no longer be avoided. The Holocaust 'industry' stepped up its remembrance of the atrocity, not because they feared a repeat of Hitler's Final Solution, but to increase Israel's negotiating leverage and moral claim to occupied Arab land.[269]

As Novick explained, "There were surprisingly few explicit references to the Holocaust in American Jewish mobilisation on behalf of Israel before the war."[270] It was only after Israel had recouped its initial losses and its survival was ensured that references to the Holocaust entered into mainstream discourse. These developments occurred within the framework of a robust US–Israeli alliance that remained fully intact[271] and it was precisely because US support for Israel was so strong that the pro-Jewish lobby felt able to demand greater demonstrations of support. American Jewish leaders did what they had always done: marched lockstep with American power.[272] Finkelstein argued that if Israel had truly been in danger of abandonment, American Jewish organisations would have reverted to their post-war posture of assimilation and conformity to ward off charges of dual loyalty and the risk of being ostracised from American society. The evoking of historic persecution was intended to deflect pressure for territorial concessions and to guarantee continued aid.

The creation of this new awareness of the Holocaust was evident across a broad spectrum of activities. Conferences were convened on the subject, notably one sponsored by the Institute of Contemporary Jewry of the Hebrew University, which brought together sixty scholars in New York City and, more importantly, was relayed to a wide audience through daily coverage in the *New York Times*.[273] Holocaust centres began to open across the US. The first of these were the Rabbi Irving Greenberg's National Jewish Conference Centre in New York and a Jewish Federation-sponsored centre in St. Louis. There was also an increase in academic discourse and courses offered on the subject at American universities matched by an increase in academic publications. One notable work was Lucy Dawidowicz's 1975 book *The War Against the Jews*, in which she argues that the destruction of European Jewry was Hitler's uppermost priority.[274]

Yet the upsurge of interest in the Holocaust did not arise solely in response to the 1973 war. It was also a product of the broader preoccupation with destruction, victimisation and survival that became pervasive in American life in the 1970s. By the mid-1970s, images of 'survivors' emerged everywhere in popular culture. The terminology for coping with daily routines, as much as actual life-and-death struggles, adopted the language of survival. 'Survival' guides began to appear in bookstores covering the whole spectrum of everyday life, from how to survive dieting and parenthood to getting a job.

Holocaust survivors are, to quote from Henry Greenspan,[275] "real survivors." Central to understanding the renewed interest in the survivors of the Final Solution is its role in the context of broader cultural trends; a vague readiness on the part society to talk about it fails to accurately delineate specific motivations for this renewed interest, although this is not to say that distance did not play an important role in Holocaust narrative. As survival became an accolade and a sought after virtue in American culture, the survivors of the Holocaust were afforded a new status in society. Wiesel embodied much of the moral prestige associated with 'surviving' and the fact that he survived, in contrast to Anne Frank, who did not, enabled this prestige to be assigned to a living person.[276]

Cultural change, combined with the determination and resourcefulness of American Jewish organisations, facilitated the swift and extensive memorialisation of the Holocaust. Within five years of the Yom Kippur War, the President of the United States, Jimmy Carter, announced the establishment of a

Presidential commission to recommend a national Holocaust memorial, a memorial that was to be more extensive than that dedicated to the American soldiers who fell in either Vietnam or the American civil war.

The Nixon–Kissinger Partnership: Final Assessment

Richard Nixon, perhaps ironically given his reputation as the President most at odds with American Jews since James Buchanan, presided over the era in which the US-Israeli special relationship was given virtually 'institutional' status. By initiating the epoch-making chain of events that gave rise to Israel's receipt of $2.2 billion in annual aid, Nixon aligned Washington with Jerusalem as firmly as any treaty commitment could have. In Washington, aid receipts elevated Israel to a new status and gave it and its supporters unprecedented power to influence the governmental decisions of a world superpower. In this way, Israel was transformed from a moral obligation and a strategic asset into an economic investment. The United States' economic stake in Israel foreclosed future opportunities for dissenters to seriously question or challenge American support.

It was also under the presidency of Nixon that the circumstances were contrived in which Israel's most threatening and powerful Arab enemy was delivered to the Western peace camp. Although condemned by Israel for its tough negotiating stance, Washington broke the Arab alignment against Israel, engaged Cairo in the direct negotiations that Jerusalem had long demanded and set the scene for the first peace agreement and recognition by an Arab state. These monumental events appeared to indicate that Nixon and Kissinger were the best friends Israel ever had in the White House.

While the benefits of the final outcome speak for themselves, many condemn the Nixon administration for its grudging policy towards Israel. Theories of its betrayal of Israel focus on three events. First, the delay in the military re-supply operation during the Yom Kippur War. The very fact that the airlift did not commence immediately is grounds amongst staunch Israeli supporters for condemning the administration. Other commentators focus more specifically on the psychology of Kissinger. It is well documented that he sought to engineer a battleground stalemate as a prerequisite for negotiations, but did he go as far as to delay the airlift as a means of achieving this? The idea is not inconceivable given his ability to tolerate thousands of avoidable deaths in Cambodia and Vietnam to secure a theoretical power balance.[277] However, the evidence is inconclusive and Kissinger and his supporters dismissed this as pure fabrication. Secondly, it was Kissinger's hastily negotiated cease-fire agreement that prevented the Israelis from securing a decisive victory over Egypt. In this instance, his supporters claim that the objective was to create a military stalemate from which a fruitful peace agreement could be derived. This leads directly to the third issue, namely the tough posture the US took in forcing Israel to relinquish territory to facilitate an agreement with Egypt. At the time the Israeli government did not consider Kissinger's actions to be in their best interest, but thirty years later, with the Israeli–Egyptian peace agreement still intact, it is one of Israel's greatest victories in securing international legitimacy and recognition.

Throughout his presidency, Nixon construed the world in terms of the superpower struggle for global supremacy. It has been argued that because he viewed events in the Middle East from this perspective, he forced Israel to make sacrifices to aid the process of détente. Yet it is precisely because Nixon was a staunch anti-Communist that he was so determined to maintain Israel's military superiority and security. Jerusalem was not slow to exploit the synergy between the President's beliefs and Israel's own military capability. It was precisely the imperatives of superpower competition combined with an ideological convergence that gave Israel the coveted status of a strategic asset.

Israel fared well under the Nixon administration, both financially and from a security perspective. Despite his criticism of American Jews, Nixon was a staunch defender of Israel, and not purely on the basis of the military benefits the state could provide. He admired the Israelis toughness and their tenacity, and irrespective of the imperatives of the Cold War, he acknowledged that he would "not [have] let Israel go down the tubes."[278] In their support for Israel, the President and his Secretary of State transcended the bounds of realpolitik and made an unprecedented commitment to another state. In terms of the time commitment made by the US, no region in the world had enjoyed such a focus of attention amongst the highest echelons of the United States government. Commencing under Nixon's leadership and continuing under that of Gerald Ford, Kissinger embarked on two years of shuttle diplomacy between Jerusalem and the Arab capitals, with more time devoted to securing this peace agreement than any other agreement in American history. Power politics offer an insufficient explanation for this chain of events when divorced from the more poignant cultural and emotional images. Over the years Kissinger has said very little about the impact of his Jewish background on his policy towards the Middle East. He offers only one direct comment on the subject throughout his extensive memoirs. Writing about his arrival in Israel on 21 October with the Yom Kippur cease-fire in hand, Kissinger recalled "ranks high on the list [of the] most moving moments of my government service."

It could be concluded that, in the short-term, Kissinger sacrificed what Israel perceived as its vital interests in forcing Jerusalem to make concessions in negotiations with Cairo that enhanced Washington's position with Moscow and drew Egypt into the Western orbit. However, it is also apparent that he did more than any other senior American official to enhance Israel's security. If not a redemptionist in the true sense of the word, he was at least a true providentialist and never questioned the belief that the US had a unique role to play in history.[279] He demonstrated this in Middle East diplomacy by unlocking the Soviet–Arab connection, which enabled him and the administration he served to initiate the peace process that culminated in the neutralisation of Israel's most dangerous enemy at Camp David.

The brokering of the Camp David Accords by the Carter administration was a remarkable achievement, with Carter himself deserving of much praise. But although Carter may not have realised it at the time, securing a peace treaty between Egypt and Israel, simultaneously sowed the seeds for the continuation of violence and unrest. The cultural dimension of American politics that mitigated against a sense of empathy with the Palestinian quest for a homeland was in stark contrast to the great lengths to which the Carter administration went to secure peace treaties to protect the Jewish homeland. By refusing to link an Israeli–Egyptian peace agreement with the question of the Palestinian refugees and the occupation of the West Bank and Gaza Strip, the US gave Israel what it most wanted – the neutralisation of Egypt, the most threatening Arab state, and continued, albeit disputed, control of Palestinian land. Once Egypt and Israel were at peace, Prime Minister Menachem Begin of Israel had little incentive to engage in negotiations with the Palestinians or to conclude peace agreements with the other Arab states. As a consequence, the Carter administration bequeathed the Republicans a frustrated Arab world and a confident, militarily strong Israel that sucked the US back in to the Middle East quagmire when it embarked on its first 'war of choice' in Lebanon in 1982.

6

REAGAN, THE NEO-CONSERVATIVES AND ISRAEL

THE POLICY OF RONALD REAGAN'S ADMINISTRATION towards Israel is characterised by contradictions. During his first term in office there were more conflicts between the United States and the government of Israel than under any previous administration, which was perhaps somewhat unexpected as Reagan was demonstrably extremely pro-Israeli. Israeli Prime Minister Menachem Begin had initially welcomed Reagan's election but throughout the early months of his presidency the atmosphere in relations between the two countries underwent a significant change. On occasions Israel came under unprecedented criticism from officials within the administration and the ability of Israel's American–Jewish supporters to influence US decision-makers was not assured. This change did not occur because of a sudden conscious reorientation of American policy to Israel's disadvantage; rather, it came about because Israel implemented policy decisions that had long been in the making – the bombing of Osiraq and the annexation of the Golan Heights – that were highly unpopular.[1]

Despite this, Israeli leaders were able to capitalise on Reagan's propensity to view international affairs as an extension of personal relationships as opposed to an expression of abstract principles. Reagan tended to "choose sides in conflicts more on the basis of friendships and loyalty than on any attempt at a dispassionate appraisal of the conditions of a particular conflict." By the time Reagan was elected to the presidency, a lifetime of experience had conditioned him to see Israel as part of the 'us' group in his 'us-against-them' mindset.[2] The 'us' referred to the American democratic world against the 'them' of the Soviet led non-democratic world. Therefore, in times of conflict in the Middle East, Reagan's natural sympathies lay with Israel, a propensity that was to consolidate and enhance the special relationship between the two countries by the time he left office.

Reagan's early life was to have a profound impact on shaping the basic premises on which he operated as President. His father was a practising Catholic and his mother, a member of the Protestant Church of the Disciples of Christ, emphasised the role of religion in everyday life.[3] As a boy, Reagan was an active participant in his religious community. He worked at the church after school and later attended a college run by the Disciples of Christ. He acquired an in-depth knowledge of the Bible and in accordance with the Disciples traditions, interpreted the Bible literally.[4] As President, Reagan quoted scripture, recounted Bible stories from his childhood and regarded Christ as his personal saviour. In a 1968, television interview with David Frost, he claimed that Jesus Christ was the historical figure he most admired.[5] His religious upbringing led him to believe that his could be the generation that would witness Armageddon, a belief that was to become a constant theme throughout his presidency. According to the Bible, Armageddon would be heralded by war in the Middle East and the destruction of Israel. Reagan's fear of Armageddon made him more inclined to support Israel's cause because he believed that Israel was the only stable democracy the US could rely on.[6]

Hollywood provided the environment in which Reagan formed his political ideas and achieved an enduring identity. Reagan once said that, "an actor knows two important things – to be honest in what he is doing and to be in touch with the audience. That's not bad advice for a politician either. My actor's instinct simply told me to speak the truth as I saw it and felt it."[7] However, what Reagan felt frequently did not correspond with reality. He recognised this and in a conflict with feelings and facts he generally gave greater weight to his feelings. In Hollywood, Reagan also encountered many more Jews than Arabs and came to consider the professional and business success of American Jews as confirmation and realisation of the 'American dream'. Many of Reagan's Hollywood friends were Jewish and during the late 1940s he spent considerable time on the banqueting circuit giving speeches at charity dinners for Jewish organisations. He believed that the Jews deserved a nation of their own and had favoured the establishment of Israel. In 1948 Reagan resigned from a lakeside country club because it refused to admit Jewish members. This belief that he owed loyalty to his Jewish friends was later to translate into his foreign policy. As President he approached Middle Eastern problems from the presumption that he was dealing with the fate of friends both on a personal and national level.[8]

Reagan was an anecdotal thinker who expressed his views through stories and communicated through anecdotes when trying to make a point. Images were the most effective way for Reagan's aides to convey a message, with his advisers briefing him through short films rather than traditional briefing books.[9] Reagan's belief in the legitimacy of the State of Israel was in part attributable to his responsibility for editing film footage brought back from the allies' liberation of the European concentration camps. Hours spent with graphic images of the horrors that had befallen the Jewish people reinforced his commitment to the Jewish homeland. His revulsion at the images of the Holocaust were replicated throughout much of American society as in 1978 NBC's presentation of the mini series *Holocaust* had brought the atrocity into the living rooms of one hundred million Americans. During his presidency, many of Reagan's opinions of world conflicts were to be influenced by CNN footage shown on American television.

As a politician, Reagan remained staunchly pro-Israeli. As an economic liberal he felt the US owed protection to the survivors of the Holocaust. As a political conservative, he came to regard Israel as a bulwark against Soviet expansionism. Reagan was a New Right neo-conservative President, and from an ideological perspective, his philosophy was commensurate with that of Begin. In Reagan, the Likud found a President who identified with their penchant for conservative realism and professed economic liberalism. On a cultural level and from a neo-conservative perspective, liberal democracy was a product of a Western culture that was not accessible to all nations of the world. Neo-conservatives identified with Israel as a part of the Western Judeo-Christian tradition, in contrast to the non-democratic and dynastic regimes of the Arab states. As Reagan once stated, "there is no nation like us except Israel."[10] The special relationship or 'meeting of ideologically aligned minds',[11] was also enhanced by the two leader's mutual obsession with the Holocaust. Reagan shared the neo-conservative belief that the world had let down the Jewish people during the Second World War and felt a strong personal commitment to Israel's security. He explained that: "My dedication to the preservation of Israel was strong. The Holocaust I believe, left America with a moral responsibility to ensure that what happened to the Jews never happens again."[12] This sense of 'moral obligation' had taken hold in the minds of countless Americans following the 1978 television mini-series *Holocaust*, one of the first popular American dramas to awaken audiences to the horrors of Nazi genocide.[13] Reagan's embedded personal and political beliefs made him susceptible to Begin's Holocaust rhetoric, consequently, in his dealings with the Jewish state, he was more patient and less inclined to pressure Israel.

Few men have come to the presidency with as clearly a defined vision of the world as Ronald Reagan. The basic tenets of Reagan's policy were virulent anti-communism, the heightening of tensions with the Soviet leadership and a dramatically increased defence budget. Reagan saw the Soviets as responsible for US problems worldwide and attributed most global conflict to the machinations of the 'evil empire'. His negativity towards the Soviet Union was openly articulated during his campaign for the presidency. "Let's not delude ourselves. The Soviet Union underlies all the unrest that is going on. If they weren't involved in this game of dominoes, there wouldn't be any hot spots in the world,"[14] Reagan stated. Similarly, in a 1983 speech, Reagan spoke of the Soviet Union in the following terms: "Let us pray for the salvation of those who live in that totalitarian darkness – pray they will discover the joy of knowing God. But until they do, let us be aware that while they preach the supremacy of the state, declare its omnipotence over individual man and predict its eventual domination of all peoples on Earth – they are the focus of evil in the modern world."

This statement demonstrates that the President's vision of the world was organised around a number of core beliefs: an ardent belief in God, alignment against the Soviet Union, a source of evil, and the curtailment of human liberty imposed by an overbearing government apparatus. Reagan's problems in government escalated when circumstances did not suit this theoretical apparatus. Every President since Eisenhower has set out the administration's foreign policy objectives and the policies it would pursue. Reagan did not do this. Instead, he spoke in general terms of his determination to thwart Soviet advancement wherever it threatened the interests of the United States, a policy that was to have disastrous repercussions in Lebanon and Central America. However, the appearance of flexibility in policy-making and apparent deviation from the New Right agenda would compromise the President's deep-seated principles and risk alienating his right-wing supporters. Compromise was only considered in cases of extreme pressure. In this way, "the administration maintained the purity of its philosophical perspective."[15]

Reagan's preoccupation with the Soviet Union was also manifest in his Middle Eastern policy. In contrast to the Carter administration, Reagan did not focus on peace-making, but on building a strategic consensus between both the Arabs and Israel aimed at blocking Soviet expansion in the area. In a 1980 speech he stated, "We must prevent the Soviet Union from penetrating the Mideast. The Nixon administration successfully moved them out; if Israel were not there, the United States would have to be there."[16] Under Reagan's leadership, the importance attached to Israel's position as a strategic asset increased, as did the military assistance it received. In conjunction with his Secretary of State Alexander Haig, Reagan also attempted to create a 'strategic consensus' whereby the military prowess of what he saw as the moderate Arabs, particularly Saudi Arabia, would be enhanced to enable them to contribute more effectively to the defence of the 'free world'. The administration believed this arrangement would be acceptable to the two parties because of the increased weaponry they would both receive. In an interview with *New York Times* reporters on 11 February 1985, Reagan justified the continued supply of arms to the Arab states on the basis that he felt "that we [America] have to make the moderate Arab states recognise that we can be their friend as well as the friend of Israel."[17] This summed up the administration's basic approach to the Middle East and highlighted one of the major causes of antagonism between the US and Israel. In pursuing this policy, Haig and Reagan ignored regional dynamics, thus limiting the effectiveness of their policies by attempting to subordinate regional issues to the conflict between East and West. They failed to appreciate that for both the Arabs and Israel, the greatest threat to their security emanated from each other and not the Soviet Union.

If the philosophy of the Reagan administration was strong on rhetoric, it tended to lack clear guidance and structure. While Reagan was a pro-Israeli and anti-Communist ideologue, he was not interested in the nuances of policy-making, leaving the interpretation and implementation of his policy directives to his advisers. Throughout his presidency, Reagan was heavily dependent on his closest advisers. As a result, his three top foreign policy advisers – Alexander Haig, Secretary of Defence Caspar Weinberger and National Security Adviser Richard Allen – exercised considerable influence over Reagan's conduct of Mideast affairs. Haig was a realist in his approach to foreign policy. He had served in the military, as Kissinger's deputy at the White House and as Nixon's chief of staff. He was pro-Israeli, supporting Israel over the Arabs, suspicious of the Soviet Union and sceptical of the Middle East peace process. Israel played a crucial role in both Reagan and Haig's conception of the strategic consensus against Moscow. Weinberger was also staunchly anti-Soviet, but his strategic conceptualisation of the Middle East contrasted with that of Reagan and Haig. Weinberger came from a business and economics background and had worked with Bechtel, a large construction company with extensive contracts in the Middle East. He was very familiar with the Arab view and saw Saudi Arabia, not Israel, as a valuable force for moderation and stability.[18] As a hereditary monarchy, Saudi Arabia was opposed to any dramatic change or regional turbulence that could potentially create social unrest. Saudi Arabia's virtually exclusive reliance on oil exports also required a quiescent regional environment and good relations with the West to ensure the uninterrupted export of oil. The competing perspectives and advice of Reagan's advisers also created inconsistency and vacillation in the formulation and implementation of policy.

Reaganism: The First Year

In the early months of Reagan's presidency, the assumption that "Israel was automatically right"[19] and that the United States would always support Jerusalem in a contest of interests with its Arab neighbours was severely challenged. The first challenge came on 7 June 1981, when Israel destroyed Osiraq, Iraq's only nuclear reactor.[20] Reagan sympathised with Israel's claim that its security interests were threatened by the Iraqi capability to produce nuclear weapons. However, until the reactor raid Reagan had believed that Israel was America's friend and was puzzled and angry that he had not been consulted before the pre-emptive strike.[21] Under the Carter administration, the US and Israel had engaged in detailed discussions on this issue. The Begin government had made it clear that if the US did not take care of 'the threat' using diplomatic means, Israel would intervene militarily. Both states agreed that Iraq presented an impending danger, but disagreements centred on how soon 'the threat' would come. The psychological environment of fear of invasion in which the Israelis lived caused Begin to call for an immediate halt to the potential nuclear threat, stating that, "If the US doesn't succeed diplomatically, we have to look after our own interests."[22] It was differences in the perception of the immediacy of the threat that caused Israel to act alone.[23]

From the perspective of Middle Eastern dynamics, the raid was a dangerous act. It undermined US claims that weaponry delivered to Israel was required for purely defensive purposes and was a clear violation of the 1952, US–Israel Mutual Defence Assistance Agreement.[24] Under the terms of the agreement, Israel had pledged to use American-supplied equipment solely to maintain its internal security and for its legitimate self-defence, and not for acts of aggression. From the Israeli perspective, the destruction of Osiraq was an act of legitimate self-defence. Washington was thus able to absolve itself of the responsibility for the actions of its client because Israel had breached the terms on which the weapons had been supplied. A parallel can be drawn with the British claim in 1999 that weapons delivered to Indonesia were for purely defensive purposes and should not have been used in the suppression of the rebellion in East Timor. However, even though the Iraqi reactor was located only ten miles outside Baghdad, Haig cited the fact that the bombing was not technically an attack on a peaceful nation (Iraq and Israel had been in a state of war with each other since 1948), as a means of legitimating the raid. Haig recalled in his memoirs that the Israelis took the decision not to notify the US of their intention because diplomatic considerations would have forced Washington to insist that Israel terminated the operation.[25]

In the testimony before the House Committee on Foreign Affairs, on 17 June 1981, the traditional dichotomy between Israel's supporters and those who were critical of Israel's misuse of US weapons was revealed.[26] For example, Representative Stephen Solarz (D.-N.Y.) claimed that Osiraq was obviously intended for the production of nuclear weapons, in contrast to Paul Findley (R.-Ill.) who was critical of the governments arms sale policy: "To my knowledge," he declared, "this new administration has not seen fit to issue any warnings whatever to the State of Israel concerning the use of US-supplied weapons."[27]

In formulating an appropriate response to the Israeli attack, both realist and emotional considerations played a role, and a clear divide emerged between the White House and the State Department. Under Secretary of State Walter J. Stoessel, Jr., expressed the view that "[W]e have condemned the Israeli attack and cannot but be dismayed by the damage which has been done to the search for peace in the Middle East."[28] In contrast, Haig argued that while US disapproval of the attack had to be demonstrated, the overt humiliation and weakening of Israel would be detrimental to the American national interest. In his memoirs Haig also claimed that, "[T]he President's deep natural sympathy for Israel and his understanding that she depended on American friendship came into play also."[29] As a means of chastising Israel for the raid, the decision was taken to delay the shipment of four F-16 aircraft. However, Weinberger leaked the decision to the press before Israel had been officially informed, thus intensifying the displeasure with which the Begin government received the news.

The bombing also raised the fundamental question as to how Israel and the US should deal with each other. The American ambassador to Israel, Samuel W. Lewis, claimed that after the attack Israeli officials were informed that their actions had had a direct impact on US interests. If Israel wanted to be America's ally, greater consultation between the two governments was required and Israel was not to inflict further surprises.[30] While the Israeli raid did not leave an indelible impression on US–Israeli relations, it did raise awkward questions about the general orientation of America's policy in the Middle East, the apparent discord between the US, the Arabs and Israel on the issue of arms policy and the real threats to state security in the region. From a US perspective, the major threat to Middle Eastern security was posed by the perceived expansionist aspirations of the Soviet Union. The administration considered it possible to create a 'strategic consensus' between Israel and the moderate Arab states whereby each party would receive advanced weapon systems from the US to be used in the defence of the region against possible Soviet encroachment. The policy failed to take into account the political perspectives of the regional states involved. Neither the Arabs nor Israel considered the Soviet Union to be a significant threat and operated on the premise that the greatest risk to their security originated with each other. The Osiraq raid coincided with another challenge to the American strategic consensus in the region – the controversy over the sale of advanced fighter aircraft to Saudi Arabia.

The AWACS Debate

Every administration that sells arms to the Arab states engenders controversy on both a domestic and international scale. For Haig, the "establishment of stronger ties with the Arab states depended upon the sale of sophisticated arms,"[31] because the lightly populated Persian Gulf states saw advanced technology as the solution to their defence requirements. The problem was how to send equipment to the friendly Arab states without weakening Israel.

Reagan inherited the controversy of the sale of five AWACS aircraft and sixty-two F-15 fighter-bombers from the Carter administration. The judgement that Saudi Arabia required these radar-equipped, technologically superior planes to deter possible attacks from revolutionary Iran and Soviet client states was "made by men deep in the American bureaucracy talking to their counterparts in the Saudi defence establishment on the basis of technical needs rather than political considerations."[32] The NSC meeting to debate the sale took place on 1 April, the day after Reagan was shot; in his absence, the meeting was punctuated by the traditional divide within the administration. In principle, Haig supported the sale of an airborne warning and surveillance system but was unconvinced that the continued security of Saudi Arabia was dependent on the sale of the five AWACS. In contrast, Weinberger vehemently endorsed the sale and convinced the NSC to sell the sophisticated equipment. He believed that strengthening Saudi Arabia would promote regional stability.[33]

Osiraq was to impact on the AWACS controversy because Israel revealed that it had flown over Saudi territory on the way to bomb the reactor. As a consequence, Saudi officials argued that they required the AWACS to defend themselves against Israeli 'aggression' and to fulfil their pan-Arab responsibilities of detecting and warning other Arab states of an impending Israeli attack. In September 1981, Begin travelled to Washington on an official visit and met with Reagan to discuss the sale. The Israeli Prime Minister was concerned that a strengthened US commitment to Saudi Arabia would increase Riyadh's leverage in Washington and undermine the US–Israeli alliance.[34] When the meeting concluded, Reagan was under the impression that Begin would not publicly campaign against the sale, accepting that the legislation was inherited from the Carter administration. However, Begin later met American Jewish leaders to lobby against the sale and spoke before an assembly of congressmen to register his opposition to the transaction. Believing that an agreement had been reached between himself and the Israeli Prime Minister, Reagan felt that he had been deliberately misled over the issue, and was infuriated that the latter had actively intensified protests against his administration.[35]

In addition to the perennial concern for the preferences of American Jewish constituents, Congress advanced two arguments against the sale: the ostensible risks to Israel's security per se and the potential risks to US security were Saudi Arabia to become 'another Iran'.[36] The exertion of congressional pressure on the White House was fuelled by the American Israeli Public Affairs Committee (Aipac) which distributed a copy of the novel *Holocaust* based on the aforementioned television mini-series, to every member of Congress,[37] in an attempt to reinforce the moral obligation of the US to Israel's security. As late as October, with administrative attention diverted towards the budget and tax cuts that would launch the 'Reagan revolution', opposition to the sale appeared insurmountable. There were counter-pressures, and the political tables were turned in part by the powerful lobbying undertaken by Boeing and United Technologies, both with evident interests in plane sales, and oil companies such as Mobil with lucrative stakes in Saudi oil.[38] But the decisive weapon in the campaign for the sale was the President himself.

Epitomised in the slogan 'Reagan or Begin', the President effectively made the AWACS sale a test of his personal prestige and authority. At a news conference on 1 October, he declared that "As President, it is my duty to define and defend our broad national security objectives . . . And while we must always take into account the vital interests of our allies, American security must remain our internal responsibility. It is not the business of any other nation to make American foreign policy."[39] His speech implied that those senators and congressman who opposed the sale were unpatriotic and put the interests of Jerusalem above those of Washington. Six days after the news conference, Anwar al-Sadat, the President of Egypt, was assassinated by a group of Islamic militants. They believed that Sadat had 'sold out' both the Arab and Islamic cause by recognising Israel's right to exist and by signing a peace treaty with the Jewish state at Camp David in 1979. Sadat's assassination intensified the executive's fear of the spread of what it termed 'Islamic Fundamentalism' and became part of the argument in favour of the AWACS sale. While Congress argued that the sale of AWACS to Saudi Arabia should be avoided in case the monarchy was overthrown and a radical government was brought to power (as occurred in Iran), the White House claimed the sale was required to prevent this by enhancing the power and stability of the monarchy.

In the last weeks of campaigning prior to the final vote, the Senate became the focus of Presidential attention. The House, with a Democratic majority, rejected the sale by a vote of 301–111, but the Senate was more vulnerable to Presidential pressure. On 7 October, Reagan held a private meeting with forty-three Republican Senators affiliated with the New Right. These legislators were among the most adamant opponents of the White House and a President they had been instrumental in bringing to office. The New Right viewed Israel as an anti-Communist bastion in the region, while some of the most militant Protestant fundamentalists involved in New Right causes had swung to Zionist policies across the board for both religious and political reasons. Jerry Falwell, founder of the Moral Majority, one of the major political organisations of the New Christian Right, was the most prominent example and was considered by Begin to be a personal friend.[40] However, the support of his organisation was insufficient to determine the outcome and in the final vote, the sale was endorsed by fifty-two votes to forty-eight.

While the sale marked a victory for the President, it was not without its price in political capital.[41] Numerous restrictions were placed on the use of the AWACS, while the F-15s were sold with smaller than usual fuel tanks and denude of bomb racks.[42] Confrontation between the two leaders over the AWACS sale resonated deeply, as Haig acknowledged:

> [T]he question of five planes is tiny when held against the universe of American politics. But every issue between two nations is a microcosm of their whole relationship, containing within itself, in a kind of genetic code, all the energy, all the goodwill and trust, all the resentment and suspicion of the parent body.[43]

Defeat over the AWACS sale encouraged Israeli leaders to seek specific evidence of their ostensibly elevated status as a strategic asset to Washington. Almost as a consolation prize the administration concluded a strategic cooperation agreement with the Israeli government in November 1981. Weinberger opposed an official alliance with Israel because of the detrimental effect it could exert on relations with the Arabs.[44] As Weinberger's department was responsible for the implementation of any security agreement, the eventual Memorandum of Understanding (MOU) between the United States and Israel outlining the parameters on strategic cooperation was a diluted version of the initial proposal. The MOU embodied the two fundamental principles of Reagan's foreign policy: the desire to form alliances against the Soviet Union and the need to protect Israel's psychological and physical security. The document advanced strategic cooperation "against the threat to peace and security of the region caused by the Soviet Union or Soviet-controlled forces from outside the region introduced into the region, joint military exercises and cooperation in R&D."[45]

The MOU received a mixed reception in Israel. While Israel's Foreign Minister Ariel Sharon was unimpressed by the substance of the agreement, Begin considered the exact terms unimportant. For him "the issue was that the US and Israel were behaving as allies. Israel was not a puppet and wanted to be treated as an ally, the security agreement offered this."[46] While Begin heralded the MOU as a major triumph, many Israelis interpreted it as a one-sided agreement that directly involved Israel in protecting the American national interest. The clause in the document that explicitly pitted Israel against the Soviet Union was the most virulently condemned. There was no corresponding US commitment to come to Israel's aid against 'aggressive' Arab forces.

On 14 December 1981, just days after the publication of the MOU, Begin inflicted a second shock on Washington. He convened a special weekend session of the Knesset to formally ratify the extension of Israeli law to the Golan Heights. The rationale behind Begin's decision is unclear. Lewis claimed that radio broadcasts of Syrian President Hafiz al-Assad's speeches, denouncing Israel and reiterating Syria's refusal to make peace, convinced Begin that he had nothing to lose by effectively annexing the territory.[47] Yet this ignores the pressure Begin was susceptible to from right-wing elements within his own party and his need to take steps to retain the support of all members within his government. The law was a superb political move but the act in itself was of minimal scope because it merely ratified the application of Israeli law, which had already been in *de facto* operation since 1969. Whatever his motivations, Begin either disregarded or failed to adequately account for Washington's reaction; his decision reflected the lack of understanding by each side of developments within the other.[48] That the US administration was caught by surprise is beyond doubt. At a news conference following the annexation Reagan stated, "We were caught by surprise. This was done without any notification to US,"[49] and following so closely after the signing of the MOU, Reagan was infuriated. The timing of the move gave the impression of US complicity, whilst the change in legal status had no relevance to Israel's security needs.[50]

Tensions ran so high that Haig and Weinberger were unified in their mutual condemnation of the Begin government.[51] In a token gesture of retaliation, the disillusioned administration suspended the MOU and temporarily suspended aircraft deliveries. Begin was outraged by the decision and vented his anger on the US ambassador. "Are we a vassal state of yours? Are we a banana republic?" he demanded. When Lewis responded that reinstatement of the MOU depended on progress in the autonomy talks and the situation in Lebanon, Begin declared that "[t]he people of Israel have lived without the MOU for 3,700 years, and will continue to live without it for another 3,700 years."[52] Yet despite the public reports of tension between the two governments, the deep-seated unity between Israel and the US appeared to cushion the American response, which was in reality quite muted. As Ed Meese, one of Reagan's closest advisors, explained:

> It's important to understand that the U.S. remains the best friend Israel could possibly have. We have been disappointed by the events in the last week. We're obviously disappointed by this reaction. Just as with friends, occasionally you may be disappointed, but that doesn't end the friendship.[53]

Even the annexing of the Golan Heights, coming so soon after the AWACS controversy and the Osiraq raid, did not exhaust Reagan's patience with Israel. This is as much attributable to calculations of realpolitik as it is to the existence of a 'special relationship'. The administration was not in a position to take too harsh a line with Israel that could seriously impair relations, for two very pragmatic reasons. First, there was the potential for domestic political backlash against the government from pro-Israeli factions. Secondly, there was the fear that international isolation would only intensify Israeli intransigence.[54] A tough American backlash could well have threatened to derail the final withdrawal of Israeli forces from Sinai, as agreed in the Camp David Accords, at a time when the credibility and presidency of Hosni Mubarak, the successor of Sadat, were in their infancy.[55] The boundaries of the permissible, as delineated by the special relationship, in conjunction with the interrelated, ever fluctuating nature of Middle Eastern politics, inevitably provided a sound basis for American restraint in its dealings with Israel. The forthcoming invasion of Lebanon was to put the special relationship to the test, but not before yet another demonstration of Reagan's inability to restrain Begin was provided.

The Israeli Invasion of Lebanon

In the context of pure Reaganism, conflicts such as those in Lebanon were considered either unimportant or symptomatic of Soviet interference. The administration had little patience for the intricacies of Lebanon's sectarian politics[56] and the country only forced itself onto the US agenda as a by-product of Israeli involvement. The war Israel fought in Lebanon was very different from previous Arab–Israeli wars. It was a long war (compared with those of 1967 and 1973), lasting almost three months, fought in densely populated urban areas and under the close scrutiny of the world's media. Moreover, Israel's participation caused dissension within Israel and outrage in the international community. America was the crucial factor in determining the course of the war because as long as the Reagan administration viewed the war as conducive to or, at least congruent with its interests, it enabled the Begin government to continue to pursue its own aims.[57]

The Israeli invasion of Lebanon in June 1982 was a product of growing tensions between Israel and the Palestinian Liberation Organisation (PLO) along the Israeli–Lebanese border. Following its eviction from Jordan in 1970, the PLO had moved its headquarters to Beirut and had established an autonomous territorial base and military infrastructure in South Lebanon. As the PLO's military capability in Southern Lebanon increased, conflicts between the Palestinians and Israelis intensified. By summer 1981, Jerusalem perceived the PLO's increasing strength in Lebanon as posing a serious threat. During the fighting of July 1981, the PLO's artillery and rockets shelled northern Galilee and Israel was unable to adequately respond. Such was the PLO's success that the future viability of settlements in the Galilee was called into question.[58] In late August, with Saudi assistance, Philip Habib, Reagan's special negotiator to the Middle East, brokered a cease-fire.[59] Habib was an Arab American from a Lebanese Christian family who had grown up in a Jewish neighbourhood in Brooklyn.[60] He was well placed to deal with the complexities of the crisis in his homeland.

Contrary to American expectations, the Israeli–PLO cease-fire agreement did not resolve hostilities. The Israeli government knew that the events of summer 1981 would repeat themselves were the cease-fire to break down. A permanent solution had not been found to the PLO's shelling of northern Galilee, and the

Israeli coffers did not have sufficient funds for the construction of an adequate shelter system.[61] As the PLO derived legitimacy and popular support from its war against Israel, from its perspective, the cessation of hostilities was virtually impossible. The Palestinians were not a monolithic group. While the PLO considered itself 'the legitimate representatives of the Palestinian people', a number of other factions vied for this role. Were PLO leader Yassir Arafat to have relented in his battle against Israel, or to have failed to retaliate against Israeli provocation, more radical groups, such as the Popular Front for the Liberation of Palestine (PFLP), would have challenged his status and credibility as the leader of the Palestinians. In an endeavour to adhere to the cease-fire and to continue its campaign against Israel, i.e., to be perceived as moderate by Israelis and radical by the Palestinians, the PLO found other means of pursuing its cause for which it did not acknowledge responsibility: terrorist attacks in Europe and against Major Sa'ad Haddad in South Lebanon were two such examples.

The primary motivation behind the Israeli invasion was the conviction that the PLO had to be driven beyond artillery range of the Israeli border. This culminated in the formulation of the 'security belt' concept, known under the code name of Little Pines, in which the PLO would be driven back 25 miles into Lebanese territory. However, while Labour party members Yitzhak Rabin and Mordechai Gur remained sceptical that a full-scale military operation could solve the problem, the Likud formulated a grand-scale plan for an invasion of Lebanon. Sharon's preferred strategy, 'Operation Big Pines' planned for operations as far north as Beirut. Sharon reasoned that once the invasion was underway, the Israeli army should advance to the Beirut–Damascus highway and link up with the Phalangists, a Christian militia force that was opposed to PLO operations in Lebanon, led by Bashir Gemayel. Gemayel's forces would then enter West Beirut and root out any remaining PLO fighters. With the Lebanese Presidential election scheduled for September 1982, the invasion provided the ideal opportunity for Israeli intervention to bring Bashir Gemayel to power. A strong central government friendly to or allied with Israel was thought to offer the solution to the defence of Israel's northern border.[62] The election of Gemayel was also viewed favourably by the US. He was well known to the CIA and in meetings with top American officials had once indicated that he thought Lebanon should become the fifty-first state.

The author Zeev Schiff describes America as an 'implicit partner' in the Israeli invasion of Lebanon.[63] Washington knew of Israel's intentions in the months preceding the war. It was only the exact timing of the invasion of which the administration was unclear. In January 1982, Sharon secretly visited Beirut to meet Phalangist commanders in an endeavour to coordinate an Israeli operation with the Maronites, the largest Christian sect in Lebanon. Sharon laid out exactly which significant military areas in and around Beirut the Israelis would have to seize to eradicate PLO strongholds. Whatever information the US had not uncovered in Israel about the forthcoming invasion was revealed to American intelligence in Lebanon,[64] when Sharon and Bashir Gemayel apparently agreed upon a joint military strategy.[65]

For Israeli attempts at a full-scale invasion of Lebanon to be successful, coordination with Washington, or at least its tacit consent, was essential. During visits to Washington in early 1982, Israeli officials outlined their ambitious plans for Lebanon. The relationship was once again complicated by the multiplicity of contacts between the two governments. The administration was divided, and Jerusalem received contradictory messages from different branches of the government. When Sharon outlined his invasion plans, Weinberger was outraged by his suggestions and threatened sanctions should Israel proceed.[66] In February 1982, Major General Yehoshua Saguy, Chief of Israeli Military Intelligence, met with officials at the Pentagon and with Haig in an attempt to discover what the US would consider an unquestionable breach of the cease-fire.[67] This was followed in March by a dispute between Begin and Habib regarding the scope of the 1981 cease-fire. Begin contended that the accord held worldwide, while Habib claimed that it applied only with regard to attacks across the Israeli–Lebanese border. Within Israel itself an agreement emerged that the point of origin of an attack was the criterion for judging whether there was a violation.[68]

One principle the Reagan administration felt strongly about was the right of every country to defend its people. Reagan would never have relinquished that right for the American people and would not deny an ally the right to defend its citizens.[69] By repeatedly informing Israeli leaders that they "would never tell Israel not to defend itself from attack,"[70] the message from Reagan and Haig, which did not include an outright 'No', was tantamount to a green light to proceed. Haig repeatedly informed the Israeli government that, if it was contemplating an invasion of Lebanon, "unless there was a clear, internationally recognised provocation – and even then, unless the reaction was proportionate to that provocation – any such course would have very grave effects in the US."[71] Sharon took Haig's message at face value: a military operation had to be quick and in response to a clear provocation. Reagan never actually issued an ultimatum warning against an invasion; he merely sent a letter to Begin urging restraint. Begin outwardly complied with this condition, stating, "We agree that you will make, in the near future, diplomatic and political efforts, provided that no attack whatsoever on Israeli citizens or territory or any border sector is carried out."[72]

The Israeli definition of a breach of the cease-fire was applied unilaterally and not just in terms of raids across the northern border.[73] Under these circumstances, all the Israelis needed was sufficient provocation. This was provided on 3 June 1982, when the Israeli ambassador to London was shot and seriously wounded. Although the attack was neither carried out nor sanctioned by the

PLO, Israel responded by bombing West Beirut on 4 June. Despite US warnings to the contrary,[74] the PLO retaliated by firing on Israeli settlements in the Galilee. As a consequence, the Israeli cabinet approved the invasion, "Operation Peace for Galilee." On 6 June, six Israeli divisions crossed into Lebanon and signalled that Israel had embarked on its first 'war of choice', a discretionary war that lay siege to an Arab capital. In response to condemnation from Lewis and Reagan, Begin reiterated that Israel does not "covet one inch of Lebanese territory" and reaffirmed Israel's objective as pushing the PLO north to a distance of 25 miles. Instead of limiting themselves to this zone as expected, Israeli forces moved forward and were within sight of Beirut by 11 June.

The Conflict Intensifies

The White House response to the invasion was muted. Reagan believed that Israel would halt its advance after establishing a 25-mile security zone along the border. Conceivably, by June 1982, the administration had come to view the war as inevitable and decided that it was better to capitalise on the potential such a war provided rather than engage in a futile attempt to prevent it. Even the escalation of the war beyond the 25-mile zone provoked only a moderate American reaction that revealed a certain tolerance for a protracted conflict.[75] Both Israel and the US believed they could gain from the severe weakening of the PLO and the establishment of a stable government in Lebanon.

American support for Israel was commensurate with the new method of successful containment the administration pursued, which provided an effective means of using force without cost to the body politic, or even the national treasury. Reagan's preferred method was not to intervene himself, but to force the Soviet Union onto the defensive. He also found it cheaper to use proxies such as South Africa and Israel to destabilise the Soviet Union's clients in Southern Africa and the Middle East. For example, during the 1980s, it cost the US only $250 million a year in military aid to the Afghan rebels to tie down 100,000 Soviet troops in Afghanistan. Washington doubled military aid to Israel immediately before the invasion of southern Lebanon in 1982, and then tacitly supported the drive across the Litani river into the heart of Beirut in the hope of 'taking out' the PLO as well as Syria, the Soviet Union's two principal clients in the region.[76]

On the second day of the war Habib flew to Jerusalem and then Damascus to press for a cease-fire. American ambassadors took on the role of intermediaries between the hostile factions, but to a large extent became conduits for conveying Israeli demands to the Syrians and PLO. Habib's willingness to convey Israeli demands to Assad that PLO men in the midst of Syria's forces leave the 25-mile zone enhanced Israel's confidence in America's support, and while Habib was waiting to meet with Assad, Israel destroyed the Syrian missile system situated beyond the 'security zone'. The Israeli strategy of escalation exceeded the limited objectives announced at the onset of the war, undermined Habib's credibility as an impartial negotiator and implied American complicity in Israeli actions.

On this occasion, Israeli action united the entire Reagan team in pressing for an immediate cease-fire.[77] Sharon appeared not to have considered the possibility of intervention from Reagan and the way scenes of violence could elicit an emotional response from him. On 9 June Reagan signed one of the harshest letters ever delivered to an Israeli Prime Minister:

> I am extremely concerned by the latest reports of additional advances of Israel into central Lebanon and the escalation of violence between Israel and Syria. . . . Menachem, a refusal by Israel to accept a ceasefire will aggravate further the serious threat to world peace and will create extreme tension in our relations.[78]

At the United Nations, a unanimous resolution was passed calling for an Israeli withdrawal and a general cease-fire.

However, the US ambassador Jeane Kirkpatrick vetoed a second UN Resolution a few days later that condemned Israeli 'aggression' and threatened sanctions. Once again the 'special' nature of US–Israeli relations interposed itself between Israeli actions and the full backlash of an American retaliatory response. When Turkey illegally used American supplied weapons in the invasion of Cyprus, the US suspended all weapons supplies to Ankara. In contrast, American condemnation of the Israeli violation of the Arms Export Control Act by using American-supplied weapons for non-defensive purposes was muted. It was not until 19 July, more than two weeks after the event, that Reagan issued an order halting further shipments of cluster bombs to Israel in response to their use on the civilian population of Beirut.[79]

By 11 June Israeli troops had cut off West Beirut, closed the Beirut–Damascus road and connected with Phalangist forces, trapping the PLO's military and political leadership inside the city. However, the Phalangist militia did not enter Beirut from the north as previously agreed with Sharon, preventing the encirclement of the city.

With Israeli forces slowly strangling Beirut, through relentless bombing and the termination of the water and electricity supply to the civilian population, Haig became the only leading administration figure who continued to oppose a tough stance against Israel. Haig believed that the US should exploit the Israeli invasion to the utmost to ensure a permanent change in the political situation in Lebanon and to drive out the PLO. Even Reagan began to speak out against Israeli actions, warning Begin that "[i]f you invade West Beirut, it would have most grievous consequences for our relationship. Should these Israeli practices continue, it will become increasingly difficult to defend the proposition that Israel's use of US arms is for defensive purposes."[80] Reagan implied that he would cease to oppose the use of statutory provisions and suspend the supply of American military equipment to Israel, the ultimate sanction, if the advance continued.

American threats did more to cast doubt on the endurance of its relationship with Israel than to weaken the resolve of the opposing forces because Washington's attempts at diplomacy undercut Israel's use of force. Threats of diplomatic sanctions failed to restrain Israel but convinced the PLO to stand their ground in Lebanon. Only Haig and Habib appeared to understand the need to use the prospective threat of an Israeli invasion of West Beirut to induce a PLO withdrawal.[81] In an insightful editorial in the *New York Times*, William Safire described the situation thus:

> While Israel moves in tanks to squeeze the West Bank, President Reagan moves from impatient scowls to vague threats to squeeze Israel. He says that Israeli advances are unhelpful to efforts to get the PLO out of Lebanon. Yet it is only the Israeli threat that makes the PLO willing to consider withdrawing.[82]

With its effective military defeat by Israeli forces the PLO could only renew its political life through the protection of a third party[83] and whether intentionally or not, the US became this third party.

When on 21 June, Begin flew to Washington for talks with Reagan, the earlier cordiality between the two leaders was gone.[84] Begin presented Israel's position to the President and Reagan replied by reading aloud from file cards prepared for him by NSC staff. The Oval Office meeting was concluded before Begin had the opportunity to respond, with the threat of sanctions imminent if Israel failed to comply with the cease-fire and withdraw. The talks continued in the presence of aides where a promise was extracted from Begin not to invade Beirut. However, at the press briefing Reagan's bland comments and Begin's emphasis on mutual points of agreement and common interest in Lebanon, made the two countries appear closer than was actually the case.[85] The public image of the meeting between the two leaders reinforced Haig's strategy of public support for Israel but was detrimental to that of the President and the majority of his aides, who favoured a de-escalation of Israeli military action.[86]

For Israel to blatantly ignore the US goes against the grain of theory which states that the dependence of a small state automatically translates into influence for the large benefactor. Such, however, was the nature of the relationship that sanctions were not perceived as credible by either Israel or the American public. No one believed that the US would abandon its ally during a military conflict, an action that would risk Israel's defeat by a Soviet-supported enemy. Reagan's threat to recall Ambassador Habib was far more credible than that of military sanctions. Consequently, there was no reason for Israel not to call

America's bluff. In the final event, sanctions were not imposed for a number of reasons. First, experience showed that the imposition of sanctions against Israel were an ineffective deterrent. Suspension of the delivery of jet aircraft to Israel after the bombing of the Osiraq reactor did not deter the annexation of the Golan, while the suspension of the shipment of cluster bombs did not prevent an escalation of the fighting in and around Beirut. Secondly, the administration believed that sanctions might encourage escalation and lead to an all-out Israeli attack. Thirdly, sanctions were not an effective lever or means of crisis management, particularly when, given the closeness of the US–Israeli alignment, they would have been imposed in a half-hearted manner.[87]

By late June, divisions within the administration had reached breaking point. Haig was now in constant opposition with Bush, Weinberger, Kirkpatrick, Clark, Baker, Deaver and Meese.[88] On 24 June Haig met with Reagan and the President accepted his resignation. However, despite Haig's departure, the orientation of American policy remained relatively unchanged. The administration continued to provide Israel with sufficient political backing in the international arena as to facilitate its imposition of a profound change in the political and military configuration in Lebanon.

With Haig's resignation, attention now turned to his successor George Shultz and his relationship with Bechtel, the large Californian contracting firm with extensive connections in the Arab world. He was more of a 'team player' than Haig and more inclined to allow a strong role for the Middle East experts in the State Department.[89] Shultz had been Weinberger's boss at Bechtel and was viewed by the Israelis with deep suspicion. At his Senate confirmation hearing Shultz referred to "the legitimate needs and problems of the Palestinian people."[90] For some, this confirmed his pro-Arab sympathies. He avoided his predecessors' extensive references to the Soviet Union and on the situation in Lebanon commented, "I believe that strength is not simply military strength, but what you do with it and what you do with the situation that may be created by it. It is not military strength that we want; it is peace that we want."[91] This statement was poignant in view of Israel's military gains and the opportunity this provided if land could be effectively negotiated for peace and security guarantees.

Certain US actions during the invasion served to undermine Israel's gains on the ground and gave impetus to the reluctance of Syria and the PLO to withdraw from Lebanon. Reagan's agreement, on 6 July, to "contribute a small contingent" of US troops to a multinational force for temporary "peacekeeping" in Beirut undermined Habib's negotiations with Assad for the relocation of the PLO to Syria and realigned the Soviets with Syria. Confronted with the prospect of US militarily involvement, Moscow and Damascus set aside their disagreements over responsibility for the Israeli defeat of Syria. Assured of Soviet backing, on 9 July, Assad rejected the plan to transfer PLO fighters to Syria.

American emphasis on diplomacy rather than the use of force strengthened the position of the PLO. Arafat became more intransigent because he felt reassured that the American preference for diplomacy and influence over Israel would deter a full-scale Israeli attack on PLO fighters in Beirut and he determined to extract a political price from Washington in exchange for withdrawal.[92]

The administration's approach to the conflict and the objectives it hoped to achieve were based on false premises. First, Washington wrongly assumed that Israel would voluntarily relinquish the security zone to a multinational force of countries that had demonstrated their hostility to Israeli actions. Secondly, the administration failed to appreciate that, while it was protecting the PLO from an Israeli attack, the organisation had little incentive to disarm and evacuate Beirut. Thirdly, Washington failed to acknowledge that Damascus would not accept PLO fighters as this would indirectly strengthen Lebanon's central government in direct contradiction of Assad's aim of extending Syrian authority over the country.[93] American diplomacy was detached from the harsh realities of Lebanese politics.

The deployment of the multinational force ushered in weeks of stalemate. The PLO leadership would not allow themselves to be pushed out of Beirut, but lacked the power to leave independently. The Israelis were reluctant to enter West Beirut because of the high casualties they were certain to incur through house-to-house combat. Habib continued the thankless task of brokering one hopeless cease-fire after another, whilst simultaneously seeking a deal that would allow the PLO to leave Beirut.

The stalemate convinced Sharon of the futility of securing a PLO withdrawal through diplomatic means. American mediation efforts had to be backed up by an Israeli show of force. On 6 August Sharon ordered the advancement of Israeli units into West Beirut. For the first time the Israeli army occupied an Arab capital in its 'war of choice' against the PLO.

The Siege of Beirut

On 12 August Israeli planes bombed West Beirut for eleven hours. The severity of the raid equated with some of the worst bombing of civilian population centres during the Second World War. It was a rare event during the Reagan presidency, and it produced an emotional reaction among all White House aides. Mike Deaver informed Reagan that, he could not "be a part of this anymore, the bombings, the killing of children. It's wrong. And you're the one person on the face of the earth right now who can stop it. All you have to do is tell Begin you want it stopped."[94] With his staff demanding intervention, Reagan personally called Begin to demand an immediate halt to the bombings.[95] "Menachem, this is a Holocaust," he told the Israeli Prime Minister. Begin replied, "Mr. President, I think I know what a Holocaust is." Begin nevertheless returned the call in twenty minutes to inform Reagan that Sharon had been ordered to stop the bombing.[96] Deaver recounts in his memoirs that when Reagan had hung up the telephone, he said "I didn't know I had that kind of power."[97] This image of US power over Israel was deceptive. In ordering the attack of West Beirut, Sharon had over reached his authority and while it appeared that Begin was misleading the White House, Sharon was in reality misleading him.[98] In response, the Israeli cabinet had ordered him to end the raids before Reagan's phone call.[99] If anything, the call delayed the process.

The Israeli bombing of Beirut came as a profound shock to Reagan. He had believed that the invasion was designed to clear a 25-mile security zone and as a result, it had been greeted with a mild US response. Reagan's reaction when he watched television footage of bodies being removed from Beirut apartment buildings after a raid was both emotional and negative. Television pictures mattered to Reagan and their importance was increased because what he was seeing was not commensurate with his fundamental beliefs about Israel. The image that most moved Reagan was that of a photograph of a baby that had lost its arms. In reality the picture was deceptive and UPI issued a correction the following month: the baby's arms had been bandaged after being burned in a PLO attack on East Beirut and he was recovering satisfactorily.[100] However the damage had been done. For Reagan, the symbol of the war had become "a baby without arms." It was this image that prompted him to order a halt to the fighting.

Before the war, Reagan had behaved as though America had no interest in pushing for a settlement of the Palestinian issue,[101] but with Shultz in the driving seat as the new Secretary of State, US attention was refocused on the peace process. Shultz believed that the Israeli invasion of Lebanon would destroy the prospects for peace in the region unless the US undertook a new initiative. However, this reorientation of American policy was still couched in terms that were favourable to Israel. Shultz stated that: "We owe it to Israel in the context of our special relationship to work with her to bring about a comprehensive peace acceptable to all the parties involved, which is the only sure guarantee of true and durable security."[102]

On 21 August, after endless negotiations, the PLO began its evacuation of Beirut. President Reagan pledged a US contingent of 100 Marines to join French and Italian troops in guaranteeing the safe departure of PLO fighters. Three days after their departure, Bashir Gemayel was elected President of Lebanon. Shultz was determined to use the period of relative calm to move forward with a peace initiative and on 1 September Reagan made his first and only major speech on the Middle East.

The Reagan Peace Plan

September 1 heralded a new phase in the Lebanese war and accentuated the contradictions between Israeli and American objectives in the Middle East. President Reagan's peace initiative highlighted the context in which the Lebanese war had been fought and the contradictions between the position of the US and Israel regarding the West Bank. From the US perspective, Jordan's 'unique and enduring character' was a fact of political life which America was committed to uphold. Therefore, the administration would not permit the removal of the Palestinians from the West Bank and the establishment of Jordan as the Palestinian homeland would not occur as a result of the peace process. Paradoxically, the Israeli invasion of Lebanon and attempts to remove the PLO shifted Palestinian issues to the front of the US agenda. Contrary to Israeli expectations, its threats placed the PLO in a position to benefit from American willingness to make concessions in the pursuit of peace. Raymond Tanter argues that the "Israeli threat of war had the unintended consequence of planting the seeds of peace in Washington."[103] These seeds grew into the Reagan peace initiative.

Ambiguity regarding the final status of the occupied territories was crucial to the success of the 1979 Camp David Accords between Israel and Egypt. In contrast, the Reagan Plan was far more ambitious. By putting forward a comprehensive solution to the Palestinian question, the plan was destined to failure, because it tried to do too much too soon. Reagan's initiative rejected both an independent Palestinian state and the Israeli annexation of the West Bank and Gaza. As an alternative, Reagan advanced four key ideas. First, "[s]elf-government by the Palestinians of the West Bank and Gaza in association with Jordan,"[104] as the solution that offered "the best chance for a durable, just and lasting peace."[105] Secondly, an immediate freeze on Israeli settlement building in the West Bank because, "[f]urther settlement activity is in no way necessary for the security of Israel and only diminishes the confidence of the Arabs that a final outcome can be freely and fairly negotiated."[106] Thirdly, Israel would not return to the narrow and indefensible borders of pre-1967. Reagan explained that "[I]n the pre-1967 borders Israel was barely 10 miles wide at its narrowest point. The bulk of Israel's population lived within artillery range of hostile Arab armies. I am not about to ask Israel to live that way again."[107] Fourthly, Jerusalem would remain undivided.

Samuel Lewis presented an advance text to Begin on 31 August without prior warning or consultation.[108] The Knesset rejected the proposal because it required Israel to relinquish the occupied territories in exchange for peace and offered an interpretation of the Camp David Accords that differed from its own.[109] Israel also feared that the agreement would culminate in the establishment of a PLO state in the West Bank that would further compromise Israeli security. As opposed to outright rejection, the Arab states, at a summit in Fez, presented a plan of their own. The plan attempted to find consensus between the differing Arab perspectives and called for the immediate Israeli withdrawal from the occupied territories followed by the creation of an independent Palestinian state with Jerusalem as its capital. It also envisaged the drawing up by the Security Council of guarantees for peace for all states of the region. Although Israel was not explicitly mentioned, US officials consoled themselves with the fact that reference to "all states of the region" included Israel. While the Arab states'offer differed in substance to the Reagan proposal, it at least provided America and the Arabs with a basis for discussion.[110]

Sabra and Shatila

The Reagan Plan over-stretched the administration by forcing it to deal simultaneously with the separate questions of Lebanon and the Palestinians simultaneously. The problem was exacerbated by Bashir Gemayel's assassination on 14 September, five days after the enunciation of the Fez Plan. Fearing that the death of the Maronite President would undermine military gains already made in Lebanon, Sharon ordered General Rafael 'Raful' Eytan to move Israeli forces into West Beirut in direct violation of the cease-fire. The objective was to rout out 2,000 Palestinian terrorists suspected of hiding in the city.[111]

Israeli operations with Phalangist forces were to have horrific consequences. On 16 September, Sharon allowed the Phalangist militia to enter the Palestinian refugee camps of Sabra and Shatila to rout out PLO installations and personnel, stating that he did not want to see "a single one of the terrorists left." By the evening, Israeli intelligence officers watching the camps intercepted radio conversations between Christian militia men, which indicated that indiscriminate violence may have been perpetrated. They relayed their suspicions to army headquarters. After several hours of confusion, General Amir Drori, the northern front commander, ordered the withdrawal of Phalangists from the camps. The order was not carried out and the following day additional Phalangists entered the camps. Through the initiative of several Israeli journalists, Foreign Minister Yitzhak Shamir was notified of events, but he chose not to investigate. It was only on the morning of 18 September, when Sharon entered the camps and witnessed the evidence of the massacres for himself, that he ordered them to leave.[112]

By 18 September the foreign media were reporting news of the massacre. The remains of 2,300 men, women and children had already been found in the camps, while dozens of additional bodies were disinterred in front of the world's media. It was reported that Israeli forces had provided the night-time illuminations that facilitated the perpetration of the massacre and that the Israel Defense Forces (IDF) had done nothing to stop it, even though it happened right under their noses.[113] Revelations of the atrocity provoked outrage in both Israel and the US, leading to the establishment in Jerusalem of a commission of enquiry.[114]

While the international community was shocked by events, reaction from inside the Reagan administration was mild and slow in coming. American officials were concerned that the premature withdrawal of the Marines had culminated in the massacre. If only by virtue of bad conscience for the refugee camp massacres, on 20 September Reagan recommitted the Marine contingent, in direct contradiction of the advice of his Secretary of Defence. Weinberger objected to the redeployment of the Multi-National Force (MNF) because they lacked a clearly defined role.[115] As a component of the MNF, the role of the Marines was understood to be neutral, with the stated mission of "enabling the Lebanese government to restore full sovereignty over its capital, the essential precondition for extending its sovereignty over the whole country."[116] Weinberger argued that the objective of the force was "demonstrably unattainable,"[117] because there was nothing neutral about the Syrian, Israeli or Lebanese forces involved in the conflict.[118]

In Israel itself, news of the massacres was greeted with a public outcry as the appearance of bloodstained corpses on national television implied that the country had been reduced to the level of its Arab neighbours. On 24 September a protest was staged by over 400,000 demonstrators in Tel Aviv's Municipality Square, condemning the government's handling of the incident. In response, on 28 September Begin announced that a commission of enquiry would be convened under the chairmanship of Yitzhak Kahan, the President of the Supreme Court. The three-man panel took testimony from all available sources: Israelis and Lebanese, military officers and journalists, Sharon and Begin.

In February 1983 the commission issued its report. While it exonerated Begin of the decision to send the Phalangists into the refugee camp, it noted that for "two days after the Prime Minister heard about the Phalangist entry, he showed absolutely no interest in their actions in the camps." The verdict against Sharon was yet more damning, with the report stating: "As an official responsible for Israel's security affairs, the defence minister had the duty . . . not to disregard . . . the [possibility] . . . that the Phalangists were liable to commit atrocities."[119] Equivalent culpability was also assigned to Shamir, Eytan and his generals.

As the cabinet debated their response to the Kahan Report, crowds gathered outside the Prime Minister's office, demanding the resignation of Sharon, Shamir and Begin. Finally a compromise was reached, whereby Sharon would step down as Minister of Defence but remain in the cabinet as a Minister without Portfolio. But by then the damage was done and the aftermath of the Lebanese war continued to polarise Israeli society until the final withdrawal of troops in 2001.

The public horror that galvanised Israeli society was not replicated to the same extent in the US. The atrocity did not cause a breach between Washington and Jerusalem because the massacre was not committed directly by Israeli forces and the government had swiftly ordered an enquiry. The US administration accepted the Israeli enquiry, considering its findings to be reputable, comprehensive and open because it was conducted by a democratic country which operated under the rule of law. Moreover, the Israeli government was perceived to have acted on the recommendations of the Kahan Report, despite the fact that all government personnel implicated through complicity in the massacres remained in office. While the administration did not approve of all Israel's actions, they continued to perceive it as a politically righteous society, deserving of their support.[120]

In America, despite public incredulity that Israel could be complicit in such an event, the people were nevertheless receptive to explanations as to why it had occurred and tended to be assuaged by newspaper reports that the Israeli government had not been directly responsible.[121] After all, allegations that Israel had perpetrated a massacre of innocent civilians did not adhere to the stereotypical image of the vulnerable and heroic Jewish state and were therefore met with resistance. In general Americans do not relate to "victims in their faraway country with their unpronounceable names and odd clothing."[122] As Philip Lopate explained, "those piles of victims are not as significant as Jewish corpses"[123] because Jews are commonly portrayed in the Western media as individuals, in contrast to the Arabs who are depicted as large, faceless masses. In sum, the American public dealt with revelations of the less palatable aspects of Israeli involvement in Lebanon "with dissatisfaction and criticism, but without ultimate alienation or withdrawal of basic support."[124]

In replicating the relatively muted response of the administration to the events at Sabra and Shatila the media collaborated in the people's apparent willingness "to see or take sufficient account of the ethical shortcomings of those with whom they share a sense of political, cultural or ideological kinship."[125] As a consequence, the atrocities of Palestinian terrorists committed against Israelis were portrayed as more egregious than those of the Israelis, even if those latter acts resulted in a far greater death toll.[126] Noam Chomsky argued that this is because the media serves a propaganda function in which the atrocities committed by official allies are not deemed newsworthy in the same way similar acts carried out by 'rouge' actors are. Furthermore, because the country is deemed to have a free press, it is illogical for the people to believe that coverage is biased[127] or that there is a misrepresentation of facts. Another equally important reason for the US willingness to 'forgive' Israeli culpability was that the majority of Americans simply did not pay attention to international events and were uninterested in the intricacies of foreign relations.[128]

To the present day, Sabra and Shatila are rarely mentioned in the American media. In 2002, on the twentieth anniversary of the massacre, the only reference to the refugee camps in the mainstream press appeared at the end of an article in the *New York Times.* Similarly, between 27 August and 10 September 2002, the *Los Angeles Times* ran a series of articles to commemorate the thirtieth anniversary of the kidnapping and murder of eleven Israeli athletes at the Munich Olympics by Palestinian terrorists. The series contained twenty articles, totalling over 18,000 words or 500 column inches. The disparity between the coverage of Israel and that of the Palestinians is self-evident.[129]

A break with Israel over Sabra and Shatila was inconceivable when it was fighting Communist-backed Arab radical states and terrorist organisations which were opposed to the values of the US and Western civilisation.[130] However, there was a growing concern for Lebanon's civilian population within the US administration, tinged with a sense of guilt, which was demonstrated through the redeployment of the multinational force and renewed efforts to convince King Hussein of the viability of the Reagan Plan.

The Failure of the Reagan Plan

American reliance on Jordanian participation in the peace accord proved to be the final insurmountable obstacle in the implementation of the plan. King Hussein considered American involvement in Lebanon to be a test of how effectively it could deal with the Palestinian issue. Hussein felt that if Washington could not get the Israelis out of Lebanon, there would be little prospect of securing their withdrawal from the West Bank. Reagan further undermined the success of his initiative by publicly stating that the Palestinian question could not be resolved until there was agreement on Lebanon.[131] In this, he effectively provided the opponents of his initiative with the means to destroy it. Begin, Assad and the Soviets took this statement as an invitation to exacerbate the difficulties in Lebanon to ensure that "another Camp David," as the Syrians dubbed it, would not succeed.[132]

The Reagan initiative included a five-year transitional period during which the territory would move from Israeli to Jordanian control. The King was reportedly tempted to accept the Reagan initiative and travelled to Washington in December 1982 for talks with the President. In exchange for his cooperation, Hussein was promised increased weapons supplies and a freeze on Israeli settlement activity in the West Bank once negotiations were underway. However, the administration overlooked the fact that they could not force Israel to comply with American promises to Hussein of a halt to settlement building.

Jordanian–US dialogue was followed up by Jordanian–PLO talks over the next few months. However, in April 1983, Hussein concluded that a joint negotiating position with the PLO could not be established. In the absence of a favourable Arab consensus, Hussein felt powerless to accept the Reagan Plan on behalf of the Palestinians. On 10 April 1983, he called Reagan to tell him that his talks with Arafat had failed and that he was not prepared to act alone.[133] Hussein had not ruled as King of Jordan for over thirty years by taking bold initiatives that risked alienating other Arab states or his Palestinian citizens. With the failure of the Reagan Plan, the US refocused its attention on Lebanon. Amin Gemayel succeeded his dead brother to the presidency and Begin set in motion steps to realise the true objective of the war – a peace agreement with Beirut that would guarantee Israeli control of South Lebanon.[134]

The Lebanese–Israeli Peace Initiative

Begin's quest for a peace agreement between Israel and Lebanon was not shared by Assad, who opposed the move for the same reason Washington and Jerusalem favoured it. The withdrawal of PLO forces and an Israeli–Lebanese peace agreement would have radically undermined Syrian influence in Lebanon. Pressure from conflicting forces put the Lebanese President in an untenable position. To maintain Christian hegemony over the Muslim population and to liberate Lebanon from the control of foreign armies required a US guarantee. By guaranteeing an Israeli–Lebanese peace agreement, America pledged to defend Gemayel against his adversaries. In the complex interaction of Mideast politics the Americans were now committed to defend the settlement against Syria, which was supported by the Soviet Union and the Lebanese Shi'ites, who were, in turn, supported by Khomeini's Iran.[135]

Tensions were heightened in April 1983 when the American embassy in Beirut was bombed, killing sixty-three people. Among the dead were seventeen Americans including Robert Ames, the CIA's chief Middle East analyst, and William Casey's *de facto* liaison officer to the PLO and an unofficial adviser to Shultz.[136] The attack was later attributed to Iranian allies of Lebanon.

Two days after the bombing, Shultz flew to Jerusalem with an agreement acceptable to the Israeli cabinet. However, Assad, whose views had not yet been sought, considered the clause that made Israeli and Syrian troop withdrawal mutually dependent on each other, as a capitulation to Israel,[137] and refused to accept the accord.

Despite Syrian intransigence, on 17 May, Israeli and Lebanese officials signed an agreement that terminated the state of war between the two countries, stipulated mutual regard for sovereignty and established a security zone in Southern Lebanon.[138] For Israel, it was a win-win proposition. If observed, the treaty offered peace; if violated – that is if Syrian and PLO forces remained in Lebanon – Israeli forces could do likewise. In this way, the US assumed responsibility for an agreement it could not implement.

Following the Soviet rearming of the Syrians, fighting resumed in Beirut. As the fighting intensified, the Israelis began to disengage from the Shouf mountains, leaving the position of the US Marines exposed. Beginning in September 1983, US offshore forces gradually became embroiled in inter-Lebanese battles and the American role changed from that of peacekeeper to co-belligerent on the side of the Lebanese Christian forces.

On 23 October, as tensions between America and Syria escalated, a truck loaded with explosives was driven into the compound of the marine barracks. The truck exploded, killing 241 American servicemen.[139] Simultaneous attacks were carried out on French and Israeli units. Reagan responded with a powerful statement condemning the attack and emphasising the inability of terrorists to change American policy. "The struggle for peace is indivisible. The United States will not be intimidated by terrorists," Reagan declared.[140] However, immediately following the attack, plans for American troop withdrawal were drawn up. The effect of this terrorist attack was to push America back into alignment with Israel, and with it the adoption of a policy designed to punish Syria.

Within days of the attack, Reagan signed National Security Decision Directive 111, outlining the parameters for strategic cooperation between Israel and the US, thereby reviving the agreement that had been suspended in December 1981. Under Secretary of State Lawrence Eagleburger believed that by restoring the strategic cooperation agreement, the American administration would be better placed to influence Israeli decisions that impacted upon American interests.[141] Impetus was given to the *rapprochement* between the US and Israel by the Israeli general election and the emergence of Yitzhak Shamir and Moshe Arens as leaders. The change in personnel in itself eased tensions between the two governments but made little difference to the situation in Lebanon. By early 1984, the politics of re-election were uppermost in the minds of Reagan's advisers. The death of American servicemen overseas was detrimental to the President's image and re-election prospects, which contributed to the decision to redeploy US forces offshore. Reagan, who had pinned American prestige on a stable settlement in Lebanon, now "cut and ran," removing the most tangible sign of that commitment. In so doing, America abandoned Lebanon to factional infighting and left it to the mercy of its two powerful neighbours.

Bitburg, Reagan and the American Jews

Reagan was renowned for his mastery of political symbolism and impeccable political instincts, but his talent appeared to desert him in 1985 when he engaged in a symbolic act of reconciliation between the US and the Federal Republic of Germany, setting him on a collision course with the American Jewish community, Israel and Congress.

The furore stemmed from an announcement that Reagan would accept an invitation from the West German Chancellor, Helmut Kohl, to participate in a symbolic act of reconciliation between Washington and Bonn to mark the 40th anniversary of V-E Day, on 8 May 1945. First reports indicated that the chosen site would be a Nazi concentration camp, but this was dropped in favour of the Kolmeshohe Cemetery at Bitburg. A fierce debate erupted when it was revealed that approximately 49 members of the *Waffen* SS were buried at Kolmeshohe.

Requests were made by the Zionist and pro-Jewish lobbies and members of the American public for Reagan to change his itinerary, and the White House received a storm of protests when he refused to do this. As a result, a storm gathered in the US Congress in response to protests from angry constituents that spilled out into the media and ultimately threatened relationships between Jews, Christians, politicians and the governments of the two countries involved.[142]

The origins of the visit dated back to 30 November 1984 when, during an informal discussion in Washington, Chancellor Kohl invited Reagan to visit Germany during the Economic Summit in May. The act of reconciliation between the two countries was to consist of a handshake and the laying of a wreath at a cemetery where American and German soldiers were buried. Unfortunately no one seemed aware that the remains of all US soldiers had long since been removed from German soil. During the discussion of the visit, Kohl presented Reagan with a number of suggested sites for inclusion in the itinerary, of which Dachau concentration camp was one.

Within days of the discussion and without explanation, the Germans asked that Dachau be withdrawn from the programme and expressed their displeasure when as late as March 1985 the camp remained on the agenda. To ease tensions between the governments, on 21 March Reagan announced that he would not visit Dachau because he didn't want to risk "reawakening the passions of the time"[143] or to offend his hosts. His aides would later contend that the West Germans were privately pleased with this decision, implying that Kohl had made the offer only as a courtesy. Yet being intensely aware of the need for good public relations and to avoid the perception that he had succumb to pressure from Bonn, Reagan inadvertently compounded the situation by stating that "since the German people have very few alive that remember even the war, and certainly none of them who were alive and participating in any way, [they should not have feelings of] guilt imposed upon them."[144]

The White House announcement on 11 April that Reagan would not visit Dachau and would instead attend a service at Kolmeshohe, gave rise to what was perhaps the worst public relations disaster of his presidency. It appeared that the President was willing to substitute a visit to a concentration camp in favour of a wreath-laying ceremony near the graves of the *Waffen* SS, who were directly and heavily involved in the perpetration of the Holocaust.[145]

In an endeavour to defuse the growing tide of public protest, on 19 April, Reagan announced that he would visit a concentration camp and chose Bergen-Belsen, explaining the delay in his decision thus: "I thought that there was no way that I, as guest of the government [of the Federal Republic of Germany] . . . could on my own take off and go some place and, then, run the risk of appearing as if I was trying to say to the Germans, 'Look what you did.'" He later elaborated on this, claiming, "I think that there's nothing wrong with visiting that cemetery where those young men are victims of Nazism also, even though they were fighting in the German uniform, drafted into service to carry out the hateful wishes of the Nazis. They were victims, just as surely as the victims in the concentration camps."[146] The shock of hearing a pro-Israeli President describing Nazi soldiers as victims reverberated around the world.

The legislature's response to the President's remarks was swift. In the Congress, 53 senators, 11 of them Republicans, signed a letter urging him to cancel the visit, while 257 representatives, including 84 Republicans, signed a letter asking Chancellor Kohl to withdraw the invitation. The following day the Senate passed a resolution urging the President to reconsider his itinerary.

The Bitburg visit generated unprecedented controversy because it exposed three controversial issues to international scrutiny. The first was the American commemoration of the Holocaust. Since the 1970s the Holocaust had occupied a sacred place in the American consciousness. Therefore any act that was considered detrimental to this memory or the uniqueness of the Jewish experience, particularly when it was initiated by the President of the United States, was destined to generate controversy.

The second was the clash between conventional politics and moral considerations. Conventional political behaviour is generally based on compromise, but when one group has a claim to moral absolutism, a compromise is no longer possible. In staging a US–German reconciliation at Bitburg, the leaders were perceived as somehow diluting the absolute evil of Nazism.[147] The visit to the cemetery was transformed into a classic political situation of confronting contradictory demands from unyielding friends. The US presidency, for all the power it wields, sometimes operates akin to a brokerage house, where the most important rule is, "they owe us one" or "we owe them".[148] This held true with regard to Bitburg. Reagan felt he "owed" Kohl who, despite considerable public and political opposition, had stood firm with Reagan on the deployment of Pershing missiles in West Germany a few years earlier. He was also seeking the Chancellor's support for the Strategic Defence Initiative. Kohl, in turn, saw Reagan's visit as an opportunity to further his own political interests and to help secure his victory in the upcoming state elections in North Rhineland Westphalia. The events and decisions leading up to and including the visit were a product of conventional politics but touched on an issue in the realm of moral absolutism. In so doing, the circumstances were created in which a clash between the administration and the American Jewish community was inevitable.[149]

The third issue concerned two national memories – that of the Jews and that of the Germans.[150] For the Jews, the memory of the Holocaust is inextricably interwoven with their concept of present-day Jewish nationhood. To Jewish people, it is inconceivable that the Holocaust should be detached from their national and ethnic experience. The efforts of Reagan and Kohl to change the frame of reference of the Holocaust, and by implication that memory, was perceived as an affront to Jewish history.[151] Set against this was the contemporary memory of modern Germany, which came into existence in 1949. The modern memory is based on the belief that the Germany of today is not responsible for the atrocities of Nazism and that the past should not impinge on the moral fibre of the present-day state. Reagan's visit to a concentration camp was, therefore, viewed as antithetical to the values of the German people.

The Bitburg visit impinged upon all three highly contentious issues, which begged the question of why Reagan agreed to a state visit that was destined to be so controversial. The answer seems to lie in the fact that the administration's decision was a political, not moral one. The Bitburg visit was about the administration's relationship with Germany and Kohl, and Reagan agreed to the visit before he fully understood the historical implications of the trip.[152] Once Reagan had given Kohl his word, it was impossible for him to recant without endangering the political goodwill he enjoyed with the Chancellor. Perhaps what is most surprising is that a staunchly pro-Israeli President would act in such a way as to antagonise both American Jewish opinion and the Israelis. But this was never Reagan's intention and he did not see a direct contradiction between a state visit to Germany and his unswerving support for the Jewish state. For Reagan, the politics of present-day Germany and the Nazi Holocaust were two distinct entities and he did not waver in his belief that his visit to Bitburg was "morally right." He was therefore able to endure the storm of protest that descended on him.[153]

Bitburg made American Jews both unhappy and uncomfortable.[154] It did not cause them to doubt the reliability of the American political system or the goodwill of the President, but it did make them aware once again of their vulnerability and how, even in a democracy, the "tune is called on high."[155] Symbols are of great salience in a pluralistic society, and Reagan was perceived to have altered the symbolic reference of the Holocaust, as the ultimate atrocity perpetrated against a distinct ethnic group, for which he was never quite forgiven.[156]

From the perspective of the general non-Jewish American majority, both the visit and Reagan's comment on SS members as victims were out of kilter with popular opinion. Popular productions such as ABC/TV's *The Winds of War* (1983) which re-enacted graphic scenes from the Final Solution, including the Babi Yar massacre of 30,000 Jews outside Kiev, abided by the conventional media representations of the Holocaust.[157] The visit was even more inappropriate as the ensuing public debate coincided with the release of Claude Lanzmann's documentary film *Shoah*, based on first-hand accounts and probing interviews with Holocaust survivors and non-Jewish bystanders. With a running time of nine hours and twenty-three minutes, *Shoah* was not intended for a mass audience, but it provided a quality representation of the Holocaust sought by intellectuals. Its commercial release received an outstanding critique and due to its length and complexity most public knowledge of the film was derived from such sources.[158]

Although over time the Bitburg controversy was sidelined, its ramifications continued to be felt by the American Jewish community.[159] But the intention of the Reagan administration was never to undermine US relations with Israel and, three years later, when Israel became involved in one of the most controversial human rights issues of its history, the Reagan White House stood firmly by its side.

The Intifada and the Shultz Plan

In more than thirty-five years of occupation of the West Bank and Gaza, Israel had not considered the costs excessive. Life for the Palestinians and the Israeli settlers had assumed a type of routine. But the illusion that "Palestinian docility under occupation would go on forever"[160] was shattered on 8 December 1988 when, in the Jebaliya refugee camp in Gaza, an Israeli vehicle crashed into an automobile carrying Palestinians to work in Israel. Four Palestinians were killed and eight others seriously injured. A Palestinian leaflet circulated in Gaza that day denouncing the Israeli action and when the funerals were held that evening stones were thrown at a nearby Israeli military post. Angry protests erupted the following day and Israeli military patrols were stoned and petrol bombed by Palestinian youths. In response, Israeli soldiers fired lived ammunition and two Arabs were killed, including a schoolboy.[161]

The disturbances, or *Intifada* as it became known, spread to the West Bank and it soon became clear that something "qualitatively new" was happening.[162] The spontaneity of the *Intifada* caught the PLO leadership by surprise[163] but they quickly endorsed it and gave the appearance of coordinating the protests with the United National Leadership of the Uprising, as the internal leadership referred to itself. Israeli Defence Minister Rabin was in Washington when the fighting broke out and "the issue was discussed at almost every meeting Rabin was to have, be it with the press, his advisers or American officials, both in

Congress and the administration."[164] CBS footage of Israeli soldiers beating Palestinian youths was broadcast worldwide and even Reagan was said to be concerned about the disturbances.[165]

One of the first criticisms of Israel's response to the *Intifada* came on 17 December 1987 from the Office of the US Secretary of State, which described Israel's actions as sometimes inconsistent with international standards. For the Israeli government, overt lack of support from Washington was both unexpected and unwelcome. This condemnation was followed up on 22 December when the UN Security Council voted unanimously (the US abstained) in favour of a resolution deploring the lack of respect for human rights Israel was exhibiting by opening fire on civilians and implementing wholesale detention without trial (over 900 Palestinians having been taken into custody since the *Intifada* began). On 3 January 1988, when Israel served deportation orders on nine Palestinians who were accused of subversive activities, the UN Security Council approved a resolution condemning the deportations, and on this occasion the US supported the motion: the first time the US had voted against Israel in the Security Council since 1981, when Israel annexed the Golan Heights. Nevertheless, further deportation orders followed.[166]

Despite international censure, the Israeli leadership intensified their violent response to the crisis. On 17 January the Israeli cabinet endorsed an "iron fist" policy, the first priority of which, according to Rabin "was to use might, power and beatings" to restore order.[167] These violent methods provoked revulsion in the US and televised pictures of children using slingshots and hurling rocks at fully armed Israeli soldiers generated sympathy for the Palestinians and improved the moral strength of the Palestinian cause worldwide.[168] The use of lethal force aroused condemnation in the West and sentiments grew that the US government should do something to bring peace to the area. From this point on, foreign journalists found it increasingly difficult to obtain official Israeli permits to cover incidents or gain information about them.[169] Even Reagan publicly condemned Israeli press censorship and, by implication, its policy of violent retaliation. "I'm a great believer in a free press and the right of people to know, and so I would have to be opposed to it [banning television coverage], thinking that they want to conduct operations in which they would rather not have public knowledge."[170]

Given the fate which had befallen the Reagan Plan, Shultz was reluctant to commit American prestige to another Middle East peace plan without some guarantee of success. The President and his Secretary of State had never considered movement towards a peace accord as a crucial objective in the region. To them, Cold War regional balance-of-power concerns took precedence. As an Israeli diplomat intimately involved in the talks with the US noted: "In the eight Reagan years you didn't have the feeling that he was a President who lost any sleep over the lack of a peace process in the Middle East."[171] But public opinion was pushing the administration towards intervention, while the Egyptian government warned that the *Intifada* could lead to the radicalisation of the entire region.

In February 1988, Shultz visited Israel with a hastily-drafted peace plan largely based on the Camp David Accords. It called for six months of negotiations – to commence on 1 May – between Israeli and joint Jordanian–PLO delegations. The objective of the plan was Palestinian autonomy, which would be implemented over a period of three years. The process was to begin with an international conference, which would include the five permanent members of the UN Security Council and representatives from all the countries involved.[172] A final settlement was to be based on Resolutions 242 and 338. But its concentration upon Jordan as the principal negotiator for the Palestinians and the inclusion of the "land for peace" formula, which was unacceptable to the Likud, meant that the plan was fatally flawed.[173]

In the months that followed his initiative, Shultz worked determinedly to overcome the objections of Israel and the Arabs. His biggest obstacle was Shamir, who stated his "strong reservations concerning the proposed international conference which . . . is not conducive to peace."[174] Despite repeated displays of intransigence, the administration was reluctant to pressurise Shamir. Starting from a position of sympathy, Reagan and Shultz tended to accept the procedural and 'security' concerns of Shamir and the Likud as genuine, particularly as these points reinforced their own feelings as to the unreliability of the Arab moderates. In contrast to Begin and Sharon, Shamir and Arens had a pragmatic style; Arens, in particular, was skilled at presenting the Likud case in Cold War/neo-conservative terms. Only when Shamir publicly stated in 1988 that the exchange of territory for peace was foreign to him, did Shultz reach the conclusion that the Likud were using procedure as an excuse.[175] Only then was pressure considered, and by then it was too late.

Although American Jewish leaders, distressed by daily television images coming from Israel, had reportedly played a significant role in persuading Shultz to resume an active American role in reviving the moribund peace process, they were unwilling to pressurise Israel to accept specific American proposals. This was in keeping with their traditional view that since the Israelis had to bear the risks of any concessions, a peace agreement should be the result of direct Arab–Israeli negotiations. At the same time, however, there was growing concern amongst the Jewish leadership that the Likud should not be perceived as obstructive to the administration's efforts to reach a peace settlement. To bring the message home to Shamir, on the eve of his visit to Washington in March 1988, thirty senators, including many of Israel's staunchest supporters, sent a letter to Secretary Shultz "to express our support for your efforts to break the dangerous Middle East stalemate that has led to the current cycle of violence and counter violence."[176] The letter reflected their misgivings over the stalemated peace process that had become widespread among their constituents and their preference for a "land for peace" formula to end the uprising.[177]

The US and the PLO

The success of the Shultz Plan, as the initiative was dubbed, was dependent upon the cooperation of King Hussein of Jordan, which Shultz tried to secure during four visits to the Middle East in the first half of 1988. However, in exerting pressure on Hussein to endorse the plan he ignored the complex regional pressures operating on the King and succeeded only in reinforcing his desire to extricate his kingdom from the negotiations. On 31 July, in an official statement, King Hussein relinquished all Jordan's legal and administrative ties to the West Bank, stating that the PLO would now be responsible for the Palestinians residing there.[178]

The *Intifada*, which had prompted Hussein's disengagement from the West Bank, shattered the American complacency that surrounded the 'peace process' and proved that peace could not be made between the Arabs and Israel without the consent and participation of the people most directly involved – the Palestinians themselves.[179] After the King's speech it became apparent that the peace process could only remain alive if it sprang from Palestinian–Israeli discussions. Yet with both the Labour Party and the Likud bloc firmly set against talks with the PLO, the initiative once again fell on the White House.

The idea of establishing direct talks between Washington and the PLO had been deliberated in the past and as early as 1974 Kissinger had authorised meetings between the PLO and Vernon Walters of the CIA.[180] But after Kissinger's declaration in 1975 that the US would not recognise or negotiate with the PLO until it acknowledged Israel's right to exist, renounced terrorism and accepted Resolution 242, contacts had been rare. By 1989 circumstances were propitious for a change in strategy and if somewhat unexpectedly it was the pro-Israeli Reagan and his equally pro-Israeli Secretary of State that reversed US policy. The establishment of a dialogue between Washington and the PLO would enable Jerusalem to talk indirectly with the PLO without having to alter its official posture. Washington was aware that Arafat was seeking to establish a dialogue, not just to gain further legitimacy for his organisation but in an endeavour to secure a role for the PLO in future peace negotiations. If talks could be established, America stood to gain as it would acquire new leverage over the organisation as both Israel and the PLO would be forced to rely upon it. If real progress were ever achieved, the US administration could take full credit, without having to share accolades with the UN or any other world power.[181]

One obstacle remained to opening a US–PLO dialogue – the 1975 commitment to Israel in which the US had pledged that it would not negotiate with the PLO until it acknowledged Israel's right to exist and accepted Resolution 242. The Reagan administration therefore required Arafat to issue a public statement adhering to these criteria, insisting that Arafat say certain words. In return, Washington would announce that it was prepared to begin substantive discussions with the PLO and that the Palestinians had the "right to pursue an independent state through negotiations."[182] On 14 December, at a special session of the UN in Geneva convened specifically to hear Arafat, who was prohibited as a terrorist from entering the US,[183] he met the American conditions when he stated his acceptance of:

> The right of all parties concerned in the Middle East conflict to exist in peace and security . . . including the state of Palestine, Israel and other neighbours according to the resolution 242 and 338.
>
> As for terrorism, I renounced it yesterday in no uncertain terms, and yet, I repeat for the record that we totally and absolutely renounce all forms of terrorism, including individual, group, and state terrorism.[184]

In response, Reagan approved the commencement of US-PLO discussions at the level of the American ambassador in Tunisia, and Washington lifted the ban on dealing with the PLO.[185] Reagan defended his administration's decision, which was objected to by members of the Likud, on the basis that it would "help Israel achieve the recognition and security it deserves."[186]

Despite this breakthrough, by the autumn of 1988, any practical plans for the peace process ran afoul of the campaign season for national elections in both Israel and the US, which fortuitously coincided in early November. In Israel, another inconclusive vote eventually produced another divided National Unity Government, this time with the reins of foreign policy more firmly in Likud's hands. In the US, the landslide victory of George Bush, the first incumbent Vice-President elected since Martin Van Buren, a century and a half before, promised a considerable measure of continuity in foreign policy. The political reality confronting the Bush administration was that the *Intifada* had greatly increased the salience of Arab–Israeli conflict management without indicating a better means to that end.[187]

Explaining the Reagan Administration's Response to the *Intifada*

While it might appear that the Reagan administration had done little to condemn Israel's "iron fist" policy in Gaza and the West Bank, a significant departure did occur from the usual convivial tone of the relationship. Reagan reiterated his concern for "the human rights of the Palestinians . . . and made it clear that we [America] oppose deportations and any denial of the due process of law."[188] He also condemned any policy that the government of Israel would want to conceal through press censorship and highlighted the "legitimate rights of the Palestinians" in the 1988 State of the Union Address.[189] More significantly, Reagan took the virtually unprecedented step of authorising the US representative at the UN to vote in favour of a resolution sanctioning Israel.

Despite these relatively superficial moments of dissension, the US–Israeli alliance remained firm throughout the period of the *Intifada* and aid levels remained unaffected. Although the widely used analogy of Israel as the tiny David fighting the Goliath of the Arab world was no longer appropriate, the sympathy Reagan felt for the Jewish state and the commitment of the American Jewish community and the administration did not falter. In reality, the most the administration did was to antagonise the Likud by advancing a peace plan that favoured a final status outcome of the Palestinian question that was almost identical to Labour's official position. As one Israeli official noted, the biggest problem for Likud was: "How can we get him [Shultz] to go home and stay home?"[190]

The reason Israeli violations of Palestinian human rights in the occupied territories elicited a relatively muted response is rooted in America's common perception of the world as democratic allies and non-democratic enemies. A statement Reagan made in 1983 reveals this mentality:

> It's no coincidence that the same forces which are destabilising the Middle East – the Soviet Union, Libya, the PLO – are also working hand in glove with Cuba to destabilise Central America. . . . The question isn't who has the most perfect democracy. The question is, who's trying to build democracy and who is determined to destroy it. Many nations, including the United States, which once condoned slavery, have evolved into better democracies over time.[191]

Even though Israel had demonstrated itself to be an imperfect democracy, it remained a democratic state that was firmly aligned with American values and interests, in contrast to the monarchical or dictatorial values of many Arab states.

Americans are quick to support any ally that is considered important to their country, particularly when that ally's values are consistent with their own. Under these circumstances they will treat their ally's defects in the same way they treat their own country's defects: with dissatisfaction, but with the acceptance that some events are unavoidable necessities. Americans who thought that Israel was ill-treating the Palestinians continued to support it because they believed that "politically evil acts are mitigated through the creation and maintenance of politically righteous societies."[192] Those Americans who say they are proud of their country but are ashamed of some aspects of its past or even its present are accepting this proposition. This same proposition is applied to Israel: while Americans, and even Reagan and his advisors, did not necessarily approve of all Israel's actions, they continued to perceive it as a politically righteous society, deserving of their support.[193] The subordination of the human rights of the 'enemy' in the pursuit of state security was deemed, if not acceptable, then at least tolerable by the administration and was a mode of behaviour subsequently adopted by Washington in dealing with suspected al-Qaeda suspects in 2002–3.

Reagan and the Neo-Conservatives

Reagan's continued support for Israel was greeted with relief by the neo-conservatives who had increasingly criticised his foreign policy since January 1984, when the White House abandoned its confrontational policy towards Moscow and began seeking a *rapprochement*. The transformation of Reagan from the "chief spokesman for realism in defence issues into a quixotic advocate of nuclear disarmament"[194] was anathema to his conservative core constituency. The neo-conservatives were unhappy with Reagan for failing to live up to the promise he had held out in 1981. Not only had there been no roll-back, no sanctions of note against the Soviet Union and no attempt to challenge Soviet control of Eastern Europe, the US had even abandoned the propaganda war which, at least, had been endorsed by John Foster Dulles. The deputy programme director of the Voice of America, who had wanted to 'destabilise' the Soviet Union and its satellites by promoting 'disaffection between people and rulers', was forced to resign.

The President's fundamental belief that the battle between Communism and democracy was the axis upon which international politics turned, and that US–Soviet relations were central to his understanding of international politics, remained unaltered.[195] What had changed during his second term in office was not his perception of the evil of Communism but his image of the Kremlin under President Mikhail Gorbachev. As Gorbachev embarked on a process of domestic liberalisation and sought to integrate the Soviet Union into the world economy, Reagan began to differentiate the Soviet leadership from "Communists" more generally, although they were part of a Communist government.

With a more congenial government in the Kremlin, Reagan turned his attention to nuclear arms reduction. He felt that the development of nuclear weapons represented a step backward for mankind[196] and wrote in his memoirs: "Looking back at the recent history of the world, I find it amazing how civilisation has retrogressed so quickly."[197] Existing arms control treaties did little to mitigate the threat of nuclear war that hung over the world. Underpinning the

President's abhorrence of nuclear weapons and MAD was his fascination with the biblical story of Armageddon.[198] To Reagan's mind, the existence of nuclear weapons threatened people around the globe and he rejected traditional approaches to arms control, such as SALT I and SALT II, which limited the growth of nuclear arsenals, so that some kind of balance between the superpowers was maintained. Reagan wanted to reduce those arsenals and he embarked on a series of summits with Gorbachev to achieve this goal.

Reagan's policy reversal achieved its stated goal of abolishing whole classes of nuclear missiles, but provoked condemnation within the right-wing of the Republican Party, who described him as "lacking the moral self-confidence to pursue measures for the nation's defence."[199] Yet what they failed to appreciate, and what Reagan seemed to understand, was that Washington was now operating from a position of strength in its dealings with Moscow. Despite the popular appeal of Gorbachev, the US held most of the cards. In 1969, the US had been engaged in Vietnam while tacitly supporting a string of dictatorships against left-wing forces. In the 1980s, the Soviet Union was saddled with a string of weak, precarious allies and economic distress. Washington held the key to Moscow's access to the global economy through its control of the world's commodity and currency markets and Reagan used economic incentives as a source of leverage to secure reductions in nuclear weapons.

Reagan's commitment to arms reduction did not mean that he was willing to bargain away the Strategic Defence Initiative (SDI) for an arms control treaty, as some neo-conservatives had feared. The Intermediate-Range Nuclear Forces Treaty (INF), which Reagan and Gorbachev signed, was designed to eliminate intermediate-range and shorter-range missiles. While this was disastrous for the Europeans, who relied on these weapons for their protection, it was a triumph for the hardliners in Washington. The neo-conservatives wished to dilute extended deterrence, while concentrating on a qualitative conventional arms race which would enable the US to confine a war with the Soviet Union to Europe, and prevail on the battlefield without recourse to nuclear weapons. Reagan understood that opposition to nuclear arms reductions would not be offset by the tremendous increase in spending on conventional weapons but he maintained that it was his role to convince the public that his approach was in America's interest.[200] While he may have been successful with the public at large, the neo-conservatives did not acknowledge the foresight of his policy until after Bush took office and the Soviet Union collapsed.

Yet the neo-conservatives' fear that arms control would lead the administration to renege on its other foreign policy commitments was without foundation and throughout his term in office Reagan did not waver in his support for Israel.

Assessing Reagan's Middle East Policy

"Israel has never had a greater friend in the White House than Ronald Reagan" is the opening line of Haig's memoirs. Four years later, in 1988, Israel's Premier Shamir echoed similar sentiments: "This is the most friendly administration we have ever worked with. They are determined that the strong friendship and cooperation will continue and even be strengthened despite the differences that crop up from time to time."[201] Similar sentiments spoken by both American and Israeli leaders reflected the fundamentals of the relationship during the Reagan presidency. Such sentiments were deeply felt by Reagan himself. On the occasion of welcoming Premier Begin to Washington in September 1981 he said, "I welcome this chance to further strengthen the unbreakable ties between the United States and Israel and to assure you of our commitment to Israel's security and well-being."[202] Reagan, of all the American Presidents, undoubtedly had the greatest sense of affinity for the State of Israel and, George Lenczowski concluded that he "strove to form an almost symbiotic relationship with Israel."[203] Yet despite this, policy throughout his presidency exhibited many similarities to that pursued by previous administrations towards the Arab–Israeli dispute.

Throughout Reagan's two terms in office, relations with Israel figured prominently on the US foreign policy agenda. This was predominately attributable to Israel's propensity for transforming its own security concerns, through unilateral action, into a potential Mideast crisis. On numerous occasions, Israel's pursuit of its own security interests led to tensions with Washington because American and Israeli national interests were not identical. However, the Reagan administration's condemnation of Israeli transgressions was always relatively muted and short-lived when compared to the extent and possible consequences of Israel's perceived misdemeanours and human rights violations during the invasion of Lebanon and the *Intifada*. This is attributable to a number of factors.

First, many of the tensions that arose between the US and Israel during the Reagan administration were a product of the two states' divergent geo-strategic and political priorities, due to their differing status within the international hierarchy and the consequent difference in perceptions of the international system. As a small state, Israel had the luxury of concentrating on a narrow range of vital interests and disregarding almost everything else. It could also disregard or discount the effects of its actions on the stability of international politics in general. For example, Israel did not need to consider the global implications of a war with an Arab state. When an Arab–Israeli dispute occurred the US would support Israel while the Soviet Union would back the Arab states. This type of indirect confrontation between the superpowers had the potential to escalate into a full-blown US-Soviet conflict. As in the case of the bombing of Osiraq and the annexation of the Golan Heights, Israel had acted unilaterally in its own interests without prior consultation with Washington. In so doing, it had failed to acknowledge the extent to which its actions affected Washington, causing Reagan great disillusionment and consternation.

Secondly, one of the notable phenomena of international relations during the Cold War was that alliances had a curious way of increasing the leverage of small states in their dealings with the big. It ceased to be the case that the "possession of superior military or economic force [could] guarantee small-power compliance with big-power interests."[204] In an increasingly interdependent world bristling with nuclear weapons, lesser allies were not only able to act independently, they were also able to use alliances to influence the policy of Great Powers and to alter the latter's policy perspectives. Both Hanoi and Havana successfully exercised leverage over Moscow from time to time, while the extent of Jerusalem's influence over Washington has been sufficient, in certain cases, to alter American perceptions of its national interest. In part, this was attributable to the open and pluralist nature of the American political system which allowed interest groups to influence political decisions and also to the perception of the Communist challenge.

Thirdly, on assuming the presidency in 1981, the most powerful initial assumption of Reaganism concerned the nature of the international system and of the American role within it. Throughout his presidency Reagan was forced to come to terms with reality, and foreign policy premises were transformed by January 1989 when Reagan left office.[205] For the first two years of his presidency, Soviet ideology was seen as the central threat to international order, and the President saw it as America's duty to support what he termed "forces of freedom" in international conflicts, utilising economic strength and national morale to provide the sinews of international assertiveness. For example, George Ball asserted that Reagan's simplistic approach to the complex problems of the Lebanese crisis was influenced by his conviction that the Soviet Union and the ideology of Marxism–Leninism were the primary cause of world tensions. Inspired by this belief, he employed a convoluted logic to produce a curious symbiosis. The fact that the Druze obtained arms from Damascus made them surrogates of the Syrians. The Syrians, in turn, obtained arms from Moscow, which made them surrogates of the Soviets. It could therefore be deduced that a successful Druze repulse of the Maronites would be a triumph for the Soviet Union which, from Reagan's perspective, was seeking to extend its influence in the Middle East. It was this "geopolitical gloss" that gave the crisis in Lebanon its importance and news worthiness.[206]

But even with the evolution of Reagan's perception of the Soviet Union and the de-escalation of tension between the superpowers, his support for Israel remained firm. This is attributable to one of the most fundamental aspects of the relationship: the prevalent belief that Israel was a politically righteous society and was deserving of Washington's virtually unconditional support.

When Reagan was succeeded by Vice-President George Bush, many observers assumed that US policy towards the Middle East would have continued in a similar vein. However, Bush was to preside over an era of great change in the international system, characterised by the disintegration of the Soviet Union and the US-led war in the Gulf against Iraq. These changes were further accentuated by Bush's very different personal feelings for Israel. For these reasons, it might have been expected that US policy towards Israel during the 1990s would be markedly different from that of the past. Superficially at least this appeared to be the case. What had been described as Reagan's overvaluation of Israel as a strategic asset and the underinvestment in peace-making[207] were reversed under Bush, but at a fundamental level many consistencies remained.

7

BUSH, THE GULF WAR AND ISRAEL

The Conservatism of George Bush Sr.

LIKE MOST INDIVIDUALS, HISTORIANS and journalists can be very selective in their interpretation and recollection of events. Nowhere is this more the case than in popular perceptions of the policy of the George Bush Sr. administration towards Israel. While Bush was never the popular choice amongst American Jews, securing only 29 percent of their vote in the Presidential election,[1] no one in 1989 would have accused him of being anti-Israeli.[2] After all, Bush's Middle East team included four American Jews – Dennis Ross, Aaron Miller, Daniel Kurtzer and Richard Haass – who were emotionally committed to the Jewish state and who devised much of the administration's policy towards the region.[3] During the course of his administration, Bush adopted a peace plan proposed by Israeli Prime Minister Yitzhak Shamir, incapacitated Iraq, Israel's most threatening neighbour, and convened a peace conference that enabled Israel to negotiate directly with its Arab neighbours while prohibiting the attendance of PLO representatives.[4] Yet by the end of his term in office, George Bush was considered by the pro-Israel lobby and many American Jews to have been the most anti-Israeli President to occupy the White House. The reality was very different from this misinformed perception and the fundamental position of the Bush administration towards an Arab–Israeli peace agreement did not differ markedly from that adopted by Johnson in 1967.

Few Presidents have assumed office with more impressive foreign affairs credentials than Bush. He was former director of the Central Intelligence Agency, head of the American diplomatic mission to China and ambassador to the United Nations and had spent eight years as Vice-President under Ronald Reagan.[5] He had also been elected to Congress, was a Texas businessman and had been national chairman of the Republican Party. Yet, while Bush's credentials were impressive, they revealed little about his own views of foreign affairs in general or the Arab–Israeli conflict in particular. It was common knowledge that he had been critical of Israel's bombing of Osiraq and had recommended that Reagan take a hard line against Israel following the invasion of Lebanon in 1982.[6] He was on good terms with the Saudi ambassador to Washington, Prince Bandar bin Sultan, and in the mid-1980s had travelled to Riyadh to urge the Saudis not to allow the price of oil to fall.[7] It was also rumoured, and based on the available evidence, that Bush did not share Reagan's emotional attachment to Israel, but given the depth of Reagan's personal affinity for the Jewish state, this was insufficient grounds to consider him anti-Israeli.

When Bush was elected President in 1988, early commentators described it as Reagan's third term. But these neo-conservatives were soon to be disappointed because Bush's brand of conservatism was marked by tradition and moderation in contrast to the ideologically motivated approach of his predecessor.[8] He defined his own political creed as conservatism and as Vice-President had told the Ripon Society, a moderate Republican research and policy organisation, that "I am a conservative. I voted along conservative lines when I was in Congress. I took conservative positions before assuming this job. I take conservative positions now."[9] There is little doubt that in the broadest sense of the word, Bush was a conservative. He tended to favour the status quo and resist innovation and perceived of the role of government in limited terms. Yet there were many on the right of the Republican Party who challenged his claim to the conservative label. These were the same people who had criticised Reagan's policy of *rapprochement* with Moscow until it contributed to the fall of the Soviet Union and they once again became devotees to Reaganism.

Bush's early commitment to conservatism was a product of his upbringing, combined with his early experience of living and working in Texas. His life was marked by wealth and privilege. He was raised in Greenwich, Connecticut, the second son of a wealthy investment banker and attended the elite educational establishment of Andover. He served with distinction as a bomber pilot during the Second World War and completed his education at Yale thereafter. Although he exhibited little interest in politics in his early years, he did acquire the values and attitudes that would later become politically relevant.[10] He embodied the "Eastern establishment creed" which was based on the maxims of 'the meek shall inherit the earth', 'real men don't boast', 'it's more blessed to give than to receive', and 'public service is the purpose for entering politics'.[11] Bush's father personified this creed and despite working long hours as a businessman he set aside time for voluntary community work and impressed upon his children the obligation of the privileged to enter public service. At the age of 55 his father entered the Senate, where he proved to be a moderate conservative with a commitment to the status quo. An overt emphasis on duty and public service was commensurate with the lack of vision that Bush was often charged with.

The conservatism in which Bush was raised was moderate, in the sense of being largely content with society and government in their current form, and against radical change, non-confrontational and relatively non-ideological, marked by civility, compassion and community. However, after graduation from Yale in 1948, he moved to Texas where he began work as a trainee in the oil industry. It was here that he came under the influence of a very different conservative tradition, based on the individualistic political culture of the Southwest. In this environment, the role models were not the traditional well born and bred elite, but self-made men from inauspicious beginnings who had carved their fortune in a region where unfettered capitalism ruled and all forms of government were despised.[12] In this part of America a neo-populist brand of conservatism dominated. It was harsher than its Eastern counterpart, lacking the sense of moderation and compassion and untempered by the belief in public service and duty. This was the brand of conservatism advocated by Barry Goldwater and it came into its own under the Reagan administration. Although his exposure to this sort of conservatism had an impact, Bush remained predominantly a product of his upbringing, an inheritance that was evident throughout his presidency.

One character trait that was to be of considerable note throughout his presidency was the emphasis Bush placed on personal relationships rather than political ideas. As his elder son, George W. Bush the current President of the US, explained: "The problem with my old man is that he thinks you can solve problems one at a time, with good character, good judgement, a good team, and all that stuff. Jebby and I understand that you need ideas, principles, based on belief."[13] Bush was a "pragmatist more attuned to the interpersonal dynamics of politics than devoted to ideology"[14] and this lack of interest in ideas was to haunt him throughout his presidency, because it was interpreted as a lack of 'vision'.

While much has been made of the insignificance of the office of the Vice-President, Reagan made noteworthy use of Bush for foreign policy purposes. By the spring of 1987 Bush had been on official visits to 73 countries, improved his comprehension of international issues and expanded the network of personal contacts that were to be crucial to the conduct of his administration's foreign policy.[15]

One essential requirement of the office of the Vice-President is the sacrifice of independence and the adoption of a position of complete deference to the President. Bush was meticulous in meeting this requirement and despite having campaigned for the Republican Party nomination on a platform at odds with Reaganism, on accepting the position as Reagan's running mate he told his staff: "We're now a wholly owned subsidiary and we're going to behave like one."[16] In the long term this was a prudent move and demonstrative of a certain amount of 'vision', for the fulfilment of his personal objective at least. His presidential ambitions demanded that he not alienate the right-wing Republicans who already doubted his neo-conservative credentials, but were a vital element in the coalition required for his 1988 election campaign.

Soon after taking office, Bush publicly expressed sentiments that were anathema to Reaganites who disliked extensive institutions of government and all they represented. When speaking to an audience of senior career bureaucrats in the federal government, he told them: "You are one of the most important groups I will ever speak to. What we really have in common is that each of us is here to serve the American people. Each of us is here because of a belief in public service as the highest and noblest calling."[17]

Bush selected like-minded individuals to be his closest advisors. As Secretary of State, he appointed James A. Baker III, a close personal friend and political ally of more than thirty years. Baker had extensive political credentials. He had managed Bush's unsuccessful Senate campaign in 1970 and on the latter's recommendation was appointed Under Secretary of State for Commerce in the Ford administration. He then ran Ford's election campaign in 1976 and did likewise for Bush in 1980. During Reagan's first term he served as Chief of Staff and in 1985 was appointed Secretary of the Treasury before managing Bush's successful bid for the presidency in 1988.[18]

Bush appointed Brent Scowcroft as his National Security Advisor. Scowcroft had a Ph.D. in international relations and was an Air Force lieutenant-general, prior to becoming Henry Kissinger's deputy at the National Security Council (NSC). He later became National Security Advisor in the Ford administration. This coincided with Bush's appointment as Director of the Central Intelligence Agency, where Scowcroft had acted as the channel through whom he reported to the President.[19]

For a President determined to retain control of foreign policy, Baker and Scowcroft were perfect choices. Their loyalty was beyond doubt and their world-view reflected that of Bush. In terms of the Bush-Baker relationship, the President had far greater knowledge of international affairs, while Baker's credentials rested on his political acumen. Their approach to politics was very similar and they were both highly pragmatic, problem-orientated and tactical in their approach. Baker was wary of grand strategy and was a manager rather than a conceptualiser. William Quandt claimed that "[i]f politics was the art of the possible, then Baker was a supreme politician."[20] Under the Reagan administration he had been criticised by conservatives for his willingness to compromise and make deals at the expense of the implementation of Reagan's ideological agenda. His lack of vision was condemned by the director of the conservative Center for Security Policy, Frank Gaffney, in a magazine article in which he said the Secretary of State "believes in success for its own sake and often finds specific goals inconvenient. That's not leadership or vision." It was this lack of vision, combined with his intention to be "the President's man at State and not State's man at the White House,"[21] that qualified Baker for the job.

In his autobiography, Bush explained that he appointed Scowcroft to be his National Security Adviser because he knew he would not transform the NSC into a policy-making agency and would accurately report the views of all council members.[22] Bush was correct in his assessment because Scowcroft defined his own role in limited terms: "The President runs the government. He has expert advice from State and Defence, and it is my job to ensure the integration to help provide a strategic concept which covers the whole field of national security."[23] He adopted a multiple advocacy approach whereby he played the final role of broker and balancer, offering the President advice and counsel. In view of the central role the NSC had played in the Iran–Contra affair, when in August 1985, the US had participated in secret dealings with Iran involving the sale of military equipment which was linked to efforts to obtain the release of American hostages held in Lebanon and funding to rebel forces in Nicaragua, it was crucial that someone whom the President could trust managed the organisation. In Scowcroft, Bush found that man.

Baker and America's Middle East Strategy

The Bush administration was often accused of undermining US–Israeli relations because its approach to the peace process was perceived by some as detrimental to Israel's interests. After all, neither Baker nor Bush shared the special regard for Israel held by Reagan, Shultz or Haig, who saw the Jewish state as simply either a sister democracy, a moral responsibility or a strategic asset.[24] The administration's approach to world affairs was based on a state-centric balance of power system; adopting a different approach than Reagan's ideologically charged vision, Bush often saw the Israelis as more of a "strategic irritant than a strategic asset."[25] Yet the personal beliefs of their key State Department advisors Ross, Miller, Kurtzer and Haass exerted a profound influence on policy. A friend of the team commented that they:

> Came to this [peace negotiations] with a sense of mission – on top of their commitment to America's interests – about trying to achieve a secure peace for Israel. They believe it's the greatest thing they can do for the Jewish people.[26]

But, as Miller acknowledged, he and his colleagues also believed "that the Arab–Israeli conflict is not a morality play, not a conflict between good and evil. It is a conflict between competing claims and competing justices"[27] and therefore must be approached from this perspective. In this they favoured the less ideologically inclined approach of the Israeli Labour party to the peace process, a policy that was inherited from the Reagan administration.

The State Department took the initiative in devising the administration's strategy towards the Middle East and it was here that those members of the administration with an emotional affinity for Israel worked. Dennis Ross believed that the *Intifada*, now in its second year, had created a new dynamic, and was a source of political ferment within Shamir's National Unity Government (NUG).[28] As the Israeli government continued to respond to the uprising with increased repression in the form of administrative detentions and deportations of Palestinian protestors, domestic politics in Israel was polarising. Labour adopted its firmest and least equivocal stance in favour of compromise with the Palestinians[29] and threatened to withdraw from the government unless Shamir abandoned his dream of a "greater Israel" and commitment to territorial maximalism.[30] Israeli Defence Minister Yitzhak Rabin, who had pursued a policy of beatings in the territories as part of an attritional strategy designed to demonstrate Israeli determination not to yield to force,[31] now believed that a military solution was not possible. As he came to understand the *Intifada* as a popular uprising he concluded that "you can't rule by force over one and a half million Palestinians."[32] These factors, combined with an apparent shift in public opinion, pushed Shamir to adopt a more flexible approach towards the territories.[33]

The State Department team considered the environment conducive to the establishment of an Israeli–Palestinian dialogue, but in view of mainstream Israeli public opinion, the Palestinian Liberation Organisation (PLO) could not be involved directly in the talks. However, Washington also acknowledged that in order to work with Palestinians from the territories, Arafat's tacit approval would be required. The vehicle for this strategy was the US–PLO dialogue in Egypt and Tunis.[34] Although the State Department was sceptical about Shamir's commitment to the peace process, attempts by Rabin to establish a dialogue with the Palestinians, amongst other things, persuaded them that a breakthrough was possible.[35]

As Labour's position on the "land for peace" question was closer to Washington's than the Likud's, there was potential for cooperation between Washington and a Labour government. This was especially true while Rabin held a senior position in the party, as one of his ostensible goals was to work closely with America to advance the peace process.[36] The short-term objectives of Washington and Rabin were also aligned as both wished to initiate a dialogue between Israel and the Palestinians from the territories that excluded the PLO from the process. On a tactical level, the views of the two parties also coincided. They both saw the perpetuation of the NUG, a coalition between Labour and the Likud, as the most effective device for drawing Israel into the negotiating process and opposed moves by Shimon Peres to bring down the government and establish what would have been a weak Labour government in its place. As a result, Baker and the State Department worked closely with Rabin during this period.[37] The secret, Ross said, "was to design a process so tailored to Israel's needs that Shamir politically couldn't afford to refuse."[38]

The difference between Shultz's and Baker's approach to negotiations was that Baker was prepared 'to play the game'. Shultz had always been reluctant to intervene in Israeli politics even to facilitate a peace agreement he endorsed. In contrast, Baker's priority was in 'doing the deal' and he was prepared to pressurise the Likud, albeit subtly, to achieve his goals. In general terms, Shultz was perceived by the Likud to have been interested in the historical and philosophical aspects of Israel; in contrast, Shamir believed Baker was "interested in what happened today, not yesterday and perhaps not even tomorrow."[39] During Baker's first visit to Israel after the Gulf War, the Likud tried to encourage greater sympathy for their position by taking him on a helicopter flight designed to demonstrate the strategic importance of the Golan Heights and the West Bank. This effort was perceived as a failure by the Israelis and Baker's subsequent visit to the Israeli Holocaust Museum, Yad Vashem, also had no discernible political impact.[40] For the Likud government, the inability of the Holocaust memory to visibly move the US Secretary of State must have been particularly frustrating, especially when Begin had successfully pursued the same strategy with Reagan.

Baker was more pragmatic than sentimental and hoped to work closely with Rabin to corner Shamir into the opening of an Israeli–Palestinian dialogue. In an endeavour to induce a positive Israeli response, Baker told the House of Representatives Appropriations Committee that if the US could not progress talks between Israel and the Palestinians, the US might be forced to look to the PLO.[41]

Despite Baker's forceful rhetoric, the administration's policy towards the peace process was initially based on a report entitled "Building for Peace," prepared prior to the 1988 Presidential election by The Washington Institute for Near East Policy. The report urged a slow "ripening" process and confidence-building moves as a precursor to full peace negotiations.[42] According to this rationale, the US should concentrate on making small efforts to improve the environment until the parties were ready to negotiate, thereby making the conflict "ripe for resolution."[43] This was a low-key strategy that did not require American pressure to be exerted on any participant or entail the risk of policy failure. Baker was unprepared to put his own credibility and that of the administration on the line to kick-start negotiations and therefore Washington would no longer be at the forefront of diplomatic initiatives. Henceforth, greater emphasis would be placed on direct co-operation between the Arabs and Israel.[44] Despite the change of personnel at the helm of US policy and their fundamentally different attitudes towards Israel, Shamir remained confident that the balance of interest on the Palestinian Question resided with Israel and not the US.

Popular Opinion and the Peace Process

By the late 1980s, the idea of Israel as a safe haven for world Jewry following the horrors of the Holocaust was a deeply ingrained tenet of American culture and foreign policy. Popular cultural representations of survivors, frequent reminders of the Second World War and the need to protect the Jews militated against the exertion of political pressure on Israel to make tangible, territorial concessions to secure a peace agreement with the Arabs. At the same time, courses on the Holocaust had become a staple of high school education and there were more than seventy centres commemorating the Holocaust across the United States. For lovers of classical music, a series of CDs were in preparation to commemorate the music of Jewish composers such as Erwin Schulhoff, Viktor Ullman and Pavel Haas, who had perished in the concentration camps.

At the dawn of the Bush presidency, the safe haven afforded to Jews by the very existence of Israel was reinforced by the increasing frequency throughout the late 1980s and early 1990s of 'personal documentaries' of return. This phenomenon had grown into what could be described as a subgenre of the Holocaust film, especially as children of survivors increasingly journeyed with a camera into Europe and into the past. In films of return, the director, often a member of the second generation, goes back to the scene of the crime or of the rescue. Some of these documentaries are investigative, such as *Loving the Dead*, *Birthplace* and *Shtel*, in which the subjects attempt to discover how their Polish Jewish parents were murdered. Some are celebratory, like *The Children of Chabannes* and *The Optimists*, which depict the rescue of Jews from, respectively, France and Bulgaria. Others are commemorative such as the Holocaust documentaries *Back in Auschwitz* and *The Last Days*,[45] the latter winning an Academy Award.

The physical return of a survivor to the ashes of European Jewry was first presented in 1980 through simple documentaries, such as *Kitty: Return to Auschwitz*. In 1990 Emanuel Rund's documentary *All Jews Out* includes interviews with the survivor and her daughter returning to their German town and the former prison of Theresienstadt. By the late 1980s, these films had also begun to seek out those who had hidden and then aided the Jews to escape. For example, the 1987 documentary *The Righteous Enemy*, directed by Joseph Rochlitz, begins with the story of his father, who was interned by the Italians, and then explores the Italian resistance and the saving of 40,000 Jews. Many of these documentaries juxtaposed images of the past with vibrant images of Jewry in the present, particularly of American Jewry. Once again the American gentiles were invited to identify with the victims of the Holocaust and to see the victims as one removed from themselves.[46]

The Holocaust rhetoric of Shamir, his devotion to the concept of a greater

Israel and opposition to a land for peace solution to the Israeli–Palestinian dispute all had a certain resonance with popular images of survivors returning to Eastern Europe and the concept of Israel as a safe haven. As a result, in the early years of the Bush presidency, it was not considered prudent for Washington to exert pressure on Israel to facilitate movement towards a peace agreement.

The American Reaction to the Shamir Plan

In May 1989, following discussions with the US administration, Israel publicly presented its four-point peace plan. The proposal was typically vague. It mentioned elections amongst the Arabs of Judea, Samaria and Gaza, but failed to specify which Arabs Israel was prepared to negotiate with and who was going to be arbiter of the debate. Washington had already stated its position that the elections be based on a mutually agreed formula, which implied modifications to the Shamir plan and the inclusion of the US as a negotiator with the Palestinians over the modalities of the elections. Baker also requested that Israel find a way to allow Palestinians from outside the territories to participate in the elections.[47] Dennis Ross embraced the plan because it gave his team something to work with and it was regarded in Washington as a plan of "constructive ambiguity."[48] Yet while ambiguity was the hallmark of success of every peace plan since UN Resolution 242, because it facilitated agreement, it was this very ambiguity that in the long term stifled progress.

The NUG was predictably divided in its response to the conditions Baker imposed on Palestinian representation. Rabin was willing to allow the electoral participation of East Jerusalem Arabs with the proviso that they voted outside the municipal boundaries. It was assumed that this would set a precedent whereby they could express their political rights in the territories and not in Jerusalem itself, which would remain an undivided part of Israel. Shamir, in representing the Likud position, took his opposition to Baker's proposal to the Israeli people. In a speech to the Likud faction of the Knesset, he opposed the participation of Arabs resident in East Jerusalem in elections and declared that Israel would never cede territory to the Arabs.[49] It was this that provoked Baker to deliver what was to become a highly controversial speech to the Aipac convention in an attempt to restore American credibility as an 'honest broker'. Baker's speech began with the traditional reiteration of the shared democratic values and strategic partnership between the two countries but then struck a discordant note when he spoke of the future of the occupied territories and the missing element in the Shamir peace plan. He spoke of "territorial withdrawal"[50] as the potential culmination of negotiations and then, making a blatant reference to the ideology of Shamir, asserted that:

> For Israel, now is the time to lay aside, once and for all, the unrealistic vision of greater Israel. Israeli interests in the West Bank and Gaza – security and otherwise – can be accommodated in a settlement based on Resolution 242. Forswear annexation. Stop settlement activity. . . . Reach out to Palestinians who deserve political rights.[51]

Baker's speech provoked outrage amongst his American Jewish audience and much consternation in Israel. The fact that he enunciated a comparable list of exacting requirements for the Palestinians did nothing to redress the balance. However, Baker's alleged lack of sympathy for Israel did not translate into sympathy for Syria or the Palestinians, and minimal effort was made to capitalise on the US-PLO dialogue begun in December 1988.[52] His speech also heralded the development of a more proactive peace effort on the part of the Bush administration, premised on the need to modify Israeli requirements, as defined in the Shamir plan, into something more palatable to the Palestinians.

The right-wing faction of the Likud now perceived the Bush administration as openly hostile and tried to withdraw the elements of 'constructive ambiguity' from the plan that the Americas so prized. Shamir argued that Baker had completely misread Israeli sentiment, with all its nuances, dilemmas and contradictions and that his speech had reinforced Israeli extremists and weakened the NUG.[53] The Likud Central Committee demanded that Shamir attach four explicit conditions to his plan: No East Jerusalemites be permitted to participate in elections, the *Intifada* be terminated before the convening of elections, Israeli settlement activity be continued and no tract of land be relinquished.[54] The Likud amendments to the Shamir plan increased tensions within the Labour–Likud alliance and even Rabin began to question the utility of continuing in the NUG under the new conditions. However, Ross warned that if Labour left the coalition it would be accused of sabotaging the peace initiative and eventually, in order to protect Israel's remaining credibility in Washington, Shamir resolved the crisis by dropping the changes to his original plan.[55]

The Ten-Point Plan

With negotiations stalled, the next initiative came from Egypt in June 1989, when the Minister of State Boutros Boutros Ghali visited Jerusalem to discuss the peace process. The Egyptians offered a 'ten-point' programme for working out the terms of elections – the centre-piece of discussions on the peace process.[56] The proposal had a number of merits: as it was submitted by an Arab party at peace with Israel and with close ties to the PLO, neither side could reject it as tainted, and as it was proposed by a regional actor, American prestige would not be directly affected by its success or failure.[57]

However, the 'ten-point' programme soon undermined the semblance of accord within the NUG because it was tailor-made to fit Labour's approach but showed no concern for the Likud's proscriptions.[58] Of the ten points, those most objectionable to the Likud were those that advocated that Arabs from East Jerusalem participate in elections, a settlement freeze be implemented, negotiations be explicitly premised on a land for peace formula and the political rights of the Palestinians be acknowledged. Despite virulent opposition from elements within Fatah, at the end of August, Arafat stipulated that the PLO would accept the ten points if the Israelis did so,[59] thereby putting the ball back in Israel's court.

The Egyptian initiative highlighted the contradictory policy pursued by different factions of the NUG. Peres adopted all ten points and, while Israel's Foreign Minister Moshe Arens travelled around the US promoting the Shamir plan, Peres followed him promoting the same ten-points the Likud had rejected.[60] Simultaneously, Baker and Rabin were trying to operationalise the Egyptian connection to the PLO to construct a compromise that would enable a meeting to be convened between Israel and the Palestinians within the confines of the NUG. While Labour and the US were permitting the PLO to play a role in the process, the Likud was activating its transnational connections to exert pressure on Congress to end the US–PLO dialogue. This highlighted the differing perceptions and ideological beliefs of the various parties. What concerned Shamir was not so much the ten points themselves as the American attitude towards them. The Americans saw the Egyptian proposal as a way to implement the Shamir plan while Shamir saw it as a contradiction to it.[61]

The US administration was reluctant to take an active position but to break the deadlock between Shamir and Rabin, on 10 October, Baker submitted a five-point proposal intended as an elaboration of the Shamir plan.[62] Israel objected to the proposal but when the administration refused to amend it, Jerusalem accepted, albeit with qualifications. These qualifications focused on the Likud's previous demands on Palestinian representation and the agenda for talks in Cairo. The divide between Israel and the Palestinians was great, and the challenge for American diplomacy was also daunting. To try to accommodate the Likud's concerns, the administration demonstrated its opposition to increasing the public role of the PLO by opposing the Arab states' attempts to have its observer status upgraded from 'observer organisation' to 'observer state'.[63] Rabin and Baker met in Washington on 18 January 1990 to try to reach a compromise on the issue of Palestinian representation, whereby the 'outsiders' would be recent deportees, and East Jerusalemites would be required to have a dual address in the territories, thereby bridging the requirements of both the Likud and the PLO.

Labour publicly accepted the American terms and, with Egyptian and PLO support virtually assured, Baker sought a commitment from the Likud.

However, the Likud stalled and Peres reacted by trying to break up the government offering Yitzhak Peretz, a leading figure in the Shas party, a Cabinet position in a Labour-led coalition.[64] Rabin tried to negate the position adopted by Peres, by continuing to work with Baker to secure Shamir's compliance. He once again submitted his compromise to the Israeli Cabinet, adding that Egypt and not the PLO would announce the names of the Palestinian delegation, while Baker continued to pressure Shamir for a positive response.

In an attempt to convince Shamir to accept the compromise, Rabin asked the Labour party to pass a resolution pledging their commitment to the integrity of Jerusalem and excluding the prospect of direct negotiations with the PLO.[65] His efforts were in vain, for although Shamir was aware that the majority of Likud ministers favoured the Rabin compromise, he remained unyielding and on 13 March, Shamir sacked Peres from the NUG. Peres then won a vote of no confidence that resulted in the collapse of the NUG. This ultimately worked to Shamir's advantage as, with the support of the ultra-Orthodox parties, he succeeded in forming the most right-wing government in the history of the Jewish state,[66] with himself at the head. The new government rejected the proposal put forward by Baker and Rabin for negotiations. Despite the change in America's government from neo-conservative to the pragmatic, 'even-handed' approach of the Bush team, American policy continued to be constrained by the radicalism of the Likud, which was reinforced domestically by the pro-Israel lobby. It was the Iraqi occupation of Kuwait on 2 August 1990 that finally broke the impasse.

The Gulf War, 1990–91

When Iraqi troops occupied Kuwait, Bush immediately demonstrated his administration's commitment to defending US interests in the Gulf. He demanded an immediate Iraqi withdrawal and announced his intention to substantiate his demands with the use of military force. On 8 August, he declared the defence of Saudi Arabia to be a vital US interest[67] and cautioned the Saudi monarchy that they too were in danger. In response, the White House received an invitation from King Fahd to station American personnel in the Saudi Kingdom and by 12 September, over 100,000 American soldiers had been deployed.[68]

Holocaust imagery figured prominently in mobilising public support for the Gulf War. Bush described Saddam Hussein as worse than Hitler[69] and although "worse than" was too strong for many commentators, the analogy stuck.[70] A columnist for the *New York Times* wrote of Saddam "carrying out his own version of the final solution"[71] while The Simon Wiesenthal Centre claimed that German firms had built "gas chambers" in Iraq.[72] Geo-political considerations, rather than fear of the perpetuation of another Holocaust, underpinned the rationale behind Operation Desert Storm, although Holocaust imagery may have contributed to building public and Congressional support.

Far from acting as an asset in the crisis, Israel was dependent on America for protection. If Israel entered the war, it was hypothesised, the Saudis, Egyptians and Syrians would withdraw from the US-led coalition, refusing to align themselves with Israel against another Arab state. Although Bush publicly stated that if Israel became directly involved in the conflict "the coalition would not fall apart,"[73] his actions belied his public rhetoric. Considerable American pressure was exerted on Shamir to resist demands by his generals to retaliate or act in the absence of close co-ordination with Washington.[74] Shamir reportedly summed up the situation by saying that, as the destruction of Iraq's military capability was the prime objective and the Americans could effectively do this, Israel should not act in any way to hamper their efforts.[75] Yet Israel's inaction cannot be attributed solely to American pressure because Jerusalem had its own reasons to desist, among them fear of catalysing a war with Jordan that had the potential to destroy the Hashemite regime. King Hussein of Jordan knew that if he opposed Iraq he risked losing his throne or his life so he had little option but to align with Saddam Hussein. As Jordan is situated between Israel and Iraq, any Israeli action would have involved entering or transversing Jordanian territory and Jordan had pledge to fight to defend itself were its sovereignty violated.[76] While Israel was confident that it could take Jordan, such an event would have been potentially damaging to the coalition.

Nevertheless, the closeness of the relationship, or the lengths to which Washington was forced to go to restrain Jerusalem, was demonstrated by the decision to grant Israel access to prime intelligence material not usually divulged to other countries.[77] Bush stated that he was "in close touch with the key players there [in Israel] in terms of our objectives,"[78] and a hotline was established between the Pentagon Crisis Situation Room and the Israeli Defence Ministry in Tel Aviv. Avi Shlaim, a professor at Oxford University, claimed that the "hot line provided a significant inducement for Israel to maintain a low profile and to closely co-operate with the United States throughout the crisis."[79]

The Gulf War was the first and only occasion that US troops physically defended Israeli territory, as the newly arrived Patriot missile batteries, intended to upgrade Israel's air defences,[80] were operated by American crews. However, the Patriots were only partially successful in intercepting the Iraqi Scud missiles fired on Tel Aviv[81] and on 11 February, Minister of Defence Moshe Arens and Deputy Chief of Staff Ehud Barak made a secret visit to Washington to urge the President to reconsider his position and give Israel a green light to intervene in the fighting.[82] Bush and his advisors were prepared to acquiesce to some of Arens' demands for weapons and financial aid, but they refused to support direct Israeli intervention and maintained their veto on operational co-ordination.[83] Shamir recalled in his memoirs that "nothing . . . went more against my grain as a Jew and a Zionist, nothing more opposed the ideology on which my life had been based"[84] than not retaliating against Iraqi Scud missile attacks.[85]

The Gulf War was replete with contradictions and paradoxes for Israel's special relationship with America and demonstrated the differing perspectives from which small states and large states operate. Operation Desert Storm achieved America's stated objective of ousting Iraqi forces from Kuwait, but not the Israeli objective of totally neutralising Iraq as a military threat. Amongst members of the Knesset, the unstated hope was that, as opposed to Israel coming to America's aid, Israel's greatest ally would seize the opportunity to defeat Israel's most powerful enemy. For the first time in its history, Israel found itself aligned with the majority of the Arab nations. However, the similarity ended there because of a fundamental difference in their approach to the crisis. The Arabs, for the most part, wanted the restoration of Kuwaiti sovereignty and the status quo, whereas Israel advocated the destruction of the Iraqi war machine.[86]

In the final outcome, Iraq's military capability was only partially destroyed, leaving Saddam with the opportunity to pose a future threat to Israel's security. Israel's own capacity to deter future Arab aggression was probably weakened by the deliberate choice to abandon its doctrine of immediate retaliation and to allow the US to act on its behalf, as this policy resulted in a perceived decrease in its capacity for conventional deterrence.[87] However, in response to Iraqi provocations, Washington co-operated with Israel's efforts to acquire advanced defences against a potential missile attack. Two batteries of US Patriot missiles costing $200 million were scheduled for deployment to Israel in late 1991.[88]

While US military actions against Iraq were beneficial to Israel, Israel was fast becoming a vast diplomatic and military liability to the US. On 12 August, ten days into the crisis, Saddam suggested that Iraq might withdraw from Kuwait if Israel withdrew from all the occupied territories and Syria withdrew from Lebanon.[89] This proposal introduced the concept of "linkage" into the Middle Eastern diplomatic lexicon. Instantaneously, the Gulf crisis and the Arab–Israeli conflict became linked in the public mind, which encouraged the direct comparison between Israeli policy and that of Iraq. Washington responded by dismissing Saddam's rhetoric as a propaganda ploy, but the damage had been done and the proposal provided the Bush administration with a difficult dilemma. At a time when the President was attempting to unite the Arab and Western worlds behind his nation's policy, he was forced to defend the unpopular actions of its client against international scrutiny. He denied a direct parallel between the Iraqi occupation of Kuwait and the Israeli occupation of the West Bank and Gaza, but pledged that once Iraq left Kuwait, a resolution of the Arab–Israeli dispute would be a top priority.[90] His policy of "deferred linkage"[91] put Israel on the defensive, because from the perspective of the Likud,

Israel's status as a 'strategic asset' had been usurped by governments that had in the last fifty years joined forces to eradicate it.[92]

By spring 1991, the administration had begun to prove that it was as good as its word and on 6 March Bush addressed a joint session of Congress stating that:

> We must do all that we can to close the gap between Israel and the Arab states and between Israelis and Palestinians . . . . A comprehensive peace must be grounded in United National Security Council Resolutions 242 and 338 and the principle of territory for peace. This principle must be elaborated to provide for Israel's security and recognition, and at the same time for legitimate Palestinian political rights. Anything else would fail the twin tests of fairness and security. The time has come to put an end to Arab–Israeli conflict.[93]

Within days of the President's speech, Baker departed on the first of eight trips to the Middle East that resembled the shuttle diplomacy of former Secretary of State Henry Kissinger. He held meetings with the leaders of Saudi Arabia, Israel, Syria and the Palestinians, culminating in the convening of the Madrid peace conference on 30 October 1991.

The Road to Madrid

The objective of the Madrid process, which was launched in autumn 1991, was to build a comprehensive peace in the Middle East. The conference brought together representatives of all the main parties to the conflict and was facilitated by the fundamental transformation in the geo-political situation both internationally and regionally. First, with the end of the Cold War, Washington and Moscow no longer viewed the Middle East as an area of superpower rivalry and were prepared to work together to advance the peace process. Secondly, Bush had pledged that once Iraqi forces had withdrawn from Kuwait, movement in the Arab–Israeli peace process would be a key US priority. Thirdly, the position of the PLO had been weakened by its support of Iraq during the Gulf crisis, which had in turn resulted in a sharp decline in Arab political and financial support.[94]

Between the Gulf War and Syria's agreement to attend the Madrid conference in July 1991, US–Israeli negotiations focused on the modalities for the conference. Shamir thought it unlikely that Damascus would attend a conference that did not guarantee in advance the return of all territory captured by Israel in the June 1967 war. Consequently his tactics consisted of conceding just enough to the Americans to prevent Israel from being accused of causing the collapse of the peace process, while holding firm on procedural formulas as a device for maintaining American pressure on the Arabs. The American intention was for a regional conference sponsored by Washington and

Moscow based on UN Resolution 242 and incorporating a Palestinian negotiating team consisting of seven individuals, none of whom were resident in Jerusalem. Shamir agreed that the conference be based on Resolution 242 on the proviso that each party was permitted to maintain their own interpretation of the resolution. The Likud believed that Israel had complied with the territorial component of the resolution when it returned the Sinai to Egypt in 1979.

Baker's main objective was to involve the Likud in the negotiating process and in this endeavour he was prepared to accommodate Shamir's demands on the composition of the Palestinian delegation. He rejected virtually all the Palestinian demands, including a request for an overt role for the PLO, partly as punishment for its alignment with Iraq in the recent war. In contrast, Jerusalem got its own way on the question of Palestinian representation to the point where Shamir was permitted to see the names of the Palestinian negotiation team prior to its announcement.[95]

On 14 July, the Syrian President Hafiz al-Assad formally agreed to attend the conference.[96] Shamir had little choice but to do likewise or risk being blamed by Washington for the breakdown of the process. American prestige was at an all-time high in the region and as Washington had made the peace process a major policy priority, it was difficult for the parties to reject the initiative. For the first time since Camp David in 1979, the US was ready and able to apply serious pressure against a Likud government that sought to deliberately stall or avoid negotiations.

Once the Israeli government accepted the fact that it had no choice but to participate, Shamir invested extensive diplomatic efforts in trying to neutralise the forum.[97] The talks in Madrid were convened on the basis of the Shamir plan[98] and Israel succeeded in excluding the PLO, confined the remit of the UN to observer status, and established that peace should emerge as a product of direct negotiations between the parties and not by superpower edict.[99]

In his opening speech on the conference's first day, Bush spoke of the need for territorial compromise but said that Washington had no map for final borders. He spoke of the need for "fairness" for the Palestinians, but said nothing about either Palestinian self-determination or statehood. Bush also made no mention of his opposition to the continued construction of Israeli settlements in the West Bank and Gaza. In defining how he saw the conference progressing, he embraced the Israeli position in its entirety. The real negotiations he said, would take place in bilateral talks between Israel and its various Arab interlocutors. Washington's role was to act as a "catalyst" or "facilitator," with the opportunity for real progress and compromise remaining in the hands of the parties themselves.[100] Ross emphasised that the considerations the President outlined in his speech demonstrated that American policy had been crafted in a manner sensitive to Israeli concerns.[101]

The delegations then progressed to the bilateral negotiations which lasted from 10–18 December. The first face-to-face meetings and speeches of the bilateral committees were of symbolic significance, although little substantive progress ensued.[102] Shamir's opening speech focused on past Jewish tragedy, particularly the Holocaust, and referred to the Jews exclusive claims to the land. He emphasised that the origins of the conflict were existential and not territorial.[103] However, the Israeli–Palestinian track did not get beyond corridor diplomacy because the Palestinian team demanded that Israel negotiate autonomy with it separately and not with the full Jordanian–Palestinian delegation. The Israelis refused to countenance this because to do so would constitute a breach of the Madrid rules on joint delegation discussions. By the third round of bilaterals, this issue had been resolved and the Palestinians submitted an outline for interim self-government that was tantamount to a state in the making. The radical elements in Shamir's government prevented him submitting a full plan for autonomy, but by the fifth round of talks, Israel proposed municipal elections and 'early empowerment' that would give the Palestinians immediate control over 19 hospitals in the territories.[104] This was rejected by the Palestinians because Israel would still retain control of the territories.

Despite the lack of progress Washington remained aloof from the negotiations. They saw the bilaterals as essentially 'getting to know you' sessions for both sides and did not expect much progress until after the Israeli elections. The American role as facilitator rather then mediator certainly adhered to Shamir's strategy on the Palestinian issue. Yet while the Americans were accommodating on procedure, they were prepared to confront Shamir over substance, and in particular the expansion of settlements.

Loan Guarantees and Settlements

From the outset, the question of loan guarantees and settlements was a source of tension in relations between the Bush administration and the Shamir government. Shamir's perception of Israeli security was based on an ideological view of the land and the assumption of Israel's intrinsic right to it.[105] For him, settlement activity was imperative to making future territorial compromise impossible and his approach to the peace process was based on this context. Shamir recognised that Bush did not support Israel's settlement policy but he relied on the fact that the President would not consider the issue crucial to American interests. As he explained to the *Jerusalem Post* in February 1990:

> There are things we do not agree on with the US government. For example settlements . . . It is an old thing. There was also no agreement with the Reagan administration. But it has not harmed the advancement of friendly ties between

> both countries. The principles in our relations with the US is that there is friendship, common interests and joint strategic co-operation, despite differences of opinion.[106]

Thus Shamir made a crucial error in underestimating Bush's strength of feeling on the question of settlement activity, which the President saw as the touchstone of American credibility in the Arab world. Following their first meeting in Washington in April 1989, the President was angered when Shamir reneged on a promise he believed had been made to slow settlement construction.[107] At the meeting Shamir had tried to present settlements as a purely domestic issue and was surprised by Bush's hostility to the subject. To end the discussion Shamir had told Bush that settlements "won't be a problem," by which he seems to have meant that as settlements were not an impediment to US–Israeli relations in the past they would not be in the future.[108] However for Bush, the settlement issue was the "litmus test" of Shamir's attitude towards the United States[109] and he understood this as the Prime Minister's commitment to curb settlement activity. When, two weeks later, a new settlement was established Bush concluded that the Israeli leader was "playing him for a fool"[110] and was outraged when Shamir told the US Ambassador to Israel, Bill Brown, that "settlements are not an earth shattering matter for the President."[111]

The administration did not permit the subject of settlements to recede to the back of the US–Israeli agenda. On 22 May, appearing before a House Foreign Affairs subcommittee, Baker overturned Reagan's policy of tacitly endorsing settlement activity and labelled the expansion of Israeli settlements a major obstacle to peace. The following day, Bush echoed this view[112] and in his June 1989 Aipac speech Baker called on Israel to "stop settlement activity."[113] However, the administration did not have a form of leverage with which to press its views until Peres mentioned the possibility of $400 million in loan guarantees to cover the cost of absorbing new immigrants. Baker asked Congress to attach a proviso to the guarantees that Israel undertake to freeze all settlement activity, otherwise US dollars would free up other money in the Israeli budget for settlement construction. Congressional reluctance to endorse Baker's request culminated in Israel obtaining the loans without a settlement freeze, but with the proviso that Israel not use the money directly for settlement activity or provide incentives for immigrants to move beyond the green line.[114]

Following congressional approval of the loan, Baker became aware that Israel was planning to build a further 12,000 new homes for settlers. When asked, Shamir's office informed the Americans that the cabinet had not approved the plans and the guarantee was granted. But three weeks later Sharon told reporters that the true figure was 13,500 homes and authorisation had already been given, alleviating the need for a cabinet agreement. Embarrassed and angered by the

Likud's actions, the administration was determined that such a situation would not be repeated.

The $10 Billion Question

On 22 January 1991, six days after coalition forces launched the air campaign against Saddam's forces in Kuwait and Iraq, Israel announced that it would shortly seek $10 billion in loan guarantees for the resettlement of Soviet Jews.[115] In acting with restraint throughout the Gulf War, the Shamir government believed it had imposed a moral claim on the administration. The President took a different view, as by his calculations, the need to protect Israel had placed a burden on the US in terms of diverted military resources. Israel's moral claim, therefore, did not produce a change in Bush's attitude towards ongoing Israeli settlement activity and the ill-timed loan guarantee request exacerbated tensions.[116]

The administration had wanted to link the guarantees to a settlement freeze or at the very least for Israel to delay its request for 120 days until after the Madrid Conference had opened. However, the Shamir government had such confidence in the special relationship, based on its congressional support,[117] that it refused both ideas and formally submitted its request on 6 September. The Israeli strategy was to use Aipac to mobilise grass roots support among Israel's sympathisers in the US. They did this by using media-friendly figures, including Deputy Foreign Minister Binyamin Netanyahu and Health Minister Ehud Olmert, to promote the message that this was 'humanitarian assistance'. Simultaneously with this, Aipac and the Israeli Embassy worked Capitol Hill to drum up legislative support behind the loan guarantees. This activity was to culminate on 12 September with a rally in Washington, D.C. supporting the application.

However, Bush undercut the position of the lobby by appealing directly to the Congress and the American people. The President asked "every single Member of Congress to defer, just for 120 days, consideration of this absorption aid package,"[118] because the construction of settlements did "not enhance the prospects for peace."[119] Following what was perceived to be the successful execution of the Gulf War, Bush's approval rating with the American people was at an all-time high. He leveraged off his popularity in a televised address in which he both reiterated American support for Israel and explained his position on the loan guarantees.

> For more than 40 years the U.S. has been Israel's closest friend in the world, and this remains the case and will as long as I am President. This is a friendship backed up by real support. Just months ago American men and women in uniform, risked their lives to defend Israel in the face of Iraqi scud missiles. And indeed, Desert

> Storm . . . achieved the defeat of Israel's most dangerous adversary. . . . The Congress charges the President with the conduct of the Nation's foreign policy . . . there's an attempt by some in the Congress to prevent the President from taking steps central to the Nation's security.[120]

Israel was financially vulnerable and Bush exploited America's unprecedented economic leverage to the full. When asked during a press conference on 23 May 1991 if he was willing to use US aid as a lever to pressure Israel, Bush claimed that he was "not pressuring anybody" and was taking "the credibility that I believe the U.S. has now in Israel and the Gulf countries and in other countries in the Middle East to try to be a catalyst for peace."[121] Shamir interpreted Bush's address as being about more than just opposition to settlement activity and claimed that it revealed the President's "true feelings and most basic attitudes towards the Jewish state."[122]

Against the backdrop of massive public support for the President, his speech undermined Israel's support in Congress and his request for a 120 day moratorium on a decision was granted. Even when negotiations recommenced in January 1992, the Israeli government was unable to mobilise sufficient support within the US to secure the guarantees on its own terms.[123] The pro-Israel lobby was reluctant to use its full force to pressure the administration and although Shamir was confident that a compromise could be reached whereby Israel would not have to commit to a settlement freeze but allow the US some control over the money granted, his optimism was misplaced.[124] The administration required a settlement freeze that was unacceptable to the radicalism of Shamir's government and by mid-March either Bush or Shamir had rejected all the compromises submitted. Yet Shamir remained confident that he would be able to extract the money at a later date as the US Presidential election drew near and Bush would be in need of Jewish money and votes. However, once again Shamir made a tactical miscalculation as Baker allegedly summed up the administration's position thus: "F**k the Jews. They don't vote for us anyway."[125]

Public acquiescence in Bush's request for a moratorium on a decision on the loan guarantees was not indicative of a decline in grassroots support for Israel, but was a reflection of a change in priorities and perceptions that occurred in the aftermath of the Gulf War. For weeks the American public had witnessed an intensive media spectacle of the coalition attack on Iraq, with coverage replicating that of the latest Hollywood blockbuster rather than a serious, newsworthy event. The American people had seen first-hand the courage and bravery of their armed forces and the precision and sophistication of American weapons systems. Their President had promised them a short and decisive war with minimal casualties and was perceived to have delivered on his promise. The US had liberated Kuwait and in so doing had once again demonstrated the nation's power to do good. In addition, US forces had risked their lives to defend Israel and in this endeavour they were also perceived to have been successful. Although Iraqi scud missiles had hit Israeli towns, casualties were minimal and US Patriot missiles had successfully intercepted a number of scuds. At the President's request, Israel had remained out of the conflict and had relied on America for its protection. Against this backdrop, the majority of the American people were in no doubt of Bush's commitment to Israel's security and believed his claim that withholding loan guarantees was not detrimental to Israel's national security and served the American national interest. In the wake of the Gulf War, Americans believed they had demonstrated their country's support for Israel. This, combined with his personal prestige and the general reticence with which the American people confront requests for foreign aid, gave Bush his victory.

Bush's decision-making was characterised by a case-by-case approach that centred on the details and circumstances immediately at hand and less on ideology or concern with consistency.[126] For Bush, settlement construction was a major 'detail' that was an obstacle to peace negotiations and with little ideological calling of his own, he was unable to comprehend Shamir's ideological commitment to them. He was not asking Israel to adopt a policy that he perceived as threatening to either its security or national interest. But by withholding the $10 billion in loan guarantees he had forced Shamir to the negotiating table and from this perspective his approach had been successful. Bush himself felt that he owed no debt to either Israel or American Jewry. On the other hand he did not want to alienate Israelis across the political spectrum and attached conditions to the loan guarantees that he knew Shamir, but not the majority of Israelis, would find impossible to accept. In so doing, he presented Shamir with a stark choice: "either halt settlements and enter into serious negotiations with the Arabs, or lose American economic and political support."[127]

The price the Shamir government paid for alienating the American President was not simply its failure to attain the loan guarantees, but the breakdown in the Likud's relationship with the administration. The consequences of this became evident in the run-up to the Israeli election, when the administration apparently tried to undermine the Likud position by intimating that the US–Israeli special relationship would be under threat if the party remained in power.[128] This was reinforced a week prior to the Israeli elections when Baker publicly accepted Rabin's campaign distinction between political and security settlements.[129] Ultimately, it was clear that in the post-Cold War world, the relationship depended on the peace index; i.e., to what extent – in American eyes – Israel was committed to the peace process. On this score, the administration had concluded that the Likud could not be trusted.

Operation Solomon

US administrations have always supported the emigration of Jews to Israel, and on this matter the Bush White House was no different; indeed it was through humanitarian gestures that Bush most overtly demonstrated his support for Israel. In 1989, as Israel resumed diplomatic relations with Ethiopia and the war that ravaged the country intensified, the Shamir government embarked on a strategy to rescue the remnant Jewish population stranded there. By late May, forces hostile to the Ethiopian President, Mengistu Haile Mariam, were converging on Addis Ababa. Jerusalem decided that the Falasha Jewish community, now acutely at risk, would have to be evacuated without delay. In fact, in the preceding months, the Israeli government had transferred $40 million into the Swiss bank accounts of influential Ethiopian ministers to facilitate precisely such an enterprise. The objective of the plan, known as Operation Solomon, was to evacuate approximately 14,000 Ethiopian Jews from Addis Ababa to Tel Aviv, in under thirty-six hours. In addition to the logistical challenge of a mass airlift, Washington's intercession proved crucial.

Mengistu made a 'covering letter' from the White House a pre-condition for allowing the Jews to be flown out and after a personal appeal from Shamir, Bush exhorted the Ethiopian government to cooperate in the Falasha evacuation.[130] Consequently, Operation Solomon was a logistical success. The Israeli air force crews managed to fit the entire refugee aggregation into thirty-three aircraft, transporting them to the safety of Israel.

Shamir recalled in his memoirs that Bush's part in the process "won him my deepest gratitude, the more so because my request for his help came at a time when he and his administration were angered by what they believed was Israel's hampering of the peace process."[131] Despite discord in both the inter-state relationship and the personal relationship between the two leaders, the Bush administration proved once again that in an extremity Jerusalem could rely on Washington. As had proved the case in the past, discord and disagreement in one area of the relationship, however serious, did not impact on the fundamental bonds that united the two states.

Bush and Rabin

Many of the periods of crises that categorised the Bush–Shamir relationship were attributable to personal conflicts and the contradictory ideological beliefs of the two leaders. As a result, progress on the peace process with Shamir in power proved impossible. The election of Rabin as Prime Minister on 23 June 1992 ushered in a turning point in US–Israeli relations. The *New York Times* claimed that from America's perspective, the election result was "a good one." Steven Spiegel, claimed that in celebrating Rabin's victory, the people were expressing more than relief. "It is a sense that our friends are back."[132]

The policy of the Labour government was predicated on the view that Israel was a normal state and not on an ideological crusade to fulfil the destiny of the Jewish people through control of the whole land of Israel. Labour did not subscribe to the view that land had an existential value and this enabled Rabin to support territorial compromise and encourage an expanded US role in the peace process, resulting in an improvement in US–Israeli relations. Bush set out to signal a warmer relationship between the two countries by evoking the language of the 'special relationship'. He referred to Israel as a 'strategic partner', and emphasised their shared commitment to "democracy, and to common values, as well as a solid commitment to Israel's security, including its qualitative military edge."[133] Immediately after the election, he invited Rabin to the United States and on 10–11 August demonstrated the personal closeness of US–Israeli ties by hosting him at his Kennebunkport home in Maine.[134] This was a meeting between political allies in the broader sense of the word and both leaders stood to gain domestically and internationally. For Bush, Rabin was a constructive player in the Middle East chess game, while Rabin acknowledged that Bush was responsible for his electoral victory and could deliver the financial wherewithal necessary to strengthen his political base at home.[135] Both parties sought to improve military cooperation and Bush demonstrated his commitment to Israel's security with the agreement to sell Apache and Black Hawk helicopters to Israel from US stockpiles in Europe.[136]

Bush and Rabin also found common ground on the question of settlements. The Israeli Prime Minister perceived a partial settlement freeze to be in Israel's interest because it facilitated territorial compromise. Rabin retained the right to increase 'security settlements' to enhance the demographic balance in the territories Israel would seek to annex in the final status agreements, but the construction of 7,000 'political' housing units were frozen and government incentives for settlement were ended. In response, the President re-evaluated his position on the loan guarantees and pledged to secure congressional approval now that the two leaders had an agreement on basic principles. Irrespective of the fact that 80 percent of Americans opposed the $10 billion loan guarantees, as part of a more general hostility to foreign aid, Bush authorised the legislation in the form of an amendment to the Foreign Aid Bill. His actions were a stark illustration of how party political Washington's involvement in the Middle East had become.[137] The seeming parity of influence in the relationship was also demonstrated when in apparent return for the loan guarantees, Rabin made only mild protests over the subsequent $9 billion sale of seventy-two F-15XFs to Saudi Arabia.[138]

Bush then urged a quick and intensive round of new negotiations which began in Washington on 24 August and lasted for a month. The administration had apparently learnt its lesson from dealing with Shamir and left the parties meeting in the talks free to pursue their own discussions. However, in September 1992 Baker departed the State Department to run Bush's re-election campaign, which signalled that, for the remaining tenure of the administration, domestic politics, not foreign affairs, would be the top priority.

Bush's Declining Fortunes

The backdrop against which the Bush administration devised its Middle East policy provided a stark contrast to that of Johnson, Nixon and Reagan, because it occurred at a time of great change in the international system and was presided over by a President and Secretary of State who had only minimal affinity for the Jewish state.[139] Given the changing international system and the diminution of the Soviet threat, had the US–Israeli relationship been based solely on American calculations of strategic or economic interest, pressure should have been exerted on Israel to relinquish territory as a form of appeasement to the Arabs. After all, there are far more Arabs than there are Israelis, and oil is to be found in abundance in the Arab world, not Israel. Yet the administration stood firmly behind Israel, adopted the peace proposal submitted by Shamir and convened a peace conference that adhered to Israel's exact criteria for negotiations.

Bush's team was convinced that security for the Jewish state would remain elusive until a peace settlement was concluded and that such a peace could not be reached without American firmness towards both sides.[140] Despite the lack of overt pressure on Israel to conclude a peace agreement, the commitment of these men to the enhancement of Israeli security was viewed with some scepticism because of public perceptions of the administration's policies. The administration came under increasing attack from Israel, the American Jewish community and members of Congress. Mel Levine, a congressman for California, told *Newsweek* reporters that "President Bush and Secretary Baker appear[ed] determined to destroy the special relationship between Israel and the United States."[141]

The paradox for Baker's team was that their administration had worked hard to tangibly improve Israel's security.[142] Bush had crippled Iraq, Israel's most threatening neighbour, won repeal of the UN resolution equating Zionism with racism; cajoled other states, most notably the Soviet Union and China, to open diplomatic relations with Israel, and helped tens of thousands of Ethiopian and Soviet Jews to immigrate to the Jewish homeland. Most of all, the Baker-generated peace talks delivered what Israel had sought since its creation: face-to-face talks with all of its Arab neighbours. Whatever the administration's critics argued, the actual conduct of the peace talks was not hostile to Israel's position. Talks followed the Camp David framework, the administration supported Israel's refusal to allow the participation of the PLO or Palestinians from East Jerusalem or the territories and refrained from putting forward its own proposal for a settlement.[143] Moreover, the US government steadfastly supported Israel's position on an interim period of autonomy and made no stipulations about the final outcome.[144] Settlement construction was not stopped during this period and once Rabin replaced Shamir as Prime Minister, Bush contravened the wishes of the American people, as expressed in the press, by granting Israel's request for financial aid.

However, these successes were overshadowed by the distorted account of the loan guarantees promoted by the Israeli leadership.[145] Shamir, in particular, was incensed by Bush's refusal to grant the loan without a settlement freeze in exchange. It was as if he believed his country had an inalienable right to financial support.[146] On the domestic front, American Jews were furious over Bush's supposed questioning of the loyalty of those who dared to lobby Congress for the guarantees.[147] If greater emphasis had been placed on publicly reassuring both American Jews and the Israeli leadership of Washington's commitment to Israel, perhaps open hostility to the administration's position might have been avoided. As Kurtzer acknowledged, "People have an uneasy feeling because of words. But the bottom line is, you have to watch what Bush and Baker have done. What they've done has been good for Israel."[148] It was the polarisation of views between the Likud and Labour that enabled Washington to advance its own agenda. If the administration acted in a way that could be considered contrary to Israel's interests, it was its ideological interests as defined by the Likud, not its security interests as defined by Labour.

The Middle East preoccupied the administration of President Bush to an unprecedented degree and he placed his credibility as President on the advancement of the Arab–Israeli peace process. The term during which he served as President is of particular note because of the minimal impact fundamental changes in the national, strategic, economic, bureaucratic and domestic spheres appeared to exert on US policy towards Israel. As the undisputed global hegemon, Washington should have been in a unique position to shape the Middle East peace process and its relations with the Jewish state. Yet even the most determined efforts at peace-making met with only limited success, and the Israeli government appeared to exert almost equal leverage as the White House in determining the course of negotiations.

8

FRAMING AMERICAN FOREIGN POLICY IN THE NEW WORLD ORDER

BETWEEN THE COLLAPSE OF THE SOVIET UNION and the Gulf War at the outset of the 1990s, and the election of George W. Bush as President of the United States and Ariel Sharon as Prime Minister of Israel, both in 2001, the relationship between the two countries confronted perhaps its most significant challenges. In the aftermath of the Cold War, Washington's strategic and geo-political priorities had shifted, and perceptions of the national interest were suddenly subject to re-evaluation.

The Strategic Interest Approach

Since the June war of 1967, Israeli politicians had attempted to ground their country's special relationship with the United States in terms of Israel's contribution to America's strategic interests. This rationale was premised on Israel's ability to act as a bulwark against the perceived threat of the Soviet Union and as both a counter to, and deterrent against, the forces of Arab radicalism. But with the evident decline of the Soviet Union, the traditional threat to American interests was considerably reduced and Israel's role as a strategic asset was called into question.

Yet in April 1990, Congressman Les Aspin stated that "the demise of the Cold War should not change our [Americas] strategic relationship with Israel."[1] He argued that the relationship was not premised on the Soviet threat but on Israel's need to deal with the threat to its own existence posed by the Arabs and on the continuing strategic needs of the United States despite the absence of any recent Soviet threat.[2] Two conclusions can be drawn from this assertion: first, that the strategic relationship should be maintained because it served Israel's strategic needs; and secondly, that Israel continued to be a strategic asset in terms of other regional threats to American interests. The events of the 1990s, however, demonstrated that Israel was hardly in a position to protect America's strategic interests in any of the areas in which they came under threat.

The Gulf War

The Gulf War challenged US perceptions of Israel as a strategic asset because the Jewish state had potentially become a dangerous liability and more dependent than ever on America for protection. In contrast to the Jordanian crisis of 1970, when Israel had been called upon to act as a US proxy,[3] Washington's efforts throughout the Gulf War centred on counselling Israel to practice restraint. As Avi Shlaim explains:

> Here was a conflict which threatened America's most vital interests in the region and the best service that Israel could render to her senior partner was to refrain from doing anything. Far from being a strategic asset, Israel was widely perceived as an embarrassment and a liability.[4]

Ironically therefore, Israel's greatest contribution to the war was to show "great understanding for the interests of the U.S. and interests of others involved in th[e] coalition,"[5] by doing nothing. In this singularly important respect, Israel emerged from the crisis as a loser and its government was forced to find a new logic to defend its status as a strategic asset.

Defending the New Strategic Interest

In a renewed effort to demonstrate Israel's continued relevance to US policy, Israeli politicians increasingly argued that the country could now play a new strategic role in the Middle East by containing the forces of radicalism and maintaining the status quo in a region where religious militancy was on the rise. Superficially at least, this appeared to be a convincing argument because the American administration still considered its interests to be under threat. It was just the nature of the threat that had changed.

In the post-Cold War world, the greatest threat Washington perceived to its interests in the Middle East derived from radical states such as Iraq and Iran, and the increasing appeal of what its opponents call Islamic Fundamentalism. This perceived threat manifested itself in three distinct ways. First, through the proliferation of non-conventional weapons, as the radical states, Iraq, Iran, Syria and North Korea, intensified their quest for non-conventional – that is, biological, chemical and nuclear – weapons. Secondly, through the threat militant Islam posed to the more traditional conservative leaders of the Middle East[6] who provided America's traditional basis of support. Thirdly, through the threat of Islamic terrorist organisations against Western targets globally. Set against this backdrop, for Israel to continue to be perceived as a strategic asset, it was necessary for the Jewish state to demonstrate how it could assist the US in preventing nuclear proliferation in the Middle East (apart from its own) and thwarting the spread of fundamentalism and terrorism.

Nuclear Proliferation

In the early 1990s, the US Defense Department turned its attention to missile proliferation in the Third World.[7] Both the Departments of State and Defence focused on those countries that had previously been armed by America: Iran under the Shah and Saddam Hussein's Iraq during the 1980s. Iran was accused of seeking to develop nuclear, biological and chemical missile systems; Iraq was suspected of being able to renew germ weapon production if UN inspections ended.[8] Yet Washington's approach to non-conventional proliferation in the Middle East was contradictory. While the government imposed stringent measures to thwart the spread of nuclear material, American decision-makers accepted Israel's somewhat oblique nuclear status and manipulated the threat of Israeli nuclear capability to constrain the radical states. Washington could therefore be seen as "selectively condemning the development of weapons of mass destruction by its 'enemies'," and "actively support[ing] weapons programmes when undertaken by its own clients and when it thus serves to consolidate US hegemony."[9]

For example, during the Gulf War, American intelligence alerted the administration to signs that indicated Israel had gone on full nuclear alert, and had moved missile launchers armed with nuclear warheads into the open, and deployed them facing Iraq. In response, and to deter Saddam Hussein from unleashing a chemical attack, Washington exploited media reports about the increasing number of Israelis who argued that a chemical attack would justify the use of nuclear weapons. For example, Secretary of Defence Richard Cheney stated on 2 February 1991 that if Iraq used chemical weapons against Israel, its government might retaliate with non-conventional weapons. Cheney's statement was significant for a number of reasons. First, because the warning was issued not in Washington's name but in Israel's, secondly because it confirmed that Israel was capable of realising a non-conventional option, and thirdly because the warning to refrain from escalation was directed solely at Iraq not Israel.[10] In this way, Washington used Israel's nuclear capability as a device for attempting to restrain the radical states and curb the spread of non-conventional weapons.

The importance placed on preventing nuclear proliferation was demonstrated in May 1995 by the level of American diplomatic activity devoted to securing the renewal and ratification of the Nuclear Non-Proliferation Treaty (NPT). The debate surrounding the ratification of the NPT is demonstrative of the complex and unconventional nature of US–Israeli relations. By signing the NPT Israel would have openly acknowledged its status as a nuclear power, thus diminishing the legitimacy of US calls to curb the global spread of non-conventional weapons. By supporting Israel's refusal to sign the treaty, Washington signalled to Iran and Iraq[11] that if they developed their own nuclear weapons programmes that threatened Israel or other American allies in the region, the US would endorse Israel's ability to retaliate in kind. In this intangible way, it could be argued, Israel maintained its position as a strategic asset while consolidating the region's existing balance of power structure.

However, the NPT offers little protection against the covert proliferation of non-conventional weapons. In March 2003, when the administration of George W. Bush resolved to take military action against Saddam Hussein's Iraq, with the stated objective of destroying weapons of mass destruction, it was London, not Jerusalem, that provided the diplomatic and military support for the war. While Israel may have temporarily thwarted the Iraqi nuclear programme with the bombing of Osiraq in 1981, the level of distrust with which it is viewed by the Arab world, meant it was unable to actively participate in either of the two subsequent US-led wars against Iraq in 1991 and 2003. From this perspective, Israel's status as a strategic asset in the traditional sense, is highly questionable.

Islamic Terror

In the eyes of the Western world, Islamic Fundamentalism and terrorism are inextricably interwoven. This is because many organisations that use terror as a political weapon, including Hamas, Hezbollah, Islamic Jihad and al-Qaeda, make selective use of Islamic doctrines to try to legitimate their actions. The US State Department's list of countries sponsoring terrorism compiled in 1995 included five supposedly Islamic Middle Eastern states: Iran, Iraq, Syria, Libya and Sudan. The reports categorised Iran, as "the premier state sponsor of international terrorism," with Sudan running a close second.[12]

During the 1990s, the battle against terrorism consolidated the US–Israeli relationship by providing a mutual enemy and a coalescence of interests in collaborating against terrorist organisations. This was one area where Israel's experience proved particularly valuable because, until 11 September 2001, Washington had been the junior partner in terms of first-hand experience of the material and psychological devastation terror inflicts on civil society. While Israel had been the habitual victim of terrorist attacks since its creation in 1948, America's first experience of terrorist activity on its soil had occurred only with the bombing of the World Trade Centre (WTC) in New York in 1993.[13] Though far less devastating than its successor, as a result of this attack, Islamic terrorism became an increasingly important factor in US policy calculations in the Middle East.[14] Given Israel's experience in defending the state against terrorism, Jerusalem became a natural ally in what Washington saw as an American-led battle to defend the world order. Reports in early 2001 that Osama bin Laden had begun to target Israel as well as the US only underscored the opportunities for collaboration.[15]

Over time, this coalescence of interests proved to be somewhat superficial. As during the Gulf War, when America acted to defend its vital interests, Israel was sometimes seen as a hindrance rather than a help. In retaliating against the terrorist attacks on the WTC and Pentagon America sought to marshal the support of the Western and Muslim worlds. In so doing, Washington relied on Britain rather than Israel to act as its foremost ally. Meanwhile, in the guise of assisting Washington, Israel's Prime Minister Ariel Sharon, exploited the situation for Israel's advantage. By describing Palestinian leader Yassir Arafat as Israel's Osama bin Laden, Sharon tried to win American acquiescence in Israel's reoccupation of Palestinian land from October 2001. In so doing, Israel inflamed regional tensions, further alienating Arab and Muslim opinion, at a time when America sought their support.

Islamic Democracy

The ability of Israel or any state to prevent the spread of militant Islam is highly questionable. This is because its real growth has often occurred at least as much through democratic elections as by state sponsorship or violent revolution. Given the value attributed to Israel's democratic status, it is ironic that it is through expressions of the popular will that fundamentalism is posing its most significant challenge to the existing political and social order. The Western world and those Middle East governments that have undertaken tightly controlled experiments in political pluralism have been shocked by its potency.[16] In the Egyptian parliamentary elections of 1987, the coalition dominated by the fundamentalist Muslim Brotherhood emerged as the biggest opposition party in a contest engineered to assure victory for the ruling elite.[17] Similarly, fundamentalists outdistanced all other opposition parties in the 1989 election for the Tunisian parliament, although the winner-takes-all system gave every seat to the ruling party.[18] In the same year, the fundamentalists nearly captured the Lower House of the Jordanian parliament and in 1990,[19] fundamentalism swept the countrywide local election in Algeria.[20] Following Algerian independence, it was only France's support of the Algerian government that prevented the expansion of Islamic democracy. For Western theorists of democracy, it was "as if the Arabs had defied the laws of gravity." Jeane Kirkpatrick went so far as to claim that: "The Arab world is the only part of the world where I've been shaken in my conviction that if you let the people decide, they will make fundamentally rational decisions."[21]

Conclusions

For decades, the strategic relationship between the US and Israel was premised on the perceived threat of the Soviet Union. However, it could be claimed that this was something of a façade because the "ease with which Washington adjusted to losing its primary rationale for strategic cooperation,"[22] indicated that the relationship was more than a military alliance based solely on hostility to another party.[23] It would therefore be inaccurate to contend that either the end of the Cold War, the impact of the Gulf War or the rise of Islamic extremism, has precluded Israel from continuing to perform the role of a strategic asset in the Middle East. On the other hand, there is more to the US–Israeli relationship than a mutuality of strategic interest. Karen Puschel provides an apt summation for the longevity of the relationship:

> It is this complex mix of motivations for strategic cooperation that serves as its greatest protection. Because there was no one imperative for strategic cooperation, there will likely never be one reason for its decline. Strategic cooperation exists, in the final analysis, because an extremely close US–Israeli relationship exists.[24]

The Economic Interest Approach

At the end of the Cold War the United States re-evaluated many of its financial commitments to its allies across the globe. Aid to Pakistan, Japan and Germany was reduced, as was America's contribution to the NATO budget. As threat perceptions initially decreased following the collapse of the Soviet Union, some diminution in foreign aid seemed a rational response to the new international reality. In this regard, Israel remained something of an anomaly because it was excluded from Washington's review of its foreign economic obligations. Aid to Israel was not revised downward from Cold War levels and in certain circumstances it was actually increased.[25] Neither the strategic interest nor the idea of an 'economic investment trap' adequately explains the economic ties between the two countries. (An 'investment trap' refers to circumstances in which a patron maintains a commitment to a client, not because it directly enhances its own well-being, but in an effort to protect previous economic and political investments and as a device for maintaining credibility or prestige.[26])

However this type of argument is not wholly convincing in the case of Israel. In the absence of the Soviet Union, or another state to rival its global supremacy, Washington could certainly have curtailed its commitment to Jerusalem without the fear that the position of influence it enjoyed would be usurped by a competing power. This argument also overlooks the fact, that economic relations were a *product* of an existing relationship between the governments of the two states, not the initialiser of relations. That the rationale for financial aid to Israel is not confined to that of economic necessity is demonstrated by the fact that the vast majority of Congress opposed foreign aid in general but consistently voted in favour of aid to Israel.

Traditionally the Republican Party for political cultural reasons – mainly their belief that the role of government in the economic sphere should be limited[27] – had been more stringent with the management of the foreign aid budget than the Democrats. In view of Republican aversion to foreign aid, their resounding victory in the 1994 congressional elections generated concern amongst the governments of the Middle East that US foreign aid commitments to the region would be reduced. When Republican Senator Jesse Helms of North Carolina, became Chairman of the Senate Foreign Relations Committee, he was critical of what he described as American "overspending" on the Arab–Israeli peace process. Helms estimated that Middle East peace had cost the US $80 billion-$100 billion since the Camp David agreement and determined to use his position to reduce future expenditure. In contrast, the Clinton administration defended foreign aid as a fundamental US commitment to the peace process and as a tangible demonstration of American credibility in the region.

Despite fierce opposition from some quarters, the special status accorded Israel across the government as a whole, was demonstrated by the congressional decision in 1995 to leave levels of assistance to the Middle East unchanged, while reducing foreign aid appropriations elsewhere. In the fiscal year 1996, the total foreign aid bill was reduced by 11 percent from $13.6 billion for the fiscal year 1995 to $12.1 billion.[28] Despite this, in accordance with the terms of the Camp David Accords, Egypt and Israel continued to receive an annual $2.15 billion and $3 billion respectively. In addition, in 1995, the US Defense Department signed contracts to buy in excess of $3 billion of military products from Israeli companies.[29] Aid to the Palestinian Authority (PA), which first began after the signing of the Oslo Accords,[30] was also increased in February 1995, when Vice-President Al Gore announced that the United States would provide $73 million to finance three projects in Gaza to generate employment for the Palestinians and to improve the region's infrastructure.[31] In June of the same year, Congress supported the White House's proposal to give $75 million in economic assistance to the PA and extended by 45 days the Middle East Facilitation Act, which permitted US aid to the Palestinians.[32]

From a realpolitik perspective, US economic support and foreign aid to Israel may be said to have exceeded the rationale for its existence, in that US influence in Israel is assured and is not challenged by any other power. Therefore, the argument that financial support was merely a product of the Cold War is greatly undermined. Similarly, economic aid is no longer linked to the need to sustain the Israeli economy, which has become one of the strongest in the Middle East. In 1998, Israel's GDP exceeded $96 billion,[33] exports totalled $30 billion and GDP per capita stood at $16,000, putting it on a par with the Western world. The increasing openness of the Israeli economy enables its large conglomerates to raise capital by floating equity issues on the New York Stock Exchange. Direct investment in Israel has reached over $2 billion and strategic alliances between foreign and domestic conglomerates have multiplied in recent years.[34]

Although aid to Israel is impacted upon by a more stringent budgetary environment in the US, the fact remains that Washington will use all the economic means at its disposal to guarantee the security of Israel and the longevity of another free market economic system and to underwrite the cost of peace in the Middle East.[35] On occasions, political reality is such that the most prudent economic policy is politically unacceptable to the nation, and non-economic benefits are considered to out-weigh the economic costs.[36] The financial commitment to Israel, therefore, is not necessarily a product of economic prudence and the rationale for its longevity must be found in another dimension of the US–Israeli relationship.

The Domestic Politics Approach

It could be argued that in the absence of the Soviet threat, the American Jewish community is perceived to have become the principal bulwark against the erosion of US support for Israel. While this offers a one-dimensional view of US–Israeli relations, it reflects the perceived power of the pro-Israel lobby and the perceived importance of the American Jewish vote in influencing Congress. According to this argument, if the pro-Israel lobby failed to support the government of Israel or if relations between Israel and the Diaspora deteriorated, US support for Israel would diminish.[37] However, this commonly held assumption was not necessarily borne out by events, and crises in relations between American Jews and the Israeli administration, were not automatically reflected in US policy towards the Jewish state. In any case, from 1982, the predilection of the government of Israel and the pro-Israel lobby in America to speak with one voice dissipated. Criticism of Israel and the policies of the Israeli government publicly emerged amongst the American Jewish community following the Israeli invasion of Lebanon in 1982 and were reinforced by the Palestinian *Intifada* of 1987. For the first time, the mass media portrayed Israel as an aggressor state and relayed televised pictures of Israeli troops breaking the bones of stone throwing Palestinian children.[38] The image of Israel as an "embattled" state was replaced by that of a regional military and economic superpower capable of acts of aggression against its Arab neighbours. This new, darker image of the Jewish state challenged the perceived need for unquestioning support from the Diaspora.

The changing nature of the Israeli state and the disunity between its citizens was also revealed by debates surrounding the direction of the peace process. The debate on the status of the occupied territories created internal divisions in the Labour and Likud parties and forced them to adopt pragmatic positions rather than concrete policies to maintain party cohesion.[39] This deep divide was reflected in public opinion in both Israel and the Diaspora. For the first time, disunity amongst the Israeli population was so great and the moral issue of the occupied territories so potent, that American Jewish organisations took sides in the political debate. Once the climate for questioning Israeli policy developed and the American Jewish consensus began to fragment, conflict between American Jewish organisations and the Israeli government openly emerged. But the disagreements were about policy and the peace process, the substance of the relationship, that of support for Israel as an entity, remained firm. It is to an analysis of changes in the transnational relationship in the 1990s that we now turn.

Israel and the Pro-Israel Lobby

One of the first examples of direct and enduring confrontation between Israel and the American Diaspora occurred following the election of Yitzhak Rabin as Prime Minister of Israel in 1992. For the first time, an Israeli Prime Minister directly charged that the lobby's attempts to aid Israel, by lobbying Congress for $10 billion in American loan guarantees,[40] had actually been detrimental to the interests of the state.[41] He claimed that the lobby's confrontational tactics had soured Israel's ties with its chief ally and that waging battles "that were lost in advance" was counterproductive. From this point on, Rabin informed the organisation, they should take their instructions from the Israeli embassy in Washington, rather than pursue their own initiatives.[42] Rabin told the American Israeli Public Affairs Committee (AIPAC) officials that he personally would conduct diplomacy directly with the White House and went so far as to demand that they not interfere.[43] But his criticism of Aipac should not be overstated and must be placed in context of his broader political style that was fundamentally different from his predecessors. His experience as Chief of Staff of the Israel Defence Forces and as ambassador to the United States, had made him direct in his approach and an advocate of one-to-one diplomacy.

However, the Israeli government was not the only critic of Aipac and prominent American Jewish figures became embroiled in Israel's domestic political battles between Labour and Likud. Israel's newspaper *Ha'aretz* argued that Aipac was involved in the "covert intelligence of American politicians, including senators and congressmen, who did not agree with Likud's policies."[44]

Israeli Labour activists, including editorial writers for *Davar*, called for the resignation of Aipac's executive director Thomas Dine, accusing him of prolonging Likud's rule by helping to secure American support for its policies.[45] The irony that the role of Aipac was ostensibly to assure the Israeli government of US support appeared to escape his accusers. It was somewhat paradoxical, given Dine's support for Likud, that he was eventually forced to resign over some unflattering remarks about Orthodox Jews that were attributed to him.[46] Tension between the Rabin government and Aipac was not easily dispelled and Harvey Friedman, the lobby's vice-president, also resigned in 1993 after revelations that he called Rabin's deputy Foreign Minister "a little slime-ball."[47]

Aipac's leaders had welcomed the defeat of George Bush and the election of Bill Clinton as President of the United States, in November 1992, because they anticipated that he would transform Capitol Hill, to use Pat Buchanan's characterisation, into "Israeli-occupied territory."[48] This relief was short lived. Although leader of one of the most pro-Israeli governments to occupy the White House, Clinton was committed to a land-for-peace formula as the device for ending the Arab–Israeli dispute – a strategy both the Israeli and American right-wing opposed. To achieve this objective, he formed a close working relationship with Rabin, who had very different views on the future of the peace process from those held by much of the pro-Israel lobby. As a result, American Jewish groups bypassed the administration and went directly to the legislature with their objections. Rabin lamented that "[n]ever before have we witnessed an attempt by U.S. Jews to pressure Congress against the policy of a legally, democratically elected government." Rabin warned that lobbying against the policies of the Labour government could cause a serious breach in Israeli relations with the American Jewish community.[49] To redress this imbalance, in 1993, the Israeli Policy Forum (IPF) was founded at the behest of Rabin and his deputy Shimon Peres, to counteract the leaders of traditional American Jewish organisations whom they felt were not sufficiently supportive of the Labour party or of the Oslo peace process.

Israel and American Jewry

Tensions between Israel and the Diaspora were not limited to relations with the official lobby, and conflict emerged between the Rabin government and members of the American Jewish community who opposed the direction of the Oslo peace process. Protests against the autonomy talks were registered in June 1995 by the 3,000 strong International Rabbinical Coalition for Israel. In a ruling issued in New York, the rabbis stated that "uprooting Jewish settlements in the Golan Heights, Judea, Samaria and Gaza Strip as part of the 'false Israeli peace' is a national crime, and it is forbidden for Jews to lend a hand to such a deed." Rabin retaliated by claming that "only those who send their children and grandchildren to the Israeli army, not some rabbis from New York, have the right to express views on the peace process."[50] Late in 1995, the Saudi Arabian ambassador to Washington found himself in the unusual position of defending the peace process to a gathering of unconvinced American Jewish leaders in New York.[51] Perhaps the ultimate discontent amongst members of the American Diaspora was registered when a right-wing zealot from Brooklyn assassinated Israeli Prime Minister Yitzhak Rabin on 4 November 1995.

The Likud victory in the 1996 elections restored some of the former equilibrium between the Israeli government and the right-wing American Jewish organisations.[52] During the election campaign, many independent Jewish organisations had been careful not to openly ally themselves with either the Labour or Likud candidate. Yet much of Aipac's leadership and Malcolm Hoenlein, the executive director of the Conference of Presidents of Major Jewish Organisations, were perceived as lukewarm in their support of the Oslo Accords and in favour of Likud leader Binyamin Netanyahu's candidacy.[53] The pro-Likud coalition in Washington comprised all the major orthodox groups and think tanks, including Aipac. The conservative Heritage Foundation in Washington, with close ties to the Republican Party, became a major forum for the enemies of Clinton and the Labour government's efforts to implement the Oslo Accords.[54] Netanyahu utilised these connections during the 1996 Israeli election campaign, when he and three former Israeli diplomats (former ambassadors to Washington Zalman Shoval, Yoran Ettinger and Yosef Ben-Aharon) travelled to Washington on several occasions to lobby lawmakers against Labour policy.[55] Netanyahu "built a certain aura around himself" that appealed to parts of the American population and he has been described as the "Israeli Ronald Reagan" in terms of his capacity to express himself to the public and on television.

Who is a Jew?

As 1996 drew to a close, the struggle over religious pluralism re-emerged as a source of tension in Israeli–Diaspora relations. Religious controversy had first appeared as a major factor in 1988, when the "Who is a Jew?" question was raised by Israel's orthodox rabbis and Israel's Shas party, a Sephardi Orthodox party, petitioned to prevent Reform and Conservative conversions to Judaism performed abroad from being recognised in Israel. The move generated an unprecedented backlash amongst America's generally non-Orthodox Jewish community and a delegation of the top US leadership flew to Israel to confer with Shamir. Pressure from the Diaspora was so great that Shamir dissolved his coalition National Unity Government and formed a new government that was not dependent on the religious parties, thus enabling him to withstand orthodox pressure and to avert a confrontation with American Jewry.

An illusion of calm returned to religious politics until 1996, when the election of Netanyahu fused the separate issues of security and religion for the first time.[56] The Likud leader slowed down the peace process and formed the most religiously right-wing dependent government in Israel's history. The "Who is a Jew?" debate came to the fore once again, with an Israeli Supreme Court decision that opened the door to non-Orthodox conversion. To forestall such a possibility, Shas proposed an amendment to the Law of Return that would have invalidated Reform and Conservative conversions to Judaism performed outside Israel. If passed, the bill would have given full conversion power to the Israeli Orthodox Rabbinate and barred non-Orthodox representatives from local religious councils.[57] This would have effectively disenfranchised 85 percent of American Jews who were either Reform or Conservative[58] and challenged their very legitimacy as Jews.[59]

On this occasion, Reform and Conservative Jews used legal means to retaliate against the bill and petitioned the Supreme Court for equal treatment under the law, including service on local and religious courts. The Supreme Court supported their claims and also demanded that ultra-Orthodox men serve in the Israeli army.[60] The ruling drew a virulent response from Israel's ultra-orthodox rabbis, who denounced the Court. They claimed that religious law transcended secular law and demanded that the Knesset pass legislation upholding the authority of Chief rabbis over religious councils. Reform and Conservative Jews responded by threatening to withhold financial support for those members of the Knesset who voted for the bill and to ban them from appearing in their synagogues.[61]

More than in previous rounds of the "Who is a Jew?" controversy, the new discourse was fraught with extreme anger and bitterness and forced Netanyahu to take action to defuse the tensions. In a visit to the United States that coincided with the debate, Netanyahu claimed that he understood the threat posed to American–Jewish–Israeli solidarity and assured American Jewish leaders that "no power on earth can rob any Jew of his or her identity."[62] However, he was careful not to directly criticise the legislation. He needed to balance the concerns of American Jews with domestic political realities – the ultra-Orthodox religious parties controlled 23 of the 66 Knesset seats in his coalition and if not appeased could have toppled his government.[63]

To avoid the perception that it was taking sides, the Netanyahu government devised a compromise. Accordingly, there would be a simultaneous moratorium on the Conversion Bill and the Reform and Conservative challenges in the courts, while a commission chaired by Finance Minister Ya'akov Ne'eman was tasked with providing a long-term solution. Although the Ne'eman commission eventually decided on a "conversion institute" that represented all three denominations, the Israeli Orthodox circles dismissed it. This did little to heal the rift with the majority of the American Jewish community.

Perhaps as a result of domestic pressure, Netanyahu apparently misread the deeply held sentiment of many American Jews. The real issue for them was that Israel, a country they supported both emotionally and materially as the legitimated homeland of the Jewish people, would refuse to recognise their brand of Judaism as valid in the Jewish state.[64] Their disillusionment with Israel's policy was registered economically when the diversion of donations from the United Jewish Appeal (UJA) to Conservative and Reform-oriented charities in Israel, contributed to a $20 million shortfall in the UJA budget.[65]

The "Who is a Jew" debate had profound implications and caused many American Jews to take a closer look at the array of political parties in the Likud government. Despite Netanyahu's 'American' background, the pivotal place of the Shas party, which represented the growing Sephardi-Orthodox population, raised feelings of discomfort regarding the right-wing elements in Israeli political culture. The controversy opened up a 'Pandora's box', as once American Jews began questioning Israel, they also questioned other aspects of Israeli policy, including its control of the West Bank and Gaza.[66]

Demographic Change in the American Jewish Community

Religious challenges to the right of American Jews to consider themselves Jewish, reflected more fundamental changes amongst the community that Israeli Jews, having enjoyed the status of nationhood for over fifty years, did not share. Although many Jewish communities were no longer persecuted, assimilation had increased and it could be legitimately argued that the American Jewish community was itself in decline.[67] The community had been experiencing a very low birth rate and a rate of intermarriage exceeding 50 percent. The low birth rate adhered to the lifestyle of traditional middleclass families, while inter-marriage showed the increasing acceptance of Jews by the non-Jewish community.[68]

As Jews become more woven into the fabric of American life their coloration becomes less distinctive.[69] The World Jewish Congress projected in 1998 that the total Jewish population outside of Israel, currently about 8 million people, would decline to approximately 4 million by 2020. This is partly because the large majority of the children of intermarried couples did not remain Jewish[70] and posed a potential threat to the longevity and future influence of world Jewry and the Diaspora's relationship with Israel.[71] Joel Meyers, the executive vice-president of the conservative movement's Rabbinical Assembly, accurately described the implications of the changing relationship between Israel and American Jewry thus:

> There is an emotional distancing going on between U.S. Jewry and Israel that is very difficult to overcome. It could have practical implications in terms of feeling part of

> the same family even politically. The American Jewish community has been a strong lobbyist on behalf of Israel. Can this still happen?[72]

This sense of pessimism appeared to be vindicated in October and November 1997, when Congress twice temporarily suspended aid to Israel. Jonathan J. Goldberg the American bureau chief for *The Jerusalem Report*, claimed that this was a direct result of a decline in American Jewish support for Israel:

> Members of Congress could get away with it because they didn't get hit with protest phone calls because American Jews are too angry at Israel now and the people who usually mobilise them are slow to move. Everybody's mad. In America being Jewish has become something you do. In Israel it's an attribute of being.[73]

At a time when conflict between the executive and legislature had brought the government to a virtual standstill, the rationale behind the decision made by Congress amounted to far more than constituency pressure. Nevertheless, it does give credence to the political importance generally attributed to the power of American Jewry to influence Congress.

The most recent and greatest testament to Jewish integration into American society and the evolving influence of American Jews was the consensus that Al Gore actually strengthened his bid for the presidency by selecting the Jewish Joseph Lieberman as his running mate in the 2000 Presidential election. Prior to this, Jonathan Goldberg explained, there had "been a sense that there is a glass ceiling that the Jews will never get past, that the highest levels in the land will be closed to us. The fact that a Jew was nominated by one of the two major parties to be Vice-President of the United States has . . . made the [2000] election a symbol of where American Judaism stands," said Ed Rettig, director of Educational Programmes on American Jewry for the American Jewish Committee.[74] While Henry Kissinger held the second most powerful office in the United States, he was appointed to this post by Richard Nixon, not popularly elected. The crucial issue in Lieberman's candidacy was the recognition amongst the major political parties that Jews are sufficiently integrated into society that the American people as an entity could elect a Jew to high office. The future of individual American Jews seems bright.[75]

The Future of Israel's Relationship with the American Diaspora Community

The American Diaspora is a voluntary community based on networks of "confederate" associations. There is no single hierarchical structure but a matrix consisting of numerous institutions tied together by crisscrossing memberships, shared purposes and common interests, whose role and power fluctuate in accordance with issues and circumstances. This built-in pluralism means that individuals and groups are free to break with the community consensus and to pursue their own agendas. As the patterns of Jewish funding and philanthropy have changed in recent years, traditional umbrella organisations have been passed over in favour of smaller groups where donors can exert more control over the agenda. Nowhere has this phenomenon been more apparent than in the realm of peace advocacy where both the political right and left have been willing to put their beliefs above traditional loyalty to the policies of the democratically elected government of Israel.

Such fragmentation has effected the functioning of the umbrella organisations that represent Israel's interests in Washington. Aipac, which in the mid-1990s was rated as the second most powerful lobby in the US, has seen its membership stagnate and its influence undermined by internal discord. The Presidents Conference, which embraced the specialised advocacy groups, has been virtually paralysed by the constant struggle between those who favour a land for peace settlement and those who oppose such a proposal.[76]

The cleavage in the American Jewish community is reflected in the polarisation of the Israeli electorate and enables both the Israeli right and left to use sympathetic segments in the Diaspora to advance their foreign policy goals. While such trends have potential implications for Israel's appeal as a symbol of Jewish unity, particularly amongst the younger generation, they can also be viewed as a reflection of the affinity between the two communities rather than a cause for concern. As Rabbi Alexander Schindler, former president of the Union of American Hebrew Congregation, explained, "I'm less nervous than other people are because from the perspective of Jewish history there was never a time in Jewish life of ideological consensus."[77]

Israel and American Christian Evangelicals

Despite tensions between Israel and some American Jews, the commitment of America's Christian evangelicals to the State of Israel remains fundamentally firm. In view of their increasing numerical superiority, in contrast to the American Jewish community which will be smaller in absolute number by the middle of the century,[78] they have been perhaps an even more important source of support. The was demonstrated in 1998 when the Christian right aligned with the Netanyahu government to undermine Clinton's policy towards the peace process. For example, Reverend Jerry Falwell told the *New York Times* that there were approximately 200,000 evangelical pastors in America and that he would ask them to go into their pulpits and use their influence to oppose pressure on the Israelis by the Clinton administration to give up more territory to the Palestinians.[79] E. Brandt Gustavson, president of the National Religious Broadcasters, sounded a similar theme when he assured Netanyahu that Christians "stand with the Prime Minister for an undivided

Jerusalem"[80] and by implication, opposed its own government's support of a land for peace formula.

Traditionally the Democrats have been considered the bastions of Israeli causes. However, this distinction effectively came to an end with the election of Ronald Reagan in 1982 on what can be described as a Christian fundamentalist/evangelical ticket.[81] In return for this support, Reagan had an obligation to address their concerns – moral, economic and social – and their support for Israel based on biblical prophecy. This was the beginning of an increasing shift in the voting patterns of evangelical Protestants that gave them control of both Houses of the Senate in 1994 and re-elected George W. Bush to the presidency in 2004. Although "evangelicals were not yet a political monolith" they were believed to "constitute a substantial Republican voting bloc"[82] and based on election results since 1982, this bloc now included at least three-fifths of the voters in this populous religious tradition. The Christian Right's campaign to increase voter turnout among evangelicals was successful, and in recent elections an average of 75 percent of those contacted cast their vote.[83] The late Arthur Kropp, president of the religious organisation People for the American Way, predicted that the Republicans would be forced to accede to many of the demands of the Religious Right. He commented that: "Precinct by precinct, Religious Right activists were the single largest organised group doing the tedious chores of voter registration and 'get out the vote' activities. He described this as "a huge political debt Republican leaders can be expected to repay with interest."[84] This alignment has perhaps reached its zenith under the presidency of George W. Bush, who has brought the neo-conservatives and Christian fundamentalists to coexist in his administration.[85] Whether Bush can maintain the alliance and continue to appease the Religious Right in his second term in office, remains to be seen. But what is important to acknowledge is the increasing political influence of a sector of the electorate that advocates American support of Israel.

It is also interesting to note that because much American Christian support for Israel is founded on the biblical prophecy that the Jews have a right to a homeland in Palestine and to the lands of Judea and Samaria, they have tended to be far less critical than American Jews of the more questionable aspects of Israeli policy. For this reason the Religious Right can be seen as an unquestioning source of support. This demonstration of the depth of Christian evangelical feeling can be traced to the original religious beliefs of the Pilgrim Fathers and the values and cultural premises on which the United States was founded. As a consequence of the increasing electoral significance of the Religious Right, support for Israel was no longer the preserve of the Democrats and became an issue both parties would highlight in future election campaigns. Given the interests of both American Jews and Christian evangelicals, it could be argued that domestic political constituencies are largely responsible for funding Middle Eastern politics.[86] Dennis Bernstein, the Jewish host of KPFA Radio's *Flashpoint* current affairs programme, has gone so far as to acknowledge that a combination of Israeli lobbyists and conservative Christian fundamentalists have in effect censored all free discussion of Israel and the Middle East out of the public domain in the US.[87]

Conclusions

In view of changes in the objective circumstances that influence decision-making, US policy in the 1990s might well have taken a somewhat different course than in previous years, with Washington determining the direction of both US–Israeli relations and the nature of the Arab–Israeli peace process. Such an eventuality did not occur and at the beginning of the twenty-first century, US–Israeli relations have defied explanation in terms of traditional inter-state relations. What we are left with is the sense that 'political culture' as a mechanism which shapes the beliefs and value systems of those who take crucial decisions and acts as a guide to policy, is perhaps worthy of further scrutiny as a means of illuminating the relationship between states of unequal power and influence.

American Political Culture and Foreign Policy in the Twenty-First Century

The last decade of the twentieth century was a time of international change as old empires crumbled and new states were born. The United States found itself at the apex of a new world order, rejoicing in the collapse of the Soviet Union, its bitterest enemy for more than forty years, but uncertain of the new dangers that would threaten both domestic and international stability. The one constant during this period was the values and beliefs of American decision-makers and the continuing role played by political culture in shaping the framework of American perceptions, expectations and aspirations in policy formulation.

The end of the Cold War had many different implications at many different levels, as the global superstructure underwent tremendous change. The Soviet Union withdrew troops from Afghanistan and other Third World states and the fall of the Berlin Wall provided the most visible symbol of how the change would affect the Western world. With the collapse of the Soviet Union, the United States became the only global superpower and by default, could claim victory in the battle for global 'freedom'. Washington once again took the lead in 'post-war' reconstruction, much as it had in the past. Wilson's Fourteen Points of January 1918, setting out his vision for a world free of strife, and Truman's 1947 programme of Marshall Aid, designed to assist countries to be free from

Communism, was followed by Bush's repackaging of 'freedom' in the "New World Order"[88] of 1990. For Bush, the idea of a new world order is a scenario "where diverse nations are drawn together in common cause to achieve the universal aspirations of mankind: peace and security, freedom, and the rule of law."[89]

Yet in contrast to his predecessors, Bush Sr., lacked one vital ingredient in motivating the American people in support of 'freedom' and domestic regeneration – an enemy with the equivalent stature of the Soviet Union to oppose. Trumpeting rock music over the walls of the Papal Nuncio's residence in Panama did not command the same enduring attention, or threat status, as earlier crusades. In fact, it brought a smile to the face of many non-Americans, although the US violation of Panama's sovereignty,[90] with thousands of troops involved, enhanced Bush's presidential rating.

'Freedom' remained the central theme in US foreign policy. Aid to former Communist East European countries was made dependent on adherence to Washington's 'democratic' criteria. The administration celebrated 'democratic' advance when the Sandinistas were defeated in the 1990 Nicaragua elections, despite the fact that Washington had contributed to the undermining of Nicaraguan democracy by arming the guerrilla opposition forces, while Wilsonian self-determination, was the publicly proclaimed reason for forcing the Iraqi withdrawal from Kuwait in the 1991 Gulf conflict.[91] Yet even in the post-Cold War world there were numerous occasions when Washington sacrificed democracy and freedom for the kind of stability that was seen as best serving the national interest.[92] For example, as the Russian Federation fumbled its way towards a new democratic and capitalist order, Bush Sr., continued to support Gorbachev, even though Boris Yeltsin had contested a democratic election and claimed victory.[93] America also reneged on promised support for oppressed minorities like the Kurds, and irredentist groups like the Shi'ites, in their struggle for political reform in Iraq.[94]

The term the 'evil empire', was redefined to exclude Communist China. The US disregarded its commitment to the democratic agenda in its relations with China, as the one billion people still living under Communism and the students in Tiananmen Square in 1989 paid a high price to discover. This selective response was not new, and indeed characterised much of American history when the pursuit of the "national interest had vied with the promotion of the national narrative."[95] The new world order was, in fact, hardly distinguishable from the old. It was still based on the status quo, on existing states, existing frontiers and the quest for stability.[96]

George Bush's State of the Union address in 1990 illuminated the long-running contradictions in US policy between freedom and order and the conflict between moral rhetoric and the national interest.

> The anchor of our world today is freedom, holding us steady in times of change, a symbol of hope to all the world. And freedom is at the very heart of the idea that is America . . . America, not just the nation, but an idea, alive in the minds of people everywhere. As this new world takes shape, America stands at the corner of a widening circle of freedom – today, tomorrow, and into the next century . . . This nation, this idea called America, was and always will be a new world – our new world.[97]

This idea of America as a symbol of goodness permeated the Clinton White House. Clinton echoed similar themes to those of his predecessors and in his State of the Union address in 1997 told the American people that:

> Fifty years ago, a farsighted America led in creating the institutions that secured victory in the Cold War and built a growing world economy. As a result, today more people than ever embrace our ideals and share our interests . . . For the first time ever, more people live under democracy than dictatorship, including every nation in our own hemisphere but one – and its day too, will come.[98]

Despite the lofty rhetoric, the resolve that characterised American actions in the Gulf, and to a lesser extent in Somalia, were not matched by comparable action in Bosnia. While American leaders sought to be viewed as moral actors, their response was circumscribed to meet the public temperament of the post-Vietnam era. In the absence of an enemy in the form of a significant 'other', demonstrations of American power in Rwanda and Bosnia were symbolic and largely ineffective in terms of their stated objectives.[99]

Under the Clinton administration, America's world role remained extensive and this activism contrasted sharply with the early months of the administration of George W. Bush, whose limited knowledge of foreign affairs contributed to the domestic orientation of policy-making. This insular approach to politics continued until the events of 11 September, 2001.

The response of the Bush administration to the September 11 terrorist attacks revealed the essence of the beliefs and values on which the state was founded. In deploring these devastating acts of terrorism, the nation's leaders returned to the rhetoric of the past and the political cultural beliefs on which America was founded, provided the rallying call for action. Perhaps nowhere was the legacy of America's cultural heritage more starkly profiled than in President Bush's first State of the Union Address, delivered to Congress on 29 January 2002, imbued with references to the values on which America was founded: 'freedom', 'liberty' and 'justice', and to the United States as an exemplary nation with a responsibility and "obligations to each other, to our country and to history." In calling on the American people to continue to bear the financial and human burden necessary to pursue the 'war' on terrorism, Bush called on the traditional American sense of mission: "We want to be a Nation that serves goals larger than self" – a belief dating back to the Puritans and enshrined in the Constitution of the United States." In declaring "we will defend liberty and justice because they are right and true and unchanging" and "we can overcome evil with greater good,"[100] Bush was effectively reverting to the timeless nature of American values. As the Founding Fathers believed that America was a "shining light amongst the nations,"[101] so Bush asserted that the United States had "been called to a unique role in human events." As God was a pervasive force for the Puritan settlers, so it remained for contemporary American's who believe and take seriously the assertions of their President that "God is near."

If the moralistic element of American foreign policy has remained undiminished for more than two hundred years, the legalistic approach to foreign affairs has remained equally pervasive. The war against terrorism was defined in legalistic terms with reference to "outlaw regimes" and the pursuit of a just cause to create a "just and peaceful world."[102] The war against Iraq of March–April 2003, was also defined in these terms as the US sought to remove the leader of a 'rogue' state from power and to prevent the proliferation of weapons of mass destruction. In defining foreign policy objectives in the legalist–moralistic language of the past, the Bush administration, like its predecessors, claimed that America was the judge of good and evil in the world and defined its allies in terms of those states that shared its values.

George W. Bush and the State of Israel

For the first eight months of George W. Bush's term in office, the US–Israeli relationship was lukewarm as the President focused his attention on domestic affairs. In early 2001, the administration had shown little interest in the escalating *Intifada* despite the increasing mortality rate amongst both Israelis and Palestinians. Repeatedly he made it clear that his administration would not be sucked into assisting the two parties in reaching a compromise on how to live together.[103] Just months after his election, Israel went to the polls and elected Ariel Sharon as their new Prime Minister. Sharon's election was greeted warmly in Washington despite the death knell it sounded for the peace process. The Likud leader categorically stated that he would not discuss the future of Jerusalem or relinquish control over East Jerusalem to the Palestinians. He then announced that the terms for a peace agreement offered by his predecessor Ehud Barak at Camp David in November 2000 had been withdrawn from the negotiating table and that the peace talks would not continue at the point at which they ended in January 2001.[104] More ominously, the Bush administration legitimated Sharon's position and compounded the stalemate by stating that commitments made by the Clinton administration to the peace process would not necessarily be honoured. This stance was particularly acute given the fact that, in the past, when negotiations foundered, the parties often looked to the United States to break the deadlock.

Sharon himself had little if any personal affinity with the power brokers in Washington. Even Netanyahu, while openly disliked by the Clinton administration, formed a firm relationship with the Republican right-wing that had effectively vetoed Clinton's attempts to pressurise Israel. As much as Sharon tried to disregard American preferences, the very nature of international relations forced him, in the first months of his premiership, to take American interests seriously and to demonstrate an element of compatibility between his policies and theirs. In the aftermath of the terrorist attacks on the World Trade Center, Sharon discovered to his cost the implications of misreading American sentiment and attempting to further the Israeli national interest at what Washington perceived to be its own expense. After initially acting and speaking uncompromisingly by calling Arafat 'Israel's Osama bin Laden', Sharon agreed to an attempted cease-fire, after Washington made both Israel and the Palestinians understand that they could not afford to cross America in its hour of need and peril. As Bush endeavoured to build the widest possible coalition before launching his counterstrike against terrorism, the televising around the Arab world of the unequal struggle in the Palestinian territories made it difficult for Muslim countries to join an alliance led by Israel's chief ally.[105] If September 11 was a turning point in how the United States dealt with terrorism, many in the Arab world hoped it would also change the American approach to the Israeli–Palestinian conflict. In late September these hopes appeared vindicated when Bush spoke of his vision for a Palestinian state.[106]

However, Hamas undermined the prospects for the reconvening of peace talks with the assassination of Rehavam Zeevi, an ultra-right Israeli minister who had just resigned from the Sharon government.[107] The killing reignited the cycle of assassinations, suicide bombings and Israeli re-occupations of Palestinian land. Less than two months after demanding a cease-fire between Israel and the Palestinians, the bombing of Afghanistan bore fruit. It then appeared that Bush's rhetoric about a Palestinian state had been nothing more than political expediency designed to secure the assistance or at least quiescence of the Muslim world. Once the immediate political objective had been realised, Washington and the American people began to identify with Israel once again as an ally in the war against terrorism.

As operations in Afghanistan uncovered the extent of the al-Qaeda network and the scale of its intended terrorist actions against Western targets, Bush became increasingly receptive to Sharon's comparisons between America's war on terror and that of Israel.[108] During late 2001 and early 2002, as Israel bombed, shelled and reoccupied Palestinian areas, America remained silent. Americans identified with the Israelis as victims of Islamic terror, further increasing the emphathetic connection between the two countries. Professor

Makiya, speaking on the BBC's *Newsnight*, stated that 77 per cent of Americans believe that Palestinian suicide bombings are terrorism in the sense of the war on terror.[109] Washington claimed that the United States had the right to undertake any action it considered necessary against perceived terrorist targets to protect its national security; this claim was tacitly extended to the Israelis in their war against the Palestinians. In contrast to his father, who fulfilled the commitment to the peace process by convening an international peace conference in Madrid, George W. Bush appeared to renege on his short-lived commitment to an Israeli–Palestinian peace process, thus increasing popular distrust of the United States in the Arab world. Even Saudi Arabia and Egypt, America's staunchest regional allies, were mystified by the fact that the US could live through September 11 and not move forcefully to resolve a dispute that appeared to encourage suicide bombing and increased the popularity of Islamic radical groups.

In early 2002, Israel, as a close ally of the United States, had been granted virtually free rein to continue a conflict that inflamed Arabs and Iranians alike and fuelled the flames of Islamic terror. In writing about the Arab relationship with the United States, Fawaz Turki, columnist for the English-language Saudi newspaper *Arab News*, questioned whether the Arabs had "been left by the wayside and become irrelevant in the global dialogue of cultures."[110] In June 2002 Bush spoke of his "road map for peace" in the Middle East, but it was only towards the end of the year, as Washington sought to marshal international support for the war against Iraq, that serious consideration was given to the Israeli–Palestinian conflict. As threats of Islamic terrorism persisted, efforts to capture Osama bin Laden failed and anti-American rhetoric increased throughout the Muslim world, the Bush administration appeared to become aware that the Israeli–Palestinian dispute could not be separated from the broader Middle East landscape and that movement in the peace process could actually serve the American national interest. To this end, in May 2003, Bush published his "Road Map for Peace in the Middle East" and his vision of the creation of a Palestinian state by 2005. The plan called on both parties to make concessions for peace but the onus has been put on the Palestinians to re-structure their government, creating a new constitution that separates the powers of government, and allows for a free-market economic system. The American approach was premised on transforming a putative Palestinian state into a US style democratic entity.

However, the Road Map was stymied by the absence of a Palestinian negotiating partner as first Sharon and then Bush refused to deal with Yassir Arafat. As the Palestinian leader was confined to his compound for more than two and a half years, the Israelis began the construction of a security barrier around Jerusalem, cutting into the West Bank and effectively moving eastwards the boundary of the city whose status is intimately tied to any negotiated peace settlement. The Israeli government defended its actions by claiming that the wall is a security measure to prevent suicide bombings and other attacks. In contrast, the Palestinian's claim it is designed to unilaterally impose a border that ensures the major Jewish settlements become part of Israel, a claim upheld by the world court in July 2004. Little condemnation has been forthcoming from Washington, which has largely upheld Israel's right to defend its citizens in any way it considers appropriate.

Simultaneously with this, the Bush Administration appeared to endorse the Israeli policy of political assassination that included Hamas' spiritual leader, the wheelchair-bound, Sheikh Ahmed Yassin. Washington's immediate response to the killing on 22 March 2004 avoided any criticism of Israel's action and branded the Hamas leader a "terrorist". The Administration only belatedly acknowledged that the assassination could have potentially catastrophic consequences for US servicemen in Iraq, as well as on its war on terror, when Hamas and an offshoot of al-Qaeda, the Abu Hafs al-Masri Brigade, threatened vengeance against America. Even so, it was difficult for Washington to offer public criticism of actions that could arguably be seen as complementary to the Bush administration's doctrine of pre-emptive action. The US appeared to exonerate the Israeli policy of political assassination, which continued 25 days later with the killing of Abdel-Aziz al-Rantissi, Yassin's successor as the leader of Hamas.

The assassination of Yassin was a forceful demonstration of resolve following Sharon's announcement in February 2004, to withdraw from virtually all Israeli settlements in the Gaza Strip, with or without signing a final peace agreement with the Palestinians. While the US gave tacit approval to his plan for "unilateral disengagement" from the Palestinians, the decision infuriated many of Sharon's supporters on the religious and secular right and within his own Likud party. The assassinations served the duel purpose of signalling that Israel intends to withdraw from Gaza in a position of strength in contrast to perceptions of its withdrawal from Lebanon and to prevent the group taking advantage of any power vacuum created by the withdrawal. At present (May 2005), 7,000 settlers occupy 23 percent of this overcrowded area of land and in order to protect them from the *Intifada* Israel keeps substantial military forces in Gaza. Sharon claims that the isolated and heavily fortified settlements are incompatible with a peace agreement.

During the past year (2004), as the plan to pull out of Gaza has been debated in the Knesset, Sharon has committed to building an increasing number of homes in the West Bank, as a means to deflect criticism and consolidate Israel's presence there. This capitalises on the fundamental shift in US policy Bush signalled when he committed the US to recognising the major Jewish colonies in the West Bank as part of Israel. In early 2005, plans to build 3,500 homes to link Maale Adumim settlement with Jerusalem, met with little criticism from

Washington, although it contravenes the 'road map' and undermines Palestinian claims to the eastern part of the city as their capital.

The most viable opportunity for peace since the outbreak of the *Intifada* was provided by the death of Yassir Arafat in November 2004. Mahmoud Abbas, a determined advocate of negotiation rather than armed struggle, succeeded him as leader of the Palestine Liberation Organisation (PLO), and on 9 January 2005 was democratically elected president of the Palestinian Authority. This democratic change in leadership won the support of the international community and Bush pledged to "spend political capital" on the Israeli–Palestinian issue in his second term. The administration also pledged $350 million in aid to the Palestinians.

Condoleezza Rice, during her first visit to the Middle East as US Secretary of State, in February 2005, met with both Abbas and Sharon and urged the Israeli prime minister to take "hard decisions" for peace, sounding more even-handed than Bush has generally been. She also announced that an additional $40 million of American aid would be disbursed within 90 days to help the Palestinians create jobs and rebuild infrastructure damaged during the *Intifada.*

In an endeavour to capitalise on the visit, Jordan and Egypt hosted a peace summit in Egypt's Red Sea resort of Sharm el-Sheikh, the following week. The Egyptian administration achieved an unequivocal pledge by both sides to an immediate cessation of hostilities – in Abbas's case, effectively declaring an end to the *Intifada.* Sharon also renewed Israel's commitment to the internationally backed road map peace plan and its intended outcome of an independent Palestinian state. Notably the US took a back seat and left the renewed bout of peace making to the local parties. Given the intractable nature of the conflict, the ability of either leader to translate the idealistic rhetoric into realities on the ground must be viewed with caution.

The difficulty of dealing with this region, and the Israeli–Palestinian question that continues to exacerbate tensions between Islam and the West, will preoccupy the Bush Administration and its successors. In Mahmoud Abbas the Israelis and Americans are prepared to consider that they have a Palestinian leader and democratic entity they can work with, but it remains unclear how much influence he will exert over the radical groups that have the power to destabilise the peace process. While the level and nature of future American engagement in the Israeli–Palestinian question is unclear, the Middle East will continue to assume a high priority on the American agenda. Policy towards the region will continue to reflect the administration's global philosophy, shaped by its political cultural beliefs.

CONCLUSIONS

THIS BOOK SOUGHT TO EXPLAIN the emotionally charged, multi-dimensional relationship the United States and Israel have shared since 1948. In so doing, the traditional explanations of US–Israeli relations have been investigated: strategic interest, economic considerations, domestic politics and bureaucratic rivalry. However, these theories offer incomplete explanations of perhaps the most atypical bilateral bond in inter-state relations. After all, Washington had aligned itself with a small state of little over five million people and negligible resources, in contrast to the vast mineral wealth of Israel's 300 million or so Arab neighbours. And even if it could be argued that the Jewish state's strategic significance was of over-riding importance during the Cold War, the argument was much more difficult to sustain after it. As for the widespread notion that US policy towards Israel is almost entirely explicable in terms of the power of the Jewish lobby, it beggars belief that some six million people, even if they are well organised, influential, articulate and well funded, could determine the policy of some 280 million Americans. Since, for more than half a century, the fundamentals of the US commitment to Israel have remained largely unchanged, an alternative explanation must exist.

It is an axiom of foreign policy that its main purpose is to serve the national interest; in its long-standing commitment to Israel, however, the US was taking a somewhat idiosyncratic view of that term. Both the American government and people were strongly imbued with values which conditioned the framework of perceptions, preferences, prejudices and expectations on which policy is based and that the notion of the American national interest was, therefore, informed by these values. Political culture – the stock of political ideas, ideals and codes of conduct that are transmitted in a society from one generation to another – was responsible for creating the perception among the Americans that their society is a beacon of 'freedom' and 'democracy', in a world in which such values were often distinguished by their absence. In effect, Americans have been encouraged to believe that they shared a political kinship with societies similarly imbued and that they had an obligation to assist where such values were under threat. Such forces as European colonialism, Fascism and Communism were seen traditionally to constitute such a threat, and latterly 'Islamic

Fundamentalism' was also held to hazard such bastions of 'freedom' and 'democratic values' as Israel and the US. Furthermore, with the Zionist lobby able to count on upward of 40 million right-wing Christian evangelical supporters in addition to the influential organisations of concerned Jews, successive administrations could ill afford to ignore its demands. With the State of Israel widely portrayed in the US as a kind of democratic David against a series of powerful Arab Goliaths, its fate, it was argued, had a continuing resonance that has made it a prime focus of American concern.

Among the elements in American political culture that conditioned official policy towards Israel, three in particular stood out as crucial:

First, Americans have always been concerned with the lot of Jews. Though America is culturally Christian, the core metaphor of its exceptionalism as the Chosen People of the New World knowingly imitated the biblical saga of the return of the Jews to Israel. A common ethical and religious belief, the Judaic tradition and the Judeo-Christian heritage, were perceived to bind the US and Israel together. While theological elements of the American fascination with the Jews have been attenuated, secularised equivalents are still played out on the stage of Arab–Israeli diplomacy and American politics and foreign policy. The feeling of moral responsibility for the preservation of Israel because of the role the US played in its creation was reinforced by revulsion and horror at the Holocaust and of American complicity through inaction in its perpetration. The 'Americanisation of the Holocaust' that has occurred since the late 1970s, as the atrocity permeated American life through media images and national memorials, accentuated feelings of guilt and the sense that the Jewish people have a 'right' to their own state and protection from external sources of persecution. That America has continued to view itself as the protector of the Jewish state is evident in Washington's approach to Middle East politics, although its actions are generally legitimated in terms of the US strategic interest, and, rather more questionably, on the important contribution Israel's democratic status makes to regional stability.

Secondly, the American Jewish community can be described as the hypotenuse of the US–Israeli triangle, because it is perceived to exercise substantial political influence for Israel. Elected officials consider it 'safe' to support policy decisions that are favourable to Israel and their political careers may suffer if they openly challenge aid to the Jewish state. However, in recent years, as American Jews have come to act as much out of their own parochial interests and ill-defined identity as for the quotidian concerns of the Jewish state, Protestant Fundamentalists have become an increasingly important source of domestic support for Israel. The growing recognition by the Republican Party of Christian Evangelicals as an important voting bloc of more than forty million people, has further increased the prominence placed on issues relating to Israel in the agendas of both major political parties.

Thirdly, personalities have made a profound contribution to the dynamics of US–Israeli relations. Ronald Reagan and Menachem Begin shared a right-wing perspective while Bill Clinton and Yitzhak Rabin also found common political ground, forming a partnership in their endeavour to implement the Oslo Accords. In contrast, George Bush Sr. and Yitzhak Shamir moved in divergent directions, while their conflicting personalities reinforced policy differences. Nevertheless, Israel continues to be perceived as an American alter ego and even George W. Bush, a man who came to office with little interest in Middle East affairs or emotional affinity for Israel, promptly came to identify closely with the Jewish state. On the other hand, while personal relations do play a role, decision-makers are a product of the political cultural environment and tend to embody the values of their society. The US–Israeli relationship therefore, is not so much determined by random collisions of egos as by real differences or similarities in perceptions and interests grounded in culture and history.

Despite this apparent congruence of cultural and ideological values, the US–Israeli partnership is, of course, an unequal one. The relationship is not without tensions, many of which are as much a product of Israel's own identity problems as any inconsistencies in American foreign policy. As a Zionist state, Israel is bent on maximal independence and dedicated to the remaking of the Jewish image from hapless victim of history to that of a people shaping its own destiny. Yet the patterns of Israeli dependence on the US, particularly since 1973, more accurately resembled those of the European Diaspora in centuries past, where the fate of Jewish communities depended on the external power brokers of the age. While Jerusalem enjoys great autonomy in its relations with Washington, it is the subordinate power and, as this book has attempted to indicate above, on occasions is forced to comply, albeit grudgingly, with the preferences of the superpower.

As the emergence of a new Palestinian leadership has signalled the opportunity for a new phase of the peace process, the positions of Washington and Jerusalem are once again closely aligned. There is general agreement on the need to end the Arab–Israeli dispute, thus promoting regional stability, combating terrorism and ensuring the survival of Israel. While discord and tension may emerge over the means to achieve these ends, they go no deeper than the nuances of the relationship. The fundamentals of commitment appear to remain unchanged. For the relationship has proved itself to be "of such a kind as to exceed or excel in some way that which is usual or common; exceptional in character, quality or degree . . . admitted to particular intimacy; held in particular esteem . . . marked off from others of the kind by having some distinguishing qualities or features; having a distinct or individual character."[1] Both in form and substance, the covenant between the United States and Israel is that of a special relationship reinforced by the notion widely shared in the former that the two countries share a common political culture based in part on mutual values, history and a congruent religious heritage.

NOTES

Abbreviations

DSB	Department of State Bulletin (Washington, D.C.)
DSD	Department of State Despatch
FRUS	Foreign Relations of the United States Diplomatic Papers (Washington, D.C.: U.S. Government Printing Office)
FT	*Financial Times*
IHT	*International Herald Tribune*
JOHI	Lyndon Baines Johnson Oral History Interviews (Austin, Texas)
PPP	Public Papers of the Presidents (Washington, D.C.: U.S. Government Printing Office)
JP	*Jerusalem Post*
NYT	*New York Times*
MECS	Middle East Contemporary Survey
WP	*Washington Post*

1 The Special Relationship

1 Quoted in Bernard Reich, *Securing the Covenant: United States-Israel relations after the Cold War* (Westport, Connecticut & London: Praeger Publishers, 1995), p. 1.

2 Margaret Thatcher, speech in Washington, 21 February 1985, quoted in H. C. Allen "A Special Relationship?" *Journal of American Studies* 19, 1985, p. 407.

3 Christopher Bartlett, *'The Special Relationship': A political history of Anglo-American relations since 1945* (London & New York: Longman, 1992), p. 145.

4 Talk to British–American Parliamentary Group, 26 June 1952, Acheson Papers, Box 67, Truman Library, quoted in Alex Danchev, *On Specialness: Essays in Anglo-American relations* (New York: St. Martin's Press, 1998), p. 2.

5 See *The Economist*, 29 September 2001, p. 6, for a discussion of the contemporary special relationship between Britain and the US.

6 Quoted in Danchev, *On Specialness*, p. 7.

7 *Ibid.*

8 *Ibid.*

9 *Ibid.*

10 Richard Neustadt, *Alliance Politics* (New York: Columbia University Press, 1970), p. 79.

11 Abraham Ben-Zvi, *The United States and Israel* (New York: Columbia University Press, 1993), pp. 12–27.

12 Henry A. Kissinger, *The White House Years* (Boston: Little, Brown, 1979), p. 90 cited in John Dumbrell, *A Special Relationship: Anglo-American relations in the Cold War and after* (London: Macmillan, 2001), p. 9.

13 Warren F. Kimball, *The Most Unsordid Act: Lend-Lease, 1939–1941* (Baltimore: Johns Hopkins Press, 1969), p. 241.

14 This statement is based on the assumption that without Lend-Lease the British would have been too under-resourced to finance the war effort, while the Americans were too inexperienced and ill-prepared to lead the Allied forces single handedly. Lend-Lease provided a solution to Britain's dollar crisis by, in Roosevelt's words, "leaving out the dollar mark in the form of a dollar debt and substituting for a gentlemen's obligation to repay in kind." *Ibid.*, p. 121.

15 Danchev, *On Specialness*, p. 11.

16 *The Economist*, 22 September 2001, p. 61.

17 John Sloan Dickey, *Canada and the American Presence* (New York: New York University Press, 1975), p. 189. North America's first encounter with Jews occurred in early September 1654, when twenty-three of them arrived at the settlement of the New Netherlands on Manhattan Island. Peter Grose, *Israel in the Mind of America* (New York: Alfred A. Knopf, 1983), p. 3.

18 See Chapter 6 for a full account of these events.

19 *The Economist*, 22 September 2001, p. 61.

20 *Ibid.*

21 Dumbrell, *A Special Relationship*, p. 13.

22 *The Economist*, 8 December 2001, p. 57.

23 Alvin Z. Rubinstein, *Soviet Policy towards Turkey, Iran and Afghanistan: The dynamics of influence* (New York: Praeger, 1982), p. viii. If a military threat, tacit or otherwise, was required for country A to force country B to comply, this would be referred to as force not influence.

24 Dumbrell, *A Special Relationship*, p. 8.

25 Quoted in Reich, *Securing the Covenant*, p. 5.

26 Vice-President Walter Mondale at the American Jewish Committee, New York, 18 May 1978. Emphasis in the original.

27 Embassy of Israel, Washington, D.C., *For Your Information*, "Presentation of the New Government: Address before Knesset by Prime Minister Designate Yitzhak Rabin, 13 July 1992."

28 *BBC Monitoring Middle East*, 27 July 1999.

29 Bush stated that he was "in close touch with the key players there [in Israel] in terms of our objectives." *Public Papers of the Presidents: George Bush*, 1990 (Washington, 1992) 8 November 1990, p. 1584.

30 For a detailed discussion of the Iran–Contra affair see Jonathan Marshall, Peter Dale Scott & Jane Hunter, *The Iran–Contra Connection: Secret teams and covert operations in the Reagan era* (Montreal & New York: Black Rose Books, 1987) and Lawrence E. Walsh, *Iran–Contra: The final report* (New York: Times Books, 1994).

31 Author's interview with Peter W. Rodman: Member of the National Security Council staff and a special assistant to Henry Kissinger 1969–1977.

32 Reich, *Securing the Covenant*, p. 101.
33 Vernon Lewis Parrington, *Main Currents in American Thought: An interpretation of American literature from the beginnings to 1920* (New York: Harcourt, Brace, 1930).
34 Author's interview with David Bar-Ilan, Israeli Director of Communications.
35 Edward Glick, *The Triangular Confrontation: America, Israel and American Jews* (London, Boston & Sydney: George, Allen & Unwin, 1982), p. 22.
36 Ellis Sendoz (ed.), *Political Sermons of the American Founding Era, 1730–1805* (Indianapolis: Liberty Press, 1991) provides accounts of sermons during the independence period that highlight the perceived similarities between the United States and Israel.
37 Samuel Langdon, *The Republic of the Israelites: An example to the American states* sermon reprinted in *ibid.*, pp. 941–68 and Grose, *Israel in the Mind of America*, p. 5.
38 Grose, *Israel in the Mind of America*, p. 5
39 Glick, *The Triangular Confrontation*, pp. 22–23.
40 *Ibid.*, p. 23.
41 Grose, *Israel in the Mind of America*, p. 3 claims that the Lost Tribes had been an obsession with medieval Christendom since their abandonment by history in 722 BC. It was believed that with their rediscovery would come redemption for all mankind; Reuben Fink, *America and Palestine* (New York: Herald Square Press, Inc., 1945), p. 14.
42 Robert Bellah, "Civil Religion in America" in David McLellan (ed.), *Political Christianity: A reader* (Wiltshire: Redwood Books, 1997), p. 98.
43 *WP*, 15 May 1994, p. X6.
44 Quoted in Fink, *America and Palestine*, p. 14.
45 Quoted in Moshe Davis (ed.), *With Eyes Towards Zion* (New York: Arno Press, 1977), p. 9.
46 Jewish nationalists often omit the remainder of Adams text: "Once restored to an independent government and no longer persecuted they would soon wear away some of the asperities and peculiarities of their character, possibly in time become liberal Unitarian Christians." Quoted in Grose, *Israel in the Mind of America*, p. 6.
47 Glick, *The Triangular Confrontation*, p. 27.
48 Quoted in Fink, *America and Palestine*, p. 432.
49 *Ibid.*, p. 32.
50 The report was prepared by the research group appointed by President Wilson to prepare material and recommendations for the American Delegation at the Versailles Peace Conference.
51 Fink, *America and Palestine*, p. 34.
52 *Ibid.*, p. 38.
53 Cited in *ibid.*, p. 41.
54 Author's interview with David Bar-Ilan.
55 See Paul. J. Hare, "Diplomatic Chronicles of the Middle East: A biography of Raymond Hare" (Washington: The Middle East Institute, 1993), p. 10 in Michael C. Hudson, "To Play the Hegemon: Fifty years of US policy towards the Middle East," *Middle East Journal*, vol. 50, no. 3, Summer 1996, pp. 329–43.

56 Author's interview with Richard Murphy, U.S. Ambassador to Syria 1974–78, to Saudi Arabia 1981–83 and Assistant Secretary of State for Near Eastern and South Asian Affairs 1983–89.
57 Hare, *Diplomatic Chronicles of the Middle East*, p. 10
58 Hoover put forward this unique scheme, first published in an article on 19 November 1945 by the *New York World-Telegram.*
59 Glick, *The Triangular Confrontation*, p. 58.
60 *Congressional Record*, 25 May 1939, p. 6167.
61 Fink, *America and Palestine*, p. 181.
62 Quoted in Zvi Ganin, *Truman, American Jewry and Israel, 1945–1948* (London & New York: Holmes & Meier Publishers Inc., 1979), p. 7.
63 Warren F. Kimball, ed., *Churchill & Roosevelt: The complete correspondence*, Vol. III (Princeton, New Jersey: Princeton University Press, 1984), p. 206. For a detailed discussion of the Jewish refugee question see Henry L. Feingold, *Politics of Rescue: The Roosevelt administration and the Holocaust,1938–1945* (New Brunswick, New Jersey: Rutgers University Press, 1970).
64 *FRUS, 1943*, Washington, D.C. 1965, pp. 336–46.
65 Peter Novick, *The Holocaust in American Life* (New York: Houghton, Mifflin & Co., 1999), pp. 48–9 and Glick, *The Triangular Confrontation*, pp. 59–60.
66 Novick, *The Holocaust in American Life*, p. 40.
67 Grose, *Israel in the Mind of America*, p. 130
68 *Ibid.*, p. 156.
69 Jim Bishop, *FDR's Last Year* (New York: William Morrow Co. Inc., 1974), p. 545.
70 Ganin, *Truman, American Jewry and Israel*, p. 17.
71 *FRUS, 1944*, Vol. V, Washington, D.C. 1965, p. 588.
72 These groups were the Zionist Organisation of America, Hadassah (the Women's Zionist Organization of America), the Mizrachi (the religious Zionists), and the Labour Zionists, who were closely tied to the socialist and kibbutz-oriented party that dominated the Jewish community of Palestine.
73 Joseph Heller, *The Birth of Israel, 1945–49* (Florida: Florida University Press, 2000), p. 21.
74 Ganin, *Truman, American Jewry and Israel*, pp. 2–3.
75 See Marc Lee Raphael, *Abba Hillel Silver: A profile in American Judaism* (New York: Holmer & Meier, 1989), Introduction, for a detailed account of Silver's early life and political beliefs.
76 Bruce Eversen, *Truman, Palestine and the Press: Shaping conventional wisdom at the beginning of the Cold War* (New York, Connecticut & London: Greenwood Press, 1992), p. 50.
77 Heller, *The Birth of Israel*, pp. 21–2, Eversen, *Truman, Palestine and the Press*, p. 51, Grose, *Israel in the Mind of America*, p. 169,
78 *Ibid.*, p. 172.
79 Quoted in *ibid.*, p. 175.
80 Eversen, *Truman, Palestine and the Press*, p. 52.
81 Ganin, *Truman, American Jewry and Israel*, p. 14.
82 *FRUS, 1948*, Vol. V, Washington, D.C., 1972, p. 26. Statement made by the

Platform of the Democratic Party, Approved by the Democratic Convention, Philadelphia, 14 July 1948. "We pledge full recognition of the State of Israel. We affirm our pride that the United States, under the leadership of President Truman, played a leading role in the adoption of the resolution of November 29, 1947, by the United Nations General Assembly for the creation of the Jewish state."

83 Heller, *The Birth of Israel*, p. 22.
84 Harry S. Truman, *Memoirs*,Vol. II (New York: Signet Books, 1965), p. 136.
85 *Ibid.*
86 The United Nations Special Committee on Palestine (UNSCOP) was created as a discussion forum for matters relating to Palestine.
87 On 29 November 1947, this proposal was adopted by the UN General Assembly by a vote of 33 to 13 with 10 abstentions.
88 Truman, *Memoirs*, pp. 183–4.
89 *Ibid.*, p. 157.
90 *FRUS, 1947*, Vol. V. Washington, D.C., 1972, p. 1283.
91 *FRUS, 1948*, Vol. V, p. 666.
92 Quoted in Ganin, *Truman, American Jewry and Israel*, pp. 150–54. In response to the failure of partition, on 19 March 1948, Ambassador Austin, US representative to the UN Security Council proposed a temporary trusteeship for Palestine to restore public order. It is unclear whether Truman had prior knowledge of Austin's announcement and evidence suggests he was not as surprised as he later made out. According to Clark Clifford, the White House Special Counsel, Truman had agreed to the trusteeship proposal under three qualifications: firstly that the conciliatory machinery of the Security Council had been completely exhausted, secondly that the Council itself must then vote to propose an alternative to partition and thirdly that the Council must vote to reject partition altogether. The president's qualifications did not appear in Austin's statement.
93 See *FRUS*, 1948, Vol. V, pp. 82–83. The Soviet Union extended *de jure* recognition to Israel on 18 May 1948. The US refused to grant *de jure* recognition until Israel held its first democratic elections.
94 Eversen, *Truman, Palestine and the Press*, p. 164.
95 Author's interview with David Bar-Ilan.
96 *Ibid.*
97 Truman, *Memoirs*, p. 154.
98 *Ibid.*, p. 132.
99 Clark Clifford with Richard Holbrooke, *Counsel to the President: A memoir* (New York: Random House, 1991), pp. 7–8.
100 *Ibid.*
101 Truman had refused to issue a statement pledging recognition of a Jewish state on the Eve of Yom Kippur, the timing of which may have boosted his domestic popularity.
102 Ganin, *Truman, American Jewry and Israel*, p. 105.
103 *Ibid.*, p. 71.
104 Clark Clifford, "Annals of Government: Serving the president in the Truman years" *New Yorker*, 25 March, 1991, p. 71.

2 Framing American Foreign Policy

1 Steven L. Spiegel, *The Other Arab–Israeli Conflict: Making America's Middle East policy, from Truman to Reagan* (Chicago & London: University of Chicago Press, 1985), p. 10.
2 *Ibid.*
3 *Ibid.*
4 Joseph Frankel, *National Interest* (London: Pall Mall Press Ltd., 1970), p. 26.
5 Geoffrey Stern, *The Structure of International Society* (London & New York: Pinter, 2000), p. 128.
6 The Brookings Institution, *Major Problems of United States Foreign Policy 1953–1954* (Washington, D.C.: The Brookings Institution, 1955), pp. 373–5 cited in Frankel, *National Interest*, p. 18.
7 Richard Little & Steve Smith, *Belief Systems and International Relations* (Oxford: Basil Blackwell, 1988), p. 5.
8 See J. W. Burton, *International Relations: A general theory* (Cambridge: Cambridge University Press, 1965).
9 Stern, *The Structure of International Society*, pp. 130–31, 143–4.
10 William Wallace, *Foreign Policy and the Political Process* (London & Basingstoke: Macmillan, 1971), p. 13.
11 Stern, *The Structure of International Society*, p. 130.
12 David Sanders, *Losing an Empire Finding a Role* (Basingstoke: Macmillan Education, 1990), p. 135.
13 Wallace, *Foreign Policy*, p. 9.
14 Karen Dawisha, *The Foundations, Structure and Dynamics of Soviet Policy towards the Arab Radical Regimes* (Ph.D. thesis: LSE, 1978), p. 131.
15 Hélène Carrère D'Encausee, *Lenin: Revolution and power* (London & New York: Longman, 1982), p. 78. Lenin argued that Russia had to choose between the liquidation of the internal bourgeois enemy and the external war with Germany.
16 Dawisha, *The Foundations, Structure and Dynamics of Soviet Policy*, p. 133.
17 Stern, *The Structure of International Society*, p. 131.
18 *Ibid.*, p. 132.
19 Wallace, *Foreign Policy*, p. 21.
20 *Ibid.*, p. 32.
21 *Ibid.*
22 William Quandt, *Decade of Decisions: American policy towards the Arab–Israeli conflict, 1967–1976* (Berkeley, Los Angeles & London: University of California Press, 1977), p. 4.
23 Graham T. Allison, *Essence of Decision: Explaining the Cuban missile crisis* (Boston: Little, Brown & Co., 1971), p. 29.
24 F. S. Northedge, *The International Political System* (London & Boston: Faber & Faber, 1981), p. 24.
25 Wallace, *Foreign Policy*, p. 33.
26 Northedge, *The International Political System*, p. 25.
27 Joseph Frankel, *The Making of Foreign Policy* (Oxford: Oxford University Press, 1963), p. 168.

28 Frankel, *National Interest*, p. 19.
29 John H. McFadden, "The Strategic Arena" in Harry S. Allen & Ivan Volgyes (eds.), *Israel, the Middle East and U.S. Interests* (New York: Praeger Publishers, 1983), p. 3.
30 Author's interview with Richard Murphy.
31 *Ibid.*
32 Bernard Reich, *Securing the Covenant: United States–Israel relations after the Cold War* (Connecticut: Greenwood Press, 1995), p. 37.
33 *Ibid.*
34 David Schoenbaum, *The United States and the State of Israel* (Oxford: Oxford University Press, 1993), p. 137 and George Lenczowski, *American Presidents and the Middle East* (Durham & London: Duke University Press, 1990), p. 71.
35 The Israeli attack on the USS *Liberty* on 8 June 1967 presented a potential challenge to the relationship.
36 See Chapter 5 for a more detailed discussion of the arms policy the Nixon administration adopted towards the Middle East.
37 Black September refers to the period during September 1970, when the PLO, operating as a state-within-a-state, hijacked three western airliners and held the passengers hostage in Amman. The actions of the PLO threatened to overthrow the Jordanian monarchy. See Chapter 5 for a more detailed account.
38 Reagan's speech was quoted in *WP*, 15 August 1979.
39 Author's interview with Norman Podhoretz, Senior Fellow, Hudson Institute and former editor-in-chief of *Commentary* 1960–95.
40 *DSB*, "U.S., Israel Agree on Strategic Cooperation," January 1982, p. 45. For Israel, the significance of the MOU stemmed from the US identification of Israel as a strategic partner rather than as a client state.
41 Reich, *Securing the Covenant*, p. 45.
42 *Ibid.*
43 Author's interview with Marshall Breger, special assistant to President Reagan and his liaison to the Jewish Community, 1982–84.
44 Author's interview with Norman Podhoretz.
45 In principle any number of states could join the Baghdad Pact, but in practice the criteria for selection was rigorous. Anglo-American planners expected potential members to share their real sense of danger posed by Soviet Union and world Communism and that all member states should see eye to eye with one another. As a consequence, a very short list of candidates was compiled which yielded only three signatories: Britain, Iraq and Turkey. Even the United States was unwilling to join. Schoenbaum, *The United States*, p. 84.
46 Daniel Yergin, *The Prize: The epic quest for oil, money and power* (New York: Simon & Schuster, 1991), p. 115.
47 Anthony Sampson, *The Seven Sisters: The great oil companies and the world they made* (Sevenoaks: Coronet Books, 1976), p. 115.
48 Henry A. Kissinger, *White House Years* (Boston: Little, Brown, 1979), pp. 1262–64.
49 Yergin, *The Prize*, p. 115.
50 Warren F. Kimball (ed.), *Churchill & Roosevelt: The complete correspondence*, Vol. III (Princeton, New Jersey: Princeton University Press, 1984), p. 17.

51 Yergin, *The Prize*, p. 115.
52 Author's interview with Richard Murphy.
53 See Chapter 5 for a more detailed account of the 1973 oil embargo.
54 Karen L. Puschel, *US–Israeli Strategic Cooperation in the Post-Cold War Era* (Jerusalem: Jerusalem Post Press, 1992), p. 157.
55 This involved the covert transfer of American military equipment to Iran, a country against which Washington had imposed sanctions, in exchange for the release of US hostages held in Lebanon. Israel acted as the intermediary in dealings between Washington and Tehran.
56 Steven W. Hook, *National Interest and Foreign Aid* (Boulder, CO & London: Lynne Rienner Publishers, 1995), p. 24.
57 David Baldwin, *Foreign Aid and American Foreign Policy: A documentary analysis* (New York, Washington & London: Frederick A. Praeger, 1966), p. 25.
58 Christopher Coker, *Reflections on American Foreign Policy Since 1945* (London: Pinter Publishers, 1989), p. 106.
59 Leopold Yehuda Laufer, "U.S. Aid to Israel: Problems and perceptions," in Gabriel Sheffer (ed.), *Dynamics of Dependence: U.S. Israeli relations* (Boulder, CO & London: Westview Press, 1987), p. 134.
60 Reich, *Securing the Covenant* p. 93.
61 *Ibid.*, p. 93.
62 *Ibid.*, p. 91.
63 *WP*, 15 May 1994, p. X6.
64 Author's interview with Lewis Roth, Representative, Americans for Peace Now, Washington, D.C.
65 There is a tendency of donors to direct aid flows to recipient countries with economic systems similar to their own. Hook, *National Interest*, p. 145.
66 A. F. K. Organski, *The $36 Billion Bargain: Strategy and politics in U.S. assistance to Israel* (New York: Columbia University Press, 1990), p. 159.
67 *Ibid.*, p. 160.
68 Hook, *National Interest*, p. 145
69 Reich, *Securing the Covenant*, p. 96.
70 *Ibid.*
71 Author's interview with Geoffrey Aronson, Director for Research and Publications, Foundation for Middle East Peace.
72 Organski, *The $36 Billion Bargain*, p. 204.
73 *Ibid.*, p. 206.
74 For both the censored and uncensored versions see "US Assistance to the State of Israel;" *Report of the Comptroller General of the United States* "US Assistance to Israel," General Accounting Office, United States, 24 June 1983, Washington 1983.
75 Michael Donelan, "The Elements of United States Foreign Policy" in F. S. Northedge (ed.), *Foreign Policies of the Powers* (London: Faber & Faber, 1972), p 45.
76 Author's interview with George R. Salem, member of the Palestinian negotiating team at Madrid talks 1991–93.
77 Quandt, *Decade of Decisions*, p. 15.

78 James N. Rosenau, "Introduction," in James N. Rosenau (ed.), *Domestic Sources of Foreign Policy* (New York: Free Press, 1967), p. 2.

79 Richard E. Neustadt, *Presidential Power and the Modern Presidents: The politics of leadership from Roosevelt to Reagan* (New York: The Free Press, Macmillan Publishing Co., 1990), p. 29.

80 Samuel Huntington, *The Common Defence: Strategic programmes in national politics* (New York & London: Columbia University Press, 1961), p. 135, cited in Robert J. Art, "Bureaucratic Politics & American Foreign Policy: A critique" *Political Sciences* 4: (1973), p. 470.

81 *Ibid.*

82 Art, "Bureaucratic Politics," p. 470.

83 Roger Hillsman, "The Foreign-Policy Consensus: An interim report" *Journal of Conflict Resolution* 3: (December 1959), p. 369 cited in Art, "Bureaucratic Politics,"p. 470.

84 Neustadt, *Presidential Power*, p. 7.

85 Camille Mansour, *Beyond Alliance: Israel in US foreign policy* (New York: Columbia University Press, 1994), p. 265.

86 Seymour Lipset & Earl Raab, *Jews and the New American Scene* (Cambridge, MA & London: Harvard University Press, 1995), p. 171.

87 Author's interview with Wayne Owens, Congressman for Utah 1972–74 and member of the Foreign Affairs Committee, Vice Chairman of the Centre for Middle East Peace and Economic Cooperation 1993–95, President of the Centre 1995–present.

88 *Ibid.*

89 Author's interview with Khalid Jahshan, President, National Association of Arab Americans, 1997–2000.

90 Cecil V. Crabb, Jr., Glenn J. Antizzo & Leila E. Sarieddine, *Congress and the Foreign Policy Process: Modes of legislative behaviour* (Louisiana: Louisiana State University Press, 2000), p. 145.

91 Ofira Seliktar, *Divided We Stand: American Jews, Israel, and the peace process* (Westport, CT & London: Praeger, 2002), p. 208.

92 Camill Mansour, *Beyond Alliance: Israel in US foreign policy* (New York: Columbia University Press, 1994), p. 241.

93 Author's interview with David Bar-Ilan.

94 For example, as early as 1956 the cotton, oil and Zionist lobbies combined forces to ensure Congress rejected the aid bill to finance the Egyptian Aswan High Dam.

95 *IHT*, 8 August 1986 p. 20.

96 Carl J. Friedrich, *Man and His Government* (New York: McGraw-Hill, 1963), chapter 11.

97 Walter Eytan, *The First Ten Years: A diplomatic history of Israel* (New York: Simon & Schuster, 1958), p. 209ff.

98 Mansour, *Beyond Alliance*, p. 248.

99 David Shribman, "Hosts not Visitors: The future of Jews in American political life," in L. Sandy Maisel (ed.), *Jews in American Politics* (Rowman & Littlefield Publishers: Lanham, Boulder, New York, Oxford, 2001), p. 276.

100 Novik, *The United States*, pp. 59–60.
101 *Los Angeles Times* "Special Report: Decision 2000, How California Voted," November 9, 2000 p. A49.
102 Stephen D. Isaacs, *Jews and American Politics* (New York: Doubleday, 1974), p. 6. These figures are reached by calculating the number of Jewish votes as a percentage of total votes cast.
103 *Ibid.*, p. 6.
104 Author's interview with Gene Burger, Member of the Israeli Policy Forum, 1995–present.
105 *Ibid.*
106 Jeffrey Helmreich, "The Israel Swing Factor: How the American Jewish vote influences US elections," *Jerusalem Center for Public Affairs* no. 446, 20 Tevet 5761 / 15 January 2001.
107 *Ibid.*, pp. 284, 64.
108 Mansour, *Beyond Alliance*, p. 248.
109 Lipset & Raab, *Jews and the New American Scene*, p. 111.
110 In contrast many Catholics have historically condemned the Jews as the killers of Christ.
111 Robert Fisk, "A strange kind of freedom," *The Independent*, 9 July 2002.
112 Grace Halsell, *Prophecy and Politics: Militant evangelists on the road to nuclear war* (Westport, Connecticut: Lawrence Hill & Co., 1986), p. 159.
113 Halsell, *Prophecy and Politics*, p.197.
114 Author's interview with Lewis Roth, Representative, Americans for Peace Now, Washington, D.C.
115 Halsell, *Prophecy and Politics*, p.155.
116 John Simpson, "Support for the Moral Majority and its Sociomoral Platform" in David Bromley & Anson Shape (ed.), *New Christian Politics* (Macon: Mercer University Press, 1984), p. 65.
117 Author's interview with Marshall Breger.
118 Albert J. Menendez, *Evangelicals at the Ballot Box* (New York: Prometheus Books, 1996), p. 145.
119 Erling Jorstad, *The New Christian Right, 1981–1988: Prospects for the Reagan decade* (Lewinston: Edwin Mellen Press, 1987), p. 130.
120 *Ibid.*, p. 144. See *Evangelicals at the Ballot Box*, pp. 135–53 for a detailed account of the changes in religious voting patterns between 1980 and 1988.
121 Author's interview with Khalid Jahshan.
122 Spiegel, *The Other Arab–Israeli Conflict*, p. 7.
123 Robert H. Trice, "Domestic Interest Groups and the Arab–Israeli Conflict: A behavioural analysis," in Abdul Aziz Said (ed.), *Ethnicity and US Foreign Policy* (New York & London: Praeger Publishers, 1977), p. 123.
124 Author's interview with George R. Salem.
125 "The Middle East: U.S. Policy, Israel, Oil and the Arabs" *Congressional Quarterly*, 4th ed. (Washington, D.C.: Congressional Quarterly, 1992), p. 97.
126 Author's interview with Wayne Owens.
127 Author's interview with David Bar-Ilan.

128 Author's interview with Khalid Jahshan.
129 Author's interview with Wayne Owens and Lewis Roth.
130 Author's interview with Khalid Jahshan.
131 *DSB*, 21 December 1970, p. 751.
132 These traits of the American national character gave rise to a foreign policy that veers from isolationism in peacetime to moral activism in wartime. John Spanier & Steven W. Hook, *American Foreign Policy Since World War II* (Washington, D.C.: CQ Press, 1997), p. xii; and Seyom Brown, *The Faces of Power: United States foreign policy from Truman to Clinton* (New York: Columbia University Press, 1994), p. 7.
133 Author's interview with Dennis Ross, Director of State Department Planning Policy 1988–92 and Special Middle East Co-ordinator 1992–2000.
134 Author's interview with Geoffrey Aronson, Director for Research and Publications, Foundation for Middle East Peace
135 Sharon Hays, "Structure and Agency and the sticky problem of culture," *Sociological Theory* 12(1), March 1994, p. 65.
136 Raymond Williams, "Culture is Ordinary" in Ann Gray & Jim McGuigen (eds.), *Studying Culture* (New York: Routledge, 1993), p. 6.
137 Clifford Geertz, *The Interpretation of Cultures* (New York: Basic Books, 1973), p. 15.
138 Stern, *International Society*, p. 144.
139 Plato, *Republic* (Oxford: Clarendon Press, 1921–22).
140 Jean-Jacques Rousseau, *The Social Contract and Discourses*, translated, with introduction by G. D. N. Cole (London: Dent, 1955), p. 43.
141 In American society, C. Wright Mills describes the power elite as the leading men in the high military, the corporate executives and the political directorate. For an in-depth discussion see C. Wright Mills, *Power, Politics and People* (London, Oxford & New York: Oxford University Press, 1963), p. 27.
142 Gramsci wrote that the key element of American politics was that the whole life of the country was organised around capitalist productive activity, from which emerged a new type of human being, a new work process, a new dynamic material culture with no feudal survivors and therefore, a weak socialist tradition in comparison to other capitalist societies. See Carl Boggs, *The Two Revolutions: Gramsci and the dilemmas of Western Marxism* (Boston, Massachusetts: South End Press, 1984), pp. 178–181.
143 *State and Civil Society* (London: Lawrence & Wishart, 1971), p. 260.
144 Barrington Moore, *The Social Origins of Democracy & Dictatorship: Lord and peasant in the making of the modern world* (London: Allen Lane, 1967), p. 486.
145 Loren Baritz, *Backfire: A history of how American culture led us into Vietnam and made us fight the way we did* (Baltimore & London: Johns Hopkins University Press, 1998), p. 331.
146 Barbara Cruikshank, "Cultural Politics: Political theory and the foundations of democratic order" in Jodi Dean (ed.), *Cultural Studies and Political Theory* (Ithaca & London: Cornell University Press, 2000), p. 67.
147 See Alasdair MacIntyre, *After Virtue: A study in moral theory* (London: Duckworth, 1985).

148 John Gibbens, "Contemporary Political Culture: An Introduction" in J. Gibbens (ed.), *Contemporary Political Culture: Politics in a post-modern age* (London: Sage, 1989), pp. 3–6.
149 Ronald Rogowski, *A Rational Theory of Legitimacy* (Princeton, NJ: Princeton University Press, 1976).
150 Henry A. Kissinger, *Years of Upheaval* (London: Weidenfeld & Nicolson, 1982), p. 465.
151 Lucian W. Pye, "Political Culture & Political Development," in Lucian W. Pye & Sidney Verba (eds.), *Political Culture & Political Development* (Princeton, New Jersey: Princeton University Press, 1965), p. 8.
152 See B. Girvin, "Change and Continuity in Liberal Political Culture" in J. Gibbens, ed., *Contemporary Political Culture: Politics in a post-modern age* (London: Sage, 1989).
153 Geertz, *The Interpretation of Cultures*, p. 408.
154 Chris Jenks, *Culture* (London & New York: Routledge, 1993), p. 53.
155 Geertz, *The Interpretation of Cultures*, p. 362.
156 David E. Apter, "Ideology and Discontent" in David E. Apter (ed.), *Ideology and Discontent* (London & New York: The Free Press, 1964), p. 62.
157 Eric Hobsbawm, "Introduction: Inventing Traditions," in E. Hobsbawm & T. Ranger (eds), *The Invention of Tradition* (Cambridge: Cambridge University Press, 1983), p. 7.
158 Geertz, *The Interpretation of Cultures*, p. 126.
159 Anthony Smith, *National Identity* (London: Penguin Books, 1991), pp. 16–17.
160 Apter (ed.), *Ideology and Discontent*, p. 62.
161 *Ibid.*
162 Hobsbawm, *The Invention of Tradition*, p. 107.
163 *Ibid.*, pp. 1–14.
164 William Bloom, *Personal Identity, National Identity and International Relations* (Cambridge: Cambridge University Press, 1990), p. 81.
165 Hobsbawm, *The Invention of Tradition*, p. 1.
166 Stern, *International Society*, p. 106.
167 *Ibid.*
168 *Ibid.*
169 Anthony Smith, *Nations and Nationalism in a Global Era* (Cambridge, Massachusetts: Polity Press, 1995), pp. 179–80.
170 Hobsbawm, *The Invention of Tradition*, p. 11.
171 Habermas, J. *Legitimating Crisis* (Boston: Beacon Press, 1975), p. 105.
172 Philip Converse, "The Nature of Belief Systems in Mass Publics" in D. Apter (ed.), *Ideology and Discontent* (New York: Free Press, 1964), p. 211.
173 See E. Gellner, *Nations and Nationalism* (Oxford: Blackwell, 1983).
174 Asher Arian, Ilan Talmud & Tamar Hermann, *National Security and Public Opinion in Israel* (Boulder, CO: Westview, 1988), p. 16.
175 *Ibid.*
176 Quoted in S. Welch *The Concept of Political Culture* (Basingstoke: Macmillan, 1993), p. 7.

177 Francis Fukuyama, *The End of History and the Last Man* (London: Hamish Hamilton, 1992), p. 15.
178 *DSB*, 16 September 1974, p. 377.
179 Hobsbawm, *The Invention of Tradition*, p. 123.
180 A. Arian, M. Shamir & R. Ventura, "Public Opinion and Political Change," *Comparative Politics*, vol. 24, no. 3, p. 317.
181 Wilson & Pronay (eds.), *The Political Re-Education of Germany and Her Allies After World War II* (London: Croom Helm, 1985).
182 Talcott Parsons, *The Social System* (London: Routledge & Kegan Paul, 1951), p. 15.
183 *Ibid.*
184 Apter, *Ideology and Discontent*, p. 43.
185 James F. Barnes, Marshall Carter & Max J. Skidmore, *The World of Politics: A concise introduction* 2nd ed. (New York: St. Martin's Press, 1984), p. 33.
186 Irvin Child, "Socialisation" in Lindzey Gardner (ed.), *Handbook of Social Psychology*, Vol. II (Boston: McGraw-Hill, New York: Oxford University Press, 1954), p. 655.
187 Emile Durkheim, cited in William Bloom, *Personal Identity and International Relations* (Cambridge: Cambridge University Press, 1990), p. 14
188 William Lyons, John M. Scheb II & Lilliard E. Richardson, Jr., *American Government: Politics & political culture* (Minneapolis/St. Paul, New York, Los Angeles, San Francisco: West Publishing Co., 1995), p. 175.
189 *Ibid.*
190 Barnes, Carter & Skidmore, *The World of Politics*, p. 174.
191 *Ibid.*
192 Almond, Gabriel & Powell, Bingham. *Comparative Politics Today*, 6th ed. (New York: Harper Collins, 1996), p. 43.
193 Barnes, Carter & Skidmore, *The World of Politics*, p. 175.
194 Geoffrey Stern, *The Rise and Decline of International Communism* (Aldershot: Edward Elgar Publishing Ltd., 1990), p. 139.
195 Harold and Margaret Sprout, *Man-Milieu Relationship Hypotheses in the Context of International Politics* (Princeton: Centre for International Studies, 1956), Introduction.
196 *Ibid.*
197 For a detailed discussion of perception and misperception in decision-making see Robert Jervis, *Perception and Misperception in World Politics* (Princeton, New Jersey: Princeton University Press, 1976), and Robert Axelrod, *Structure of Decision: The cognitive maps of political elites* (Princeton, New Jersey: Princeton University Press, 1976).
198 John Volger, "Perspectives on the Foreign Policy System: Psychological approaches," in Michael Clarke & Brian White (eds.), *Understanding Foreign Policy: The foreign policy systems approach* (Aldershot: Edward Elgar Publishing Ltd., 1989), p. 136.

3 American Political Culture

1 Daniel J. Elazar, *The American Mosaic: The impact of space, time, & culture on American politics* (Boulder, San Francisco, Oxford: Westview Press, 1994), p. 201.
2 *Ibid.*
3 *Ibid.*
4 P. M. Kattenburg, *The Vietnam Trauma in American Foreign Policy, 1945–75* (New Brunswick: Transaction books, 1980), p. 69 ff. This is not to suggest that America is the only society that is defined by principles and ideas. It is the degree to which this has been the case in America when combined with its vast size and population diversity that makes the US somewhat exceptional in this regard.
5 Elazar, *American Federalism*, p. 106.
6 Vance Packard, *The Hidden Persuaders* (London: Longmans, 1962), p. 201.
7 Peter Woll & Stephen J. Rockwell, *American Politics and Realities* (New York: Longman, 2000), p. 31.
8 William Lyons, John M. Scheb II & Lilliard E. Richardson, Jr., *American Government: Politics & political culture* (Minneapolis/St. Paul, New York, Los Angeles, San Francisco: West Publishing Co., 1995), p. 25.
9 Packard, *The Hidden Persuaders*, p. 201.
10 *Ibid.*, pp. 181–2.
11 The head of a Chicago research firm that conducted psychoanalytically orientated studies for merchandisers, Louis Cheskin, summed up motivation research as "the type of research that seeks to learn what motivates people in making choices. It employs techniques designed to reach the unconscious or subconscious mind because preferences generally are determined by factors of which the individual is not conscious . . . Actually in the buying situation the consumer generally acts emotionally and compulsively, unconsciously reacting to the images and designs which in the subconscious are associated with the product." Quoted in Packard, *The Hidden Persuaders*, p. 8.
12 Lyons, Scheb II & Richardson Jr., *American Government*, p. 25.
13 Christopher Coker, *Reflections on American Foreign Policy Since 1945* (London: Pinter, 1989), p. 1.
14 *Ibid.*, p. 2.
15 *Ibid.*, p. 4.
16 Samuel Huntington, *American Politics in the United States* (New York: St. Martin's Press, 1987), p. 6.
17 Robert Bellah, *Beyond Belief: Essays on religion in a post-traditional world* (Berkeley & Oxford: University of California Press, 1970), pp. 182–3.
18 David McLellan "Introduction" in David McLellan (ed.), *Political Christianity: A reader* (Wiltshire: Redwood Books, 1997), p. 97.
19 Michael Novak, *The Spirit of Democratic Capitalism* (London, IEA Health and Welfare Unit, 1991), quoted in David McLellan "Introduction" in *ibid.*, pp. 97–8.
20 David Ryan, *US Foreign Policy in World History* (London & New York: Routledge, 2000), p. 23.
21 *Ibid.*, pp. 24–5.
22 Louis Hartz, *The Liberal Tradition in America: An interpretation of American political thought since the revolution* (New York: Harcourt Brace, 1955), p. 38.

23 Byron Shafer, *Introduction*, in Byron Shafer (ed.), *Is America Different?* (Oxford: Oxford University Press, 1991), p. v.
24 *DBS*, 6 December 1976, p. 677.
25 Daniel Bell, "The Hegelian Secret: Civil society and American exceptionalism" in Byron Shafer (ed.), *Is America Different?* (Oxford: Oxford University Press, 1991), pp. 50–51.
26 Vernon van Dyke, *Human Rights, the United States and the World Community* (Oxford: Oxford University Press, 1970), quoted in Coker, *Reflections on American Foreign Policy*, p. 10.
27 Daniel Boorstin, *The Image, or What Happened to the American Dream* (London: Weidenfeld & Nicolson 1961), p. 244.
28 David L. Larson, *The Puritan Ethic in United States Foreign Policy* (New York: D. van Nostrand Co. Ltd., 1966), p. 12.
29 See Christopher Thorne, "American Political Culture and the End of the Cold War," *Journal of American Studies* 26, 1992, p. 316.
30 *DSB*, 6 December 1976, pp. 677–8.
31 James Burns, *The American Idea of Mission* (New Brunswick: Rutgers University Press, 1957), p. 14.
32 Cited in William Herberg, *Protestant-Catholic-Jew* (New York: Doubleday, 1960), p. 258n.
33 John Foster Dulles, *War, Peace or Change* (New York: Harper & Row, 1939).
34 Zbigniew Brzezinski, "Remarks before the Women's National Democratic Club, Washington, D.C., 21 February 1980," *White House Press Release* (21 February 1980).
35 Coker, *Reflections on American Foreign Policy*, p. 18.
36 Fredrick Turner, *The Frontier in American History* (New York: Dover Publications, 1996), pp. 1–3.
37 Cecil V. Crabb, Jr. *American Foreign Policy in the Nuclear Age* (New York: Harper & Row, 1960), p. 32.
38 Scott Lucas, *Freedom's War: The US crusade against the Soviet Union, 1945–56* (Manchester: Manchester University Press, 1999), p. 2.
39 There has generally been an implicit but clear division of function between the civil religion and Christianity. Bellah, *Beyond Belief*, p. 176.
40 Robert Bellah, "Civil Religion in America" in David McLellan (ed.), *Political Christianity: A reader* (Wiltshire: Redwood Books, 1997), p. 98.
41 Lipset argued that American religion, at least since the early nineteenth century has been predominately activist, moralistic and social rather than contemplative, theological, or innerly spiritual. Seymour Martin Lipset, "Religion and American Values" in *The First New Nation* (New York: Basic Books, 1964), chapter 4.
42 Bellah, *Civil Religion*, p. 98.
43 Hans J. Morgenthau, *Politics Among Nations: The struggle for power and peace* (New York: McGraw-Hill, Inc., 1993), p. 13.
44 Crabb, Jr., *American Foreign Policy in the Nuclear Age* (New York: Harper & Row, 1960), p. 32.
45 Bellah, *Civil Religion*, p. 102.
46 Michael Donelan, "The Elements of United States Policy" in F. S. Northedge

(ed.), *Foreign Policies of the Powers* (London: Faber & Faber, 1974), p. 62.

47 George F. Kennan, *Realities of American Foreign Policy* (London: Oxford University Press, 1954), p. 13. R. A. Packenham writes that "Nowhere in the world has the United States knowingly supported, directly or indirectly, actively or by cool responses to those in power, genuinely radical movements, groups or individuals. This seems to be strong evidence that under no circumstances are radicalism and revolution appropriate for economic and political development." R. A. Packenham, *Liberal America and the Third World: Political development ideas in foreign aid and social science* (Princeton: Princeton University Press, 1973), p. 144.

48 Japan and the Philippines are two such examples.

49 Lucas, *Freedom's War*, p. 279.

50 Michael Donelan, "The Ideas of American Foreign Policy", p. 62.

51 During the Eisenhower administration, George Humphrey, the Secretary of the Treasury, argued that "We should . . . stop talking so much about democracy, and make it clear that we are quite willing to support dictatorships of the right if their polices are pro-American." See Lucas, *Freedom's War*, p. 279.

52 George Kennan, *American Diplomacy, 1900–1950* (Chicago: Chicago University Press, 1953), p. 94.

53 *Ibid.*

54 Banks, *Foreign Policy*, p. 47.

55 *Ibid.*, p. 48.

56 See transcript of President George W. Bush's first State of the Union address, delivered to Congress on 29 January 2002. <www.whitehouse.gov/news/releases/2002/01/20020129-11.html>.

57 Henry Kissinger, *The White House Years* (Boston: Little, Brown, 1979), p. 911.

58 William Fulbright wrote that "inevitably our major impact on the world is not what we do but what we are: the way we govern ourselves." William Fulbright, *The Arrogance of Power* (London: Cape, 1967).

59 Fernand Braudel, *The Identity of France, Vol. 1: History & Environment* (London: Collins, 1988), p. 18.

60 Pitirim A. Sorokin, *The Crisis of Our Age* (London & Sydney: Angus & Robertson, 1942), p. 104.

61 Leon Samson, *Towards a United Front: A philosophy for American workers* (New York: Faber & Rinehart, 1933), pp. 16–17.

62 David Apter, "Introduction: Ideology and Discontent" in David E. Apter (ed.), *Ideology and Discontent* (London & New York: The Free Press, 1964), pp. 18–21.

63 Carl Boggs, *The Two Revolutions: Gramsci and the dilemmas of Western Marxism* (Boston, MA: South End Press, 1984), p. 179.

64 Lucas, *Freedom's War*, pp. 1, 7.

65 Ryan, *US Foreign Policy*, p. 1.

66 Edward Weisband, *The Ideology of American Foreign Policy: A paradigm of Lockean liberalism* (London & Beverly Hills: Sage Publications, 1973), p. 62.

67 Cited in Donald Devine, *The Political Culture of the United States* (Boston: Little, Brown, 1972).

68 Weisband, *The Ideology of American Foreign Policy*, p. 62.

69 Noam Chomsky, "The Old and the New Cold War" in James Peck (ed.), *The Chomsky Reader* (New York: Pantheon Books, 1987), p. 218.

70 Two foreign policy analysts observed in the lead article in a 1993 edition of *Foreign Policy* that "Underpinning U.S. world order strategy is the belief that America must maintain what is in essence a military protectorate in economically critical regions to ensure that America's vital trade and financial relations will not be disrupted by political upheaval." Christopher Layne, senior fellow of the Cato Institute, and Benjamin Schwarz, international policy analyst at RAND, *Foreign Policy*, Fall 1993, cited in Noam Chomsky, *World Orders Old and New* (New York: Columbia University Press, 1996), pp. 31–2. See Lucas, *Freedom's War*, p. 2 for a contrary discussion of this issue.

71 Donelan, 1974, *"The Elements"*, p. 67.

72 See Geoffrey Stern, *The Rise and Decline of International Communism* (Aldershot: Edward Elgar Publishing Ltd., 1990), pp. 253–4 for a discussion of the changes Gorbachev made to the Soviet bureaucracy that contributed to the demise of the Soviet Union.

73 In a 2002 survey, 77% of Americans said they viewed Palestinian suicide bombings as terrorism in the sense of the war on terror. Professor Makiya, Brandeis University, speaking on *Newsnight* BBC 1, 4 April 2002.

74 Fawas A. Gerges, *America and Political Islam: Clash of cultures or clash of interests* (Cambridge: Cambridge University Press, 1999), p. 6.

75 Abraham Ben-Zvi, *The United States and Israel* (New York: Columbia University Press, 1993), pp. 15–16.

76 New York Post, 2 April 1943, p. 29 and January 1943 Gallup poll cited in Deborah Lipstadt, *Beyond Belief: The American press and the coming of the Holocaust, 1933–45* (New York: The Free Press, 1986), pp. 240–41.

77 Norman G. Finkelstein, *The Holocaust Industry: Reflections of the exploitation of Jewish suffering* (London & New York: Verso, 2000), p. 14.

78 Within a short period of time following the end of the Second World War the American conception of the Soviet Union changed from that of an ally to the image of a totalitarian state bent on unlimited expansion through conquest and subversion. Deborah Welch Larson, *Origins of Containment: A psychological explanation* (Princeton, New Jersey: Princeton University Press, 1985), p. 4.

79 See Hannah Arendt, *The Origins of Totalitarianism* (London: George, Allen & Unwin, 1962), for an in-depth discussion of the totalitarian movement and totalitarianism in power and the similarities between Nazism and Soviet Communism.

80 Novik, *The United States*, p. 92.

81 *Ibid.*

82 Report No. 2 from Hollywood representative, 15 October 1948, NCRAC Papers, Box 51, cited in *ibid.*, p. 95.

83 Report No. 10, 23 May 1949, NCRAC Papers, Box 51, cited in *ibid.*, p. 95.

84 Finkelstein, *The Holocaust Industry*, p. 16.

85 Norman Podhoretz, *Making It* (New York: Random House, 1967), p. 101.

86 Novik, *The United States*, pp. 95–6.

87 *Ibid.*, p. 114.

88 Alan Mintz, *Popular Culture and the Shaping of Holocaust Memory in America* (Seattle & London: University of Washington Press, 2001), p. 5.
89 Novik, *The United States*, p. 113.
90 Mintz, *Popular Culture*, p. 7.
91 *Ibid.*, p. 10.
92 See Nathan Glazer, *Ethnic Dilemmas, 1964–82* (Cambridge, MA: Harvard University Press, 1983).
93 Morris Dickstein, "Black Humor and History," in Gerald Howard (ed.), *The Sixties* (New York: Washington Square Press publication of Pocket Books, 1982), pp. 272–92, cited in Judith Doneson, *The Holocaust in American Film* (Syracuse: Syracuse University Press, 2002), p. 107.
94 Novik, *The United States*, p. 128.
95 Author's interview with Marshall Breger, special assistant to President Reagan and his liaison to the Jewish Community, 1982–84.
96 Howard Sachar, *A History of Israel from the Rise of Zionism to Our Time* (New York: Alfred A. Knopf, 1996), p. 555.
97 *Ibid.*, p. 556.
98 Mintz, *Popular Culture*, pp. 12–13.
99 *Ibid.*, p. 16.
100 Annette Insdorf, *Indelible Shadows: Film and the Holocaust* (Cambridge University Press: Cambridge, 2003), p. 7.
101 *Ibid.*, p. 7.
102 Joyce Antler, "Three Thousand Miles Away: The Holocaust in recent works for the American theater," in Hilene Flanzbaum, *The Americanization of the Holocaust* (Maryland: Johns Hopkins University Press, 1999), p. 125.
103 *Ibid.*, p. 149.
104 Doneson, *The Holocaust*, p. 53.
105 Antler, "Three Thousand Miles Away", p. 150.
106 *Ibid.*, pp. 150–51.
107 Sara R. Horowitz, "The Cinematic Triangulation of Jewish American Identity: Israel, America, and the Holocaust" in Hilene Flanzbaum, *The Americanization of the Holocaust* (Maryland: Johns Hopkins University Press, 1999), pp. 155–6.
108 *Ibid.*, p. 156.
109 "Man's Long, Rough Pursuit of Justice," *Life*, 15 December 1965, pp. 121–3, cited in Mintz, *Popular Culture* p. 92.
110 Bosley Crowther, "Hollywood's Producer of Controversy," *NYT Magazine*, 10 December 1961, pp. 76–7.
111 Pierre Sorlin, *The Film in History: Restaging the past* (Totowa, NJ: Barnes & Noble Books, 1980), p. 44, cited in Doneson, *The Holocaust*, p. 97.
112 Insdorf, *Indelible Shadows*, p. 8.
113 *Ibid.*
114 Mintz, *Popular Culture*, p. 91.
115 Insdorf, *Indelible Shadows*, p. 8.
116 Doneson, *The Holocaust*, p. 112.
117 Bosley Crowther, "Screen: *The Pawnbroker* Opens at Three Theatres," *NYT*, 14 April 1965.

118 Mintz, *Popular Culture*, p. 113.
119 *Ibid.*, p. 115.
120 See Glazer, *Ethnic Dilemmas.*
121 Novik, *The United States*, p. 209.
122 Mintz, *Popular Culture*, p. 26.
123 Horowitz, "Cinematic Triangulation," p. 72.
124 Mintz, *Popular Culture*, p. 151.
125 Lawrence Langer, *Versions of Survival* (Albany: State University of New York Press, 1982), pp. 1–65 cited in Mintz *Popular Culture*, p. 153.
126 Hilene Flanzbaum "Introduction: The Americanisation of the Holocaust" in Hilene Flanzbaum (ed.), *The Americanisation of the Holocaust* (Baltimore & London: The Johns Hopkins University Press, 1999), p. 13.
127 James E. Young, "Memory and the Politics of Identity" in Flanzbaum (ed.), *The Americanisation of the Holocaust*, p. 72.
128 Mintz, *Popular Culture*, pp. 41, 81.
129 Bernard Reich, *Securing the Covenant: United States–Israel relations after the Cold War* (Westport, Connecticut & London: Praeger Publishers, 1995), p. 11.
130 "Democracy in America," remarks by Governor Bill Clinton, University of Wisconsin, Milwaukee, October 1, 1992, p. 1, quoted in Reich, *Securing the Covenant*, p. 12.
131 The theme of the American Israel was used, almost from the beginning, as a justification for the appalling treatment of the American Indians. It can be overtly or implicitly linked to the idea of manifest destiny and has been used to legitimate imperialist adventures since the nineteenth century. Bellah, *Beyond Belief*, p. 182.
132 Reich, *Securing the Covenant*, pp. 12–13.
133 *DSB*, 26 July 1976, pp. 106–15.
134 William Quandt, *Decade of Decision: American policy towards the Arab–Israeli conflict, 1967–1976* (Berkeley, Los Angeles, London: University of California Press, 1977), p. 35.
135 *DSB*, 7 June 1976, p. 721.
136 *Ibid.*, p. 720.
137 Michael H. Hunt, *Ideology and U.S. Foreign Policy* (New Haven, CT: Yale University Press, 1987), pp. 15–16.
138 George Lenczowski, *American Presidents and the Middle East* (Durham and London: Duke University Press, 1990), p. 47.

4 The Johnson Administration and US Policy towards Israel

1 William B. Quandt, *Peace Process: American diplomacy and the Arab–Israeli conflict since 1967* (Washington, D.C. & Berkeley, Los Angeles: The Brookings Institution & University of California Press, 1993), p. 25.
2 Barbara Kellerman & Ryan J. Barilleaux, *The President as World Leader* (New York: St. Martin's Press, 1991), p. 74.
3 Steven L. Spiegel, *The Other Arab–Israeli Conflict: Making America's Middle East policy, from Truman to Reagan* (Chicago & London: The University of Chicago Press, 1985), p. 118.

4 Louis Gomolak, *Prologue: LBJ's foreign affairs background, 1908–48*, Ph.D. diss., University of Texas, Austin, 1981), pp. 30–35, 44–51, 94–6. cited in Douglas Little, "Choosing Sides: Lyndon Johnson and the Middle East" in Robert A. Divine (ed.), *The Johnson Years*, p. 152.
5 *Ibid.*
6 H. W. Brands, *The Wages of Globalism: Lyndon Johnson and the limits of American power* (New York & Oxford: Oxford University Press, 1995), p. 187.
7 *Public Papers of the Presidents: Lyndon Johnson*, 1968 (Washington, 1969): 10 September 1968. Johnson delivered this speech at the 125th Anniversary Meeting of B'nai B'rith.
8 Spiegel, *The Other Arab–Israeli Conflict*, p. 124.
9 Lyndon Baines Johnson, *The Vantage Point: Perspectives of the presidency, 1963–1969* (New York: Holt, Rinehart & Winston, 1971), p. 297.
10 *PPP*, 1966 (Washington, 1967), 2 August 1966, p. 573.
11 *PPP* 1963–64 (Washington, 1965),14 April 1964, p. 462.
12 Quandt, *Peace Process*, p. 25.
13 Brands, *The Wages of Globalism*, p. 187.
14 Eban, *An Autobiography*, p. 355.
15 David Schoenbaum, *The United States and the State of Israel* (New York & Oxford: Oxford University Press, 1993), p. 154. In his personal correspondence McPherson recalled that "The impression I have is that I simply reached up one day and found the 'Jewish affairs' hat on my head."
16 Harry McPherson, JOHI, 16 January 1969, tape 4, p. 22.
17 See Donald Neff, *Warriors for Jerusalem: The six days that changed the Middle East* (Simon & Schuster, 1984), pp. 80–85, 156–8 and Abba Eban, *An Autobiography* (New York: Random House, 1977).
18 Spiegel, *The Other Arab–Israeli Conflict*, p. 128.
19 *Ibid.*, p. 129.
20 Harry McPherson, claimed that Johnson was "never a friend of the Oil and Gas Industry. Harry McPherson, 5 December 1968, tape 1, pp. 21–2, JOHI Interview.
21 Brands, *The Wages of Globalism*, p. 188.
22 Divine, *The Johnson Years*, p. 152.
23 Brands, *The Wages of Globalism*, p. 188.
24 George Lenczowski, *American Presidents and the Middle East* (Durham & London: Duke University Press, 1990).
25 Christopher Coker, *Reflections on American Foreign Policy Since 1945* (London: Pinter Publishers, 1989), p. 87.
26 Kellerman & Ryan J. Barilleaux, *The President as World Leader*, p. 74. For more detailed accounts of the origins and evolution of the American commitment to the security of Southeast Asia see Robert Divine, "The Johnson Revival: A bibliographical appraisal" in Robert Divine (ed.), *The Johnson Years*, pp. 16–17 and Dean Rusk, *As I Saw It* (New York: Penguin Books, 1990), pp. 430, 442.
27 Loren Baritz, *Backfire: A history of how American culture led us into Vietnam and made us fight the way we did* (Baltimore & London: Johns Hopkins University Press, 1998), p. 128.

28 *Ibid.*, p. 38.
29 Just days after Kennedy's death Secretary of State Dean Rusk, summed up the new President's view of America's world role thus: "We [America] made a national decision to involve ourselves in the fate of the world [after WWII] because, among other things, our own fate was deeply involved in what happens elsewhere." Philip Geyelin, *Lyndon B. Johnson and the World* (New York, Washington & London: Praeger 1966), p. 70.
30 *PPP*, 11 May 1966, p. 497.
31 Geyelin, *Lyndon B. Johnson*, pp. 71–2.
32 See for example, *PPP*, 1965 (Washington, 1966), 28 May 1965, p. 593.
33 See for example, *DSB*, 8 November 1965, pp. 736–7.
34 Spiegel, *The Other Arab–Israeli Conflict*, p. 122.
35 Nasser's speech at Port Said, broadcast on Radio Cairo, 23 December 1964, quoted in William B. Quandt, *U.S. Policy in the Middle East: Constraints and choices* (Santa Monica: Rand Corporation, 1970), p. 38.
36 Geyelin, *Lyndon B. Johnson*, p. 261. It is interesting to note that while in Congress, Johnson had voted to halt aid to Nasser unless Israeli shipping was permitted to pass through the Suez Canal.
37 Interview with Myer Feldman quoted in Spiegel, *The Other Arab–Israeli Conflict*, p. 95.
38 *Public Papers of the Presidents: John Kennedy*, 1962 (Washington, 1963), Memorandum of Presidential Conversation with Israeli Foreign Minister Meir, 27 December 1962, p. 5.
39 Howard Sachar, *A History of Israel from the Rise of Zionism to Our Time* (New York: Alfred A. Knopf, 1996), p. 552.
40 Jeffrey Shandler, "Aliens in the Wasteland: American encounters with the Holocaust on 1960s science fiction television" in Hilene Flanzbaum (ed.), *The Americanisation of the Holocaust* (Baltimore & London: The Johns Hopkins University Press, 1999), p. 35.
41 *Ibid.*, p. 36.
42 *Ibid.*, p. 37.
43 Yitzhak Rabin, *The Rabin Memoirs* (London: Weidenfeld & Nicolson, 1979), p. 49.
44 The United Arab Republic (UAR) was formed in 1958 when the Syrian army convinced Egypt to unify with Syria to prevent the growth of communism in the country.
45 Spiegel, *The Other Arab–Israeli Conflict*, p. 131.
46 From the time the Communists came to power in China in 1948, until Nixon's overtures of friendship in the early 1970s, the United States pursued a policy of isolating China from the rest of the world and tried to deter other states from forming diplomatic or trade relations with the Communist regime.
47 Spiegel, *The Other Arab–Israeli Conflict*, p. 131.
48 Shimon Peres, *David's Sling* (London: Weidenfeld & Nicolson, 1970), p. 106.
49 *Ibid.*, pp. 105–6.
50 *Ibid.*, p. 104.
51 Schoenbaum, *The United States*, p. 143. Revelations of the tank shipments had the

effect Bonn had sought to avoid and pushed Nasser closer to the Soviets and East Germany. Nasser received increased aid from the Soviet Union and, in January 1965, the East German leader Walter Ulbricht travelled to Cairo to sign a $78 million credit package with him.

52 Peres, *David's Sling*, p. 108.

53 Komer to Bundy, 8 February 1966, NSF, Name File, Box 6, "Komer Memos, vol. 2," LBJ Library.

54 Peres, *David's Sling*, p. 108. Jordan apparently preferred the design of the F-104s over the Skyhawks.

55 Spiegel, *The Other Arab–Israeli Conflict*, p. 134 and Rabin, *The Rabin Memoirs*, p. 50.

56 By late 1966, Soviet arms sales to the Middle East had totalled $2.3 billion.

57 Spiegel, *The Other Arab–Israeli Conflict*, p. 135.

58 Benjamin Read to Walt Rostow, 30 April 1966, NSF, Country File, box 139, "Israel, vol. 5," LBJ Library.

59 See Avner Cohen, *Israel and the Bomb* (New York: Columbia University Press, 1998), chapter 9.

60 Seymour Hersh, *The Samson Option: Israel's nuclear arsenal and american foreign policy* (New York: Random House, 1991), pp. 124–6.

61 Divine, *The Johnson Years*, pp. 170–71.

62 Theodore Draper, *Israel and World Politics: Roots of the third Arab–Israeli war* (New York: Viking Press, 1968), p. 58.

63 Richard B. Parker, "The June War: Whose conspiracy?" *Journal of Palestine Studies* vol. XXI, no. 4 (Summer 1992) p. 21. In a statement to the Knesset on 22 May 1967, Prime Minister Eshkol described the closure of the Straits as "the latest development is a link in a chain of tension, the source of which lies in Damascus." Israel. Ministry of Foreign Affairs, vols. 1–2: 1947–1974, XI. The Six Day War, "Statement to the Knesset by Prime Minister Eshkol," 22 May 1967. Available at <http://www.mfa.gov.il/mfa/go.asp?MFAH0dya0>.

64 Schoenbaum, *The United States*, p. 150.

65 *DSB*, 16 November 1966, pp. 974–8.

66 Divine, *The Johnson Years*, p. 172.

67 Maj.-Gen. Indar Jit Rikhye, *The Sinai Blunder: Withdrawal of United Nations Emergency Force leading to the Six Day War of June 1967* (London: Frank Cass, 1980), p. 158; Draper, *Israel and World Politics*, p. 44.

68 Rikhye, *The Sinai Blunder*, p. 160.
The letter read: "The Government of the United Arab Republic has the honour to inform your Excellency that it has decided to terminate the presence of the United Nations Emergency Force from the territory of the United Arab Republic and Gaza Strip. I request that the necessary steps be taken for the withdrawal of the forces as soon as possible."

69 Terence Prittie, *Eshkol of Israel: The man and the nation* (London: Museum Press, 1969), p. 252.

70 Abba Eban, *Personal Witness: Israel through my eyes* (London: Jonathan Cape, 1993), p. 355.

71 *Ibid.*
72 In early July 1967 the UN published a report on the withdrawal of the UNEF in the *UN Monthly Chronicle*, vol. IV, no. 7, July 1967. "The withdrawal of United Nations Emergency Force (UNEF)." Report by the Secretary-General published by the United Nations office of Public Information (OP1/275–17584). The report exacerbated criticism of U Thant's role.
73 Johnson, *Vantage Point*, p. 290.
74 The UNEF had provided a buffer between Israel and Egypt for more than a decade and had made an important contribution to keeping the peace during that time. U Thant's actions were subject to criticism for a number of reasons. Firstly, the decision was unparalleled in its speed. U Thant's response was delivered within 75 minutes of receipt of the letter to which it made reply. Secondly, the decision was taken before consultation with Israel or the governments that contributed troops to the force. Thirdly, no appeal was made to Nasser to reconsider. Finally and perhaps most crucially, U Thant's determination that a request for partial withdrawal was "tantamount to a request for complete withdrawal" had never been endorsed by any international institution.
75 Johnson, *Vantage Point*, p. 290
76 Michael Bar-Zohar, *Embassies in Crisis: Diplomats and demagogues behind the Six Day War* (Englewood Cliffs, NJ: Prentice-Hall, 1970), pp. 40–41.
77 Michael Brecher, *Decisions in Israel's Foreign Policy* (London: Oxford University Press, 1974), p. 375.
78 Gamel Nasser's speech was published in *Al-Ahram* (Cairo), 23 May 1967, reprinted in Draper, *Israel and World Politics*, p. 214.
79 Moshe Dayan, *Dairy of the Sinai Campaign* (London: Weidenfeld & Nicolson, 1966), p. 203.
80 Rabin, *The Rabin Memoirs*, p. 79.
81 Moshe Dayan, *Story of My Life* (London: Sphere Books Ltd., 1977), pp. 339, 345.
82 The Pentagon adopted the contrary perspective and claimed that delays in an Israeli or international response actually weakened the Egyptians.
83 *Public Papers of the Presidents: Lyndon Johnson*, 1967 (Washington, 1968); 23 May 1967, pp. 561–3.
84 Dayan, *Story of My Life*, p. 345.
85 George Lenczowski, *American Presidents and the Middle East* (Durham and London: Duke University Press, 1990), p. 107.
86 Gideon Rafael, *Destination Peace: Three decades of Israeli foreign policy* (London: Weidenfeld & Nicholson, 1981), p. 153.
87 Rabin, *The Rabin Memoirs*, p. 76.
88 Eban, *Personal Witness*, p. 374. In a statement to the Council of Ministers of France on the Middle East De Gaulle stated that "the state that would be the first – wherever it might be – to take up arms will not have either her approval and even less her support." Israel. Ministry of Foreign Affairs, available at <www.mfa.gov.il/mfa>.
89 Harold Wilson, *The Chariot of Israel* (London: Weidenfeld & Michael Joseph, 1981), p. 358.

90 Schoenbaum, *The United States*, p. 15.
91 Robert McNamara, US Secretary of Defense, 1961–68, speaking on *Dead in the Water: The USS Liberty*. Source Films for the BBC, 4 June 2003.
92 *Congressional Record*, Senate, vol. 113, pt. 10, 23 May 1967, pp. 13481, 7222.
93 Spiegel, *The Other Arab–Israeli Conflict*, pp. 144–5.
94 Johnson, *Vantage Point*, pp. 295–96.
95 *Ibid.*, p. 295.
96 *Ibid.*, pp. 295–6.
97 *Ibid.*, p. 293 and Eban, *Personal Witness*, p. 358.
98 Johnson, *Vantage Point*, p. 295.
99 Churchill & Churchill, *The Six Day War*, p. 33.
100 In a broadcast to the nation on the 5 June 1967, Eshkol described the objective of the pact as to "encircle us with an ever-tightening noose." <http://www.mfa.gov.il/mfa/go.asp?MFAH0dyr0>.
101 Lucius Battle and David Nes, then deputy Chair of the US mission in Cairo, were convinced as early as January 1967 that Nasser was planning a showdown with Israel and the West. See Draper, *Israel and World Politics*, p. 105 and Churchill & Churchill, *The Six Day War*, p. 33.
102 Spiegel, *The Other Arab–Israeli Conflict*, pp. 143–4.
103 Mohamed Heikal, *Nasser: The Cairo documents* (London: New English Library, 1972) p. 221.
104 Michael Bar-Zohar, *Embassies in Crisis: Diplomats and demagogues behind the Six Day War* (Englewood Cliffs, New Jersey: Prentice-Hall, 1970), p. 157, states that on 30 May, after Jordan threw in its lot with Egypt, Walt Rostow expressed the opinion that he no longer saw a political solution. Quoted in Quandt, *Peace Process* p. 45.
105 William Quandt, *Decade of Decisions: American policy towards the Arab–Israeli conflict: 1967–1976* (London, Berkeley & Los Angeles: University of California Press, 1977) pp. 43, 46.
106 Edward Weisband, *The Ideology of American Foreign Policy: A paradigm of Lockean liberalism* (London & Beverly Hills: Sage Publications, 1973).
107 Brands, *The Wages of Globalism*, p. 205.
108 Spiegel, *The Other Arab–Israeli Conflict*, p. 149.
109 Johnson, *Vantage Point*, p. 297.
110 Israel: Ministry of Foreign Affairs. Message from Prime Minister Eshkol to King Hussein of Jordan, 5 June 1967. Transmitted the through Chief of Staff of UNTSO. "We are engaged in defensive fighting on the Egyptian sector, and we shall not engage ourselves in any action against Jordan, unless Jordan attacks us. Should Jordan attack Israel, we shall go against her with all our might." <www.mfa.gov.il/mfa>.
111 This was the estimate Israel's Major General David Elazar gave of the time it would take the Israeli army to reach Damascus. Schoenbaum, *The United States*, p. 159.
112 Brands, *The Wages of Globalism*, p. 207.
113 Washington later advocated the withdrawal of all forces from the Sinai including Egyptian troops, in flagrant contravention of Egypt's sovereign rights. Lenczowski, *American Presidents*, p. 109.

114 The Six Day War also provided the first occasion in which the hotline connecting Washington with Moscow was used. The superpowers were to use the hotline on almost two dozen occasions throughout the six day crisis. Schoenbaum, *The United States*, p. 159, Spiegel, p. 151, Quandt, *Peace Process*, p. 52.

115 Sydney Bailey, *The Making of Resolution 242* (Dordrecht, Boston & Lancaster: Martinus Nijhoff Publishers, 1985), p. 89.

116 Schoenbaum, *The United States*, p. 159.

117 Johnson, *Vantage Point*, p. 299.

118 Lenczowski, *American Presidents*, p. 113.

119 Brands, *The Wages of Globalism*, p. 163.

120 Schoenbaum, *The United States*, p. 155.

121 *Congressional Record*, 6 June 1967, vol. 113, part 11, p. 14745.

122 Johnson, *Vantage Point*, pp. 298–99.

123 Spiegel, *The Other Arab–Israeli Conflict*, p. 153.

124 Brands, *The Wages of Globalism* p. 163.

125 US Cryptological History Report, "Attack on a Sigint Collector, the USS *Liberty*," 1981, p. 37.

126 James M. Ennes, Jr., *Assault on the Liberty: The true story of the Israeli attack on an American intelligence ship* (New York: Randon House, 1979) p. 96. Israel admitted to the torpedo attack, which killed 28 of the sailors, but claimed this was a response to the boats being fired upon by the *Liberty*. "The USS Liberty," Jewish Virtual Library, A division of the American–Israeli Cooperative Enterprise, <www. jewishvirtuallibrary.org/jsource/History/liberty.html>.

127 Author's interview with James M. Ennes, Jr., crew member, USS *Liberty*.

128 *Ibid.*

129 *Ibid.*

130 Ennes, *Assault on the Liberty*, p. 96.

131 Deputy Secretary of Defense Cyrus Vance notified the Commander-in-Chief of the US Navy Europe by phone at 17.00 hours, on 8 June 1967, that all news regarding the *Liberty* would be made at Washington level. The crew were told not to speak to reporters about the attack. National Security Agency, US Cryptological History Report, "Attack on a Sigint Collector, the USS *Liberty*," 1981, p. 38.

132 Author's interview with James Ennes.

133 National Security Agency, "Aftermath of Israeli Attack on USS *Liberty*," 22 June 1967.

134 Rabin, *The Rabin Memoirs*, p. 86.

135 For a comprehensive analysis of Israel's account of the incident see A. Jay Cristol, *The Liberty Incident* (Washington, D.C.: Brassey's Inc., 2002). Recently declassified US government documents on the incident are available at <www. nsagov/ docs/efoia/released/liberty.html>.

136 Quoted in Ennes, *Assault on the Liberty*, p. 111.

137 Joseph A. Califano, Jr., *The Triumph & Tragedy of Lyndon Johnson* (New York: Simon & Schuster, 1991), p. 206.

138 Clark Clifford with Richard Holbrooke, *Counsel to the President: A memoir* (New York: Random House, 1991), p. 447.

139 Lucius D. Battle, former US ambassador to Egypt and assistant secretary of state for Near East and South Asian Affairs, speaking on *Dead in the Water: The USS Liberty* Source Films for the BBC, 4 June 2003.
140 Johnson, *Vantage Point*, p. 293, Eban, *Personal Witness*, pp. 300–1 and quoted in Lenczowski, *American Presidents*, p. 111.
141 Califano, Jr., *The Triumph and Tragedy*, p. 206.
142 Robert McNamara, US Secretary of Defense, 1961–68, speaking on *Dead in the Water: The USS Liberty* Source Films for the BBC, 4 June 2003.
143 Lucius D. Battle, former US ambassador to Egypt and assistant secretary of state for Near East and South Asian Affairs, speaking on *Dead in the Water: The USS Liberty* Source Films for the BBC, 4 June 2003.
144 Lenczowski, *American Presidents*, p. 111.
145 Brands, *The Wages of Globalism*, p. 212.
146 *Congressional Record*, 8 June 1967, vol. 113, part 11, p. 15270.
147 Author's interview with James Ennes.
148 Author's interview with David Bar-Ilan, Israeli Director of Communications and "The USS Liberty," Jewish Virtual Library, A division of the American–Israeli Cooperative Enterprise, <www.jewishvirtuallibrary.org/jsource/ History/ liberty.html>.
149 Geoffrey Stern, "Moral Judgments and Political Prejudice," *Contemporary Review*, May 1975, pp. 231–2.
150 Tom Gorman, "Worthy and Unworthy Victims: Munich matters, Sabra and Shatila don't," *CounterPunch*, 21 September 2002, p. 4.
151 Goldman, *The Tragedy of Lyndon Johnson* (New York: Knopf, 1969) p. 63.
152 Norman G. Finkelstein, *The Holocaust Industry: Reflections of the exploitation of Jewish suffering* (London & New York: Verso, 2000), pp. 20–1.
153 *Ibid.*, p. 20.
154 *Ibid.*, p. 22.
155 "Talking Points for Prime Minister Eshkol," memorandum for the president, 5 January 1968, National Security Files (Washington) 1963–69.
156 At a press conference on 13 June, Johnson abrogated both himself and his Administration of the responsibility for presenting a solution to the post-war stalemate with the statement that "what happens will depend a good deal on the nations themselves." *PPP*, 19 June 1967, p. 633.
157 Spiegel, *The Other Arab–Israeli Conflict*, p. 153.
158 Quandt, *Peace Process*, p. 55.
159 In 1967, of Israel's population, 90% majority favoured retaining the West Bank, Sharm-el-Sheikh and the Golan, while 85% favoured holding at least part of Gaza. Schoenbaum, *The United States*, p. 160.
160 Jonathan Rynhold *Israeli Political Culture in Relations with the U.S. over the Palestine Question, 1981–96* (Ph.D. thesis, University of London, London, 1998), pp. 266, 160.
161 Quandt, *Peace Process*, p. 55.
162 *PPP*, 19 June 1967, p. 633.
163 Israel: Ministry of Foreign Affairs. Eshkol made a statement on 27 June 1967 in

which he made direct negotiations a pre-requisite for a peace agreement. A copy of the statement is available at the <www.mfa.gov.il/mfa/go.asp?MFAH0e150>.

164 Coker, *Reflections on American Foreign Policy*, p. 90.

165 Eisenhower had sent American troops into South Korea in 1950 to protect the people's right to self-determination against the Communist forces of the North.

166 Rafael, *Destination Peace*, p. 177.

167 Schoenbaum, *The United States*, p. 161.

168 Rafael, *Destination Peace*, p. 179.

169 Eban, *An Autobiography*, p. 443.

170 Bailey, *The Making*, p. 126.

171 Eban, *An Autobiography*, p. 445.

172 Howard Sachar, *A History of Israel from the Rise of Zionism to Our Time* (New York: Alfred A. Knopf, 1996), p. 673.

173 David A. Korn, *Stalemate: The war of attrition and great power diplomacy in the Middle East, 1967–1970* (Boulder, CO: Westview Press, 1992) pp. 84–6.

174 Abba Eban, "Jarring, Lyndon Johnson, Richard Nixon and '242'" in Lord Carandon et al. *U.N. Security Council Resolution 242: A case study in diplomatic ambiguity* (Washington, D.C., 1981), p. 48.

175 Schoenbaum, *The United States*, p. 164.

176 Rafael, *Destination Peace*, pp. 185, 188.

177 J. J. Goldberg, *Jewish Power: Inside the American Jewish establishment* (Reading, Massachusetts: Addison Wesley, 1996) pp. 230.

178 *Ibid.*

179 Rafael claims that the sponsors of Resolution 242 were aware of the Arab design to turn the refugee issue into a political weapon and therefore the word "Palestinian" was not included. Rafael, *Destination Peace*, p. 190.

180 Rabin, *The Rabin Memoirs*, p. 114.

181 Quandt, *Decade of Decisions*, p. 66.

182 Steven Spiegel, "Israel and Beyond: American Jews and US foreign policy" in L. Sandy Maisel (ed.), *Jews in American Politics* (Lanham, Boulder, New York, Oxford: Rowman & Littlefield Publishers, 2001), p. 261.

183 *Gallup Opinion Index*, Report 25, July 1967, p. 5 cited in Spiegel, *The Other Arab–Israeli Conflict*, p. 158.

184 Coker, *Reflections on American Foreign Policy*, p. 93.

185 Doneson, *The Holocaust*, p. 118.

186 Irving Kristol, "A Matter of Fundamentals" *Commentary* (April 1961), pp. 55–6.

187 *Ibid.*, p. 66.

188 *Congressional Record*, 26 June 1967, vol. 113, part 13, p. 17305.

189 Author's interview with Norman Podhoretz, Senior Fellow, Hudson Institute and former editor-in-chief of *Commentary*, 1960–95.

190 Memorandum From Harold H. Saunders of the National Security Council Staff to the President's Special Assistant Rostow, 14 October 1968, Johnson Library, National Security File, Country File, Israel, vol. X, Cables and Memos, 6/68–11/68.

191 Quandt, *Decade of Decisions*, p. 67.

192 *Ibid.*

193 Spiegel, *The Other Arab–Israeli Conflict*, p. 165.
194 *Ibid.*

5 Nixon, Kissinger and US Policy towards Israel

1 Jonathan. J. Goldberg, *Jewish Power: Inside the American Jewish establishment* (Reading, Massachusetts: Addison Wesley, 1996), p. 246.
2 Author's interview with Peter W. Rodman, Member of the National Security Council staff and a special assistant to Henry Kissinger 1969–1977. Nixon was to establish a special channel of communication between US National Security Adviser Henry A. Kissinger and Israeli Ambassador Yitzhak Rabin that circumvented Secretary of State William Rogers and the State Department.
3 Richard Nixon, *The Memoirs of Richard Nixon*, vol. I (New York: Warner Books, 1978), p. 339.
4 George Lenczowski, *American Presidents and the Middle East* (Durham and London: Duke University Press, 1990), pp. 120–21.
5 *Ibid.*
6 For a more detailed account of "linkage" politics see Robert S. Litwak, *Détente and the Nixon Doctrine: American foreign policy and the pursuit of stability, 1969–1976* (Cambridge, New York, New Rochelle, Melbourne & Sydney: Cambridge University Press, 1984).
7 Nixon's mother came from a long line of Quakers and his father converted from Methodism to Quakerism at the time of his marriage.
8 Richard Nixon, *RN* (New York: Touchstone, 1990), p. 16
9 *Ibid.*, p. 14.
10 *Ibid.*, p. 27.
11 Nixon, *Memoirs*, p. 27.
12 Author's interview with William Quandt, former National Security Council aide, Nixon and Carter administrations.
13 Henry A. Kissinger, *Years of Upheaval* (London: Weidenfeld & Nicolson & Michael Joseph, 1982), p. 202.
14 For a discussion of Nixon's apparently negative attitude towards the American Jewish community see Anthony Summers, *The Arrogance of Power: The secret world of Richard Nixon* (New York: Viking, Penguin Group, 2000), pp. 354–5.
15 Author's interview with William Quandt.
16 Summers, *The Arrogance of Power*, p. 354.
17 Henry A. Kissinger, *White House Years (*Boston: Little, Brown, 1979), p. 370.
18 Summers, *The Arrogance of Power*, p. 354.
19 Author's interview with William Quandt.
20 Summers, *The Arrogance of Power*, p. 353 and Jonathan J. Goldberg, *Jewish Power*, p. 248.
21 Author's interview with William Quandt.
22 Kissinger, *Years of Upheaval*, p. 203
23 *Ibid.*, pp. 201–2.
24 Author's interview with Peter Rodman.
25 Kissinger, *Years of Upheaval*, p. 203.

26 Goldberg, *Jewish Power*, p. 238.
27 Defence Secretary James Schlesinger quoted in Walter Isaacson, *Kissinger: A biography* (London: Faber & Faber, 1992), p. 521.
28 Author's interview with William Quandt.
29 Jean A. Garrison, *Games Advisors Play: Foreign policy in the Nixon and Carter Administrations* (Texas: Texas A&M University, 1999), p. 8.
30 Kissinger, *Years of Upheaval*, p. 202.
31 Richard Nixon, *The Memoirs of Richard Nixon* vol. I (New York: Warner Books, 1978) p. 591.
32 Lenczowski, *American Presidents*, p. 121.
33 Author's interview with Norman Podhoretz, Senior Fellow, Hudson Institute and former editor-in-chief of *Commentary* 1960–95.
34 Lenczowski, *American Presidents*, p. 121.
35 Nixon *Memoirs*, p. 596.
36 Author's interview with Norman Podhoretz.
37 Nixon, *Memoirs*, p. 591.
38 *Ibid.*, p. 350.
39 *Ibid.*, p. 595.
40 Author's interview with Peter Rodman.
41 Nixon *Memoirs*, p. 596.
42 Annette Insdorf, *Indelible Shadows: Film and the Holocaust* (Cambridge: Cambridge University Press, 2003), p. 47.
43 Judith Doneson, *The Holocaust in American Film* (Syracuse: Syracuse University Press, 2002) pp. 123, 125.
44 For a fuller account of the film see Hilene Flanzbaum (ed.), *The Americanisation of the Holocaust* (Baltimore & London: The Johns Hopkins University Press, 1999), pp. 95, 199.
45 Doneson, *The Holocaust*, pp. 127–8.
46 Author's interview with Peter Rodman.
47 Nixon, *Memoirs*, p. 339.
48 Garrison, *Games Advisors Play*, p. 7.
49 Nixon *Memoirs*, p. 340.
50 The NSC provided the President with genuine foreign policy alternatives through the constant flow of memoranda and policy studies that situated foreign policy formulation in a broader context than had been available to previous presidents. These National Security Study Memoranda (NSSM) were discussed by a Senior Review Group (SRG), then referred to the NSC for decision before a National Security Decision Memorandum (NSDM) was issued.
51 Joan Hoff, *Nixon Reconsidered* (New York: Basic Books, 1994), p. 157.
52 Garrison, *Games Advisors Play*, p. 7.
53 Steven L. Spiegel, *The Other Arab–Israeli Conflict: Making America's Middle East policy, from Truman to Reagan* (Chicago & London: The University of Chicago Press, 1985), p. 174.
54 Kissinger, *Years of Upheaval*, p. 48, cited in Spiegel, *The Other Arab–Israeli Conflict*, p. 174.

55 William Quandt, *Peace Process: American diplomacy and the Arab–Israeli conflict since 1967* (Washington D.C. & Berkeley, Los Angeles: The Brookings Institution & University of California Press, 1993), pp. 67–8.
56 William Quandt, *Decade of Decisions: American policy towards the Arab–Israeli conflict: 1967–1976* (London, Berkeley & Los Angeles: University of California Press, 1977), p. 75.
57 Quandt, *Decade of Decisions*, pp. 75–6.
58 Nixon, *RN*, p. 477.
59 Kissinger, *White House Years*, p. 348.
60 Nixon news conference on 27 January, 1969, *DSB*, vol. 60 (17 February, 1969), pp. 142–3.
61 Kissinger, *White House Years*, p. 348.
62 Alvin Rubinstein, *Red Star on the Nile: The Soviet–Egyptian influence relationship since the June war* (Princeton: Princeton University Press, 1977), p. 87. With the Four Powers talks in a situation of stalemate and the US determined to press ahead with the SALT talks irrespective of disputes in other areas, Moscow had little to loose by supporting Nasser in the War of Attrition.
63 Moshe Dayan, *Story of My Life* (London: Sphere Books Ltd., 1977), pp. 369–70.
64 *PPP, 1969*, p. 18.
65 Yitzhak Rabin, *The Rabin Memoirs* (London: Weidenfeld & Nicolson, 1979), p. 115.
66 Spiegel, *The Other Arab–Israeli Conflict*, p. 184.
67 Kissinger, *White House Years*, pp. 367–9, 370–2.
68 Author's interview with Ira Sharkansky, political scientist, Hebrew University of Jerusalem. Some analysts of US–Israeli relations claim that Meir was able to form a good working relationship with the Nixon administration because she "spoke English better than she spoke Hebrew."
69 Author's interview with Peter Rodman.
70 Spiegel, *The Other Arab–Israeli Conflict*, pp. 185–6.
71 Joint US–USSR Working Paper, Fundamental Principles (The Rogers Plan), October 28, 1969.
72 *NYT*, 28 March 1969 p. 14 and *DSB*, 14 April 1969, p. 305
73 Full text in the *NYT*, 11 December 1969 and in the *DSB*, 5 January 1970.
74 Spiegel, *The Other Arab–Israeli Conflict*, p. 183.
75 Rabin, *The Rabin Memoirs*, p. 96.
76 Abba Eban, *An Autobiography* (London: Weidenfeld & Nicholson, 1978), p. 463.
77 Rabin, *The Rabin Memoirs*, p. 115.
78 *Arab Report and Record*, Dec. 16–31, 1969, no. 24, p. 549.
79 For a more detailed account of the response of the different parties to the Rogers Plan see Spiegel, *The Other Arab–Israeli Conflict*, pp. 181–92.
80 Nixon, *RN*, p. 478.
81 Kissinger, *White House Years*, pp. 372, 376.
82 *Ibid.*, pp. 351–2.
83 Henry Kissinger made this comment in 1975 at the end of his tenure in office, quoted in Leslie H. Gelb, "The Kissinger Legacy," *New York Times Magazine*, 31 October 1976, p. 85.

84 Kissinger, *White House Years*, pp. 354, 361.
85 Author's interview with Peter Rodman.
86 Kissinger, *White House Years*, pp. 354, 361.
87 Kissinger's description of negotiations in the Arab–Israeli peace process, as recollected to the author by Peter Rodman.
88 Rabin, *The Rabin Memoirs*, p. 118.
89 See Seymour Hersh, *The Price of Power: Kissinger in the Nixon White House* (New York: Summit Books, 1983), p. 217.
90 Rubinstein, *Red Star on the Nile*, p. 115.
91 Walter Laqueur, *Confrontation: The Middle East and world politics* (New York: Quadrangle, 1974), p. 4.
92 Israel. Ministry of Foreign Affairs. "Soviet involvement in the War of Attrition," Government Statement, 29 April 1970. <www.mfa.gov.il/mfa>.
93 Moshe Dayan, *Story of My Life* (London: Sphere Books Ltd., 1977), pp. 366–7.
94 David A. Korn, *Stalemate: The war of attrition and great power diplomacy in the Middle East 1967–1970* (Boulder, San Francisco & Oxford: Westview Press, 1992), p. 198.
95 Quandt, *Decade of Decisions*, p. 94.
96 Kissinger, *Years of Upheaval*, p. 563.
97 *PPP*, 1970, pp. 119, 120, 154, 180.
98 Nixon made this announcement at a press conference on 30 January 1970. Quoted in Helen Thomas (ed.), *The Nixon Press Conferences* (London: Heyden, 1978), p. 82.
99 Kissinger, *White House Years*, p. 565.
100 Nixon, *RN*, pp. 479–80 and Korn, *Stalemate*, p. 200.
101 Spiegel, *The Other Arab–Israeli Conflict*, p. 192.
102 *NYT*, 4 March, 1970, p. 3 and Kissinger, *White House Years*, p. 566.
103 Rabin, *The Rabin Memoirs*, p. 171 and Spiegel, *The Other Arab–Israeli Conflict*, p. 191.
104 Eban, *An Autobiography*, p. 466.
105 Quandt, *Peace Process*, p. 89. Meir considered this to be the first time Israel had officially accepted UN Resolution 242, although Israel's ambassador to the UN had publicly done so in 1968.
106 Kissinger, *White House Years*, p. 572.
107 *DSB*, vol. 63, 10 August 1970, pp. 178–9.
108 *NYT*, 3 July,1970, p. 1.
109 *NYT*, 4 July 1970, p. 1 and Marvin Kalb and Bernard Kalb, *Kissinger* (London: Hutchinson, 1974), p. 193.
110 *PPP*, 1 July 1970, p. 558.
111 Mohamed Heikal, *The Road to Ramadan* (London: Collins, 1975), p. 95.
112 Nadav Safran, *Israel: The embattled ally* (Cambridge, MA: Belknap Press, 1981), p. 443.
113 Kissinger, *White House Years*, pp. 584–5.
114 *DSB*, vol. 63, 17 August 1970, pp. 185–7.
115 In a statement to the Knesset Meir stated that she believed that Nixon was

committed to preserving Israel's security. Israel. Ministry of Foreign Affairs, vols 1–2: 1947–1974. "The War of Attrition and Cease Fire," Statement to the Knesset by Prime Minister Meir, 4 August 1970. Available at <http://www.mfa.gov.il/mfa/go.asp?MFAH0e2w0>.

116 *JP*, 5 August, 1970, p. 3, Prime Minister Meir's speech to the Knesset, 4 August, 1970.

117 David Schoenbaum, *The United States and the State of Israel* (Oxford: Oxford University Press, 1993), p. 177.

118 Spiegel, *The Other Arab–Israeli Conflict*, p. 194

119 Nixon, *RN*, p. 482.

120 On the 13 August 1970, in a statement to the Knesset, Defence Minister Dayan stated that the matter of Egyptian cease-fire violations were being "discussed between us [Israel] and the US Government on the basis of our insistence on the return of the launching sites to their previous positions because their being brought forward was and is a violation of the agreement." Israel. Ministry of Foreign Affairs. See <www.mfa.gov.il/mfa>. for the complete text of the statement.

121 *NYT*, 5 September 1970, p. 1.

122 Nixon, *RN*, p. 482.

123 Christopher Coker, *Reflections on American Foreign Policy Since 1945* (London: Pinter Publishers, 1989), p. 137.

124 Nixon, *RN*, p. 482.

125 Hoff, *Nixon Reconsidered*, p. 258 and Nixon, *RN*, p. 483.

126 *Congressional Record*, part 121, 1 September 1970, pp. 30723–4.

127 On 26 July 1972, in a statement to the Knesset, Meir acknowledged that the Egyptians had used the cease-fire as an opportunity to advance their ground-to-air missiles to the Canal line. Israel. Ministry of Foreign Affairs. Statement to the Knesset by Prime Minister Meir, 26 July 1972, vols. 1–2: 1947–1974, <www.mfa.gov.il/mfa/go.asp?MFAH0e3p0>.

128 Kissinger, *White House Years*, p. 594.

129 Quandt, *Peace Process*, p. 98.

130 *NYT*, 2 September 1970, p. 2.

131 Spiegel, *The Other Arab–Israeli Conflict*, p. 196.

132 *NYT*, 7 September 1970, pp. 1–2.

133 Kalb & Kalb, *Kissinger*, p. 206.

134 Seymour Hersh, *The Price of Power* (London: Faber, 1983), pp. 235–6.

135 Quandt, *Peace Process*, p. 101.

136 *Ibid.*, p. 103.

137 *NYT*, 19 September 1970, p. 8.

138 Kissinger, *White House Years*, p. 620.

139 *PPP*, 3 November 1969, pp. 548, 905.

140 Schoenbaum, *The United States*, p. 181.

141 For a full account of Kissinger's discussions with Rabin see Rabin, *The Rabin Memoirs*, pp. 146–9.

142 Kissinger, *White House Years*, p. 625.

143 Isaacson, *Kissinger*, p. 303.

144 Kissinger and Sisco conveyed to Rabin Hussein's preference for Israeli ground action inside Syria not Jordan, although such a move increased the probability of Soviet intervention against Israel.
145 Isaacson, *Kissinger*, p. 303.
146 Hafez al Assad, head of the Syrian air force, refused to enter the war, leaving Syrian ground forces exposed to Jordanian air attacks.
147 Isacson, *Kissinger*, p. 312.
148 Quandt, *Decade of Decisions*, p. 122
149 Spiegel, *The Other Arab–Israeli Conflict*, p. 201
150 Hoff, *Nixon Reconsidered*, p. 260.
151 Heikal, *The Road to Ramadan*, p. 115.
152 For a copy of Jarring's memorandum and the Israeli and Egyptian response see *Arab Report and Record* March 1–15, 1971, pp. 158–9.
153 "Israel's Search for Peace: An extensive survey of Israel's political and security position given by the Prime Minister to the Knesset." Quoted in Golda Meir with Marie Syrkin (ed.), *Golda Meir Speaks Out* (Jerusalem: Weidenfeld & Nicolson, 1973), p. 207.
154 Kissinger, *White House Years*, p. 1285.
155 *Ibid.*, p. 1279.
156 Korn, *Stalemate*, p. 272.
157 Schoenbaum, *The United States*, p. 196. Sadat allowed the Soviet Union to retain naval facilities at Alexandria, Port Said and to a lesser degree at Ras Banas on the Red Sea. Rubinstein, *Red Star on the Nile*, p. 191.
158 Michael Handel, *The Diplomacy of Surprise, Hitler, Nixon, Sadat* (Cambridge, MA: Centre for International Affairs, Harvard University, 1981), pp. 278–9.
159 Israel. Ministry of Foreign Affairs. Statement to the Knesset by Prime Minister Meir, 26 July 1972. "The War of Attrition and its Aftermath." vols. 1–2: 1947–1974, <www.mfa.gov.il/mfa/go.asp?MFAH0e3p0>.
160 Schoenbaum, *The United States*, p. 197.
161 Handel, *The Diplomacy of Surprise*, pp. 276–7.
162 Schoenbaum, *The United States*, p. 197.
163 Notes on memo Nixon sent to Kissinger, cited in Kissinger, *Years of Upheaval*, p. 212. Italics in the original.
164 Heikal, *The Road to Ramadan*, p. 102.
165 Kissinger, *Years of Upheaval*, pp. 224–5. By the end of Meir's visit, Kissinger and Rabin had agreed a formula whereby Kissinger would explore a new approach with Egypt based on Egyptian sovereignty over the entire Sinai in exchange for an Israeli security presence on some Egyptian territory. This was never put to the Egyptians because news of the US–Israeli arms deal undermined Washington's position in Cairo. See Rabin, *The Rabin Memoirs*, p. 216 for a more detailed account of the negotiations.
166 William Bundy, *A Tangled Web: The making of foreign policy in the Nixon presidency* (London & New York: I. B. Tauris, 1998), p. 433.
167 Nixon, *RN*, p. 922.
168 Author's interview with Peter Rodman.

169 Hoff, *Nixon Reconsidered*, p. 271.
170 Mohamed Anwar al-Sadat, *In Search of Identity* (London: Collins, 1978), p. 238.
171 Author's interview with Peter Rodman.
172 Nixon, *RN*, p. 920.
173 Conversation between Kissinger and Meir, 1 March 1973, quoted in Kissinger, *Years of Upheaval*, p. 220.
174 Author's interview with James Schlesinger, Director of the Central Intelligence Agency, February-May 1973 and Secretary of Defence 1973–1975.
175 Ray S. Cline, "Policy without Intelligence," *Foreign Policy*, no. 17 (Winter 1974–75) pp. 121–35.
176 Kissinger, *Years of Upheaval*, p. 465.
177 Nixon, *RN*, p. 920.
178 Quandt, *Peace Process*, p. 150.
179 *New York Times*, 7 October 1973, p. 1 reported that "Secretary of State Kissinger was caught by surprise when the crisis developed." As late as 5 October, Golda Meir sent a message to Kissinger asking him to reassure the Arabs that Israel did not plan to attack. Matti Golan, *The Secret Conversations of Henry Kissinger: Step-by-step diplomacy in the Middle East* (New York: Quadrangle Books, 1976), pp. 37–9.
180 Nixon, *RN*, p. 921.
181 Dayan, *Story of My Life*, pp. 379, 388. Kissinger reminded Haikal during their meetings following the war that the US had not made an issue out of the fact that the Egyptians and Syrians initiated hostilities. See "Interviews: Kissinger Meets Haikal," *Journal of Palestine Studies*, vol. 3 (Winter 1974), p. 213
182 Dayan, *Story of My Life*, p. 921.
183 Washington proposed a cease-fire to put America on the record as favouring a prompt termination of the conflict, even though they knew Moscow would reject it. Richard Thornton, *The Nixon–Kissinger Years: Reshaping America's foreign policy* (New York: Paragon House, 1989), p. 236.
184 Quandt, *Peace Process*, p. 153.
185 Nixon, *RN*, p. 921.
186 Dayan, *Story of My Life*, p. 921–4.
187 In a speech delivered to the Pacem in Teris III Conference, Washington, D.C., 8 October 1973, Kissinger reminded the Soviets of their obligations under détente. "Our policy with regard to détente is clear: We shall resist aggressive foreign policies. Détente cannot survive irresponsibility in any area, including the Middle East." Printed in *DSB*, vol. 69, 29 October 1973, pp. 525–31.
188 Nixon, *RN*, p. 920.
189 Author's interview with James Schlesinger.
190 *Ibid.*
191 Quoted in Kissinger, *Years of Upheaval*, p. 478.
192 *Ibid.*
193 Author's interview with Dr John Lehman, Secretary of the US Navy 1981–87.
194 Kissinger, *Years of Upheaval*, p. 478.
195 Author's interview with James Schlesinger.

196 Kissinger, *Years of Upheaval*, p. 477.
197 Nixon, *RN*, p. 922.
198 *NYT*, 9 October 1973, p. 1.
199 Schoenbaum, *The United States*, p. 201.
200 Author's interview with James Schlesinger and *NYT*, 10 October 1973, pp. 1, 18.
201 Golda Meir, *My Life* (London: Futura, 1976) p. 427, Quandt, *Decade of Decisions*, pp. 174–5 and Hersh, *The Price of Power*, chapter 17.
202 Author's interview with Geoffrey Aronson.
203 William Quandt, "How Far Will Israel Go?," *Washington Post Book World*, 20 November 1991, p. 10. Nadav Safran, *Israel: The embattled ally* (Harvard University Press, 1978), p. 483, assumes that Kissinger was motivated by a fear that Israel might resort to nuclear weapons.
204 Michael Brecher with Benjamin Geist, *Decisions in Crisis: Israel, 1967 and 1973* (Berkeley: University of California Press, 1980), p. 214.
205 Spiegel, *The Other Arab–Israeli Conflict*, p. 254.
206 *Congressional Record*, vol. 119, part 28, 15 October 1973, p. 36270.
207 Nixon, *RN*, p. 926.
208 Author's interview with James Schlesinger.
209 Kissinger, *Years of Upheaval*, p. 522.
210 Anne Hessing Cahn, "United States Arms to the Middle East, 1967–1976" in Milton Leitenberg & Gabriel Sheffer (eds.), *Great Power Intervention in the Middle East* (New York, Oxford: Pergamon, 1979), p. 122, Isaacson, *Kissinger*, p. 513 and Nixon, *RN*, p. 927.
211 Isaacson, *Kissinger*, p. 513.
212 Goldberg, *Jewish Power*, p. 241.
213 Isaacson, *Kissinger*, p. 519.
214 Goldberg, *Jewish Power*, p. 242.
215 *DSB*, vol. 69, 19 November 1973, p. 624.
216 Author's interview with Dr John Lehman.
217 Kissinger, *Years of Upheaval*, p. 485 and Quandt, *Decade of Decisions*, p. 175.
218 Isaacson, *Kissinger*, pp. 513–17.
219 Kissinger, *Years of Upheaval* p. 522.
220 A. F. K. Organski, *The $36 Billion Bargain*, pp. 163, 48.
221 Goldberg, *Jewish Power*, p. 246.
222 William B. Quandt quoted in Goldberg, *Jewish Power*, p. 246.
223 *Ibid.*
224 *Ibid.*
225 Author's interview with Khalil Jahshan, Executive Vice-President, American–Arab Anti-Discrimination Committee.
226 Goldberg, *Jewish Power*, p. 246.
227 Peter Novick, *The Holocaust in American Life* (New York: Houghton, Mifflin & Co., 1999), p. 156
228 *Ibid.*, pp. 155–7.
229 I. L. Kenen, "Twisted Comparison Cheapens Memory of Holocaust," *Near East Report*, 22, 3 May 1978.
230 Novick, *The Holocaust in American Life*, p. 158.

231 William Bundy, *A Tangled Web: The making of foreign policy in the Nixon presidency* (London & New York: I. B. Tauris, 1998), p. 429.
232 Author's interview with James Schlesinger.
233 *MNOC*, p. 144. The letter received no more that a note of acknowledgement. It was later claimed that the letter was the work of the Saudi government. Whatever the letters origin, the actions of the oil companies apparently did not impact directly on the administration's behaviour.
234 Author's interview with James Schlesinger.
235 *Congressional Record*, vol. 119, part 26. 15 October 1973, p. 34161.
236 *WP*, 2 September 1973 and *NYT*, 16 October 1973 pp. 1, 19.
237 *NYT*, 16 October 1973 pp. 1, 19.
238 Spiegel, *The Other Arab–Israeli Conflict*, p. 257. During this period Aramco worked to enforce the Saudi oil embargo and assist the Arab war effort. They supplied the Egyptians and Iraqis with oil, and refused to supply American military in the area in accordance with Saudi instructions. Aramco Chairman Frank Jungers claimed that "The important thing was to give the immediate image of being *with* the [Saudi Arabian] government, not trying to fight it." Anthony Sampson, *The Seven Sisters: The great oil companies and the world they made* (Sevenoaks: Coronet Books, 1976), p. 253.
239 Nixon, *RN*, p. 932.
240 Hoff, *Nixon Reconsidered*, p. 265.
241 Thomas, *The Nixon Press Conferences*, p. 370.
242 Nixon, *RN*, p. 931.
243 Anatoly Dobryin, *In Confidence: Moscow's ambassador to America's six cold war presidents* (New York: Random House, 1995), p. 292 and Kissinger, *Years of Upheaval*, pp. 550–1.
244 Bundy, *A Tangled Web*, p. 440. Nixon's memoirs emphasise his preoccupation with countering the Soviets and preserving his own position in office – the impending Middle East cease-fire is not even mentioned. The Soviet Ambassador Anatoly Dobryin later claimed in his memoirs that "this very important message, if implemented, could have changed the whole future course of a Middle East settlement." Dobryin, *In Confidence*, pp. 292–3.
245 Nixon, *RN*, p. 936.
246 Meir, *My Life*, p. 438.
247 Kissinger, *Years of Upheaval*, p. 575.
248 In a statement to the Knesset on 13 November 1973, Meir claimed that the Egyptians continued fighting after the cease-fire had gone into effect and the IDF fought back. Israel. Ministry of Foreign Affairs, vols 1–2: 1947–1974, XIII. "The Yom Kippur War and Aftermath," Statement to the Knesset by Prime Minister Golda Meir, 13 November 1973, <www.mfa.gov.il/mfa/go.asp?MFAH0dzr0>.
249 Nixon, *RN*, pp. 938–9.
250 Nixon wrote in his memoirs that at the press conference Kissinger held the morning after the alert a reporter commented, "As you know, there has been some line of speculation this morning that the American alert might have been prompted as much perhaps by American domestic requirements as by the real requirements of diplomacy in the Middle East." See Nixon, *RN*, p. 940. See *Weekly Compilation of*

Presidential Documents, vol. 9, 29 October 1973, pp. 1287–94 for Nixon's official account of events surrounding the alert.

251 Dayan, *Story of My Life*, p. 544.

252 Coker, *Reflections on American Foreign Policy*, p. 137.

253 Author's interview with Peter Rodman.

254 Howard Sachar, *A History of Israel from the Rise of Zionism to Our Time* (New York: Alfred A. Knopf, 1996), p. 784.

255 Kissinger, *White House Years*, p. 610.

256 Dickinson, *Kissinger and the Meaning of History*, p. 86.

257 Goldberg, *Jewish Power*, p. 244.

258 Kissinger, *Years of Upheaval*, p. 798.

259 William Burr (ed.), *The Kissinger Transcripts* (New York: The New York Press, 1998), pp. 331–2.

260 Henry A. Kissinger, "Central Issues of American Foreign Policy" in Kermit Gordon (ed.), *Agenda for the Nation* (New York: Doubleday, 1969), p. 611.

261 Henry Kissinger, *DSB*, 29 October 1973, p. 535; Richard Nixon, *DSB*, 7 July 1974, p. 3; Joseph Sisco, *DSB*, 8 July 1974, p. 56.

262 George H. Gallup, *The Gallup Poll: Public opinion, 1972–77*, vol. 4 (Wilmington Scholarly Resources, 1978), 4–7 April 1975.

263 *WP*, 13 November 1974, p. A9, quoted in Spiegel, *The Other Arab–Israeli Conflict*, p. 221.

264 Spiegel, *The Other Arab–Israeli Conflict*, p. 221.

265 Edward Luttwak, "The Defence Budget and Israel," *Commentary*, February 1975, pp. 27–37. According to Spiegel, sixty-one articles appeared in US technical military journals in 1974 on the tactics and hardware of the October war and twenty-four additional articles appeared in 1975.

266 Sara Horowitz, "Cinematic Triangulation of Jewish American Identity" in Flanzbaum, Hilene (ed.), *The Americanisation of the Holocaust* (Baltimore & London: The Johns Hopkins University Press, 1999), pp. 156–7.

267 Novick, *The Holocaust in American Life*, p. 151.

268 Leonard Fein, "Right in the First Place," *Moment* 1, September 1975, p. 28.

269 Norman G. Finkelstein, *The Holocaust Industry: Reflections of the exploitation of Jewish suffering* (London & New York: Verso, 2000), p. 27.

270 Novick, *The Holocaust in American Life*, p. 148.

271 Finkelstein, *Image and Reality of the Israel-Palestine Conflict* (New York: Verso, 1995), chapter 6.

272 Finkelstein, *The Holocaust Industry*, p. 23.

273 Israel Shenker, *NYT*, 4, 5, 6, March 1975.

274 Doneson, *The Holocaust*, pp. 149–56.

275 Henry Greenspan, "Testimony and the Rise of Holocaust Consciousness" in Hilene Flanzbaum (ed.), *The Americanisation of the Holocaust* (Baltimore & London: The Johns Hopkins University Press, 1999), p. 57.

276 Alan Mintz, *Popular Culture and the Shaping of Holocaust Memory in America* (Seattle & London: University of Washington Press, 2001), p. 21.

277 Goldberg, *Jewish Power*, p. 242.

278 Nixon, *RN*, p. 924.
279 Coker, *Reflections on American Foreign Policy*, p. 74.

6 Reagan, the Neo-Conservatives and Israel

1 Alexander Haig, *Caveat: Realism, Reagan, and foreign policy* (New York: Macmillan Publishing Company, 1984), p. 167.
2 Wolf Blitzer, *Between Washington and Jerusalem: A reporter's notebook* (New York & Oxford: Oxford University Press, 1985), p. 238.
3 Albert J. Menendez, *Evangelicals at the Ballot Box* (New York: Prometheus Books, 1996), p. 145.
4 Garry Wills, *Reagan's America: Innocents at home* (Garden City, NY: Doubleday, 1987), pp. 17–18.
5 Lou Cannon, *President Reagan: The role of a lifetime* (New York: Simon & Schuster, 1991), p. 288.
6 Blitzer, *Between Washington and Jerusalem*, p. 240. Despite Reagan's sympathetic discussions with fundamentalists preachers about the fulfilment of biblical prophecies of Armageddon, he was forced to publicly modify his stance in response to a statement by the Roman Catholic Bishop, Thomas Gumbleton, that "it is disturbing that any political leaders – especially leaders with responsibility for decisions affecting war and peace – might identify themselves with extremists who believe that nuclear Armageddon is inevitable and imminent." See Menendez, *Evangelicals at the Ballot Box*, p. 145.
7 Cannon, *President Reagan*, p. 38.
8 Blitzer, *Between Washington and Jerusalem*, pp. 238–9.
9 Beth A. Fischer, *The Reagan Reversal: Foreign policy at the end of the cold war* (Columbia & London: University of Missouri Press, 1997), p. 118.
10 Pat Golden, *Quiet Diplomat: A biography of Max Fisher* (New York: Herzl Press, 1992), p. 424 quoted in Jonathan Rynhold *Israeli Political Culture in Relations with the US over the Palestine Question, 1981–96* (Ph.D. thesis, University of London, London, 1998), p. 129.
11 For a practical example of the personal closeness of the relationship see the "Dear Menachem" salutation and signature of "Ron" in "Letter to Prime Minister Menachem Begin," 16 February 1982, *PPP*, vol. 2 1982, p. 177 and "Letter from Prime Minister Begin to President Reagan, 5 September 1982." Israel. Ministry of Foreign Affairs, vol. 8: 1982–84, <www.mfa.gov.il/mfa/go.asp?MFAH0ics0>.
12 Ronald Reagan, *An American Life* (London: Hutchinson, 1990), p. 410.
13 Judith Doneson, *The Holocaust in American Film* (Syracuse: Syracuse University Press, 2002), p. 149.
14 From an interview cited in Karen Elliott House, "Reagan's World," *Wall Street Journal*, 3 June 1980, p. 1, quoted in William Quandt, *Peace Process: American diplomacy and the Arab–Israeli conflict since 1967* (Washington D.C. & Berkeley, Los Angeles: The Brookings Institution & University of California Press, 1993), p. 338.
15 Steven L. Spiegel, *The Other Arab–Israeli Conflict: Making America's Middle East policy, from Truman to Reagan* (Chicago & London: University of Chicago Press, 1985), p. 400.

16 Blitzer, *Between Washington and Jerusalem*, p. 240. This was the conclusion Nixon reached in agreeing to the use of Israel as a US proxy during the Jordanian crisis of September 1970.
17 *PPP*, 1985, 11 February 1985.
18 Quandt, *Peace Process*, p. 337.
19 Cannon, *President Reagan*, p. 391.
20 The Iraqi nuclear reactor Osiraq was constructed by French and Italian technicians.
21 Author's interview with Samuel W. Lewis, U.S. Ambassador to Israel 1977–85, Chief State Department Policy Planning / Assistant Secretary of State, Policy Planning 1992–95.
22 *Ibid.*
23 Reagan was unaware of past discussions on this issue and when he was presented with the 'full history' surrounding Israel's actions, relations were smoothed over and Begin was invited to Washington for talks.
24 *DSB*, August 1981, p. 79.
25 Haig, *Caveat*, pp. 182.
26 George Lenczowski, *American Presidents and the Middle East* (Durham & London: Duke University Press, 1990), p. 257.
27 "Israeli Attack on Iraqi Nuclear Facilities," Hearings before the Subcommittees on International Security and Scientific Affairs, on Europe and the Middle East, and on International Economic Policy and Trade of the Committee on Foreign Affairs, House of Representatives, Ninety-Seventh Congress, First Session, June 17 and 25, 1981 (Washington D.C.: Government Printing Office, 1981), p. 15. Paul Findley later lost his government seat and blamed his electoral defeat on the pro-Israel lobby's smearing of his campaign and its financial support of his opponent.
28 Lenczowski, *American Presidents*, p. 258.
29 Haig, *Caveat*, p. 184.
30 Author's interview with Samuel W. Lewis.
31 Haig, *Caveat*, p. 168.
32 *Ibid.*, p. 175.
33 *MECS*, 1981–82, p. 27.
34 *Ibid.*, p. 28.
35 Blitzer, *Between Washington and Jerusalem*, p. 247.
36 The term 'another Iran' refers to the administration's fear that the Saudi monarchy could be overthrown by an Islamic revolution as had been carried out against the Shah of Iran in 1979.
37 Peter Novick, *The Holocaust in American Life* (Boston & New York: Houghton Mifflin Company, 1999), p. 156.
38 Nimrod Novik, *The United States and Israel: Domestic determinants of a changing US commitment* (Boulder, CO: Westview Press/Tel Aviv: The Jaffee Centre for Strategic Studies, Tel Aviv University, 1984), pp. 127–9.
39 Laurence I. Barrett, *Gambling with History: Ronald Reagan in the White House* (Garden City, New York: Doubleday & Co., Inc., 1983), p. 275.
40 *Ibid.*

41 Author's interview with Marshall Breger, special assistant to President Reagan and his liaison to the Jewish Community, 1982–84.
42 Lenczowski, *American Presidents*, p. 259.
43 Haig, *Caveat*, p. 191.
44 Author's interview with Samuel W. Lewis.
45 For the text of the Memorandum of Understanding, see *DSB*, December 1981, pp. 45–6 and *NYT*, 1 December 1981, p. A 14.
46 Author's interview with Samuel W. Lewis.
47 *Ibid.*
48 Steven Spiegel, "The Middle East: A consensus of error," *Commentary*, vol. 73, no. 3, March 1982, p. 22.
49 *PPP*, 1981, 17 December 1981.
50 Barrett, *Gambling with History*, p. 277.
51 Weinberger stated that the annexation constituted a "clear violation" of UN resolutions and the Camp David agreements. Lenczowski, *American Presidents*, p. 262.
52 Author's interview with Samuel W. Lewis.
53 Meese spoke on "Meet the Press," 20 December 1981, quoted in Barrett, *Gambling with History*, p. 278, (Ed Meese was Reagan's transitional director when he assumed the presidency in 1980) and John Durke, *The Institutional President* (Maryland: Johns Hopkins University Press, 1992), p. 140.
54 Barrett, *Gambling with History*, p. 278.
55 Mubarak succeed Sadat as President of Egypt following Sadat's assassination by Islamic extremists on 6 October 1981. The completion of the Israeli withdrawal from Sinai and the return of Egyptian land to Egypt, under the terms of the Camp David agreement, was a key test of Mubarak's ability to govern the country. Had the Israeli withdrawal been delayed, the US feared that Mubarak would be ousted from power and replaced by a more radical, Islamic leader.
56 This view is expressed in Quandt, *Peace Process*, p. 340.
57 *MECS*, 1981–82, p. 109.
58 Zeev Schiff, "The Green Light" *Foreign Policy*, pp. 73–85, vol. 50, Spring 1983, p. 76.
59 The three most significant direct consequences of this agreement were:1) Saudi assistance convinced the administration that the sale of the AWAC jets was a positive decision, 2) the success of diplomacy in the region was demonstrated, 3) Habib increased in stature, particularly in the eyes of the President. Spiegel, *The Other Arab–Israeli Conflict*, p. 415.
60 George P. Shultz, *Turmoil and Triumph: My years as secretary of state* (New York: Charles Scribner's Sons, 1993), p. 45.
61 *MECS*, 1981–82, pp. 109–10.
62 *Ibid.*, p. 111.
63 Schiff, "The Green Light," p. 73.
64 *Ibid.*, p. 78.
65 *MECS*, 1981–82, p. 111.
66 David Schoenbaum, *The United States and the State of Israel* (New York & Oxford: Oxford University Press, 1993), p. 283.

67 Schiff, "The Green Light," p. 79.
68 Raymond Tanter, *Who's at the Helm? Lessons of Lebanon* (San Francisco & Oxford: Westview Press, 1990), p. 80.
69 Author's interview with Samuel W. Lewis.
70 *Ibid.*
71 Haig, *Caveat*, pp. 326–7.
72 *Ibid.*, p. 333.
73 In a statement to the Knesset Begin argued that Israel could not accept an agreement that only prevented terrorist attacks on Israel from Southern Lebanon and that did not extended to the protection of Jews everywhere. Israel. Ministry of Foreign Affairs, vol. 8: 1982–1984, Statement to the Knesset by Prime Minister Begin, 8 June 1982, <www.mfa.gov.il/mfa/go.asp?MFAH0icu0>.
74 Author's interview with Samuel W. Lewis. The US advised Arafat not to respond to Israeli raids as Begin was looking for an excuse to launch a larger scale attack.
75 Schiff, "The Green Light," p. 83.
76 Fred Halliday, "The Reagan Administration and the Middle East," *Atlantic Quarterly*, 2:3 (Autumn 1984), p. 229.
77 Spiegel, *The Other Arab–Israeli Conflict*, p. 415.
78 Translated from the Hebrew version of the letter from Reagan to Begin, 9 June 1982, as published by Ayre Naor, *Cabinet at War* (in Hebrew) (Tel Aviv: Lahav, 1986) p. 76, quoted in Quandt, *Peace Process*, p. 342.
79 Lenczowski, *American Presidents*, p. 220.
80 Shultz, *Turmoil and Triumph*, p. 54.
81 Tanter, *Who's at the Helm?*, p. 131.
82 William Safire, *NYT*, editorial, 5 August 1982 quoted in *ibid.*, p. 186.
83 Robert Tucker, "Lebanon: The case for the war," *Commentary*, vol. 74, no. 4, October 1982, p. 21.
84 Begin had wanted a private meeting with Reagan because he thought this would provide the opportunity for him to convince the President of Israel's way of thinking. It was finally agreed that the two leaders would meet in the presence of their respective ambassadors, Sam Lewis and Moshe Arens.
85 Schiff, "The Green Light," p. 84.
86 It was left to Weinberger, Vice-President Bush, and Senator Charles Percy, chairman of the Foreign Relations Committee to reassure the Arabs, on the occasion of King Khalid's funeral in Riyadh. Spiegel, *The Other Arab–Israeli Conflict*, p. 415.
87 Tanter, *Who's at the Helm?*, pp. 186–9.
88 Haig became the highest ranking American decision-maker to counsel against a tough course of action against Israel. Spiegel, *The Other Arab–Israeli Conflict*, p. 415.
89 Coral Bell, *The Reagan Paradox: US foreign policy in the 1980s* (New Jersey: Rutgers Univeristy Press, 1989), p. 95.
90 Shultz, *Turmoil and Triumph*, p. 21.
91 See "Nomination of George P. Shultz." Hearings, House Committee on Foreign Relations. Washington, 1982, for a full account of the statements delivered during the nomination hearings.

92 Tucker, "Lebanon: The case for the war," p. 21.
93 Tanter, *Who's at the Helm?*, p. 134.
94 Michael K. Deaver, *Behind the Scenes* (New York: William Morrow, 1987), p. 166.
95 Howard Sachar, *A History of Israel from the Rise of Zionism to Our Time* (New York: Alfred A. Knopf, 1996), p. 909.
96 Spiegel, *The Other Arab–Israeli Conflict*, p. 285.
97 Deaver, *Behind the Scenes*, p. 166.
98 Author's interview with William Quandt, former National Security Council aide, Nixon and Carter administrations.
99 Spiegel, *The Other Arab–Israeli Conflict*, p. 417.
100 *WP*, 2 August 1982, p. A 16.
101 Tucker, "Lebanon: The case for the war," p. 30.
102 Shultz, *Turmoil and Triumph*, p. 22.
103 Tanter, *Who's at the Helm?*, pp. 89–90.
104 Bell, *The Reagan Paradox*, p. 94.
105 *DSB*, 1 September 1982.
106 *PPP*, 1 September 1982, p. 1095.
107 *Ibid.*
108 Israel was not consulted about the Plan because Washington feared a leak. *MECS*, 1995, p. 31 and Author's interview with Samuel W. Lewis.
109 Spiegel, *The Other Arab–Israeli Conflict*, p. 420. The text of Begin's speech to the Knesset on the Reagan Plan, delivered on 8 September 1982, is available at Israel. Ministry of Foreign Affairs. vol. 8 1982–84, <www.mfa.gov.il/mfa /go.asp? MFAH0icn0>.
110 Quandt, *Peace Process*, p. 345. For more detailed accounts of the Fez Plan see *Foreign Broadcast and Information Service*, 10 September 1982, A 17–18 and Spiegel, *The Other Arab–Israeli Conflict*, p. 420.
111 Spiegel, *The Other Arab–Israeli Conflict*, p. 422.
112 Sachar, *A History of Israel*, p. 914.
113 Yossi Beilin, *Israel: A concise political history* (London: Weidenfeld & Nicolson, 1992), p. 124.
114 *MECS*, 1995, p. 31.
115 Caspar Weinberger, *Fighting for Peace: Seven critical years at the Pentagon* (London: Michael Joseph Ltd., 1990), p. 105.
116 *PPP*, September 1982, pp. 1187–9.
117 Weinberger, *Fighting for Peace*, p. 105.
118 Schoenbaum, *The United States*, p. 283.
119 Report by the Kahan Commission, quoted in Sachar, *A History of Israel*, p. 915.
120 Earl Raab, "Is the Jewish Community Split?" *Commentary*, vol. 74, no. 3, March 1982, p. 23.
121 Author's interview with William Quandt and Marshall Breger.
122 Epstein, "A Dissent on Schindler's List," *New York Review of Books*, 41 (21 April 1994), cited in Peter Novick, *The Holocaust in American Life* (New York: Houghton, Mifflin & Co., 1999), p. 235.
123 Philip Lopate, "Resistance to the Holocaust," *Tikkun*, 4 (May–June 1989), p. 58.
124 Raab, "Is the Jewish Community Split?," p. 23.

125 Geoffrey Stern, "Moral Judgments and Political Prejudice," *Contemporary Review*, May 1975, pp. 231–2.
126 Tom Gorman, "Worthy and Unworthy Victims: Munich matters, Sabra and Shatila don't," *CounterPunch*, 21 September 2002, p. 2.
127 Edward Herman & Noam Chomsky, *Manufacturing Consent.*
128 Author's interview with William Quandt.
129 Gorman, "Worthy and Unworthy Victims," p. 1.
130 Norman Podhoretz, "J'Accuse," *Commentary*, vol. 74, no. 3, September 1982, p. 31.
131 William B. Quandt, "Reagan's Lebanon Policy: Trial and error," *Middle East Journal*, vol. 38 (Spring 1984) pp. 241–2.
132 Quandt, *Peace Process*, p. 347.
133 The text of "Jordan's Statement on Its refusal to Join the Reagan Peace Initiative," appeared in the *NYT*, 11 April, 1983, p. A12.
134 George W. Ball, *Error and Betrayal in Lebanon: An analysis of Israel's invasion of Lebanon and the implications for US–Israeli relations* (Washington D.C.: Foundation for Middle East Peace, 1984), p. 63.
135 Schoenbaum, *The United States*, p. 283.
136 *Ibid.*, p. 293.
137 *DSB*, June 1983, pp. 62–4.
138 Quandt, *Reagan's Lebanon Policy*, pp. 237ff.
139 Quandt, *Peace Process*, pp. 348–9.
140 *PPP*, 24 October 1983.
141 Helena Cobban, *The Superpowers and the Syrian-Israeli Conflict: Beyond crisis management?* (New York: Praeger, 1991), pp. 87–8.
142 Ilya Levkov, *Bitburg and Beyond: Encounters in American, German and Jewish history* (New York: Shapolsky Publishers, 1987), p. 22.
143 *PPP*, 21 March 1985.
144 *WP*, 21 March 1985.
145 Levkov, *Bitburg and Beyond*, p. 24.
146 *PPP*, 18 April 1985.
147 Levkov, *Bitburg and Beyond*, p. 27.
148 Raul Hilberg, "Bitburg as a Symbol" in Geoffrey Hartman (ed.), *Bitburg: In moral and political perspective* (Bloomington: Indiana University Press, 1986), p. 19.
149 Levkov, *Bitburg and Beyond*, p. 27.
150 Author's interview with Norman Podhoretz, Senior Fellow, Hudson Institute and former editor-in-chief of *Commentary*, 1960–95.
151 Levkov, *Bitburg and Beyond*, p. 27.
152 Author's interview with Norman Podhoretz.
153 *PPP*, 23 April 1985.
154 Author's interview with Marshall Breger, special assistant to President Reagan and his liaison to the Jewish Community, 1982–84.
155 Hartman, *Bitburg*, p. 9.
156 Author's interview with Norman Podhoretz.
157 Annette Insdorf, *Indelible Shadows: Film and the holocaust* (Cambridge: Cambridge University Press, 2003), p. 23.

158 Judith Doneson, *The Holocaust in American Film* (Syracuse: Syracuse University Press, 2002), p. 199.
159 Author's interview with Norman Podhoretz. Some authors like Norman Finkelstein take the view that because the avowed concern of American Jews for the Holocaust was contrived for use as a "chip in a high-stakes power game" they quickly forgave Reagan for his visit to Bitburg. See Norman G. Finkelstein, *The Holocaust Industry: Reflections of the exploitation of Jewish suffering* (London & New York: Verso, 2000).
160 Uri Avnery, "The Intifada: Substance and illusion," *New Outlook* (December 1989), p. 13 cited in Mark Tessler, *A History of the Israeli–Palestinian Conflict* (Indiana: Indiana University Press, 1994), p. 707.
161 Edgar O'Balance, *The Palestinian Intifada* (London: Macmillan Press, 1998), p. 26.
162 Quandt, *Peace Process*, p. 364.
163 Sachar, *A History of Israel*, p. 964.
164 *JP*, 18 December 1987, p. 5.
165 F. Robert Hunter, *The Palestinian Uprising: A war by other means* (London & New York: Tauris & Co., 1991), p. 82.
166 O'Balance, *The Palestinian Intifada*, pp. 35–6.
167 *JP*, 17 January 1988.
168 Hunter, *The Palestinian Uprising*, p. 149 and Tim Youngs, *Developments in the Middle East Peace Process, 1991–2000* (London: House of Commons Library, 2001), p. 13.
169 O'Balance, *The Palestinian Intifada*, p. 33.
170 *PPP*, 10 March 1988, p. 314.
171 Y. Melman and D. Raviv, *Friends in Deed: Inside the US–Israeli alliance* (New York: Hyperion, 1994), p. 408.
172 O'Balance, *The Palestinian Intifada*, p. 38.
173 Hunter, *The Palestinian Uprising*, p. 150.
174 *PPP*, 16 March 1988, p. 343.
175 Shultz, *Turmoil and Triumph*, p. 1026.
176 George Gruen, "Impact of the Intifada on American Jews" in Robert O. Freedman (ed.), *The Intifada: Its impact on Israel, the Arab world, and the superpowers* (Florida: Florida International University Press, 1991), p. 238.
177 In May 1989 a New York Times/CBS poll asked a national American sample, "Do you believe Israel has done enough to prove that it is interested in peace, or hasn't it done enough?" 17% voted 'Yes', while 70% of respondents voted 'No'. See "The New York Times/CBS News Poll Foreign Policy Survey, May 9–11 1989 cited in George Gruen, "Impact of the Intifada on American Jews" in Robert O. Freedman (ed.), *The Intifada: Its impact on Israel, the Arab world, and the superpowers* (Florida: Florida International University Press, 1991), p. 240.
178 Sachar, *A History of Israel*, p. 960.
179 Hunter, *The Palestinian Uprising*, p. 149.
180 Quandt, *Peace Process*, p. 368.
181 Hunter, *The Palestinian Uprising*, p. 159.
182 Quandt, *Peace Process*, p. 373.
183 Sachar, *A History of Israel*, p. 975

184 Yassir Arafat, quoted in Quandt, *Peace Process*, p. 375.
185 Quandt, *Peace Process*, p. 375.
186 *PPP*, 15 December 1988, p. 1627.
187 David Pollock, "The American Response to the Intifada" in Robert O. Freedman (ed.), *The Intifada: Its impact on Israel, the Arab world, and the Superpowers* (Florida: Florida International University Press, 1991), p. 116.
188 *PPP*, 28 January 1988, p. 135.
189 *PPP*, 25 January 1988, p. 102.
190 Shultz, *Turmoil and Triumph*, p. 1023.
191 *PPP*, p. 848, 10 June 1983. Remarks at the Annual Convention of the Anti-Defamation League of B'nai B'rith.
192 Earl Raab, "Is the Jewish Community Split?" *Commentary*, vol. 74, no. 3, March 1982, p. 23.
193 *Ibid.*
194 Patrick Glynn, "Reagan's Rush to Disarm," *Commentary*, vol. 85, no. 3, March 1988, p. 19.
195 Beth A. Fischer, *The Reagan Reversal: Foreign policy and the end of the Cold War* (Columbia & London: University of Missouri Press, 1997), p. 81.
196 *Ibid.*, p. 103.
197 Ronald Reagan, *An American Life* (London: Hutchinson, 1990), p. 549.
198 Fischer, *The Reagan Reversal*, p. 106.
199 Glynn, "Reagan's Rush to Disarm," p. 28.
200 *Ibid.*, p. 61.
201 *WP*, 22 April 1988.
202 *PPP*, 9 September 1981, p. 767.
203 Lenczowski, *American Presidents*, p. 255.
204 Robert O'Keohane, "The Big Influence of Small Allies," *Foreign Policy* (Spring 1975), no. 2, pp. 23–4.
205 Joseph Hogan (ed.), *The Reagan Years: The record in presidential leadership* (Manchester & New York: Manchester University Press, 1990), pp. 263–4.
206 Ball, *Error and Betrayal in Lebanon*, p. 78.
207 Author's interview with William Quandt.

7 Bush, the Gulf War and Israel

1 *NYT*, Thomas L. Friedman, "Special Relationship Reaches Its Limits," 21 October 1990.
2 William Quandt, *Peace Process: American diplomacy and the Arab–Israeli conflict since 1967* (Washington, D.C. & Berkeley, Los Angeles: The Brookings Institution & University of California Press, 1993), p. 388.
3 *Newsweek*, 1 June 1992, p. 57.
4 *NYT*, 16 May 1992, p. 2.
5 Quandt, *Peace Process*, p. 383.
6 *MECS*, 1989, p. 15
7 Quandt, *Peace Process*, p. 384.
8 Author's interview with Norman Podhoretz, Senior Fellow, Hudson Institute and

former editor-in-chief of *Commentary* 1960–95 and Marshall Breger, special assistant to President Reagan and his liaison to the Jewish Community, 1982–84.

9 Robert Shogan, *The Riddle of Power: Presidential leadership from Truman to Bush* (New York: Dutton, 1991), p. 259.

10 George Bush with Victor Gold, *Looking Forward* (London: The Bodley Head, 1988), p. 81.

11 Fitzhugh Green, *George Bush: An intimate portrait* (New York: Hippocrene Books, 1991), p. 78.

12 David Mervin, *George Bush and the Guardianship Presidency* (London: Macmillan, 1996), pp. 17–18.

13 George W. Bush, quoted in Ruth Shalit, "What I Saw at the Devolution," *Reason*, 9 March 1993, pp. 27–33, cited in Mervin, *George Bush*, p. 20.

14 Ronald Elving, "House Service Set Course for New President," *Congressional Quarterly Weekly Report*, 14 January 1989, pp. 55–7.

15 Bush, *Looking Forward*, p. 234.

16 Gail Sheehy, *Character: America's search for leadership* (New York: Bantam Books, 1990), p. 198.

17 Burt Solomon, "Bush's Lack of Ambitious Policies . . . Makes His Plans Seem Thin Gruel," *National Journal*, 6 May 1989, no. 18, p. 1102.

18 Baker also managed Bush's unsuccessful bid for re-election in 1992.

19 Henry Allen, "The Quintessential Establishment," *Washington Post National Weekly Edition*, 9–15 January 1989.

20 Quandt, *Peace Process*, p. 384.

21 Christopher Ogden, "Vision Problems at State . . . " *Time* (International Edition), 25 September 1989, p. 36.

22 Bush, *Looking Forward*, p. 174.

23 *NYT*, 3 November 1989, p. A16.

24 Author's interview with Dennis Ross, Director of State Department Planning Policy 1988–92 and Special Middle East Co-ordinator 1992–2000.

25 Jonathan Rynhold, *Israeli Political Culture in Relations with the US over the Palestine Question, 1981–96* (Ph.D. thesis, London School of Economics & Political Science: London, 1998), p. 180.

26 *Newsweek*, 1 June 1992, p. 59.

27 *Ibid.*

28 James Baker III, *Politics and Diplomacy* (New York: Putnam Publishing, 1995), p. 117.

29 Howard Sachar, *A History of Israel from the Rise of Zionism to Our Time* (New York: Alfred A. Knopf, 1996), p. 967.

30 Shamir's commitment to 'greater Israel' was a product of religion and ideology, both of which had been key issues in the 1988 Israeli elections. For a more detailed account of their salience and influence on policy see Robert Freedman, "Religion, Politics, and the Israeli Elections of 1988," *Middle East Journal*, Winter 1989.

31 E. Inbar, "Rabin and Israeli National Security," *BESA Security and Policy Study*, no. 25 1996.

32 *JP*, 24 March 1988, p. 3.

33 Sachar, *A History of Israel*, p. 967.

34 Quandt, *Peace Process*, pp. 385–8.
35 Baker, *Politics and Diplomacy*, pp. 116–18.
36 Author's interview with Dennis Ross.
37 Moshe Arens, *Broken Covenant: American foreign policy and the crisis between the US and Israel* (London: Simon & Schuster, 1995), p. 75 and Baker, *Politics and Diplomacy*, pp. 116–18.
38 Author's interview with Dennis Ross.
39 Yitzhak Shamir, *Summing Up: An autobiography* (London: Weidenfeld & Nicolson, 1994), p. 201.
40 Arens, *Broken Covenant*, p. 219 and James Baker, *Politics and Diplomacy* (New York: Putnam Publishing, 1995), p. 421.
41 Arens, *Broken Covenant*, pp. 55–7.
42 For complete details of the Report see, The Washington Institute Presidential Study Group, "Building for Peace: An American strategy for the Middle East," (Washington: The Washington Institute for Near East Policy, 1988).
43 Ben Zvi, *The United States and Israel: The limits of the special relationship* (New York: Columbia University Press, 1993), p. 165.
44 Quandt, *Peace Process*, p. 387.
45 Annette Insdorf, *Indelible Shadows: Film and the Holocaust* (Cambridge: Cambridge University Press: Cambridge, 2003), p. 300.
46 Peter Novick, *The Holocaust in American Life* (Boston & New York: Houghton Mifflin Company, 1999), p. 235.
47 Baker, *Politics and Diplomacy*, pp. 120–1.
48 *FBIS*, 23 January 1989, p. 31.
49 *MECS*, 1989, pp. 71, 74.
50 Shlaim, *War and Peace*, p. 469.
51 *DSB*, July 1989, pp. 24–7.
52 Christison, Kathleen. "Splitting the Difference: The Palestinian–Israeli policy of James Baker" *Journal of Palestine Studies*, vol. XXIV, no. 1 (Autumn 1994), p. 44. The US began a dialogue with the PLO began under the Reagan administration and with the full knowledge and consent of then Vice-President George Bush.
53 Shamir, *Summing Up*, p. 203. For a detailed account of the religious and political composition of the Knesset during this period and its impact on policy see Shmuel Sandler, "Israel's 1988 Knesset Elections and the Transformation of the Israeli Polity," *Middle East Review*, no. 1, 1989–90.
54 *MECS*, 1989, p. 22.
55 Author's interview with Dennis Ross.
56 Eytan Bentsur, *Making Peace in the Middle East: A first-hand account of the Arab–Israeli peace process* (Westport, CT & London: Praeger, 2001), p. 23.
57 *MECS*, 1989, p. 24.
58 *Ibid.*, p. 73.
59 *MECS*, 1989, p. 24.
60 Arens, *Broken Covenant*, pp. 75, 78.
61 *MECS*, 1989, p. 73.
62 Bentsur, *Making Peace in the Middle East*, p. 27.
63 Author's interview with Dennis Ross.

64 *FBIS*, 16 February 1990, p. 25.
65 *MECS*, 1990, pp. 105–7.
66 Mark Tessler, *A History of the Israeli–Palestinian Conflict* (Indiana: Indiana University Press, 1994).
67 *MECS*, 1992, p. 28. The US was concerned that if Saddam Hussein's military forces were left intact and occupying Kuwait, he would be able to threaten Saudi Arabia and force the House of Saud to follow foreign and oil-pricing policies dictated by Baghdad. This combination could have effectively allowed Saddam to control 20% of world oil reserves and thus the global price of oil. Kenneth Pollack, "How Saddam Misread the United States," in Micah Sifry & Christopher Cerf (eds.), *The Iraqi War Reader* (New York: Touchstone, 2003), p. 76.
68 *Ibid.*, p. 28.
69 *PPP*, 1990, 1 November 1990, p. 1509.
70 Novick, *The Holocaust in American Life*, 249.
71 *NYT*, 9 April 1991, p. A25.
72 David Willis, "Germans Built Gas Chambers for Iraq, Wiesenthal [Centre] Says," *Forward*, 15 February 1991, p. 20, cited in Novick, *The Holocaust in American Life*, p. 249.
73 *PPP*, 18 December 1990, p. 1807.
74 Arens, *Broken Covenant*, p. 184.
75 *Jerusalem Report*, 31 January 1991, p. 10.
76 Shamir, *Summing Up*, pp. 221–3.
77 Shlaim, *War and Peace*, p. 477.
78 *PPP*, 8 November 1990, p. 1584.
79 Shlaim, *War and Peace*, p. 477.
80 *PPP*, 1 October 1990, p. 1334. The Patriot success rate was 41 for 42: 42 scuds were engaged and 41 were intercepted. Not every intercept resulted in total destruction, but Bush claimed that the Patriot was proof positive that missile defence worked. *PPP*, 1991, 15 February 1991, p. 150 and Karen L. Puschel, *US–Israeli Strategic Cooperation in the Post-Cold War Era: An American perspective* (Jerusalem: Jerusalem Post Press, 1992), p. 133.
81 This was the first occasion Israel itself had been subject to aerial attack since 1948.
82 Puschel, *US–Israeli Strategic Cooperation*, p. 125 and Shlaim, *War and Peace*, p. 481.
83 Shlaim, *War and Peace*, p. 481.
84 Shamir *Summing Up*, p. 217.
85 For a more detailed account of the impact the Gulf War exerted on Israel see Ze'ev Schiff, "Israel after the [Gulf] War," *Foreign Affairs*, February 1991.
86 Shlaim, *War and Peace*, pp. 473–4.
87 Author's interview with David Bar-Ilan, Israeli Director of Communications & Policy Planning, 1996–1999, and Puschel, *US–Israeli Strategic Cooperation*, p. 133.
88 *MECS*, 1992, p. 25.
89 *Ibid.*, p. 31.
90 Dilip Hiro, *Desert Shield to Desert Storm* (London: Paladin, 1992), p. 449.
91 Shlaim, *War and Peace*, p. 474.
92 Shamir, *Summing Up*, p. 221.
93 *WP*, 7 March 1991, p. 1.

94 Tim Youngs, *Developments in the Middle East Peace Process 1991–2000* (London: House of Commons Library, 2001), p. 17.
95 Baker, *Politics and Diplomacy*, pp. 497, 504.
96 The dramatic change in Syria's position was attributable to the collapse of the Soviet Union which had been its main source of support and the defeat of Iraq which had been seen as providing strategic depth in its confrontation with Israel. Hiro, *Desert Shield to Desert Storm*, p. 451.
97 Neill Lochery, *The Israeli Labour Party: In the shadow of the Likud* (Reading: Ithaca Press, 1997), p. 189.
98 *NYT*, 16 March 1992, p. 3. The Likud government would not agree to talks on any other basis. F. Robert Hunter, *The Palestinian Uprising: A war by other means* (Berkeley, Los Angeles: University of California Press, 1993), p. 278.
99 *The Economist*, 2 November 1991, p. 80. The results of the conference were not binding and it only served as a preamble to bilateral talks scheduled to take place in Washington five weeks later. Lochery, *Israeli Labour Party*, p. 189.
100 Address by President George Bush, *PPP*, 30 October 1991, p. 80.
101 Bentsur, *Making Peace in the Middle East*, p. 166.
102 Youngs, *Developments in the Middle East*, p. 18.
103 Israel, Ministry of Foreign Affairs, Address by Israeli Prime Minister Yitzhak Shamir, "Opening Remarks at the Madrid Peace Conference," 31 October 1991, <ww.mfa.gov.il/mfa/go.asp?MFAH0bvt0>.
104 *MECS*, 1992, p. 124.
105 Rynhold, *Israeli Political Culture*, p. 266.
106 *JP*, 23 February 1990.
107 *NYT Magazine*, Maureen Dowd & Thomas L. Friedman, "The Fabulous Bush & Baker Boys," p. 42.
108 *MECS*, 1989, p. 19.
109 *Ibid.*, p. 27.
110 See Dowd & Friedman, "The Fabulous Bush & Baker Boys," pp. 34–67, for a more detailed account of the settlement issue.
111 Melman & Raviv, *Friends in Deed: Inside the U.S.–Israel alliance* (New York: Hyperion, 1994), p. 410.
112 *NYT*, 23 May 1991, p. 5 and *NYT*, 24 May 1991, p. 3.
113 *MECS*, 1989, p. 21.
114 Frankel, *Israeli Political Culture*, p. 298.
115 Baker, *Politics and Diplomacy*, p. 544.
116 Sachar, *A History of Israel*, p. 981. On 11 February 1991, Baker told Defence Minister Moshe Arnes, that it "is inappropriate to request aid at a time when United States soldiers [are] dying in a war beneficial to Israel."
117 Glenn Frankel, *Beyond the Promised Land: Jews and Arabs on the hard road to a new Israel* (New York: Simon & Schuster, 1994), pp. 292–302.
118 *PPP*, 6 September 1991, p. 1121. Ironically, although the pro-Israel lobby accused Bush and Baker of anti-Semitism, Haass wrote Bush's comments in September 1991, criticising Israel's congressional push for loan guarantees.
119 *PPP*, 23 May 1991, p. 547.

120 *PPP*, 12 September 1991, p. 1140.
121 *PPP*, 23 May 1991, p. 547.
122 Shamir, *Summing Up*, p. 234.
123 Rynhold, *Israeli Political Culture*, p. 247.
124 *FBIS*, 3 February 1992, p. 26.
125 *New York Post*, 6 March 1992; *MECS*, 1992, p. 18.
126 David Hoffman, "One Hundred Days of Solicitude," *Washington Post National Weekly Edition*, 8–14 May 1989, p. 13, cited in Mervin, *George Bush*, p. 86.
127 *NYT*, 25 June 1992, p. 14, and Christison, "Splitting the Difference," p. 46.
128 *WP*, 9 February 1992.
129 *Washington Jewish World*, 14 June, 1992, p. 17.
130 Sachar, *A History of Israel*, p. 982.
131 Shamir, *Summing Up*, p. 216.
132 *NYT*, 25 June 1992, p. 14.
133 *NYT*, 12 August 1992.
134 Ofira Seliktar, *Divided We Stand: American Jews, Israel, and the peace process* (Westport, CT & London, Praeger, 2002), p. 120.
135 Leon T. Hadar, "Thawing the American–Israeli Chill," *Journal of Palestine Studies* vol. XXII, no. 2 (Winter 1993), p. 82.
136 *MECS*, 1992, p. 19.
137 Neill Lochery, *The Difficult Road to Peace in the Middle East* (Lebanon: Ithaca Press, 1999), p. 212.
138 Hadar, "Thawing the American–Israeli Chill," p. 82.
139 Author's interview with Marshall Breger.
140 *Ibid.*
141 *Newsweek*, 1 June 1992, p. 57.
142 *Ibid.*
143 *NYT*, 16 May 1992, pp. 2–3.
144 *WP*, 6 March 1992, p. 2.
145 Steven Spiegel argues that the damage inflicted on the Bush administration's relationship with American Jews by the President's refusal to authorise the loan guarantees, was not redressed by the convening of the Madrid conference. Steven Spiegel, "Israel and Beyond: American Jews and US foreign policy" in L. Sandy Maisel (ed.), *Jews in American Politics* (Lanham, Boulder, New York, Oxford: Rowman & Littlefield Publishers, 2001), p. 264.
146 Jonathan J. Goldberg, *Jewish Power: Inside the American Jewish establishment* (Reading Massachusetts: Addison Wesley, 1996), p. 248. Following congressional ratification of Nixon's decision to grant Israel a $2.2 billion aid appropriation, Goldberg argued that Israel came to view financial aid as a right.
147 Author's interview with Dennis Ross.
148 Kurtzer, quoted in *Newsweek*, 1 June 1992, p. 58.

8 Framing American Foreign Policy in the New World Order

1 Les Aspin, "Session IV, Congressman Les Aspin, Chairman, House Armed Services Committee," in *The Soref Symposium: The Middle East in an era of changing super-*

power relations, Washington D.C., April 29–30, 1990, David Segal (ed.) (Washington, D.C.: The Washington Institute for Near East Policy, 1990), p. 40 quoted in Bernard Reich, *Securing the Covenant: United States-Israel relations after the Cold War* (Connecticut: Greenwood Press, 1995), pp. 58–9.

2 Reich, *Securing the Covenant*, pp. 58–9.

3 See chapter 5 for a detailed explanation of the Jordanian crisis of September 1970.

4 Avi Shlaim, "Israel and the Conflict," in A. Danchev & D. Keohane (eds.), *International Perspectives on the Gulf Conflict 1990–91* (London: Macmillan, 1994), p. 77.

5 *PPP*, 1991, 17 January 1991, p. 47

6 Uri Savir, *The Process: 1,000 days that changed the Middle East* (New York: Vintage Books, 1998), p. 4.

7 *JP*, 30 March 1992.

8 *MECS*, 1997, p. 17.

9 Nafeez Mosaddeq Ahmed, *Behind the War on Terror: Western secret strategy and the struggle for Iraq* (East Sussex: Clairview, 2003), p. 155.

10 Shlaim, *The Iron Wall*, pp. 480–1.

11 In securing ratification of the Nuclear Non-Proliferation Treaty (NPT), US efforts focused on Iran and Iraq. No significant pressure was exerted on Israel. *MECS*, 1995, p. 34.

12 *MECS*, 1995, p. 30.

13 In contrast to the American experience, Israel has been a victim of habitual terrorist attacks since its creation in 1948.

14 *MECS*, 1997, p. 17.

15 *JP*, 14 February 2001, p. 2.

16 Martin Kramer, "Islam vs. Democracy," *Commentary*, vol. 95, no. 1, January 1993, p. 36.

17 Daniel Price, *Islamic Political Culture, Democracy, and Human Rights: A comparative study* (Westport, CT & London: Praeger, 1999), p. 60.

18 Kramer, "Islam vs. Democracy," pp. 36–7.

19 Price, *Islamic Political Culture*, p. 55.

20 *Ibid.*, p. 118.

21 Kramer, "Islam vs. Democracy," p. 37.

22 Karen L. Puschel, *US–Israeli Strategic Cooperation in the Post-Cold War Era: An American persepctive* (Jerusalem: Jerusalem Post Press, 1992), p. 155.

23 Reich, *Securing the Covenant*, p. 3.

24 Puschel, *US–Israeli Strategic Cooperation*, p. 155.

25 In 1991, following the Gulf War, Israel received an additional $2 billion in aid – $5 billion as compared with the usual $3bn annual payment.

26 Leopold Yehuda Laufer, "U.S. Aid to Israel: Problems and perceptions," in Gabriel Sheffer (ed.), *Dynamics of Dependence: US Israeli relations* (Boulder, CO & London: Westview Press, 1987), p. 3.

27 David Baldwin, *Foreign Aid and American Foreign Policy: A documentary analysis* (New York, Washington & London: Frederick A. Praeger, 1966), p. 5.

28 *MECS*, 1995, pp. 30–9.

29 *Mideast Mirror*, 24 March 1995, p. 3.
30 Under the Oslo provision, a $2 billion fund was established to restore the Palestinian economy, of which a quarter was to come from the US. For a more detailed account of Israeli and American Jewish responses to aid packages resulting from the Oslo Accords see Ofira Seliktar, *Divided We Stand: American Jews, Israel, and the peace process* (Westport, CT & London: Praeger, 2002), p. 136.
31 These projects included: $40 million to improve the sewage system of Gaza City; $25 million to provide thousands of public works jobs; and $8 million to pave streets and upgrade shelters for the elderly and ill in refugee camps. See *MECS*, 1995, p. 29.
32 This budget was administered by USAID, the official aid organisation of the US. Denis Sullivan, "International Aid and the Peace Process" in *Structural Flaws in the Middle East Peace Process* (Hampshire & New York: Palgrave, 2001), p. 171.
33 David Rothkopf, *The Price of Peace: Emergency intervention and US foreign policy* (Washington, D.C.: The Brookings Institution Press, 1998), p. 54.
34 Simson Bichler, "Between Capitalism and Jewish Voters: Electoral economics in Israel, 1977 to 1997" in J. W. Wright, Jr. (ed.), *Structural Flaws in the Middle East Peace Process* (Hampshire & New York: Palgrave, 2001), p. 218.
35 The US financial commitment to the peace process is crucial as if peace is to take root in the wake of conflict, economic growth is vital. Economic failures can quickly reverse political and military successes. Rothkopf, *The Price of Peace*, p. 6.
36 Richard J. Trethewey, "International Economics and Politics: A theoretical framework" in Robert A. Bauer (ed.), *The Interaction of Economics and Foreign Policy* (Charlottesville: University Press of Virginia, 1975), p. 24.
37 *JP*, 27 March 1989.
38 F. Robert Hunter, *The Palestinian Uprising: A war by other means* (London & New York: Tauris & Co., 1991), p. 82.
39 Neill Lochery, *The Israeli Labour Party: In the shadow of the Likud* (Reading: Ithaca Press, 1997), p. 267.
40 Financial assistance was requested by Israel to meet the cost of absorption of Soviet Jews.
41 Leon T. Hadar, "Thawing the American–Israeli Chill," *Journal of Palestine Studies*, vol. XXII, no. 2, Winter 1993, p. 84.
42 *NYT*, 22 August 1992, p. 2.
43 Leon Hadar, "The Friends of Bibi (FOB's) vs. The New Middle East," *Journal of Palestine Studies*, vol. XXVI, no. 1, Autumn 1996, p. 90.
44 Quoted in "AIPAC Charged with Maintaining a Blacklist to Silence Criticism of Israel's Lobby is Also Criticised by Prime Minister Rabin," *Special Interest Report* published by American Council of Judaism (Sept.–Oct. 1992), in Hadar "Thawing the American–Israeli Chill," p. 84.
45 Hadar "Thawing the American–Israeli Chill," p. 84.
46 *NYT*, 14 July 1996, p. 2.
47 Seliktar, *Divided We Stand*, p. 10
48 Hadar, "Thawing the American–Israeli Chill," p. 85.
49 *NYT*, 30 September 1995, p. 1.

50 *MECS*, 1995, p. 371.
51 Hadar, "The Friends of Bibi," p. 91.
52 Seliktar, *Divided We Stand*, p. 152.
53 *MECS*, 1996, p. 385.
54 Hadar, "The Friends of Bibi," p. 92.
55 Leading newspaper columnists, including William Safire and A. M. Rosenthal of the *New York Times* and Charles Krauthammer and George Will of the *Washington Post* were transformed into the American media's voice of the Likud. Similarly, Netanyahu appeared so often on *Nightline*, that the wags began referring to "Ted Netanyahu" and "Bibi Koppel". See Hadar "The Friends of Bibi," p. 93. The part played by a small, but highly influential group of American Jewish businessmen in Netanyahu's rise to power also deserves attention. The group included Mervyn Adelson, the former chairman of Lorimar-Telepictures and the former US ambassador to Austria, Rinald Lauder. This clique had reportedly spent years financing Netanyahu's career and introducing him to congressmen and State Department officials. Nurturing shared views on the peace process, Lauder was said to be active in raising funds for Likud and reportedly connected Netanyahu with Republican political consultant Arthur Finkelstein. See *MECS*, 1996, p. 385.
56 Shmuel Sandler, Robert O'Freeman & Shibley Telhami, "The Religious-Secular Divide in Israeli Politics" *Middle East Policy*, vol. VI, no. 4, June 1999, p 142.
57 Seliktar, *Divided We Stand*, p. 161.
58 *NYT*, 17 November 1997, p. 1.
59 Meryl Hyman, *Who is a Jew? Conversion, not conclusion* (Woodstock, VT: Jewish Light Publishing, 1998), p. 178.
60 *FT*, 10 December 1998, p. 8.
61 Sandler, O'Freeman & Telhami, "The Religious-Secular Divide," p. 143.
62 *NYT*, 26 November 1997, p. 26.
63 *NYT*, 17 November 1997, p. 1.
64 Horowitz, "Cinematic Triangulation of Jewish American Identity," p. 386.
65 Ira Stoll, "Conversion Crisis Will Cause $100 Million Drop in American Giving to Israel, Reform Leaders Warn," *Forward*, 8 January 1999.
66 Author's interview with Lewis Roth, Assistant Executive Director, Americans for Peace Now, Washington, D.C.
67 Irving Kristol, "Why Religion is Good for the Jews," *Commentary*, vol. 98, no. 2, August 1994, p. 19.
68 Seymour Lipset & Earl Raab, *Jews and the New American Scene* (Cambridge, MA & London: Harvard University Press, 1995), p. 206.
69 David Shribman, "Hosts not Visitors: The future of Jews in American political life," in L. Sandy Maisel (ed.), *Jews in American Politics* (Lanham, Boulder, New York, Oxford: Rowman & Littlefield Publishers, 2001), p. 276.
70 *NYT*, 16 November 1998, p. 8.
71 There is a feeling in some circles that funds raised by American Jews should not be sent to Israel but used in the US to retard the process of assimilation and "Jewish disappearance." Author's interview with Ira Sharkansky, political scientist, Hebrew University of Jerusalem.

72 *Jerusalem Report*, 1 March 1999, p. 32, cited in Sandler, O'Freeman & Telhami, "The Religious–Secular Divide," p. 143.

73 *NYT*, 16 November 1997, p. 8.

74 *JP*, 7 November 2000.

75 Shribman, "Hosts not Visitors," p. 276.

76 *Ibid.* p. 208.

77 *NYT*, 16 November 1997, p. 8.

78 Lipset & Rabb, *Jews and the New American Scene*, p. 206.

79 *NYT*, 21 January 1998, p. 6 and *Chicago Tribune*, 21 January 1998, p. 9.

80 *Mideast Mirror*, 20 January 1998, vol. 12, no. 12, p. 18.

81 Reagan's appeal to the fundamentalists appeared to translate into votes with 22 million Christian fundamentalists and evangelists shifting from a pro-Democratic 56–43% margin in 1976 to an 81–19% Republican sweep in 1984. See Albert J. Menendez, *Evangelicals at the Ballot Box* (New York: Prometheus Books, 1996), pp. 135–183 for a detailed account of changes in religious voting patterns between 1980 and 1994.

82 Stephen Bates, *Battleground* (New York: Poseidon Press, 1993), p. 301.

83 Menendez, *Evangelicals at the Ballot Box*, p. 177.

84 Quoted in *ibid.*, p. 183.

85 Both neo-conservatives and Christian fundamentalists hold senior positions within the George W. Bush administration. John Ashcroft, the Attorney General is a Christian fundamentalist and Paul Wolfowitz, the Deputy Secretary of Defence is a neo-conservative. Alain Frachon & Daniel Vernet, "The Strategist and the Philosopher," *CounterPunch*, 2 June 2003.

86 Author's interview with George R. Salem, member of the Palestinian negotiating team at the Madrid talks 1991–93.

87 Robert Fisk "A strange kind of freedom," *The Independent*, 9 July 2002.

88 Scott Lucas, *Freedom's War: The US crusade against the Soviet Union, 1945–56* (Manchester: Manchester University Press, 1999), p. 283.

89 President Bush's Speech to Congress, *PPP*, 6 March 1991.

90 Noam Chomsky, *World Orders Old and New* (New York: Columbia University Press, 1996), pp. 12–13. The US vetoed two Security Council Resolutions condemning its aggression, along with the General Assembly resolution that denounced the invasion as a violation of international law and of the independence, sovereignty and territorial integrity of states.

91 David Ryan, *US Foreign Policy in World History* (London & New York: Routledge, 2000), p. 186.

92 Avi Shlaim, *War and Peace in the Middle East* (New York: Penguin Books, 1995), p. 135.

93 Ryan, *US Foreign Policy in World History*, p. 186.

94 Shlaim, *War and Peace*, p. 135.

95 Ryan, *US Foreign Policy in World History*, p. 187.

96 Shlaim, *War and Peace*, p. 135.

97 Bush's address at <http://odur.let.rug.nl/~usa/P/gb41/speeches/su90ghwb.htm>.

98 Clinton address at <http://www.usis.usemb.se/speeches/stateoft.html>. quoted in Lucas, *Freedom's War*, p. 283.

99 David Ryan, "Asserting US Power" in Philip Davies (ed.), *An American Quarter*

Century: US politics from Vietnam to Clinton (Manchester: Manchester University Press, 1995), pp. 120–1.

100 Transcript of President Bush's first State of the Union address, delivered to Congress on 29 January 2002. <www.whitehouse.gov/news/ releases/2002/01/20020129–11.html>.

101 Byron Shafer, "Introduction," in Byron Shafer (ed.), *Is America Different?* (Oxford: Oxford University Press, 1991), p. v.

102 <www.whitehouse.gov/news/releases/2002/01/20020129–11.html>.

103 *The Economist*, 26 May 2001, p. 11.

104 *Middle East International*, 9 March 2001, p. 3

105 *The Economist*, 22 September 2001, p. 61.

106 *IHT*, 4 February 2002, p. 5.

107 Author's interview with Lewis Roth.

108 Author's interview with William Quandt, National Security Council aide, Nixon and Carter administrations.

109 Professor Makiya, Brandeis University, speaking on *Newsnight*, BBC 1, 4 April 2002.

110 Fawaz Turki, quoted in *IHT*, 4 February 2002, p. 5.

Conclusions

1 See Alex Danchev, *On Specialness: Essays in Anglo-American relations* (New York: St. Martin's Press, 1998), p. 7.

BIBLIOGRAPHY

Primary Sources

American Officials

Marshall Breger: special assistant to President Reagan and his liaison to the Jewish Community, 1982–84.

Samuel W. Lewis: U.S. Ambassador to Israel 1977–85, Chief State Department Policy Planning / Assistant Secretary of State, Policy Planning 1992–95.

John Lehman: Secretary of the US Navy 1981–87.

Richard Murphy: U.S. Ambassador to Syria 1974–78, to Saudi Arabia 1981–83 and Assistant Secretary of State for Near Eastern and South Asian Affairs 1983–89.

Wayne Owens: Congressman for Utah 1972–74 and member of the Foreign Affairs Committee, Vice Chairman of the Centre for Middle East Peace and Economic Cooperation 1993–95, President of the Centre 1995–present.

William Quandt: National Security Council aide, Nixon and Carter administrations.

Peter W. Rodman: Member of the National Security Council staff and a special assistant to Henry Kissinger 1969–1977. Participant in nearly all of Kissinger's negotiations and missions 1972–1977. Principal research and editorial assistant to Kissinger in the preparation of his memoirs.

Dennis Ross: Director of State Department Planning Policy 1988–92 and Special Middle East Co-ordinator 1992–2000.

James Schlesinger: Director of the Central Intelligence Agency, February–May 1973 and Secretary of Defence 1973–1975.

American Jewish Community

Geoffrey Aronson: Director for Research and Publications, Foundation for Middle East Peace.

Gene Burger: Member of the Israeli Policy Forum, 1995–present.

Norman Podhoretz: Senior Fellow, Hudson Institute and former editor-in-chief of *Commentary*, 1960–95.

Lewis Roth: Assistant Executive Director, Americans for Peace Now.

American Arab Community

Khalil Jahshan: Executive Vice-President, American–Arab Anti-Discrimination Committee.

George R. Salem: member of the Palestinian negotiating team at Madrid talks 1991–93.

Other Americans

James M. Ennes, Jr.: crew member, USS *Liberty*.

Israeli Officials

David Bar-Ilan: Israeli Director of Communications & Policy Planning, 1996–1999.

Israeli Academics

Ira Sharkansky: political scientist, The Hebrew University of Jerusalem.

Government Documents

Congressional Hearings.
Congressional Record.
Department of State Bulletin (Washington, D.C.).
Department of State Despatch (Washington, D.C.).
Israel. Ministry of Foreign Affairs. "Egypt and the Suez Canal, 1948–56," Jerusalem, 1956.
Israel. Ministry of Foreign Affairs. "Egypt's Unlawful Blockade of the Gulf of Aqaba," Jerusalem, 1967.
Israel. Ministry of Foreign Affairs. "Message from Prime Minister Eshkol to King Hussein of Jordan," Jerusalem, 5 June 1967.
Israel. Ministry of Foreign Affairs. "Statement to the Knesset by Prime Minister Eshkol," Jerusalem, 27 June 1967.
Israel. Ministry of Foreign Affairs. "Soviet involvement in the War of Attrition," Government Statement. Jerusalem, 29 April 1970.
Israel. Ministry of Foreign Affairs. Statement to the Knesset by Prime Minister Meir. Jerusalem, 26 July 1972.
Israel. Ministry of Foreign Affairs. "The War of Attrition," Defence Minister Dayan statement to the Knesset. Jerusalem, 13 August 1970.
Israel. Ministry of Foreign Affairs. "The Yom Kippur War and Aftermath," Statement to the Knesset by Prime Minister Golda Meir. Jerusalem, 13 November 1973.
Israel. Ministry of Foreign Affairs, "Statement to the Knesset by Prime Minister Begin," Jerusalem, 8 June 1982.
Israel. Ministry of Foreign Affairs, "Prime Minister Begin's speech to the Knesset on the Reagan Plan," Jerusalem, 8 September 1982.
Israel: Ministry of Foreign Affairs. "Address by Israeli Prime Minister," Yitzhak Shamir, Jerusalem, 31 October 1991.
Lyndon Baines Johnson Oral History Interviews (Austin, Texas).
National Security Agency, US Cryptological History Report, "Attack on a Sigint Collector, the USS *Liberty*," 1981.
National Security Agency, "Aftermath of Israeli Attack on USS *Liberty*," 22 June 1967.
National Security Files "Talking Points for Prime Minister Eshkol," memorandum for the president, 5 January 1968 (Washington) 1963–69.
Public Papers of the Presidents: Lyndon Johnson, 1963–64 (Washington, 1965);

Lyndon Johnson, 1967 (Washington, 1968); Richard Nixon, 1969 (Washington, 1971); Richard Nixon, 1970 (Washington, 1972); Ronald Reagan, 1981 (Washington, 1982); Ronald Reagan, 1982 (Washington, 1983); Ronald Reagan, 1985 (Washington, 1986); George Bush, 1990 (Washington, 1992); George Bush, 1991 (Washington, 1993).

United States: *Weekly Compilation of Presidential Documents* (Washington, D. C.).

United States. Department of State. Joint US-USSR Working Paper, Fundamental Principles (The Rogers Plan), October 28, 1969.

United States. Department of State. *Foreign Relations of the United States, 1943* Washington, D.C. 1965; *FRUS, 1945* Vol. VII, Washington, D.C. 1965; *FRUS, 1945* Vol. VII, Washington, D.C. 1965; *FRUS, 1946* Vol. VIII, Washington, D.C. 1965; *FRUS, 1947* Vol. V. Washington, D.C. 1972; *FRUS, 1948* Vol. V. Washington, D.C. 1972.

United States. Congress: House Committee on Foreign Affairs. "The Impact of the October 1973 War," Washington, D.C., 1974.

United States. House of Representatives. Committee on Foreign Affairs. "The Multinational Force and Observers (MFO) for the Sinai." Washington, D.C., 1982.

United States. Hearings, House Committee on Foreign Relations. "Nomination of George P. Shultz." Washington, 1982.

United States. "US Assistance to the State of Israel," *Report of the Comptroller General of the United States,* Washington 1983.

United States. "US Assistance to Israel," *General Accounting Office,* 24 June 1983.

United States. The Washington Institute Presidential Study Group, "Building for Peace: An American Strategy for the Middle East" (Washington: The Washington Institute for Near East Policy, 1988).

Secondary Sources

Articles

Allen, H.C. "A Special Relationship?" *Journal of American Studies* 19 (1985).

Art, Robert J. "Bureaucratic Politics & American Foreign Policy: A Critique" *Political Sciences* 4 (1973).

Boniface, Pascal. "Reflections on America as a World Power," *Journal of Palestine Studies, 115,* vol. XXIX, no. 3 (Spring 2000).

Christison, Kathleen. "Splitting the Difference: The Palestinian–Israeli Policy of James Baker," *Journal of Palestine Studies,* vol. XXIV, no. 1 (Autumn 1994).

Cline, Ray S. "Policy without Intelligence," *Foreign Policy,* no. 17 (Winter 1974–75).

Clifford, Clark. "Annals of Government: Serving the President in the Truman Years," *New Yorker* 25 (March 1991).

Cordesman, Anthony. "The Middle East and the Cost of the Politics of Force," *Middle East Journal* (Winter 1986)

Fein, Leonard. "Right in the First Place," *Moment* 1 (September 1975).

Frank, Charles & Mary Baird, "Foreign Aid: Its Speckled Past and Future Prospects," *International Organisation* 29 (Winter 1975).

Freedman, Robert O. "Religion, Politics, and the Israeli Elections of 1988," *Middle East Journal* (Winter 1989).

Gorman, Tom. "Worthy and Unworthy Victims: Munich Matters, Sabra and Shatila Don't," *CounterPunch*, 21 September 2002.
Grimmett, Richard. "Conventional Arms Transfers to the Third World, 1983–1990," *Congressional Research Service* (Washington, 2 August 1991).
Hadar, Leon T. "Clinton's Tilt," *Journal of Palestine Studies*, vol. XXII, no. 4 (Summer 1993).
Hadar, Leon T. "The Friends of Bibi (FOB's) vs. The New Middle East," *Journal of Palestine Studies*, vol. XXVI, no. 1 (Autumn 1996).
Halliday, Fred. "The Reagan Administration and the Middle East," *Atlantic Quarterly* , 2:3 (Autumn 1984).
Hays, Sharon. "Structure and Agency and the Sticky Problem of Culture," *Sociological Theory*, vol. 12, no. 1 (March 1994).
Helmreich, Jeffrey. "The Israel Swing Factor: How the American Jewish Vote Influences US Elections," *Jerusalem Centre for Public Affairs*, no. 446, 20 Tevet 5761 / 15 January 2001.
Hilsman, Roger. "The Foreign-Policy Consensus: An Interim Report." *Journal of Conflict Resolution*, vol. 3 (December 1959).
Hudson, Michael C. "To Play the Hegemon: Fifty Years of US Policy towards the Middle East," *Middle East Journal*, vol. 50, no. 3 (Summer 1996).
Inbar, E. "Rabin and Israeli National Security," *BESA Security and Policy Study*, no. 25, 1996.
Kenen, I. L. "Twisted Comparison Cheapens Memory of Holocaust," *Near East Report* 22, 3 May 1978.
Khalidi, Walid. "The Ownership of the U.S. Embassy Site in Jerusalem," *Journal of Palestine Studies*, 116, vol. XXIX, no. 4 (Summer 2000).
Kramer, Martin. "Islam vs. Democracy," *Commentary*, vol. 95, no. 1 (January 1993).
Kristol, Irving. "Why Religion is Good for the Jews," *Commentary*, vol. 98, no. 2, August 1994.
Lewis, Samuel. W. "The United States and Israel: Evolution of an Unwritten Alliance," *Middle East Journal*, vol. 53, no. 3 (Summer 1999).
Luttwak, Edward N. "The Defence Budget and Israel," *Commentary*, (February 1975).
Luttwak, Edward N. "Strategic Aspects of U.S.-Israeli Relations," *Israel Affairs*, vol. 2, no. 3&4 (Spring/Summer 1996).
Muravchik, Joshua. "Misreporting Lebanon," *Policy Review* (Winter 1983).
Neff, Donald. "The Clinton Administration and UN Resolution 242," *Journal of Palestine Studies*, vol. XXIII, no. 2 (Winter 1994).
Parker, Richard B. "The June War: Whose Conspiracy?" *Journal of Palestine Studies*, vol. XXI, no. 4 (Summer 1992).
Quandt, William B. "Reagan's Lebanon Policy: Trial and Error," *Middle East Journal*, vol. 38 (Spring 1984).
Sandler, Shmuel. "Israel's 1988 Knesset Elections and the Transformation of the Israeli Polity," *Middle East Review*, no. 1, 1989–90.
Schiff, Ze'ev. "The Green Light," *Foreign Policy*, vol. 50 (Spring 1983).
Shribman, David. "Hosts not Visitors: The Future of Jews in American Political Life," in Maisel, L. Sandy. (ed.), *Jews in American Politics* (Lanham, Boulder, New York,

Solomon, Burt. "Bush's Lack of Ambitious Policies . . . Makes His Plans Seem Thin Gruel," *National Journal*, no. 18, 6 May 1989.

Stern, Geoffrey. "Moral Judgments and Political Prejudice," *Contemporary Review*, May 1975.

Stock, Raymond. "Prestige Press at War," *Middle East Journal* (Summer 1985).

Stoll, Ira. "Conversion Crisis Will Cause $100 Million Drop in American Giving to Israel, Reform Leaders Warn," *Forward*, 8 January 1999.

Telhami, Shibley. "From Camp David to Wye: Changing Assumptions in Arab–Israeli Negotiations," *Middle East Journal*, vol. 53, no. 3 (Summer 1999).

Thorne, Christopher. "American Political Culture and the End of the Cold War," *Journal of American Studies*, vol. 26 (1992).

Wald, Kenneth D., James L. Guth, Cleveland R. Fraser, John C. Green, Corwin E. Smidt, & Lyman A. Kellstedt, "Reclaiming Zion: How American Religious Groups View the Middle East," *Israel Affairs*, vol. 2, no. 3 & 4 (Spring/Summer 1996).

Ze'ev Schiff, "Israel after the [Gulf] War," *Foreign Affairs*, February 1991.

Books

Ahmed, Nafeez. *Behind the War on Terror: Western Secret Strategy and the Struggle for Iraq* (East Sussex: Clairview, 2003).

Allison, Graham. *Essence of Decisions* (New York: Little, Brown & Co., 1999).

Almond, Gabriel & Powell, Bingham. *Comparative Politics Today*, 6th ed. (New York: HarperCollins, 1996).

Apter, D. E. (ed.), *Ideology and Discontent* (London & New York: The Free Press, 1964).

Arens, Moshe. *Broken Covenant: American Foreign Policy and the Crisis between the U.S. and Israel* (New York: Simon & Schuster, 1995).

Arian, Asher, Ilan Talmud & Tamar Hermann. *National Security and Public Opinion in Israel* (Boulder, CO: Westview, 1988).

Axelrod, Robert. *Structure of Decision: The Cognitive Maps of Political Elites* (Princeton, New Jersey: Princeton University Press, 1976).

Badeau, John S. *The American Approach to the Arab World* (New York: HarperCollins, 1968).

Bailey, Sydney D. *The Making of Resolution 242* (Dordrecht, Boston & Lancaster: Martinus Nijhoff Publishers, 1985).

Baker, J. *Politics and Diplomacy* (New York: Putnam Publishing, 1995).

Baldwin, David. *Foreign Aid and American Foreign Policy: A Documentary Analysis* (New York, Washington & London: Frederick A. Praeger, 1966).

Ball, George W. *Error and Betrayal in Lebanon: An Analysis of Israel's Invasion of Lebanon and the Implications for US–Israeli Relations* (Washington, D.C.: Foundation for Middle East Peace, 1984).

Bar-Zohar, Michael. *Embassies in Crisis: Diplomats and Demagogues Behind the Six Day War* (Englewood Cliffs, NJ: Prentice-Hall, 1970).

Bard, Michael. "Ethnic Group Influence on Middle East Policy," in Mohammed Ahrari (ed.), *Ethnic Group Influence and U.S. Foreign Policy* (Westport: Greenwood, 1987).

Barnes, James F., Marshall Carter, & Max J. Skidmore. *The World of Politics: A Concise Introduction*, 2nd ed. (New York: St. Martin's Press, 1984).

Barrett, Laurence I. *Gambling with History: Ronald Reagan in the White House* (Garden City, New York: Doubleday & Co., Inc., 1983).

Bartlett, Christopher. *'The Special Relationship': A Political History of Anglo-American Relations since 1945* (London & New York: Longman, 1992).

Baritz, Loren. *Backfire: A History of How American Culture Led us into Vietnam and Made us Fight the Way We Did* (Baltimore & London: Johns Hopkins University Press, 1998).

Beilin, Yossi. *Israel: A Concise Political History* (London: Weidenfeld & Nicolson, 1992).

Bell, Coral. *A Study in Diplomatic Management* (Oxford: Oxford University Press, 1971).

Bell, Daniel. "The Hegelian Secret: Civil Society and American Exceptionalism" in Byron Shafer (ed.), *Is America Different?* (Oxford: Oxford University Press, 1991).

Bellah, Robert. *Beyond Belief: Essays on Religion in a Post-Traditional World* (Berkeley & Oxford: University of California Press,1970).

Bellah, Robert. *The Broken Covenant: American Civil Religion in Time of Trial* (New York: Seabury Press, 1975).

Bellah, Robert, R. Madsen, W. Sullivan, A. Swidler S. Tipton. *The Good Society* (Alfred A. Knopf: New York, 1991).

Bentsur, Eytan. *Making Peace in the Middle East: A First-Hand Account of the Arab–Israeli Peace Process* (Westport, CT & London: Praeger, 2001).

Ben-Zvi, Abraham. *The United States and Israel* (New York: Columbia University Press, 1993).

Bichler, Simson. "Between Capitalism and Jewish Voters: Electoral Economics in Israel, 1977 to 1997" in J. W. Wright, Jr. (ed.), *Structural Flaws in the Middle East Peace Process* (Hampshire & New York: Palgrave, 2001).

Bishop, Jim. *FDR's Last Year* (New York: William Morrow Co. Inc., 1974).

Blitzer, Wolf. *Between Washington and Jerusalem: A Reporter's Notebook* (New York & Oxford: Oxford University Press, 1985).

Bloom, William. *Personal Identity, National Identity and International Relations* (Cambridge: Cambridge University Press, 1990).

Boggs, Carl. *The Two Revolutions: Gramsci and the Dilemmas of Western Marxism* (Boston, Massachusetts: South End Press, 1984)

Boorstin, Daniel. *The Image, or What Happened to the American Dream* (London: Weidenfeld & Nicolson, 1961).

Boulding, Kenneth. *The Image* (Ann Arbor: Michigan University Press, 1956).

Brands, H. W. *The Wages of Globalism: Lyndon Johnson and the Limits of American Power* (New York & Oxford: Oxford University Press, 1995).

Braudel, Fernand. *The Identity of France, Vol. 1: History & Environment* (London: Collins, 1988).

Brecher, Michael. *Decisions in Israel's Foreign Policy* (London: Oxford University Press, 1974).

Brecher, Michael with Benjamin Geist. *Decisions in Crisis: Israel, 1967 and 1973* (Berkeley: University of California Press, 1980).

Brenner, Lenni. *Jews in America Today* (London: Al Saqi Books, 1986).

Brint, Michael. *A Genealogy of Political Culture* (Boulder, CO: Westview Press, 1991).

Bromley, David & Anson Shape (ed.), *New Christian Politics* (Macon, GA: Mercer University Press, 1984).

Brown, Seyom. *The Faces of Power: United States Foreign Policy from Truman to Clinton* (New York: Columbia University Press, 1994).

Bundy, William. *A Tangled Web: The Making of Foreign Policy in the Nixon Presidency* (London & New York: I. B. Tauris, 1998).

Burr, William (ed.), *The Kissinger Transcripts* (New York: The New York Press, 1998).

Bush, George with Gold, Victor. *Looking Forward* (London: The Bodley Head, 1988).

Califano, Jr., Joseph A. *The Triumph & Tragedy of Lyndon Johnson* (New York: Simon & Schuster, 1991).

Cannon, Lou. *President Reagan: The Role of a Lifetime* (New York: Simon & Schuster, 1991).

Lord Carandon et al. *U.N. Security Council Resolution 242: A Case Study in Diplomatic Ambiguity* (Washington D.C., 1981).

Carl Boggs, *The Two Revolutions: Gramsci and the Dilemmas of Western Marxism* (Boston, Massachusetts: South End Press, 1984).

Carrere D'Encausee, Helene. *Lenin: Revolution and Power* (London & New York: Longman, 1982).

Child, Irvin. "Socialisation" in Lindzey Gardner (ed.), *Handbook of Social Psychology*, vol. II (Boston: McGraw-Hill & New York: Oxford University Press, 1954).

Chomsky, Noam. "The Old and the New Cold War" in James Peck (ed.), *The Chomsky Reader* (New York: Pantheon Books, 1987).

Chomsky, Noam. *World Orders Old and New* (New York: Columbia University Press, 1996).

Churchill, Randolph S. & Winston S. Churchill. *The Six Day War* (London: Heinemann,1967).

Clifford, Clark with Richard Holbrooke. *Counsel to the President: A Memoir* (New York: Random House, 1991).

Cobban, Helena. *The Superpowers and the Syrian–Israeli Conflict: Beyond Crisis Management?* (New York: Praeger, 1991).

Cohen, Avner. *Israel and the Bomb* (New York: Columbia University Press, 1998).

Coker, Christopher. *Reflections on American Foreign Policy Since 1945* (London: Pinter, 1989).

Crabb, Jr. Cecil V. *American Foreign Policy in the Nuclear Age* (New York: Harper & Row, 1960).

Crabb, Jr., Cecil V., Glenn J. Antizzo & Leila E. Sarieddine. *Congress and the Foreign Policy Process: Modes of Legislative Behaviour* (Louisiana: Louisiana State University Press, 2000).

Cristol, A. Jay. *The Liberty Incident* (Washington, D.C.: Brassey's Inc., 2002).

Cruikshank, B. "Cultural Politics: Political Theory and the Foundations of Democratic Order" in Jodi Dean (ed.), *Cultural Studies and Political Theory* (Ithaca & London: Cornell University Press, 2000).

Danchev, Alex. *On Specialness: Essays in Anglo-American Relations* (New York: St. Martin's Press, 1998).

Davis, Moshe (ed.), *With Eyes Towards Zion* (New York: Arno Press, 1977).

Dawisha, Karen. *The Foundations, Structure and Dynamics of Soviet Policy towards the Arab Radical Regimes* (Ph.D. thesis: LSE, 1978).

Dayan, Moshe. *Dairy of the Sinai Campaign* (London: Weidenfeld & Nicolson, 1966).
Dayan, Moshe. *Story of My Life* (London: Sphere Books Ltd., 1977).
Deaver, Michael K. *Behind the Scenes* (New York: William Morrow, 1987).
Dickey, John Sloan. *Canada and the American Presence* (New York: New York University Press, 1975).
Dickinson. *Kissinger and the Meaning of History* (Cambridge: Cambridge University Press, 1978).
Divine, Robert A. (ed.), *The Johnson Years: Vol. 3* (Lawrence, Kansas: University Press of Kansas, 1994).
Dobryin, Anatoly. *In Confidence: Moscow's Ambassador to America's Six Cold War Presidents* (New York: Random House, 1995).
Donelan, Michael. "The Ideas of American Foreign Policy" in F. S. Northedge (ed.), *Foreign Policies of the Powers* (London: Faber & Faber, 1968).
Donelan, Michael. "The Elements of United States Policy" in F. S. Northedge (ed.), *Foreign Policies of the Powers* (London: Faber & Faber, 1974).
Doneson, Judith. T*he Holocaust in American Film* (Syracuse: Syracuse University Press, 2002).
Draper, Theodore. *Israel and World Politics: Roots of the Third Arab–Israeli War* (New York: Viking Press, 1968).
Dumbrell, John. *A Special Relationship: Anglo-American Relations in the Cold War and After* (London: MacMillan, 2001).
Durke, John. *The Institutional President* (Maryland: Johns Hopkins University Press, 1992).
Eban, Abba. *An Autobiography* (New York: Random House, 1977).
Eban, Abba. *Personal Witness: Israel Through My Eyes* (London: Jonathan Cape, 1993).
Elazar, Daniel J. *American Federalism: A View from the States* (New York: Thomas Y. Crowell Co., 1966).
Elazar, Daniel J. *The American Mosaic: The Impact of Space, Time, & Culture on American Politics (*Boulder, San Francisco, Oxford: Westview Press, 1994).
Ennes, Jr., James M. *Assault on the Liberty: The True Story of the Israeli Attack on an American Intelligence Ship* (New York: Randon House, 1979).
Eveland, Wilbur Crane. *Ropes of Sand* (New York: W. W. Norton & Co. Inc., 1980).
Eversen, Bruce. *Truman, Palestine and the Press: Shaping Conventional Wisdom at the Beginning of the Cold War* (New York, Connecticut & London: Greenwood Press, 1992).
Eytan, Walter. *First Ten Years: A Diplomatic History of Israel* (New York: Simon & Schuster, 1958).
Feingold, Henry L. *Politics of Rescue: The Roosevelt Administration and the Holocaust,1938–1945* (New Brunswick, New Jersey: Rutgers University Press, 1970).
Fink, Reuben. *America and Palestine* (New York: Herald Square Press, Inc., 1945).
Finkelstein, Norman. *Image and Reality of the Israel–Palestine Conflict* (New York: 1995)
Finkelstein, Norman. *The Holocaust Industry: Reflections of the Exploitation of Jewish Suffering* (London & New York: Verso, 2000).
Fischer, Beth A. *The Reagan Reversal: Foreign Policy at the End of the Cold War* (Columbia & London: University of Missouri Press, 1997).

Flanzbaum, Hilene (ed.), *The Americanisation of the Holocaust* (Baltimore & London: The Johns Hopkins University Press, 1999).
Frankel, Glenn. *Beyond the Promised Land Jews and Arabs on the Hard Road to a New Israel* (New York: Simon & Schuster, 1994).
Frankel, Joseph. *National Interest* (London: Pall Mall Press Ltd., 1970).
Frankel, Joseph. *The Making of Foreign Policy* (London: Oxford University Press, 1963).
Friedrich, Carl J. *Man and His Government* (New York: McGraw-Hill, 1963).
Fukuyama, Francis, *The End of History and the Last Man* (London: Hamish Hamilton, 1992).
Gallup, George H. *The Gallup Poll: Public Opinion, 1972–77*, vol. 4 (Wilmington Scholarly Resources, 1978), 4–7 April 1975.
Ganin, Zvi. *Truman, American Jewry and Israel, 1945–1948* (London & New York: Holmes & Meier Publishers Inc., 1979).
Garrison, Jean A. *Games Advisors Play: Foreign Policy in the Nixon and Carter Administrations* (Texas: Texas A&M University, 1999).
Geertz, Clifford. *The Interpretation of Cultures* (New York: Basic Books, 1973).
Gerges, Fawaz A. *American and Political Islam: Clash of Cultures or Clash of Interests?* (New York: Cambridge University Press, 1999).
Gerth, H. H. & C. Wright Mills. *From Max Weber: Essays in Sociology* (London: Routledge & Kegan Paul, 1948).
Geyelin, Philip. *Lyndon B. Johnson and the World* (New York, Washington & London: Praeger, 1966).
Gibbens, John. "Contemporary Political Culture: An Introduction" in J. Gibbens (ed.), *Contemporary Political Culture: Politics in a Post-Modern Age* (London: Sage, 1989).
Gilboa, Etyan. *American Public Opinion Towards Israel and the Arab–Israeli Conflict* (Lexington: Lexington Books, 1987).
Glazer, Nathan. *Ethnic Dilemmas, 1964–82* (Cambridge, MA: Harvard University Press, 1983).
Glick, Edward. *The Triangular Confrontation: America, Israel and American Jews* (London, Boston & Sydney: George, Allen & Unwin, 1982).
Golan, Matti. *The Secret Conversations of Henry Kissinger: Step-by-Step Diplomacy in the Middle East (*New York: Quadrangle Books, 1976).
Goldberg, Jonathan J. *Jewish Power: Inside the American Jewish Establishment (*Reading Massachusetts: Addison Wesley, 1996).
Goldman, *The Tragedy of Lyndon Johnson* (New York: Knopf, 1969).
Goldstein, Judith & Robert Keohane (eds.), *Ideas, Beliefs, Institutions, Political Change and Foreign Policy* (Ithaca: Cornell University Press, 1993).
Gomolak, Louis. *Prologue: LBJ's Foreign Affairs Background, 1908–48* (Ph.D. thesis: University of Texas, Austin, 1981).
Gordon, Kermit (ed.), *Agenda for the Nation* (New York: Doubleday, 1969).
Gowers, Andrew and Walker, Tony. *Behind the Myth* (London: W. H. Allen, 1990).
Grose, Peter. *Israel in the Mind of America* (New York: Alfred A. Knopf, 1983).
Haig, Alexander. *Caveat: Realism, Reagan, and Foreign Policy* (New York: Macmillan Publishing Company, 1984).
Halliday, Fred. *Two Hours that Shook the World* (London: Saqi Books, 2002).

Halperin, Morton H. *Bureaucratic Politics and Foreign Policy* (Washington, D.C.: The Brookings Institution, 1974).

Halsell, Grace. *Prophecy and Politics: Militant Evangelists on the Road to Nuclear War* (Westport, Connecticut: Lawrence Hill & Co., 1986).

Hamilton, Michael P. (ed.), *American Character and Foreign Policy* (Michigan: William B. Eerdmans Publishing Co., 1986).

Hammond, Paul Y. *LBJ and the Presidential Management of Foreign Relations* (Austin: University of Texas Press, 1992).

Handel, Michael. The Diplomacy of Surprise, Hitler, Nixon, Sadat (Cambridge, MA: Center for International Affairs, Harvard University, 1981).

Hartz, Louis. *The Liberal Tradition in America* (New York: Harecourt Brace & World: 1955).

Hastedt, Glenn P. (ed.), *American Foreign Policy: Past, Present, Future* (Englewood Cliffs: Prentice-Hall, 1997).

Heikal, Mohamed. *Nasser: The Cairo Documents* (London: New English Library, 1972).

Heikal, Mohamed. *The Road to Ramadan* (London: Collins, 1975).

Heller, Joseph. *The Birth of Israel, 1945–49* (Florida: Florida University Press, 2000).

Hersh, Seymour. *The Price of Power: Kissinger in the Nixon White House* (New York: Summit Books, 1983).

Hersh, Seymour. *The Samson Option: Israel's Nuclear Arsenal and American Foreign Policy* (New York: Random House, 1991).

Hessing Cahn, Anne. "United States Arms to the Middle East, 1967–1976," in M. Leitenberg & G. Sheffer (eds.), *Great Power Intervention in the Middle East* (New York: Pergamon, 1979).

Hiro, Dilip. *Desert Shield to Desert Storm* (London: Paladin, 1992)

Hobsbawm, Eric. "Introduction: Inventing Traditions," in Hobsbawm, E. & Ranger, T. (eds), *The Invention of Tradition* (Cambridge: Cambridge University Press, 1983).

Hoff, Joan. *Nixon Reconsidered* (New York: Basic Books, 1994).

Hogan, Joseph (ed.), *The Reagan Years: The Record in Presidential Leadership* (Manchester & New York: Manchester University Press, 1990).

Holsti, Ole R. & James N. Rosenau, *American Leadership in World Affairs: Vietnam and the Breakdown of Consensus* (Boston: Allen & Unwin, 1984).

Hook, Steven W. *National Interest and Foreign Aid* (Boulder, CO & London: Lynne Rienner Publishers, 1995).

Horowitz, Sara R. "Cinematic Triangulation of Jewish American Identity" in Flanzbaum, Hilene (ed.), *The Americanisation of the Holocaust* (Baltimore & London: The Johns Hopkins University Press, 1999).

Hunt, Michael H. *Ideology and U.S. Foreign Policy* (New Haven, CT: Yale University Press, 1987).

Hunter, F. Robert. *The Palestinian Uprising: A War by Other Means* (Berkeley, Los Angeles: University of California Press, 1993).

Huntington, Samuel. *American Politics in the United States* (New York: St. Martin's Press, 1987).

Huntington, Samuel. *The Common Defence: Strategic Programmes in National Politics* (New York & London: Columbia University Press, 1961).

Hyman, Meryl. *Who is a Jew? Conversion, Not Conclusion* (Woodstock, VT: Jewish Light Publishing, 1998).
Insdorf, Annette. *Indelible Shadows: Film and the Holocaust* (Cambridge: Cambridge University Press, 2003).
Isaacs, Stephen D. *Jews and American Politics* (New York: Doubleday, 1974).
Isaacson, Walter. *Kissinger: A Biography* (London & Boston: Faber & Faber, 1992).
Jawad, Haifaa A. (ed.), 2nd ed., *The Middle East in the New World Order* (Macmillan Press Ltd., 1997).
Jenks, Chris. *Culture* (London & New York: Routledge, 1993).
Jervis, Robert. *Perception and Misperception in World Politics* (Princeton, New Jersey: Princeton University Press, 1976).
Johnson, Lyndon Baines. *The Vantage Point: Perspectives of the Presidency, 1963–1969* (New York: Holt, Rinehart & Winston, 1971).
Jorstad, Erling. *The New Christian Right, 1981–1988: Prospects for the Reagan Decade* (Lewinston, Queenston: Edwin Mellen Press, 1987).
Kalb, Marvin & Bernard Kalb. *Kissinger* (London: Hutchinson, 1974).
Kattenburg, P. M. *The Vietnam Trauma in American Foreign Policy, 1945–75* (New Brunswick: Transaction Books, 1980).
Kellerman, Barbara & Ryan J. Barilleaux. *The President as World Leader* (New York: St. Martin's Press, 1991).
Kennedy, Paul. *The Rise and Fall of the Great Powers: Economic Change and Military Conflict from 1500 to 2000* (London: Fontana, 1989).
Kennan, George F. *American Diplomacy, 1900–1950* (Chicago: Chicago University Press, 1953).
Kennan, George F. *Realities of American Foreign Policy* (London: Oxford University Press, 1954).
Kent, George. "Congress and American Middle East Policy" in William A. Beling (ed.), *The Middle East: Quest for an American Policy* (Albany: State University of New York Press, 1973).
Kimball, Warren F. (ed.), *Churchill & Roosevelt: The Complete Correspondence* Vol. 3 (Princeton, New Jersey: Princeton University Press, 1984).
Kimball, Warren F. *The Most Unsordid Act: Lend-Lease, 1939–1941* (Baltimore: Johns Hopkins Press, 1969).
Kissinger, Henry A. "Central Issues of American Foreign Policy" in Kermit Gordon (ed.), *Agenda for the Nation* (New York: Doubleday, 1969).
Kissinger, Henry A. *White House Years* (Boston: Little, Brown, 1979).
Kissinger, Henry A. *Years of Upheaval* (London: Weidenfeld & Nicolson & Michael Joseph, 1982).
Korn, David A. *Stalemate: The War of Attrition and Great Power Diplomacy in the Middle East, 1967–1970* (Boulder, CO: Westview Press, 1992).
Langer, Lawrence. *Versions of Survival* (Albany: State University of New York Press, 1982).
Laqueur, Walter. *Confrontation: The Middle East and World Politics* (New York: Quadrangle, 1974).
Larson, D. L. *The Puritan Ethic in United States Foreign Policy* (New York: D. van Nostrand Co. Ltd., 1966).

Larson, Deborah Welch. *Origins of Containment: A Psychological Explanation* (Princeton, New Jersey: Princeton University Press, 1985).

Laufer, L. Y. "U.S. Aid to Israel: Problems and Perceptions," in Gabriel Sheffer (ed.), *Dynamics of Dependence: U.S.–Israeli Relations* (Boulder, CO & London: Westview Press, 1987).

Lehman, J. *The Executive, Congress and Foreign Policy* (New York, Washington & London: Praeger Publishers, 1974).

Lenczowski, George. *American Presidents and the Middle East* (Durham and London: Duke University Press, 1990).

Lindblom, C. E. *The Policy Making Process* (Englewood Cliffs, NJ: Prentice-Hall, 1968).

Little, Richard. "Belief Systems in the Social Sciences" in Little, Richard & Smith, Steve (eds.), *Belief Systems in International Relations* (London: Blakwell, 1990).

Lipset, S. M. & E. Raab. *Jews and the New American Scene* (Cambridge, MA & London: Harvard University Press, 1995).

Lipset, S. M. *The First New Nation* (New York: Basic Books, 1964).

Lipstadt, D. *Beyond Belief: The American Press and the Coming of the Holocaust, 1933–45* (New York: The Free Press, 1986).

Little, Richard & Steve Smith. *Belief Systems and International Relations* (Oxford: Basil Blackwell, 1988).

Litwak, Robert S. *Détente and the Nixon Doctrine: American Foreign Policy and the Pursuit of Stability, 1969 – 1976* (Cambridge, New York, New Rochelle, Melbourne, Sydney: Cambridge University Press, 1984).

Luckas, Yehuda (ed.), *Documents on the Israeli–Palestinian Conflict* (Cambridge: Cambridge University Press, 1984).

Lochery, Neill. *The Difficult Road to Peace in the Middle East* (Lebanon: Ithaca Press, 1999).

Lochery, Neill. *The Israeli Labour Party: In the Shadow of the Likud* (Reading: Ithaca Press, 1997).

Lucas, Scott. *Freedom's War: The US Crusade Against the Soviet Union, 1945–56* (Manchester: Manchester University Press, 1999).

Lyons, William, John M. Scheb II, Lilliard E. Richardson, Jr., *American Government: Politics & Political Culture* (Minneapolis/St. Paul, New York, Los Angeles, San Francisco: West Publishing Co., 1995).

MacIntyre, A. *After Virtue: A Study in Moral Theory* (London: Duckworth, 1985).

Mansour, Camille. *Beyond Alliance: Israel in US Foreign Policy* (New York: Columbia University Press, 1994).

Marshall, Jonathan, Peter Dale Scott & Jane Hunter. *The Iran–Contra Connection: Secret Teams and Covert Operations in the Reagan Era* (Montreal & New York: Black Rose Books, 1987).

Mazlish, Bruce. *Kissinger: The European Mind in American Policy* (New York: Basic Books, 1976).

McFadden, John H. "The Strategic Arena" in Harry S. Allen & Ivan Volgyes (ed.), *Israel, the Middle East and U.S. Interests* (New York; Praeger Publishers, 1983).

McLellan, David (ed.), *Political Christianity: A Reader* (Wiltshire: Redwood Books, 1997).

McPherson, Harry. *A Political Education* (Boston, 1972)

Meir, Golda with Syrkin, Marie (ed.), *Golda Meir Speaks Out* (Jerusalem: Weidenfeld & Nicolson, 1973).

Meir, Golda. *My Life* (London: Futura, 1976).

Menendez, Albert J. *Evangelicals at the Ballot Box* (New York: Prometheus Books, 1996).

Mervin, David. *George Bush and the Guardianship Presidency* (London: Macmillan, 1996).

Mills, C. Wright. *Power, Politics and People* (London, Oxford & New York: Oxford University Press, 1963).

Mintz, Alan. *Popular Culture and the Shaping of Holocaust Memory in America* (Seattle & London: University of Washington Press, 2001).

Moore, Barrington. *The Social Origins of Democracy & Dictatorship: Lord and Peasant in the Making of the Modern World* (London: Allen Lane, 1967).

Morgenthau, Hans J. *Politics Among Nations: The Struggle for Power and Peace* (New York: McGraw-Hill, Inc., 1993).

Neff, Donald. *Warriors for Jerusalem: The Six Days That Changed the Middle East* (New York: Simon & Schuster, 1984).

Neustadt, Richard. E. *Alliance Politics* (New York: Columbia University Press, 1970).

Neustadt, Richard E. *Presidential Power and the Modern Presidents: The Politics of Leadership from Roosevelt to Reagan* (New York: The Free Press, Macmillan Publishing Co., 1990).

Nixon, Richard. *RN* (New York: Touchstone, 1990).

Nixon, Richard. *The Memoirs of Richard Nixon*, vol. I (New York: Warner Books, 1978).

Northedge, F. S. *The International Political System* (London & Boston: Faber & Faber, 1981).

Novick, Peter. *The Holocaust in American Life* (Boston & New York: Houghton Mifflin Company, 1999).

Novik, Nimrod. *The United States and Israel: Domestic Determinants of a Changing US Commitment* (Boulder, CO: Westview Press; Tel Aviv: The Jaffee Centre for Strategic Studies, Tel Aviv University, 1984).

Organski, A. F. K. *The $36 Billion Bargain: Strategy and Politics in U.S. Assistance to Israel* (New York: Columbia University Press, 1990).

Packard, Vance. *The Hidden Persuaders* (London: Longmans, 1962).

Packenham, R. A. *Liberal America and the Third World: Political Development Ideas in Foreign Aid and Social Science* (Princeton: Princeton University Press 1973).

Parrington, Lewis, Vernon. *Main Currents in American Thought: An Interpretation of American Literature from the Beginnings to 1920* (New York: Harcourt, Brace, 1930).

Parsons, Talcott. *The Social System* (London: Routledge & Kegan Paul, 1951).

Peres, Shimon. *David's Sling* (London: Weidenfeld & Nicolson, 1970).

Plato. *Republic* (Oxford: Clarendon Press, 1921–22).

Podhoretz, Norman. *Making It* (New York: Random House, 1967).

Pollack, Kenneth. "How Saddam Misread the United States," in Micah Sifry & Christopher Cerf (eds.), *The Iraqi War Reader* (New York: Touchstone, 2003).

Polk, William R. *The United States and the Arab World* (Cambridge: Harvard University Press, 1965).

Price, Daniel. *Islamic Political Culture, Democracy, and Human Rights: A Comparative Study* (Westport, CT & London: Praeger, 1999).

Prittie, Terence. *Eshkol of Israel: The Man and the Nation* (London: Museum Press, 1969).

Puschel, Karen L. *US–Israeli Strategic Cooperation in the Post-Cold War Era* (Jerusalem: Jerusalem Post Press, 1992).

Pye, Lucian W. & Verba, Sidney (eds.), *Political Culture & Political Development* (Princeton, New Jersey: Princeton University Press, 1965).

Quandt, William B. *U.S. Policy in the Middle East: Constraints and Choices* (Santa Monica: Rand Corporation, 1970).

Quandt, William B. "Domestic Influences on U.S. Foreign Policy in the Middle East: The View from Washington" in William A. Beling (ed.), *The Middle East: Quest for an American Policy* (Albany: State University of New York Press, 1973).

Quandt, William B. *Decade of Decisions: American Policy Towards the Arab–Israeli Conflict: 1967–1976* (Berkeley, Los Angeles, London: University of California Press, 1977).

Quandt, William B. *Peace Process: American Diplomacy and the Arab–Israeli Conflict Since 1967* (Washington D.C. & Berkeley, Los Angeles: The Brookings Institution & University of California Press, 1993).

Quandt, William B. "How Far Will Israel Go?," *Washington Post Book World*, 20 November, 1991.

Rabin, Yitzhak. *The Rabin Memoirs* (London: Weidenfeld & Nicolson, 1979).

Rafael, Gideon. *Destination Peace: Three Decades of Israeli Foreign Policy* (London: Weidenfeld & Nicholson, 1981).

Raphael, Marc Lee. *Abba Hillel Silver: A Profile in American Judaism* (New York: Holmer & Meier, 1989).

Reagan, Ronald. *An American Life* (London: Hutchinson, 1990).

Reich, Bernard. *Securing the Covenant: United States-Israel Relations After the Cold War* (Westport, Connecticut & London: Praeger Publishers, 1995).

Reich, Bernard. *The United States and Israel* (New York & Eastbourne: Praeger, 1984).

Rikhye, Indar Jit. *The Sinai Blunder: Withdrawal of United Nations Emergency Force Leading to the Six Day War of June 1967* (London: Frank Cass, 1980).

Robertson, David. *The Penguin Dictionary of Politics* (London: Penguin Books, 1993).

Roberts, Geoffrey. *A Dictionary of Political Analysis* (London: Longman, 1971).

Rosenau, James N. (ed.), *Domestic Sources of Foreign Policy* (New York: Free Press, 1967).

Rosenau, James N. "Introduction," in James Rosenau (ed.), *International Politics and Foreign Policy* (New York: Free Press, 1969).

Rousseau, Jean-Jacques. *The Social Contract and Discourses*, translated, with introduction by G. D. N. Cole (London: Dent, 1955).

Rubinstein, Alvin Z. *Red Star on the Nile: The Soviet–Egyptian Influence Relationship Since the June War* (Princeton: Princeton University Press, 1977).

Rubinstein, Alvin Z. *Soviet Policy towards Turkey, Iran and Afghanistan: The Dynamics of Influence* (New York: Praeger, 1982).

Rusk, Dean. *As I Saw It* (New York: Penguin Books, 1990).

Ryan, David. *US Foreign Policy in World History* (London & New York: Routledge, 2000).

Ryan, David. "Asserting US Power," in Philip Davies (ed.), *An American Quarter Century: US Politics From Vietnam to Clinton* (Manchester: Manchester University Press, 1995).

Rynhold, Jonathan. *Israeli Political Culture in Relations with the U.S. over the Palestine Question, 1981–96* (Ph.D. thesis, University of London, London, 1998).
Sachar, Howard. *A History of Israel from the Rise of Zionism to Our Time* (New York: Alfred A. Knopf, 1996).
Sacks, J. *Crisis and Covenant: Jewish Thought after the Holocaust* (Manchester: Manchester University Press, 1992).
Sadat, Mohamed Anwar al-. *In Search of Identity* (London: Collins, 1978).
Said, Edward W. *The Question of Palestine* (New York: Random House, 1979).
Safran, Nadav. *Israel: The Embattled Ally* (Cambridge, MA: Belknap Press, 1981).
Sampson, Anthony. *The Seven Sisters: The Great Oil Companies and the World They Made* (Sevenoaks: Coronet Books, 1976).
Samson, Leon. *Towards a United Front: A Philosophy for American Workers* (New York: Faber & Rinehart, 1933).
Schiff, Ze'ev. *A History of the Israeli Army* (New York: Macmillan, 1985).
Schoenbaum, David. *The United States and the State of Israel* (New York & Oxford: Oxford University Press, 1993).
Seliktar, Ofira. *Divided We Stand: American Jews, Israel, and the Peace Process* (Westport, CT & London: Praeger, 2002).
Sendoz, Ellis (ed.), *Polticial Sermons of the American Founding Era, 1730–1805* (Indianapolis: Liberty Press, 1991).
Shafer, Byron (ed.), *Is America Different?* (Oxford: Oxford University Press, 1991).
Sheehy, Gail. *Character: America's Search for Leadership* (New York: Bantam Books, 1990).
Shlaim, Avi. *The Iron Wall: Israel and the Arab World* (New York & London: W.W. Norton & Co., 2000).
Shlaim, Avi. *War and Peace in the Middle East* (New York: Penguin Books, 1995).
Shribman, David. "Hosts Not Visitors: The Future of Jews in American Political Life," in L. Sandy Maisel (ed.), *Jews in American Politics* (New York, Oxford: Rowman & Littlefield Publishers: Lanham, Boulder, 2001).
Shultz, George P. *Turmoil and Triumph: My Years as Secretary of State* (New York: Charles Scribner's Sons, 1993).
Simon, Herbert. *Models of Man* (New York: Wiley, 1957).
Simpson, John. "Support for the Moral Majority and its Sociomoral Platform" in David Bromley & Anson Shape (ed.), *New Christian Politics* (Macon: Mercer University Press, 1984).
Smith, Anthony. *National Identity* (London: Penguin Books, 1991).
Spanier, John & Hook, Steven W. *American Foreign Policy Since World War II* (Washington, DC: CQ Press, 1997).
Spiegel, Steven L. *The Other Arab–Israeli Conflict: Making America's Middle East Policy, from Truman to Reagan* (Chicago & London: The University of Chicago Press, 1985).
Spiegel, Steven L. "Israel and Beyond: American Jews and US Foreign Policy" in L. Sandy Maisel (ed.), *Jews in American Politics* (Lanham, Boulder, New York, Oxford: Rowman & Littlefield Publishers, 2001).
Sprout, Harold & Margaret. *Man-Milieu Relationship Hypotheses in the Context of International Politics* (Princeton: Centre for International Studies, 1956).

Stephanson, Anders. *Manifest Destiny: American Expansion and the Empire of Right* (New York: Hill and Wang, 1995).
Steven, Stewart. *The Spymasters of Israel* (New York: Ballantine Books, 1980)
Stern, Geoffrey. *The Rise and Decline of International Communism* (Aldershot: Edward Elgar Publishing Ltd., 1990).
Stern, Geoffrey. *Leaders and Leadership* (London: London School of Economics, 1993).
Stern, Geoffrey. *The Structure of International Society* (London & New York: Pinter, 2000).
Sullivan, Denis. "International Aid and the Peace Process" in *Structural Flaws in the Middle East Peace Process* in J. W. Wright, Jr. (ed.), *Structural Flaws in the Middle East Peace Process* (Hampshire & New York: Palgrave, 2001).
Summers, Anthony. *The Arrogance of Power: The Secret World of Richard Nixon* (New York: Viking, Penguin Group, 2000).
Tanter, Raymond. *Who's at the Helm? Lessons of Lebanon* (San Francisco & Oxford: Westview Press, 1990).
Tessler, Mark. *A History of the Israeli–Palestinian Conflict* (Indiana: Indiana University Press, 1994).
Thomas, Helen (ed.), *The Nixon Press Conferences* (London: Heyden, 1978).
Thornton, Richard. *The Nixon–Kissinger Years: Reshpaing America's Foreign Policy* (New York: Paragon House, 1989).
Tocqueville, Alexis de. *Democracy in America* J. P. Myers (ed.), and trans. George Laurence (New York: Doubleday, 1969).
Travis, Jr., Martin. "The Control of U.S. Foreign Policy" in Philip Buck & Martin Travis, Jr. *Control of Foreign Relations in Modern Nations* (New York: W. W. Norton & Co.: New York, 1957).
Trethewey, Richard J. "International Economics and Politics: A Theoretical Framework" in Bauer, Robert A. (ed.), *The Interaction of Economics and Foreign Policy* (Charlottesville: University Press of Virginia, 1975).
Trice, Robert H. "Domestic Interest Groups and the Arab–Israeli Conflict: A Behavioural Analysis," in Said, Abdul Aziz (ed.), *Ethnicity and US Foreign Policy* (New York & London: Praeger Publishers, 1977).
Truman, Harry S. *Memoirs* Vol. 2 (New York: Signet Books, 1965).
Turner, Fredrick *The Frontier in American History* (New York: Dover Publications, 1996).
Uri Dan, *Blood Libel* (New York: Simon & Schuster, 1987).
Volger, John. "Perspectives on the Foreign Policy System: Psychological Approaches," in Clarke, Michael & White, Brian (eds.), *Understanding Foreign Policy: The Foreign Policy Systems Approach* (Aldershot: Edward Elgar Publishing Ltd., 1989).
Wallace, William. *Foreign Policy and the Political Process* (London & Basingstoke: Macmillan, 1971).
Walsh, Lawrence E. *Iran–Contra: The Final Report* (New York: Times Books, 1994).
Weinberger, Caspar. *Fighting for Peace: Seven Critical Years at the Pentagon* (London: Michael Joseph Ltd., 1990).
Williams, Raymond. "Culture is Ordinary" in Ann Gray & Jim McGuigen (eds.), *Studying Culture* (New York: Routledge, 1993).

Wills, Garry. *Reagan's America: Innocents at Home* (Garden City, N.Y.: Doubleday, 1987).

Wilson, Harold. *The Chariot of Israel (*London: Weidenfeld & Michael Joseph, 1981).

Woll, Peter & Rockwell, Stephen J. *American Politics and Realities* (New York: Longman, 2000).

Wright, Quincy. *The Control of American Foreign Relations* (London: Macmillan, 1922).

Yergin, Daniel, *The Prize: The Epic Quest for Oil, Money and Power* (New York: Simon & Schuster, 1991).

Young, James E. "Memory and the Politics of Identity" in Hilene Flanzbaum (ed.), *The Americanisation of the Holocaust* (Baltimore & London: The Johns Hopkins University Press, 1999).

Young, Stephen D. "Ethnicity and the Indo-China War: Reasons for Conflict" in van Horne, Winston & Tonnesen, Thomas V. (eds.), *Ethnicity and War* (Madison: University of Wisconsin, 1984).

Youngs, Tim. *Developments in the Middle East Peace Process 1991–2000* (London: House of Commons Library, 2001).

Newspapers

Arab Report and Record
BBC Monitoring Middle East
BBC Summary of World Broadcasts
Congressional Quarterly
Evening Standard
Financial Times
Foreign Broadcast and Information Service
International Herald Tribune
Jerusalem Post
Jerusalem Report
Los Angeles Times
Middle East Policy
Mideast Mirror
National Journal
New Yorker
New York Times
Newsweek
The Economist
The Guardian
The Observer
Washington Post
Washington Post Book World

INDEX

Note: Administrations are listed in chronological order. All other references are listed alphabetically.